£35-

THE GEOGRAPHY OF MULTINATIONALS

CROOM HELM SERIES IN GEOGRAPHY AND ENVIRONMENT

Edited by Alan Wilson, Nigel Thrift, Michael Bradford and Edward W. Soja

The Geography of Multinationals

Studies in the Spatial Development and Economic
Consequences of Multinational Corporations

Edited by Michael Taylor and Nigel Thrift

CROOM HELM
London & Sydney

©1982 M.J. Taylor and N.J. Thrift
Croom Helm Ltd, Provident House, Burrell Row,
Beckenham, Kent, BR3 1AT

Croom Helm Australia Pty Ltd, Suite 4, 6th Floor,
64-76 Kippax Street, Surry Hills, NSW 2010, Australia

Reprinted 1983 & 1986

British Library Cataloguing in Publication Data

The Geography of the multinationals — (Croom Helm
    series in geography and environment)
    1. International business enterprises
    I. Taylor, Michael II. Thrift, Nigel
    338.8'8   HD2755.5

    ISBN 0-7099-2403-8

Printed and bound in Great Britain by
Antony Rowe Ltd, Chippenham

CONTENTS

FIGURES

TABLES

PREFACE

The purpose of this volume is to examine, through a series of international case studies, the nature and the geographical implications of the development of multinational corporations.[1] Of course, the development of such corporations had a long history prior to the Second World War (see, for instance, Chandler, 1980; Sampson, 1973; Wilkins, 1970; 1974b). But it has been in the post-war period that multinational corporations have gained their present, more general economic significance as an extra-national network of inter- and intra-firm linkages spreading rapidly over the globe. It is on this latter period of expansion that this volume concentrates and, in particular, on the current phase of corporate restructuring and readjustment in response to world-wide recession.

The significance of multinational corporations in the world economy (and, indeed, as part of the world economy) bears little repetition since it is the subject of almost continuous discussion.[2] Many such corporations have consolidated sales that total more than the Gross National Product of significant nation states and, by the early 1970s, the value added by multinational corporations was equal to about 20 per cent of the Gross National Product of countries with mixed and market economies. By the same date as much as one-third of the imports and exports of countries like the USA, UK, West Germany and Sweden could be attributed to intra-firm transactions (UNESCO, 1978). Such an estimate is now regarded as too conservative; (Lall, 1978; Plasschaert, 1979; Helleiner, 1981; Helleiner and Lavergne, 1979).

Figures like these mean that justification for the study of multinational corporations is self-apparent. The major problem is rather what aspects of such an extensive phenomenon are to be studied. This volume is therefore quite limited in its scope, to the explanation of the development of multinational corporations in space, and the consequences of such patterns of development, set against the background of a world economy that now appears to be going through a number of quite fundamental changes.

As a consequence the volume is divided into two parts. In the first part each of the five constituent chapters considers a particular aspect or set of aspects of the problem of how multinational corporations have developed and will develop. In the second part of the volume the six chapters that have been included consider different aspects of the economic and social impacts of these corporations. As in any edited volume, the unremitting assignment of chapters to one or the other theme minimises the very real connections between the two parts and the chapters in them. Perhaps the common theme that links all the papers is their emphasis on careful historical analysis of different forms of spatial organisation and their transformation into other, different forms (Taylor and Thrift, 1982). The chapters show that the days when ideal-type models reigned supreme in industrial geography are over. It is now realised that all models must be bounded in space and by time; they are otherwise too abstract and therefore not abstract enough (Zeleny, 1980).

In any volume of this kind too many colleagues have contributed to its final form for them all to be listed. However, we would like to acknowledge, in particular, the assistance provided by Jane Hirst, and we must also point to the research facilities and the intellectual focus provided by the Department of Human Geography at the Australian National University as it has moved to its current major preoccupation with the internationalisation of production in the Pacific Basin.

Notes

1. The question of what constitutes a satisfactory definition of a multinational corporation has yet to be resolved. (Linge and Hamilton, 1981.) In this volume the term is used in its broadest sense to refer to large business organisations with a number of operations abroad.

2. The best review is in UNESCO (1978).

PART ONE:

**THE SPATIAL DEVELOPMENT SEQUENCES OF
MULTINATIONAL CORPORATIONS**

1 INTRODUCTION

M.J. Taylor and N.J. Thrift

The 1970s can now be seen as a period in which a major shift took place in the structure of the world economy which can be interpreted as either the start of, or a period of transition to, a new phase of internationalisation of production. This new phase has as both its medium and outcome the development of a new form of multinational corporation which we call in this volume the *global corporation*.[1] A host of new terms have been coined to describe the symptoms of this current period of crisis: 'deindustrialisation', the 'new international division of labour', the 'fiscal crisis of the state', and so on and so forth. In essence, however, these terms describe only the national aspects of adjustments to the same thing; the emergence of a truly global system of production having at its heart the global corporation.

In 1950 most large multinational corporations were, in fact, only barely multinational. But, as Table 1.1 shows, by 1970 this situation had changed dramatically. Increasingly, large multinationals had subsidiary networks that spanned the globe. Having a presence in most areas of the globe meant that such corporations could no longer follow the diffusionist policies[2] that had prevailed in the period from 1950 to 1970, policies that involved the setting up of foreign subsidiaries in familiar areas first and then gradual movement to the less familiar areas of the world. The frontier, at least in spatial terms, was fading fast. With a global network of subsidiaries set up, the question for most large multinationals had changed from what would be the most profitable area in which to expand next to which of the existing areas could be relied upon to produce the highest returns.

Table 1.1: The Foreign Manufacturing Subsidiary Networks of 315 Large Multinational Corporations in 1950 and 1970

Number of enterprises with subsidiary networks including:	180 US-based MNCs		135 MNCs based in the UK and Europe	
	1950	1970	1950	1970
6 countries	138	9	116	31
6-20 countries	43	128	16	75
20 countries	0	44	3	29

Source: Vernon, 1979, p. 258.

1

The general decrease in opportunities for spatial expansion has coupled with two other equally important factors to produce the global corporation. First, large multinationals have begun to represent their environment and manage it in increasingly sophisticated ways. There are a number of reasons for this development. The advent of the computer has enabled more and more information about more and more topics to be stored *and* interpreted. Increasingly efficient telecommunications, and especially the satellite, have enabled the information to be transmitted at greater speeds. The development of administrative science has enabled information to be analysed and represented in all manner of new ways.[3] All these factors, and more, have combined to allow information to become increasingly centralised and control increasingly decentralised (Aglietta, 1979). Perhaps the chief indication of this new sophistication is the growth of the grid form of organisation, based on matrix management techniques, that allows greater flexibility of response.[4] Grid organisation allows the new global corporations to become more and more aware of their environment and enables them to react more swiftly to changes in it. Second, the multinational corporation has become increasingly financially oriented. The reasons for this development are complex and interrelated. Thus, fiscal measures of corporate performance have been incrementally adopted over time. The problems of financing larger and larger projects at the world scale and uneven government regulatory frameworks have led to the Eurocurrency and other international money markets and institutions. Currency differentials, and the ability of multinationals to exploit them, have become sources of profit in themselves. The result, at least, is clear. The multinational corporate structure has become as efficient a vehicle for monetary transfers as the banks or the capital markets and, in effect, the corporate headquarters now operates increasingly as a relatively autonomous and specialised banker's firm.

These two new developments have, in turn, resulted in an *acceleration* of the movement of capital (Teulings, 1981). Capital has become more footloose and, as a consequence, individual corporations are now more able to unlock resources held at one location and transfer them quickly to a more profitable location, especially through the medium of acquisition. This acceleration in the movement of capital has coincided with a period in which the degree of control of the world economy exercised by United-States-based multinationals has decreased. United-States-based multinationals must now share the stage with those from, at least, Europe and Japan. Indeed, the multinationalisation of Japanese corporations has been one of the major economic themes of the latter part of the 1960s and the 1970s, as the old subordinate relationships of Japanese capital to US capital have been sloughed off. Importantly, Japanese capital has expanded mainly into developing countries and especially those in the Pacific Basin. Of the total number of employees in Japanese overseas subsidiaries at the end of March 1978, 416,000 were employed in Asian countries, 126,000 in North America, 37,000 in Africa, 29,000 in Europe, 28,000 in Oceania and 14,000 in the Middle East. And, as Table 1.2 shows, Japan is now the largest direct investor in South Korea, Thailand, Malaysia, Indonesia and Iran (Nakase, 1981). If the giant Japanese business groups backed up by a bank can be considered as coherent business organisations, then six now rank, at least in terms of turnover, far above the other major world multinationals (Table 1.3). This internationalisation of Japanese business has also been accompanied by the internationalisation of Japanese banks. The Japanese banks have followed the same phases of internationalisation of banking as have all other multinational banks, but the sequence has been concertinaed into a far shorter period of time (Table 1.4). Most major Japanese banks are now fully international (Hughes, 1980; Ishigaki and Fujita, 1981; Rowley, 1981). By the end of March 1979 the geographical distribution of these banks in one survey was as in Table 1.5. Japanese banks, which came fairly late to the Eurocurrency and Eurobond markets and suffered a number of set-backs in the early 1970s, had all but caught up with the US and European competition by 1979, as Table 1.6 shows. The upshot of these and other developments has been a rearrangement of the world economy into a set of more regionally based zones of production dependent on a dominant regional power (the United States, Europe, Japan) in which resources, labour and capital are brought together in varying combinations at the most optimally profitable locations (Forbes, 1982).

Table 1.2: Accumulated Japanese Direct Investment in Ten Countries

	At End March 1978 (US$ million)	At End March 1979 (US$ million)	At End March 1980 (US$ million)
United States	4,770	6,049	7,394
Indonesia	3,130	3,739	3,888
Brazil	2,070	2,329	2,738
United Kingdom	1,690	1,756	1,823
Australia	960	1,168	1,734
South Korea	790	1,007	1,102
Saudi Arabia & Kuwait	880	926	1,068
Iran	470	855	431
Hong Kong	560	715	939
Canada	630	715	808

Source: Nakase, 1981, p. 64.

Table 1.3: Some of the World's Largest Multinational Corporations, Ranked by Turnover

	Country of Origin	1976 Turnover ($ million)	1978 Turnover ($ million)
Mitsubishi Group	Japan	75,000	106,400
DKB Group	Japan	54,500	79,300
Sumitomo Group	Japan	51,200	78,100
Mitsui Group	Japan	48,800	76,500
Fuyo Group	Japan	57,000	71,200
Sanwa Group	Japan	46,100	64,500
General Motors	USA	47,200	63,200
Exxon	USA	48,600	60,300
Royal Dutch-Shell	Netherlands/UK	36,100	44,000
Ford	USA	28,800	42,800
IBM	USA	16,300	21,100
General Electric	USA	15,700	19,700
Unilever	Netherlands/UK	15,800	18,900
ITT	USA	11,800	15,300
Philips	Netherlands	11,500	15,100
Hoechst	W. Germany	9,300	12,100
US Steel	USA	8,600	11,100
Nestlé	Switzerland	7,600	11,000
El du Pont	USA	8,400	10,600
Thyssen	W. Germany	7,900	9,200
ICI	UK	7,500	8,700
British Steel	UK	5,000	5,700

Source: Nakase, 1981, p. 86.

However, it is not only that new sources of capital have grown up. It is also that there has been an increasing *interpenetration* of this capital as each of the global corporations has spread itself over the whole of the world arena. Thus, to take but two examples, the largest amount of Japanese direct investment still goes to the United States (Table 1.2). And European multinationals have also, of course, increasingly moved into the United States (McConnell, 1980). At a smaller-scale level, European investment has increasingly moved into the UK and UK investment has increasingly moved into Europe. It is often forgotten that the current pattern of world investment of capital is by no means solely towards the periphery; it is also back to or within the core and, particularly, towards the lucrative markets offered as a result of US Federal State expenditure (Teulings, 1981).

Table 1.4: Phases of Internationalisation of Banking

Phases	First Phase	Second Phase	Third Phase
Method of inter-nationalisation by customer companies	Export-import	Active direct overseas invest-ment	Multinational corporations
Associated banking operations	Mainly foreign exchange opera-tions connected with foreign trade. Capital trans-actions are mainly short-term	Overseas loans and investments become import-ant, as do medium- and long-term capital transactions	Non-banking fringe activities (e.g. relevant banking, leasing, consulting) are constructed. In the later part of this phase retail banking is taken up
Methods of banking internationalisation	Correspondence contracts with foreign banks	Overseas branches and offices are strengthened	Now includes strengthening of overseas branches and offices, capital participation, busi-ness affiliations, establishing non-bank fringe busi-ness firms, in order to raise funds and lend on global basis
Type of customer	Mainly domestic	Mainly domestic	Various nationali-ties

Source: Adapted from Ishigaki and Fujita, 1981, p. 24.

Table 1.5: The Geographical Distribution of the Overseas Branches, Representative Offices and Affiliates[a] of Japanese Banks (in per cent) in 1978

	Branches	Representative Offices	Affiliates
North America	36	22	17
Central and South America	3	14	11
Europe	33	13	32
Middle and Near East	0	12	4
Asia	25	22	29
Oceania	0	12	4
Africa	0	3	0
Others	0	0	4
Total	100	100	100

Note: [a]Overseas financial affiliates with more than 50 per cent equity links with Japanese banks.

Source: Adapted from Ishigaki and Fujita, 1981, p. 17.

Table 1.6: The Top Ten Managing Bank Groups in Syndicated
Euro-loans in 1979

Banking Group	Volume (US$ billion)	Number of Loans
Lloyds Bank	23,178	106
Bank of Tokyo	21,408	95
Crédit Lyonnais	21,247	116
CIBC	20,600	81
Citicorp	20,037	97
Bank of Montreal	19,093	102
Chase	17,666	109
Mitsubishi	17,411	77
Midland Bank	17,401	111
Sumitomo	17,071	100

Source: *Far Eastern Economic Review*, 8-14 May 1981, p. 68.

The increasing acceleration and interpenetration of capital registers most dramatically as the loss of jobs in certain core countries as part of the so-called 'new international division of labour' (Fröbel, Heinrichs and Kreye, 1980; Tharakan, 1980; Thrift, 1980; Seidman and O'Keefe, 1980; Clegg, 1980; Hansen, 1981). The old international division of labour, based upon the exchange of raw materials by underdeveloped countries for core manufactured goods is now being paralleled, and perhaps to some extent superseded, by a new division of labour based on the 'relocation'[5] of manufacturing, mainly of labour-intensive production processes, to less developed countries where labour is cheaper and more plentiful. In the literature this new international division of labour is sometimes depicted simply as a crude reaction to the cheaper labour costs and more tractable workers to be found in the periphery, the whole process being set in motion as a result of various enabling conditions like new developments in transport and communications. Whilst this depiction is certainly an important component in current changes the reasons for 'relocation' are usually far more complex than this and stem from the fact that global corporations now have a world-wide character. They are therefore able to pick and choose locations for particular production processes and react to prevailing political and fiscal conditions faster and more efficiently than previously in a continual process of *locational rationalisation* that causes the fixed capital of a production plant of a multinational corporation, although it may well be remunerative by its own standards, to be checked continuously against more profitable employment of capital elsewhere.

Table 1.7: The Coats Patons Table of Comparative Labour Costs as at 21 April 1981

Country	Single Shift Total Cost per hr.	Index	Double Shift Total Cost per hr.	Index	Treble Shift Total Cost per hr.	Index
UK (base)	2.678	100	3.186	100	3.481	100
Italy	3.259	122	3.499	110	4.943	121
West Germany	3.561	133	3.696	116	3.913	115
Canada	3.596	134	3.564	112	3.613	109
United States	3.134	117	3.134	98	3.157	96
Portugal	1.076	40	1.177	37	1.799	42
Colombia	0.950	36	1.121	35	1.304	26
Brazil	0.840	31	1.009	32	1.065	31
Peru	0.611	23	0.620	19	0.637	19
India	0.342	13	0.345	11	0.416	11
Philippines	0.276	10	0.276	9	0.282	8
Indonesia	0.166	6	0.169	5	0.168	5

Source: *Financial Times*, 29 June 1981, p. 11.

Table 1.8: The Changing Division of Labour within Eight West-German-based Multinational Companies

	Employees (thousands)									
	1971		1973		1974		1975		1976	
	FRG	Abroad	FRG	Abroad	FRG	Abroad	FRG	Abroad	FRG	Abroad
AEG-Telefunken	146	21	150	25	144	26	133	29	132	30
BASF	78	15	87	21	89	22	89	23	89	23
Bosch	90	25	82	31	79	35	70	35	72	34
Daimler-Benz	127	20	134	22	130	25	129	2	133	28
Hoechst	97	45	105	52	107	72	105	77	104	79
Mannesmann	73	12	91	19	91	21	85	23	84	25
Siemens	234	72	222	81	221	88	207	89	208	96
Volkswagenwerk	160	42	161	54	142	62	118	59	124	59

Source: Adapted from Fröbel, Heinrichs and Kreye, 1980, p. 286.

Table 1.9: The Proportional Distribution of Employment within Philips, 1964-76 (per cent)

	1964	1970	1976
Netherlands	35	27	22
Europe	53	55	49
United States and Canada	12	5	10
Rest of the world		13	19

Source: Teulings, 1981.

Figure 1.1: Employment in Coats Patons World-wide, 1979

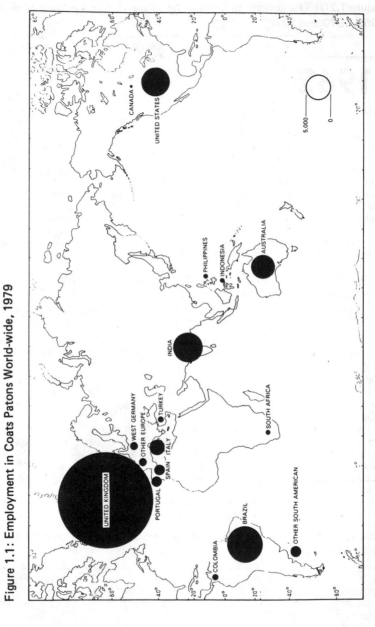

Source: *Financial Times*, 29 June 1981, p. 11.

Figure 1.2(a) The Growth of CRA Ltd in Cross-section for the Years 1962, 1970 and 1978[a]

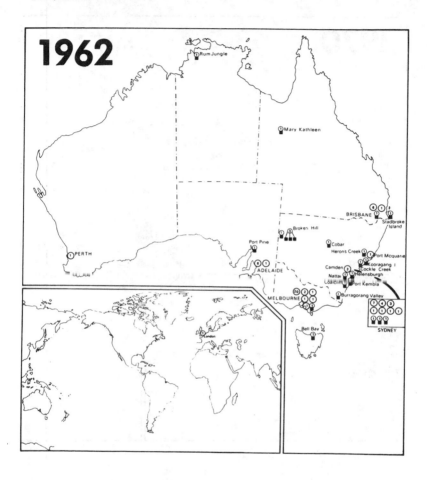

1.2(b)

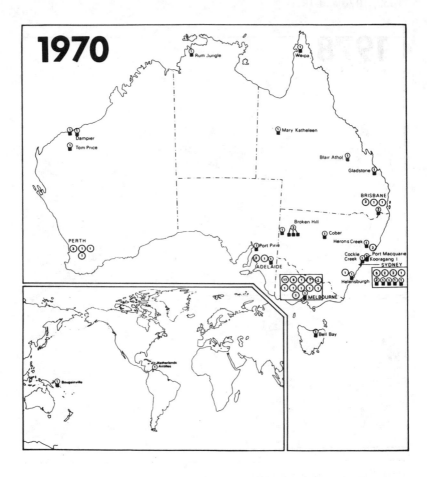

1.2(c)

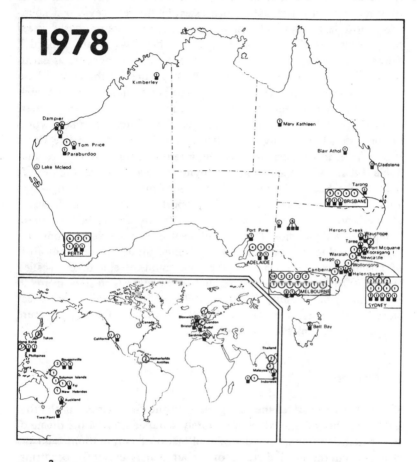

Note: [a] Circles denote offices of subsidiary companies; figure in each circle denotes number of operative companies at each site if more than one; black squares denote production sites.

With a world-wide arena in which to work the most profitable employment of capital seems to be found increasingly, at least in terms of labour-intensive production processes, in the less developed countries. Most large multinational corporations now continuously assess the profitability of each country in which they have plants. Table 1.7 shows dramatically the difference between various countries as calculated by the British textiles concern, Coats Patons, on the basis of base wage rates in each country, the charges on labour in each country such as national income and payroll taxes, and the latest exchange rates, while Figure 1.1 shows the Coats Patons labour force around the world in some detail. Certainly most multinational corporations like Coats Patons have, in the current recession, internationalised as never before. Table 1.8 shows the shifts in employment of a set of multinationals based in the Federal Republic of Germany from 1971 to 1976, whilst Table 1.9 shows, in some detail, the proportional shifts in employment of the large Dutch-based multinational, Philips, from 1964 to 1976. Philips has actively moved its employment out of the Netherlands into the less developed countries and the United States. The current crisis of unemployment in many of the core countries and their so-called 'deindustrialisation' is strongly related to these kinds of movements in employment opportunity (Morgan, 1979), although until more exact labour market studies are carried out our knowledge of the exact nature of such connections will remain oblique.

The Chapters

This summary provides the background to the five chapters in the first section of this volume which are loosely grouped around the theme of the spatial development paths of multinational corporations, and the changing international division of labour that is currently occurring. Extant geographical models of the spatial development of firms are clearly unequal to the task of making general statements about the changing spatial form that large multinationals take. For instance, Figure 1.2 shows the development sequence of CRA Ltd, the Australian subsidiary of the British mining house, Rio-Tinto Zinc, in cross-section for 1962, 1970 and 1978. Over this period this subsidiary has itself become a fully fledged multinational, moving into the Pacific and back into Europe and the UK. Why and how paths like this have happened, how representative they are and how it might be possible to provide an adequate account of them is the subject of the first chapter by *Taylor and Thrift*. It is certain that a more historical approach than has previously been adopted in industrial geography will be the first prerequisite for any adequate account or, more likely, set of accounts. The chapters by *Newfarmer and Topik* and *Watts* provide useful insights into the development of multinational corporations in particular historical periods. Thus *Newfarmer and Topik* consider the development of the world electrical industry within a dependency theory framework (cf. *International Organization*, 1979). In particular, they show how the centralisation of the industry that has continued to the present has adversely affected the development of an indigenous electrical industry in Brazil. *Watts* considers the influx of German multinationals into the UK in the 1970s, both in aggregate and by means of a case study of the development sequence of Hoechst AG. *Clarke* investigates the changing international division of labour within one multinational corporation, the British chemical giant ICI, in the 1970s. Finally, *Hirst, Taylor and Thrift* examine the development pattern of the Australian trading banks in an attempt to move from the predominantly mining and manufacturing focus of most work on the geography of multinationals to a consideration of what are now, in effect, financial multinationals (Weston, 1980; Rugman, 1981).

Notes

1. This concept is closest in conception to Karpik's (1977, 1978) idea of technological capitalism.
2. Policies like those based on the product cycle or on 'follow-the-leader' behaviour.
3. The structural contingency model is the paradigm here.
4. Grid organisation spread first through US- and Dutch-based multinationals and is only now diffusing through others (Channon, 1973; Knight, 1976).
5. The term 'relocation' is intended to signify export of capital and productive facilities overseas by a multinational, rather than the actual physical relocation of a plant from one location to another.

2 MODELS OF CORPORATE DEVELOPMENT AND THE MULTINATIONAL CORPORATION

M.J. Taylor and N.J. Thrift

The development of multinational corporations is often regarded as part of a natural progression in the evolution of enterprise structures in market and mixed economies that relates to major advances that have occurred in technology, marketing organisation and the form of oligopolistic competition in past decades. Indeed, there is a tendency in the already vast literature on multinationals to regard this form of corporate enterprise as simply the current end point of a continuum of development that begins with the small privately owned, single-plant firm to which so much attention is currently being directed. This conventional wisdom is spelled out in, for instance, the UK Bolton Report (1971) on small firms, where it is contended that 'small firms provide the means of entry into business for new entrepreneurial talent and the seedbed from which large companies will grow to challenge and stimulate the established leaders of industry' (Bolton Committee, 1971). This proposition of a relatively unimpeded trajectory of growth is implicit in the array of models of corporate growth that have been developed most extensively in industrial economics, for both national (e.g. Marris, 1972; Penrose, 1959; Downie, 1958; Macintosh, 1963; for example) and multinational firms (e.g. Vernon, 1971; 1978) and in the geographical literature (e.g. Taylor, 1975; Håkanson, 1979; McNee, 1974; McDermott, 1977; Watts, 1980a). We review these contributions below.

However, more recent contributions to the burgeoning literature on multinational corporations and on corporate development in general tend to call such a proposition into question (e.g. Devine *et al.*, 1979; Taylor and Thrift, 1980). In particular, static, *ahistorical* models of corporate development can now be seen to be incapable of depicting corporate development paths. Based upon the situation as it exists at only one point in time, and upon cross-sectional data for validation, such models can depict only *potential development sequences* unique to the moment and not *actual development paths*, since these are conditioned by the exigencies of history and the progression of inter-related events in absolute time. It is unfortunate that these actual and potential development paths have been conflated in both the economic and the geographic literature since this unwarranted juxta-position has considerably enhanced the possibilities for confusion. Additions in the past few years to the economic and geographic litera-ture would suggest that the large multinational is a very different animal to either the smaller, national enterprise or the much publicised smaller firm. The implication is that there no longer is, if indeed there ever was, a single corporate development sequence. To foreshadow the argument, it would appear that there may be at present at least four different sequences, each one appropriate to only one particular set of enterprises:

    (1) a newly developing set of 'global' corporations;
    (2) the larger national and smaller multinational corporations;
    (3) smaller quoted companies; and
    (4) the smaller firms.

Each of these sets of enterprises, and to a lesser extent the individual enterprises within each set, have a different magnitude of resources at their disposal and a differing degree of power in the networks of institutions and organisations which comprise their operational environ-ments or milieux (Averitt, 1968; Benson, 1966; Karpik, 1977; Taylor and Thrift, 1980; Devine *et al.*, 1979). The movement of individual enterprises between these sets appears to occur predominantly by take-over and merger.[1]

The purpose of this introductory chapter, then, is to establish the uniqueness of the multinational corporation not as the ultimate organisational form to which all firms, enterprises and corporations can aspire, but as a relatively discrete set of organisations within the capital-ist system, set apart from others by virtue of the size and power of its members together with their ability to maintain and reinforce that power by economic and political means.

Models of Corporate Growth and Industrial Economics

In industrial economics a number of models of firm growth have been proposed. These all begin with the assumption that there are no effec-tive constraints on the sizes of firms, only constraints on their rates of growth (Marris, 1972). Size in these models is, therefore, simply a by-product of growth and the multinational corporation is no more than the end point of a development continuum. Within these models, attention has been focused on three sets of variables as explanations of rates of growth — financial constraints, demand constraints and managerial constraints — with different authors laying particular emphasis on one or other of these sets. Thus, for Downie (1958), rates of firm growth depend, in the first instance, upon financial and demand considerations; the funds needed to expand capacity and the customers needed to absorb production. The rate of profit links the operation of these limiting factors in Downie's model. Capacity varies directly with the rate of profit while the rate of profit varies inversely with the rate of customer expansion and the growth of demand. As a direct result, the model identifies an upper limit to the rate of expansion of a firm but no upper limit to the absolute size of the enterprise. By inference, therefore, all firms are endowed with the same growth potential.

Penrose (1959) produces a somewhat different model of firm growth which intentionally emphasises internal managerial restraints on expansion, but which does not ignore the significance of both demand and financial restraints. Penrose contends that the rate of efficient managerial expansion is limited by the nature, learning abilities and teaching abilities of management teams. Allied to this point of view, it is maintained that different firms can combine the same resources in different ways and with differing degrees of skill and thus obtain very different *'productive services'* from them. Diversification is also seen as a normal avenue of firm growth owing to the changing opportunity costs to the firm of its own resources when existing markets become less profitable than others. In short, the Penrose model emphasises the growth potential of a firm's inherited resources, highlighting the uniqueness of that potential for individual firms. Among others, Barna (1962) and Richardson (1964) have provided empirical support for the Penrose model, but it is still implicit within this model that only the rate of growth of a firm is constrained and not the extent of that growth.

A more formal model of firm growth has been constructed by Marris (1972), combining the financial, managerial and demand factors that were previously considered by Downie and Penrose. However, in this model a particular emphasis is placed upon financial constraints and the discipline of the stock market through the development of a theory of take-over. Central to this model is a theory of stock market valuation in which shareholders seek to maximise the return on their investments in a firm while managers seek to maximise the rate of growth of the same enterprise. Funds for expansion can be obtained from three sources; borrowing, new share issues and retained earnings. Managers can only borrow for expansion to a finite extent, since the higher gearing ratio of the firm exposes both the lender and the borrower to increased risk. There is also a finite limit to the funds that can be raised through new share issues for, when expected profitability falls below the level necessary to maintain earnings on existing shares, there will eventually be no takers for the new shares. The only other source of funds open to the firm is retained earnings, but here there must be a trade-off with the dividends expected by shareholders. The consequence of this set of financial constraints is that the rate of growth of the firm is severely restricted. The discipline of the stock market also forces management teams to maintain the profitability of their firms owing to the threat of take-over. Take-over occurs in the Marris model when the actual market value and the valuation ratio of a firm fall below the subjective value placed upon them by a potential bidder. Clearly, then, if a firm's profitability declines, so does its market value and valuation ratio, increasing the threat of take-over. The essence of this model is, therefore, the identification of pressures on the firm to sustain the maximum rate of growth that is possible given the financial limitations within which it must live. Again, no limit is envisaged to the absolute size that the firm can attain, with the implication that the small single-plant firm and the multinational corporation can be elements of the same continuum of organisational development.

Nowhere is this contention of a uniform growth potential across all sizes of firm more clearly demonstrated than in a number of economists' work on Gibrat's Law — the law of proportionate effect — in which the probability of a firm growing at a given rate in a specified period of time is said to be independent of the size of the firm at the beginning of the period in question. Not surprisingly, the law is difficult to test and contradictory results have been produced in statistical analyses (e.g. Eatwell, 1971; Simon and Bonini, 1958; Samuels and Chester, 1972; Hannah and Kay, 1977). Garnering the results that have been produced, Pickering (1976) has maintained that 'there is quite strong evidence that the initial size of firms does not have a marked influence on the average rate of growth over a succeeding period of time' (p. 118). However, in a more recent and more critical review of this same literature, Devine *et al*. (1979) concludes that '[Gibrat's] law does not in fact appear to hold' (p. 181, footnote 86).

The principal problem confronting verification of the models of firm growth explored in this introduction is, in fact, the variable definitions of company size and the variable populations of firms that have been used in empirical investigations. Thus, for example, 'small' firms in some studies have fewer than 100 employees while in other studies 'small' firms are small public companies (Meeks and Whittington, 1975) or the smallest entries in a top 1,000 list (Hymer and Pashigian, 1962). Four areas of concern have received attention in these models in empirical studies; the interrelationships between size, growth and profitability together with the relationships between market valuation and the incidence of take-overs. Abstracting from the work of a wide range of authors, Devine *et al.* (1979) was able to draw four sets of very general conclusions. The principal conclusions on the relationship between size and firm growth were that:

(1) there is less variability in the rate of growth of larger compared with smaller firms; and
(2) there is a weak tendency for the growth rates of larger firms to be somewhat higher than those of smaller firms.

Relating profitability to size:

(1) there is a weak tendency for profitability to decline with size; but
(2) there is much less variability in the profit rates of larger compared with smaller firms.

On the relationship between growth and profitability there was found to be agreement on a strong positive relationship between the two variables with the least variability in rates of growth and profitability occurring amongst the larger firms irrespective of the industries to which they belonged. On the issues of take-over, the valuation ratio proposed by Marris (1972) was judged to be of very little use for explaining the incidence of take-over and merger. By contrast, size of firm was thought to be very important in this particular context. A study by Singh (1973), for example, suggests a relative immunity to take-over amongst the smaller quoted companies, with their greater incidence of either family control or shares held in only a few hands. Above this smaller size, the same study found the incidence of take-over to decline at an increasing rate with increased size.

The most important general feature to emerge from this review of work on industrial economics on the growth of firms is the special position of 'large' firms in relation to growth, profitability and take-over. Large firms have the least variable rates of growth and performance, a feature which seems to be independent of the industrial sectors to which they belong. In short, larger firms have a competitive advantage as a result of their size. However,

> This is not to suggest that there is a continuous relationship between size and competitive advantage; rather, it is to suggest that there exists a threshold above which firms on average enjoy advantages by comparison with those below . . . [A] theory of the competitive process . . . needs to distinguish between big business, i.e. the competitive sector, with the relationship between the sectors of some importance (Devine, 1979, p. 177).

Indeed, Devine (1979, Ch. 3) has identified a similar need to distinguish between the oligopolistic and competitive sectors of business for the construction of a more adequate general theory of the firm.

By inference, therefore, there may be no single development sequence for all organisations, but rather a series of development sequences. From the corporate growth literature alone, three such sequences might be conjectured:

(1) the small firm sequence, with 'small' defined on ownership and size, and with size a historically variable factor;

(2) a competitive sector sequence related to the smaller quoted companies that are most susceptible to take-over; and

(3) an oligopolistic sector sequence related to the larger national and multinational corporations, as this is a principal characteristic of the sectors of the economy within which they operate (Vernon, 1970; Stopford and Wells, 1972).

What is more, since a number of empirical studies, for example those of Singh (1975) and Meeks and Whittington (1975), have recognised a time-specific element to the nature of the relationship between size, profitability and firm growth, it can be suggested that these three growth sequences may exist only at present, or at least only since the 1950s. Their existence before the Second World War, for instance, is open to doubt and it is possible that there may have been only one, or more likely two, development sequences for firms at that particular time. Nevertheless, the weight of the argument developed on the evidence from industrial economics is that multinationals are a group of enterprises, set apart from other types of business organisations, which may enjoy separate and distinctive forms of development.

Models of Multinational Development and the Corporate Development Continuum

Even in models of multinationals' development, it is often implied that this type of corporation is simply the end point of a single development continuum, for the emphasis of this work is placed squarely on the reasons why firms move from national into multinational and global spheres of activity. To a certain extent, this bias in models of multi-national development is to be expected, since these models are closely related to the more general theory of the firm in economics and the theories of corporate growth discussed in the preceding section of this chapter. Within this body of literature a massive array of 'motivations'[2] for multinational development has been identified and a number of (usually monocausal) models have been proposed.

Perhaps the most distinctive set of motivations that has been distinguished relates to the oligopolistic behaviour of corporations involved with the exploitation of location-specific resources – either in the mineral or agricultural industries (e.g. Reuber, 1973; Fieldhouse, 1978). This set of motives is said to have created the export-oriented corporations which are so characteristic of dominion-capitalist countries such as Australia, New Zealand, Canada and South Africa (e.g. McKern, 1976; Bambrick, 1979; Fitzgerald, 1974; Smith, 1978; Beddgood, 1978). Extractive operations apart, there are also many enterprises that have established multinational manufacturing operations. Fieldhouse (1978) has divided these enterprises into two broad groups, those seeking to exploit the market available in a foreign country and those seeking to take advantage of favourable production factors in a particular country – be they raw materials, labour costs, exchange rates or government incentives. This, however, is only an initial caricature of a more complex problem of motivation and decision-making. Wertheimer (1971), for example, has catalogued the range of variables that might need to be taken into consideration (Table 2.1).

The development of a list of reasons for the internationalisation of a firm's production has been accompanied by a profusion of theories of multinational growth (Thomas, 1980) of which seven can be usefully distinguished (Buckley and Casson, 1976).

The first of these sets of theories has stressed the advantages which multinationals have over indigenous enterprises in such aspects of their operations as marketing, managerial skills, access to finance and technology and economies of scale (Hymer, 1960; Kindleberger, 1969).

Table 2.1: Reasons for Establishing Sales Offices and Production Units Overseas *ALSo* *OUeL* *PAGe*

1. Cost-related Reasons
   a. To take advantage of differences in technological development, labour potential, productivity and mentality, capital markets and local taxes
   b. Reduction of transport costs
   c. Avoidance of high tariff barriers
   d. To take advantage of local talents when establishing R & D overseas

2. Sales Volume Reasons
   a. Foreign middlemen unable to meet financial demands of expanded marketing
   b. For quicker adaptation to local market changes and better adaptation to local conditions
   c. Following important customers abroad
   d. Keeping up with competitors
   e. Persuasion and coercion of foreign host governments
   f. To obtain a better international division of labour, larger production runs and better utilisation of available economies of scale
   g. To avoid home country regulations, e.g. fiscal and anti-trust legislation

3. Reasons Related to Risk Factors
   a. To avoid exclusion from customers' and suppliers' markets promoting forward and backward integration
   b. To counter inflexibility and avoid country-specific recessions
   c. To reduce risks of social and political disruption by establishing operations in a number of host countries

Source: After Wertheimer, 1971.

Extending these ideas, Aliber (1970) has suggested that the specific factors of currency areas and investor myopia cause enterprises from certain home countries to establish multinational operations through investment in specific sets of host countries. However, to authors such as Caves (1971), overseas investment masks a conscious effort by an enterprise to diversify its interest and, therefore, spread its risks, a line of reasoning which has led Markowitz (1970) to examine multinational development in the context of portfolio theory. In contrast to these propositions, Aharoni (1966) maintains that the movement of enterprises into the multinational sphere is a behavioural phenomenon with the tendency to invest abroad being a function of the frequency and strength of internal (managerial) and external (environmental) stimuli. These proportions are closely related to the behavioural theory of the firm (Cyert and March, 1963) and to parallel aspects of the structural contingency models developed in organisation theory (Kast and Rosenzweig, 1973).

However, the most widely accepted theories of multinational development are those that have been proposed and elaborated upon by Vernon (1966; 1971) in relation to notions of the product cycle in the first instance, but latterly in relation to oligopolistic competition. In the product cycle explanation (Stopford and Wells, 1972; Ansoff, 1965), new products developed in the advanced core countries are seen to necessitate the acquisition of new markets as they progress to the mature stage of the cycle. With the maturity of a product, there is increased concern over production costs, a drive to export output as a first step to expand markets followed, eventually, by production abroad if labour cost differentials between the host and home country are sufficiently attractive. In the early 1970s, Vernon (1971) modified these ideas, introducing oligopoly as a prime mover in the process of multinationalisation. Oligopolists, it was suggested, would seek to prevent new firm entry and, in the second phase of the product cycle as products matured, they would seek to stabilise market shares and would move to negate any advantage a rival may gain from being the first to move into a new country. This would be achieved by locating their own facilities in that country in a follow-the-leader fashion. Competition, it was thought, would only return in the final stage of the product cycle under oligopolistic conditions.

However, Vernon's work shows the rub. In a recent paper, Vernon (1979) himself points out that the product cycle model of corporate development appears to be historically bounded:

The evidence is fairly persuasive that the product cycle hypothesis had strong predictive powers in the first two or three decades after World War II, especially in explaining the composition of US trade and in projecting the likely patterns of foreign direct investment by US firms. But certain conditions of that period are gone. For one thing, the leading MNC's have now developed global networks of subsidiaries; for another, the US market is no longer unique among national markets either in size or factor cost configuration. It seems plausible to assume that the product cycle will be less useful in explaining the relationship of the US economy to other advanced industrialised countries or to developing countries, but strong traces of the sequence are likely to remain.

The product cycle model will therefore still have some explanatory power but predominantly among smaller innovating firms and amongst 'the new multinationals' (O'Brien, 1980), developing country firms operating in international markets.

The problem, then, is how to insert models of multinational corporate development back into history. Figure 2.1 tries to summarise one such attempt for multinational corporations with their origin in market and mixed economies. At least three stages of firms' development can be identified. The nineteenth century (I) is the period of classical competitive capitalism. There are high birth and death rates as mainly (by later standards) quite small firms compete with one another. There is only one development sequence. However, beginning in the late nineteenth century and extending to the mid-twentieth century (II), a new set of development sequences gradually grows up that consists of a set of large oligopolistic business organisations with their own distinctive development sequence. As these organisations grow in size and power, so does their consequent ability to take over successful smaller firms. The result is that the smaller firm's chances of becoming a large business organisation rapidly diminish. The smaller firm develops its own limited sequence as substantial growth becomes 'a rather exceptional process' (Stanworth and Curran, 1976, p. 98). Some of the large business organisations remain, in the first instance, determinedly national, whilst others become multinational early on. Wilkins (1974a) identifies two stages in the typical multinational development sequence for US companies in this period which have more general applicability. In the first stage the approach to investment abroad is 'monocentric', that is the parent company keeps a tight grip on foreign subsidiaries, branches and affiliates and the main functions of companies abroad are to market goods made in the 'home' nation. In the European context these have been referred to as 'mother-daughter' relationships by Franko (1976). Gradually, however, the foreign subsidiaries, branches and affiliates take on a life of their own (and their own semi-independent development sequences) as a result of starting to produce goods through backward integration and so on. In the second stage, which grows out of the first, the company becomes 'polycentric' as it becomes based on a multidivisional organisational structure. Each foreign subsidiary, branch or affiliate

> [t]ake[s] on larger functions, integrating its operations and introducing new products. It might acquire other firms: it might recruit its own product planning staff; in time it might come to do its own

Figure 2.1: Corporate Growth Paths in a Historical Context

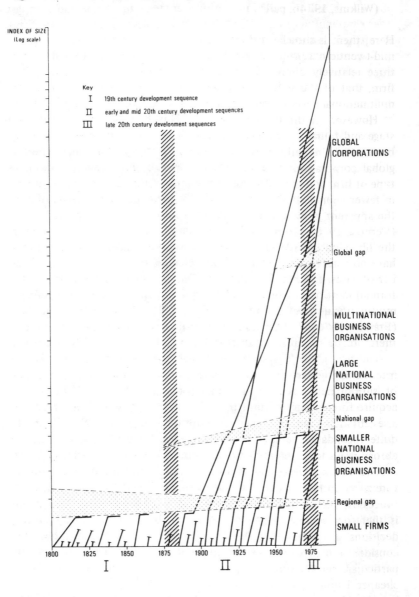

INDEX OF SIZE
(Log scale)

Key
I   19th century development sequence
II   early and mid 20th century development sequences
III late 20th century develonment sequences

GLOBAL
CORPORATIONS

Global gap

MULTINATIONAL
BUSINESS
ORGANISATIONS

LARGE
NATIONAL
BUSINESS
ORGANISATIONS

National gap

SMALLER
NATIONAL
BUSINESS
ORGANISATIONS

Regional gap

SMALL FIRMS

1800   1825   1850   1875   1900   1925   1950   1975
        I   II   III

research; it might make its own foreign [third country] investments (Wilkins, 1974b, p. 417).

Here, then, is the classical multinational. To summarise, the early and mid-twentieth century can therefore be characterised as consisting of three relatively discrete development sequences – that of the smaller firm, that of the national large business organisation and that of the multinational corporation.

However, in the late twentieth century it is possible to see a third stage and fourth development sequence developing (III), one which has been widely remarked upon in the 1970s – what might be called the global corporation. It is important to make a distinction between this type of firm and the more localised multinational corporation operating in fewer countries. The distinction is particularly important because of the apparent growth in the number of multinationals during the 1970s (Vernon, 1978). Growing corporate size on an absolute time scale and the liberalisation of the international financial system (Aliber, 1971) have obviously made multinational operations feasible in a greater number of cases. Further, the post-war years have also been marked by the formation of trading blocs, such as the EEC, which have encouraged the multinational development of corporations between member nations (Franko, 1976; Watts, 1980c). Recent multinational developments may therefore be more of a definitional nicety than an economic reality.

The new global corporation is the result of the complex process of interlocking between the relatively autonomous development sequences of subsidiaries, branches and affiliates, especially as multinationals acquire foreign *and* domestic firms that themselves have foreign subsidiaries, branches and affiliates. Some multinationals therefore grow into quite formidably complex international economic networks. Business abroad is no longer confined to several foreign centres, a few products or one or two major production processes, but exists in numerous foreign countries and in a wide range of quite different products and processes. The affiliation of the global corporation to the home country is therefore bound to be more tentative, especially since investment decisions are increasingly based on purely fiscal measures and the consideration of what therefore is the location with highest return. In particular, certain production processes, especially those that employ cheaper labour, have been moved abroad to take advantage of the lower wage rates and better worker discipline of the periphery (Fröbel, Heinrichs and Kreye, 1980).[3] In organisational terms, the old international divisions are gradually replaced by 'grid' structures, helped into existence by the new technology of computers, satellite communication and so on. Finally, in order to raise finance for increasingly large projects, the global corporations group into consortia, especially in the resource sector (Table 2.2). Thus, in the late twentieth century at least four development sequences are operating (Figure 2.1).

Table 2.2: Deep Sea-bed Mining Consortia in 1979

---

1. Kennecott Copper Corporation (US):
   Noranda (Canada)
   Consolidated Gold Fields (UK)
   Rio Tinto Zinc (UK)
   British Petroleum (UK)
   Mitsubishi (Japan)

2. Ocean Mining Associates:
   Essex Minerals Co. (a US corporation owned by United States Steel
      Corporation (US))
   Union Seas (a US corporation owned by Union Miniere, SA Belgium)
   Deepsea Ventures, Inc. (a US corporation and service contractor to Ocean
      Mining Associates)

3. Ocean Minerals Company:
   Lockheed Missiles and Space Co. Inc. (US)
   Amoco Minerals Co. (US)
   Billiton International Metals, BV (Netherlands)
   Bos Kalis Westminster Dredging (Netherlands)

4. Ocean Management, Inc.:
   INCO Ltd (Canada)
   SEDCO, Inc. (US)
   AMR Group (West Germany):
   Preussag AG
   Metallgesellschaft AG
   Salzgitter AG
   DOMCO Group (led by Sumitomo of Japan)

5. Afernod (France):
   CNEXO
   CEA
   BRGN
   Le Nickel
   France-Dunkirk

Source: *South*, 1981, p. 21.

Models of Corporate Spatial Development

In accord with the models of corporate growth developed in economics, the models developed in human geography of the spatial expansion of national and multinational enterprises have also postulated a single development sequence beginning with the small, single-plant firm and culminating with the multinational expansion of the enterprise. These explicitly geographic models can be divided into two groups. First, there are those which have taken the individual organisation as their primary focus (McNee, 1974; Blackbourn, 1974; Taylor, 1975; Erlandsson, 1975; Håkanson, 1979, for example) and, second, there are those which have attempted to stress the interrelationships between organisations as these interrelationships might influence the corporate development sequence (Rees, 1978; Watts, 1980a, 1980b).

The first set of studies, stressing internal structural metamorphosis associated with growth, owes much to the development sequence initially proposed by Ansoff (1965) and Chandler (1962) in which an enterprise was thought to pass through four distinct stages: *market penetration, product development, market development* and *diversification* (Figure 2.1). Subsequent studies have expanded specific elements of this sequence from the subnational to the multinational scale, and this progressive elaboration is demonstrated in Figure 2.2.

Figure 2.2: Four Models of Stages of Corporate Development

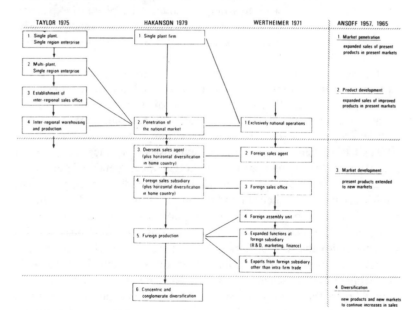

The subnational development sequence envisaged by Taylor (1975) traces the organisation from a single-plant firm, operating more frequently in the founders' home town, through a risk-minimising diffusion sequence involving the establishment of, first, an inter-regional sales office and then inter-regional warehousing and production. The essence of this model is a spatial learning process involving nested action spaces (defined by material linkages), information spaces (defined by information flows) and decision spaces (the space within which an investment decision might be made). The propositions that this model advances have proved controversial (McDermott, 1977; Harrison, Bull and Hart, 1980) and are not wholly supportable. Nevertheless, at the conclusion of this subnational development sequence, the organisation is at 'the national-multinational threshold although it may have been trading multinationally for some time' (Taylor, 1975, p. 322).

Within the geographical literature, Håkanson (1979) and Hamilton (1981) have extended this development sequence abroad. An organisation's penetration of the national market is followed by a risk-minimising diffusion sequence similar to the national sequence involving, in the first instance, the setting up of sales agencies and sales subsidiaries in order to gain access to foreign markets. This phase of expansion is then followed by a foreign production phase and, finally, 'a new phase with an integrated national subsystem in the overseas area' (Hamilton, 1981, p. 29).

Håkanson (1979) also introduces an additional element of reality into this corporate development sequence by adding the complication of product diversification – horizontal, vertical, concentric or conglomerate – as a sectoral strategy to complement, supplement or, indeed, replace a purely spatial development strategy. However, Wertheimer (1971) has spelled out the foreign expansion sequence, albeit in an essentially single-product situation, in far more detail (Figure 2.2). Håkanson's foreign production phase is elaborated to encompass, first, foreign assembly and then the extension of a foreign subsidiary's managerial and control functions to include, possibly, research and development, marketing and even financial functions. The final phase of this sequence is for the foreign subsidiary to take on export functions that go beyond intra-firm trade. The implications of this final phase in Wertheimer's (1971) scheme are plain. The foreign subsidiary may well embark upon this same risk-minimising diffusion sequence which had brought about its own creation by its parent (see also Blackbourn, 1974). However, the final phases of the sequence of development proposed by Wertheimer are not altogether supported by empirical findings, especially those relating to the structure and operation of US subsidiaries in Canada (Cordell, 1971; Government of Canada, 1972; Brown and Schneck, 1979).

Thus, empirical studies in Canada have identified two types of US subsidiary, the 'miniature replica' subsidiary, with an apparently major degree of autonomy of action, and the 'rationalised' or 'truncated' subsidiary whose operations are tightly constrained and controlled by its foreign parent. Wertheimer's sequence would suggest increasing numbers of 'miniature replica' subsidiaries emerging over time. In fact, the reverse has been true in Canada with US subsidiaries becoming progressively more bureaucratised, especially in sectors such as the automobile industry (Litvak *et al.*, 1971). However, it is important to qualify this statement, since reduced autonomy has been particularly evident in the most conspicuous US corporations and it is Hickson *et al.*'s (1974) contention that it is probably erroneous to assume that this is a general characteristic of all US ownership in Canada. It would seem equally plausible that two distinct sub-sequences of development may be open to a foreign subsidiary depending upon the inclinations, strategies and fortunes of its parent. On the one hand there might be continued spatial diffusion, while on the other hand there may be rationalisation, integration and rigid control of a foreign subsidiary's operations (cf. Taylor and Thrift, 1981c).

However, this first set of studies of corporate development has tended to treat individual organisations in isolation and not in relation to the actions and activities of the competing, controlling and complementary counterparts of their operational environments. The significance of such interdependence has been examined in a far smaller set of studies within the geographic literature which have sought, by and large, to elaborate the spatial ramifications of oligopolistic models of multinational development. Watts (1980a, 1980b) has made the greatest contribution in this respect, demonstrating not only in a simple hypothetical schema (Watts, 1980a) but also, more concretely, in an analysis of the British sugar industry in the 1920s (Watts, 1980b), the distortions of the simple spatial diffusion and accretion models which occur under conditions of oligopoly. Reinforcing his results for the British sugar beet industry with the findings of studies of the US sugar beet industry and the Mid-west meat-packing industry, Watts (1980b) has been able to identify five characteristics which characterise the spatial aspects of the interaction between firms in oligopolistic environments:

(1) *defensive, space-reserving methods* to deny potential sites to competitors;
(2) *acquisition of small-scale, rival operations*;
(3) *development of links with pressure groups* to stifle rival schemes close to current locations;
(4) *exploitation of disagreements within existing firms* to gain access to a particular region or location; and
(5) *collusive agreements with rival firms* which, though they may be short-lived, can have a major impact when they are in effect at the time of location decision-making.

Watts' studies have concentrated on large corporations which are not necessarily multinationals. However, the spatial development of multinationals under conditions of oligopoly has been examined explicitly, if only in an exploratory fashion, by Rees (1978) in relation to the operations of large rubber companies. Building on Knickerbocker's (1973) findings concerning 187 companies, in the twenty years to 1967, that 50 per cent of foreign subsidiaries had been located in three-year time clusters, Rees was able to identify elements of a similar 'move-counter move' strategy between the two largest companies in his sample, Firestone and Goodyear. The largest company, Goodyear, was established in the largest foreign tyre markets while its rival, Firestone, invested in more peripheral but growing markets, especially in Latin America. It was significant that, apart from these two largest companies, the smaller rubber manufacturing companies were neither the leaders nor the led in this pattern of point and counterpoint. Particularly striking, however, was the degree of spatial concentration associated with these cases of oligopolistic reaction in the rubber industry. Rees tentatively identified clusters of plants centred on the world's major urban regions and this pattern was particularly clear in Latin America where they centred on Buenos Aires and São Paulo (see also Cunningham, 1981). This predisposition of multinational enterprises to locate their operations in countries' major population centres near other multinational operations has also been recognised in a wide range of geographic studies covering the UK, the Netherlands, the Irish Republic, France, Germany and Europe as a whole (Watts, 1980c; Blackbourn, 1974; O'Farrell, 1975; Kemper and de Smidt, 1980; Hamilton, 1976; Labasse, 1975; McDermott, 1977, for example).

However, as with the models of corporate and multinational growth that have been developed in economics, these geographic models suffer significant limitations and shortcomings. First, and perhaps most importantly, these models also exist in only relative time, with the implication that the spatial development sequence of individual organisations is the same irrespective of when and where they are set up. This is quite clearly erroneous. The time when a firm is born and the cohort of firms it is born into is extremely important for its growth potential and the development sequence it can have in the future. Thus, Taylor and Thrift (1980, 1981a) have pointed out that access to finance has become increasingly uneven over time, favouring some firms and not others (Figure 2.1). This unevenness finds expression as *finance gaps* of which at least three can be identified (Thomas, 1978; Taylor and Thrift, 1980). The first, which has gradually diminished in importance, relates to access to banking capital and was a particular problem in the process of industrialisation in the UK in the first half of the nineteenth century, for example. Banks remain a principal source of funds for most small organisations to the present day and the establishment of a satisfactory credit profile is still a considerable hurdle to small-firm expansion (Bolton Committee, 1971). The second finance gap emerged in the late nineteenth century and became known in the UK as the 'MacMillan gap' or the venture capital gap. This barrier consists of a set of problems associated with the raising of equity finance and investment from institutional sources such as merchant banks, insurance companies and pension funds. Since the 1920s there have been problems associated with creating a market in small share issues and there are very pronounced economies of scale involved in the costs of any new share issue (Davis and Yeomans, 1974). Further, as the financial institutions have themselves grown larger, so the number of firms that are sufficiently large to satisfy their stringently conservative investment requirements have become fewer, and the finance gap confronting many enterprises has become correspondingly wider. Finally, since the Second World War, a third finance gap has emerged as a result of the internationalisation of the financial system (Aliber, 1971), bringing with it the development of international bond and currency markets. This has made finance more readily available, often on a partnership or consortium basis, to global corporations than to more localised multinational enterprises.

Quite obviously, unequal access to finance is not the only reason why there is a segmentation of development sequences according to firm type, be it smaller firm or multinational corporation. Other factors, as simple as the financial resources of a firm (which are the result of historical development, of course), which may make one firm large enough to take over or merge with other firms and another small enough to be taken over, can be equally important. But a range of factors like these, when placed in juxtaposition, does seem to create significantly different and relatively discrete spatial development sequences, according to the period and the location being studied. A firm set up at present, for example, would have to negotiate all three of the finance barriers discussed above. In contrast, a firm set up in the 1880s would have far fewer development constraints to overcome in terms of finance gaps. Certainly, it would seem reasonable to suggest that the greater the number of firms that cross a particular barrier, the more reinforced it becomes and the harder it is to cross.

Conclusion

In terms of spatial development, the propositions outlined above would deny the vast majority of present-day firms affected by the banking, finance and other gaps the opportunity to expand much beyond the restricted sub-national scale of spatial operations. Similarly, the equity and institutional finance and other gaps would deny opportunities for expansion to the multinational scale, while the existence of a more international finance and other gaps would deny many quite large multinational enterprises the chance to achieve a global scale of operations. In short, present-day expansion for the majority of firms depends upon the cohort to which they belong. Rather than the simple development sequence that may have existed in the late nineteenth century paralleled by a straightforward spatial diffusion arrangement, it is now more likely that there exists a series of truncated development sequences amongst which those followed by multinational and global corporations are quite distinctive, if not unique.

Notes

1. Take-over and merger have been classified by Whittington as a form of corporate death. Indeed, take-over undeniably involves the loss of corporate identity.

2. 'Motivation' is, of course, an unsatisfactory word because an anthropomorphic term is being used. It implies that the corporation has conscious choice. This is only partly true.

3. This movement results, of course, in the so-called 'new international division of labour' (Thrift, 1980; Fröbel, Heinrichs and Kreye, 1980).

3 TESTING DEPENDENCY THEORY: A CASE STUDY OF BRAZIL'S ELECTRICAL INDUSTRY

R.S. Newfarmer and S. Topik

Introduction

In one of the most insightful of recent articles on dependency theory, Theodore Moran (1978) asserts that dependency theorists have largely failed to test rigorously the hypotheses about multinational corporations (MNCs) that can be distilled from their overall model. He accepts his own challenge and presents three propositions he considers integral to dependency analysis. First, the benefits of foreign direct investment are 'unequally' or 'unfairly' distributed between MNCs and host countries in favour of the former, and so, in effect, MNCs are able to siphon off investible surplus. Second, MNCs create distortions in the local economy by squeezing out local business, using inappropriate technology, acting to worsen the distribution of income, and, finally, distorting consumer tastes. Third, foreign investors pervert or subvert host country political processes. To analyse these dependency propositions, Moran attempts to open a 'dialogue' between dependency theorists and other social scientists. By breaking the propositions down into component hypotheses he indicates how non-dependency theories such as theories of oligopolistic competition and bilateral monopoly might be used to verify or falsify these dependency propositions.

This chapter builds on Moran's analysis and shows the great usefulness of his theoretical formulation as well as the possible weakness of some of his preliminary conclusions. Following Moran's suggestion, we use theories of oligopolistic rivalry and bilateral monopoly in a case study of the development of Brazil's electrical industry from 1880 to 1945. The first section of this chapter elaborates slightly on aspects of the dependency propositions. The second section examines the early international electrical industry and the modes of oligopolistic rivalry among firms at the international level, and the third looks at their consequences for Brazilian development. A final section re-examines the dependency propositions in the light of Brazil's experience with the electrical MNCs.

Bilateral Monopoly and Oligopolistic Rivalry

To test his first proposition that the benefits of foreign direct investment are distributed unfairly between MNCs and host countries, Moran argues that Kindleberger's notion of bilateral monopoly is a helpful conceptualisation. The notion is that MNCs (individually or collectively) monopolise certain factors or products while the state in developing countries 'monopolises' the terms of access available to MNCs entering the local market or exploiting the local resource. Within certain bounds,[1] the distribution of gains from the MNC activity in the host country will be determined by the relative economic and political power that MNCs and host countries can muster.

Gains do not only include accounting profits, however. As Vaitsos (1974a) has shown, 'returns' from MNC activity include present earnings (including earnings of subsidiaries, from export sales, from sales of technology, from intra-firm sales, and in the form of interest on parent-held debt to subsidiaries) as well as future earnings through 'control' of the market. Control allows the firm to continue to collect all the other forms of returns. If control represents the present value of the discounted future stream of earnings, it is evident that this portion is the more important element of benefits.

The degree of competition in the international industry is obviously important to the bargaining position over gains of both the MNCs and the state. On the basis of Vernon's product cycle theory, Moran asserts that international competition among MNCs is increasing. As MNCs create and expand sales of a product, technological barriers to entry fall, and new foreign and then domestic firms enter the market. Most MNC markets, the theory postulates, pass through a relatively rapid cycle of monopoly and oligopoly that ends in workable competition. Over time, then, competition among MNCs is likely to increase in most markets and monopoly profits (Moran's Proposition I) and any distortions due to the foreign presence (Proposition II) will both decrease. In fact, Vernon (1978) extrapolates from this process and suggests that domestically controlled firms in developing countries will soon enter MNC-dominated markets and the level of foreign control (or denationalisation) of an industry will tend to fall. The theory would posit, then, that new competition will limit both the monopoly earnings and the 'control' components of returns going to MNCs in an industry of a developing country. Although Moran and Vernon make their assertions for the contemporary period, if the product cycle model has any validity in explaining changes in competitive behaviour or denationalisation, we could apply it to a longer historical period and arrive at similar conclusions.

The questions for our historical analysis of the international electrical industry then are: did MNCs at first monopolise the international industry and then rapidly evolve into a state of workable competition that transmitted the benefits of advanced technology and products to Brazil? If not, why did the predictions of the product cycle model not hold? Finally, what were the consequences for Brazilian industrial development?

The International Electrical Oligopoly

The Birth of the Large Electrical Firms

The nearly simultaneous demonstrations of the lightbulb in 1879 by Thomas Edison in the United States and Joseph Swan in England marked the birth of the electrical industry. The event triggered the growth of new technologies to supply electricity to the new demand created by lamps throughout the USA, Great Britain and Western Europe. In the decade after 1879, a handful of firms in the United States, Germany and, to a lesser extent, the other European countries gained legal access to the technology and began producing lamps and electrical equipment.

In each of these national markets, initially intense competition led to mergers and shake-outs, and convinced the surviving dominant firms of the benefits of reducing competition to raise prices and profits. In Europe, manufacturing associations sprang up to moderate competition and fix prices in the respective national markets (Jones and Marriott, 1970; Stocking and Watkins, 1946). In the US, where anti-trust laws constituted a growing obstacle to overt collusion, General Electric and Westinghouse signed a patent exchange agreement in 1896. They pooled their patents and proportioned their business out on a basis of 62.5 per cent to GE and 37.5 per cent to Westinghouse. The agreements facilitated oligopolistic pricing that substituted for the overt collusion possible in European markets (Passer, 1953). In lieu of price competition, rivalry among American firms often took non-price forms, particularly in invention and innovation, patent acquisition, product differentiation and, at first, foreign investment.

The Internationalisation of the Industry

As early as the 1880s, the largest producers turned their attention to markets abroad in search of quick profits from the new technology. The industry rapidly became 'international'. The history of the international industry may be divided into three periods, which correspond roughly to the evolution of MNCs' behaviour in the world market. From about 1880 to 1900, they competed vigorously in each other's markets. However, the major international firms soon realised the costs of competition and turned to the allocation of markets to each other via patent licences (about 1900-30); and then, with the Great Depression, the MNCs entered into overt international collusion (about 1930-45) to organise world markets.

The First Attempts to Capture Foreign Markets through Foreign Investment: 1880 to 1900

With the development of lamp and related electrical technology, the three major US electrical companies quickly sought to reap the returns of their inventions abroad. In the 1880s Edison Electric set up marketing agreements with Edison Swan in England, Deutsche Edison Gesellschaft (the AEG predecessor) company in Germany, and the Societa Edison per la Fabbricazione delle Lampade in Italy. The Thomson-Houston company set up Thomson-Houston International in the late 1880s, through which it established British Thomson-Houston to market arc lamps and incandescent bulbs in England in 1890. It also organised the Société Française Thomson-Houston in France (Jones and Marriott, 1970). These foreign operations fell under single management with the merger of Edison and Thomson-Houston to form General Electric in 1892. Finally, Westinghouse established British Westinghouse to market and manufacture its products in Britain in 1899, as a minority-owned affiliate (FTC, 1928). Meanwhile, the Siemens brothers, owners of the only European company of sufficient strength, tried to enter the United States market. It organised manufacturing subsidiaries in Chicago in 1892 (Passer, 1953).

By the late 1890s, however, these forays of direct investment overseas had shown themselves ineffective. The competition was keen and the American concerns had problems managing their affiliates from such a long distance. They had difficulty in obtaining patent protection from local host governments, which were often sympathetic to the claims of their nationals. Not infrequently, domestic companies simply pirated designs or tied up the foreign affiliates in patent suits (FTC, 1928). Consequently, the major firms ceased to expand in each other's markets, and in some cases liquidated their holdings.[2] These liquidations formed part of a broader pattern of behaviour that muted competition among producers.

International Licensing Arrangements to Allocate Markets: 1900 to 1930

As early as 1883, Werner Siemens was concerned about foreign competition and had written to his brother William: 'I believe it would be good policy to make peace with Edison *in the whole world*. It will make us ruler of the electrical industry' (quoted in Epstein and Mirow, 1977). In fact, Henry Villard, an eminent railway financier who organised the merger to create General Electric, had close connections with Siemens and Halske in Germany, and he planned to create a world cartel in electrical equipment (Chandler, 1977). Still it took another decade and a half to quell the heated competition in markets and courts of law. The leading international firms then turned to a system of international co-ordination similar to that adopted by GE and Westinghouse in 1896: patent licensing agreements. These were cross-licensing arrangements in which each party recognised the patent rights of the other, and exchanged their patented technology, subject to specified conditions.[3]

Cross-licences among international firms had been used as early as 1892, the date of one of the early Thomson-Houston agreements with France's Compagnie Française pour l'Exploitation des Procedes Thomson-Houston (FTC, 1928). Legal contracts probably became more important after the turn of the century and as international leaders established uneasy *détente* in multiple markets. References to contracts appear between General Electric and AEG in 1903, then between General Electric and Japan's Tokyo Electric beginning in 1904, and with Shibaura Engineering in 1905. Their duration ranged from 3 years to 100 years. By 1926 GE had licensing arrangements with over 19 separate foreign companies (FTC, 1928).

Moreover, as the world's dominant firm, General Electric began purchasing equity shares in its licencees and by 1935 had gained minority shares in most major European and Japanese leading electrical companies. In developing countries, GE maintained full equity control of GE SA in Brazil, Mexicana Lampadas and China General Electric, all of which it had established before the First World War (Stocking and Watkins, 1946). Other US leaders, such as Westinghouse and RCA, adopted licensing tactics similar to GE's.

Division of the World's Markets. The international patent agreements and cross-equity investments reduced international competition through the clauses in the licences that divided up world markets. The signers were allowed to use each other's patents and inventions, but only within well defined territories. The agreements divided the world into exclusive territories, non-exclusive territories and territories excluded from the agreements. Agreements stipulated where products could be sold, where they could be manufactured, and often which firms could set the price in a given market (FTC, 1928).

GE's contracts with AEG and Osram of Germany illustrate how these arrangements effectively allocated world electrical products. A contract with Osram dated 1921 divided up the world market for lamps for the 15-year duration of the contract (Osram was the lamp manufacturing joint venture of AEG, Siemens and Auer). Later in the 1920s, GE purchased Auer's share (UKBT, 1947). The agreement with AEG covered electrical apparatus and was to continue for 20 years, 'and thereafter unless terminated by not less than three years notice by either party'. In both contracts, GE reserved as its exclusive territory the North American continent, Cuba, the West Indies and the United States possessions, colonies and protectorates (except the Philippines in the Osram contract). The contracts granted as exclusive territory to AEG and Osram the countries of Germany, Denmark, Norway, Poland, Austria, Hungary, Czechoslovakia, Sweden and Finland. In addition to these, AEG also received Memel, Danzig, Estonia, Latvia and Lithuania (FTC, 1928).

The agreements excluded territories where GE had concluded separate agreements with other licensees, such as Philips in Belgium and Luxemburg, Française Thomson-Houston and CGE of France in Spain, Portugal and Greece. The remainder of the world was described as non-exclusive territory, and although products could be exported to those areas, no domestic production was allowed (FTC, 1928).

These agreements were revised and renewed at the end of the contractual period. In the case of GE's agreements with AEG and Osram, contract renewals took place on 7 October 1938. The territorial definitions changed slightly. More importantly, the foreign exchange shortage of many of the non-exclusive territories evinced some domestic investment in the industry in many of these companies' product lines. The threat of competition from national industry prompted AEG and GE to change the provision prohibiting manufacture in these areas with each other's technology. Both agreed to allow manufacture in some of the hitherto non-producing countries (UKBT, 1947).

Similar international arrangements were concluded among the other dominant world producers. All in all, the products covered by licences with territorial restrictions included the great bulk of sales in the electrical industry. During the 1920s and 1930s, agreements among international major companies divided up the world markets for lamps, electrical machinery, household appliances, motion picture equipment, phonographs, radio equipment, typewriters and other products (Hexner, 1946).

Another tool for dividing markets in addition to cross-licences was patent pooling, used most effectively in consumer electronics. Pools were formed in most industrialised countries, each with allocated areas of the world for exports. For example, the companies belonging to the US patent pool in radios and vacuum tubes received Canada, the US and its possessions. The Philips-led pool in the Netherlands received Czechoslovakia, Denmark, Estonia, Finland, Latvia and Lithuania, Norway, Sweden and Switzerland together with their colonies. This prevented export competition among the majors in the allocated areas (FTC, 1923; UKBT, 1947).

A third tactic to allocate markets was joint ventures. For example, in October 1921, ITT and the other three large telecommunications companies of the world entered into an agreement to eliminate competition between themselves in the South American market. The companies formed a single, continent-wide 'committee' with two representatives on the board from each company to manage jointly the former competitors (UKBT, 1947).

These agreements fostered a co-operative environment out of which more severe restrictive practices could grow as the grip of world-wide depression became felt.[4]

The Era of Extensive International Cartelisation: 1930-45

The onset of the Depression had a dramatic destabilising effect on the international interdependent equilibrium that had been organised under cross-licences. Producers frantically searched for new markets to keep their plants busy. Since home demand had almost evaporated and new competition was depressing export prices, the largest transnational enterprises finally turned to collusion to preserve their hunting grounds from outside poaching and to maintain prices to non-producing countries.

The most effective way to eliminate the threat of increased competition was to arrive at formal and binding agreements. On 13 December 1930, nine of the world's largest electrical manufacturers met in the Paris office of International General Electric Company, and signed the

Figure 3.1: The Territorial Division of the World according to the
International Notification and Compensation Agreement (INCA) of
1930

◯ FOREIGN COMPANIES WITH WHICH INTERNATIONAL GENERAL ELECTRIC
COMPANY, INC. HAS PATENT LICENSES AND KNOW-HOW EXCHANGE CONTRACTS

German
1 Osram Kommanditgesellschaft
2 Allgemeine Elektricitaets Gesellschaft
3 Juilus Pintsch Akhengesellschaft
4 Veremiate Gluhlampen und Electricitaets A.G.
5 Electrische-Gluhlampenfabrik "Watt" A.G.

Austrian
6 Joh. Kremenezky Fabrik fur Elektrische Gluhlampen (Vienna)

Hungarian
7 Ungorische Wolfram Lampenfabrik, Joh. Kremenezky A.G. (Budapest)

Dutch
8 Philips Glow Lamp Works, Ltd.

Belgian
9 Usines Corels Freres

French
10 Compagnie Francaise pour l'Exploitation des Procedes
   Thomson-Houston
11 La Compagnie Generals d'Electricite

Spain and Portugal
12 Compagnie Francaise pour l'Exploitation des Procedes
   Thomson-Houston

Great Britain
13 General Electric Co. Ltd.
14 British Thomson-Houston Co. Ltd.

Italian
15 Societa Edison Clerici, Fabbrica Lampada
16 Franco To: Societa Anonima

Japanese
17 Tokyo Electric Co. Ltd.
18 Shibaura Engineering Works, Ltd.

Brazilian
19 General Electric Sociedad Anonima

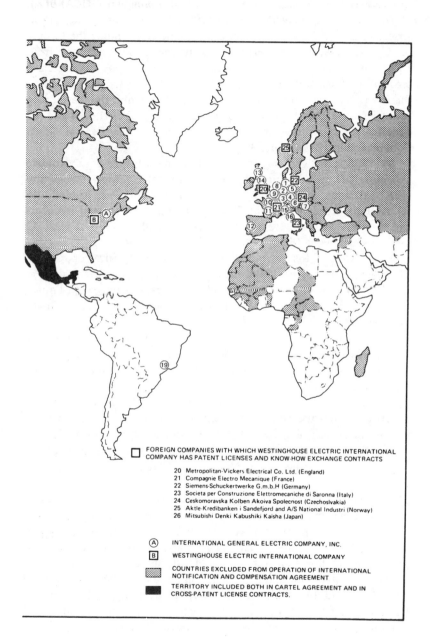

FOREIGN COMPANIES WITH WHICH WESTINGHOUSE ELECTRIC INTERNATIONAL
COMPANY HAS PATENT LICENSES AND KNOW-HOW EXCHANGE CONTRACTS

20 Metropolitan-Vickers Electrical Co. Ltd. (England)
21 Compagnie Electro Mecanique (France)
22 Siemens-Schuckertwerke G.m.b.H (Germany)
23 Societa per Construzione Elettromecaniche di Saronna (Italy)
24 Ceskomoravska Kolben Akoiva Spolecnost (Czechoslvakia)
25 Aktie-Kredibanken i Sandefjord and A/S National Industri (Norway)
26 Mitsubishi Denki Kabushiki Kaisha (Japan)

Ⓐ INTERNATIONAL GENERAL ELECTRIC COMPANY, INC.

Ⓑ WESTINGHOUSE ELECTRIC INTERNATIONAL COMPANY

COUNTRIES EXCLUDED FROM OPERATION OF INTERNATIONAL
NOTIFICATION AND COMPENSATION AGREEMENT

TERRITORY INCLUDED BOTH IN CARTEL AGREEMENT AND IN
CROSS-PATENT LICENSE CONTRACTS.

International Notification and Compensation Agreement (INCA), a formal cartel to restrain trade in electrical equipment (FTC, 1948). The INCA agreements re-enforced existing market allocation arrangements established through the cross-licences among the leading producers. Indeed, these territories were specifically excluded from INCA's provisions because in general they were already the exclusive territories of leading companies. Instead, INCA cartelised exports to the non-exclusive territories of the world, mainly the developing countries. A map of the excluded (hence protected) territories and the cartelised, non-exclusive areas was prepared by the Federal Trade Commission in 1948 (Figure 3.1).

By 1936, producers felt the need for a more formal administrative apparatus and so they formed the International Electrical Association (IEA) in Zurich, Switzerland, to administer INCA. It was divided into 16 sections based on separate product groups.[5] Additional members and sections were rapidly admitted. By the end of 1936 at least 42 members had joined (FTC, 1948).

The advent of the Second World War disrupted cartel operations. The war fragmented the cartel into separate factions on each side. The cartel survived in Britain through the war years, but only with limited participation of some British, American, Swedish and Swiss MNCs (Monopolies Commission, 1957).

In 1944 the US Federal Trade Commission announced an investigation of the American firms' participation in the cartel, charging that they had violated US anti-trust laws by illegally conspiring to restrain international trade. After three years of investigation and legal manoeuvring, a consent decree was issued in March of 1947. The American companies were legally enjoined from further participation in any international cartel (FTC, 1948). The International Electric Association, however, continued to operate as a cartel embracing the major European producers (see Newfarmer, 1978).

The Effects of the International Oligopolists' Tactics. The numerous cross-licensing, patent pooling and joint venture agreements and later formal cartel arrangements effectively reduced competition throughout the markets of the world. First, they eliminated potential foreign competition in the home markets of the industrialised nations, buttressing the concentrated structure of production there and in the international market. Second, by 'sharing a monopoly' of technology, the dominant international firms ensured that potential domestic competitors could not use the advanced technology of foreign rivals to enter the home market. Third, by allocating export markets to specific producers, the agreements typically prevented competition that would lower prices in exports to developing countries. Fourth, agreements to share technology only among themselves prevented independent firms in developing countries from gaining access to patented technology and breaking into MNC export markets. Finally, the post-1930 cartel arrangements regulated the prices of almost all international electrical equipment exports with the objective of raising prices above the competitive level.

The strategies and tactics adopted by the international oligopoly had important ramifications for the development of one of the territories allocated in the patent and cartel agreements — Brazil.

Dependent Development in Brazil's Electrical Industry

The Context: the Economic and Class Structure of Early Brazil

Industry and the Industrialists. During the first decades of the 1900s, foreign trade was the motor that drove the Brazilian economy. Agriculture, particularly coffee, provided over 90 per cent of Brazil's foreign exchange before 1945.

The export economy did foster some industrialisation. By 1910, Brazilian industry accounted for approximately half of all manufactured products; they were mostly light consumer goods (Dean, 1969). The First World War accelerated industrial production by dramatically reducing imports. The volume of industrial production grew by 50 per cent during the war and tripled by 1923 (Baer, 1965; Recenseamento, 1920). The industries that thrived had in common low capital and technological barriers to entry. For example, textiles and foodstuffs supplied nearly three-quarters of factory production. In addition, paper, glass, cigarettes, soap and matches were produced in significant quantities and several noteworthy foundries manufactured hardware, agricultural machinery and railway wagons (Recenseamento, 1920).

The textile industry experienced particular success, despite competition from imports from Europe and North America. By 1907, the average factory of the country's textile centre, Rio de Janeiro, employed almost 300 workers. By 1920, Brazilian factories had expanded to a scale comparable to their foreign competition and met virtually all the demand for textiles (Stein, 1957). Brazilians were able to get textile technology because Great Britain, having lost its competitive advantage in textiles to the US and other European producers, began selling relatively inexpensive technology (Hobsbawm, 1968).

The success of Brazilian industrialists in non-electrical machinery after the First World War also demonstrates the ability of Brazilian entrepreneurs to prosper in sectors where technological barriers to entry were relatively low and profits relatively high. Brazilian manufacturers of non-electrical machinery, whom Nathaniel Leff terms 'brilliant mechanics', had already captured an important share of the market by 1920 and by 1947-9 domestic suppliers provided approximately 61 per cent of all Brazilian capital goods (Leff, 1968).

Most industrial capital originated with planters or merchants, who viewed industry as complementary to their other activities.[6] Many planters moved into industries that processed the crops that they grew, such as sugar mills and textile factories. Some of the planters invested in industry because they had the advantage of political influence. For example, they invested in railways that received government-guaranteed profits. Non-planter merchants who established factories usually chose sectors in which they enjoyed protection from the peculiarities of the duty schedule or because of high international transport costs.[7]

The absence of a strong industrial class that perceived its interests as distinct from those of agriculture and commerce and the political supremacy of an export-oriented oligarchy precluded a more nationalist government policy of encouraging the substitution of local manufactures for imports. Planters, who exercised considerable political hegemony between 1880 and 1945, primarily promoted agricultural interests. The planter-dominated federal government derived two-thirds of this revenue from import duties since it did not want to tax land or incomes (derived from Villela and Suzigan, 1975). As a result, the government could not erect prohibitive barriers to imports without suffering a serious loss of revenue. Even the most prosperous and efficient industries such as textiles only won a measure of duty protection after they proved themselves capable competitors in the open market. Government officials opposed duties to protect infant industries, not only because such action would jeopardise their budget, but also because they believed that protection bred inefficiency and monopoly. Moreover, they feared that a tariff wall might lead foreign governments to retaliate by raising their own barriers against Brazilian production. Politicians exempted from duties the most sophisticated imports, such as electric lights, tram cars and telephones in order to encourage private entrepreneurs to equip Brazil with the trappings of modernity (Stein, 1957; PAU, 1903; Luz, 1975).

In contrast to the European and Japanese experience, Brazilian interest groups controlling government policy did not provide the development of national industry in the more sophisticated products, but left the door open to foreign goods. One of these product groups was electrical equipment.

The Beginnings of the Demand for Electricity. The birth of demand for electrical products came when Dom Pedro II installed six electrical arc lamps in the central railway station in Rio de Janeiro in 1879, the same year that Edison invented the incandescent light bulb. Foreign investors became the dominant source of funding for the electrical power industry. With ready access to large amounts of capital, they bought up many of the larger municipal utilities established by Brazilians, once demand spurred the need for greater capital investments.

The Canadian investors who founded the Brazilian Traction, Light and Power Company began by providing electricity for nearly all of São Paulo's tramways, lighting and power in 1901. Four years later the same people founded the Rio de Janeiro Tramway, Light and Power Company which, in addition to providing the city with electricity, operated its tramways, lighting, gas, power and telephones (Wileman, 1909; Souza Lima, 1962).

Another group entered with foreign financing: the Electric Bond and Share Company. This company was born as a financial subsidiary of General Electric in the United States in the early 1880s. It was established partially to finance customers for GE electrical products from the abundant profits of the manufacturing enterprise. Although it financed utilities from the turn of the century on, it expanded in the 1920s by buying up seven major and many minor Brazilian-owned companies. By 1930, the company served most of Brazil's major cities outside Rio and São Paulo.[8] This group was later acquired by American and Foreign Power Company, subsequently controlled by ITT.

The North American penetration was not without competition from Brazilians. Guinle and Gaffree, who owned one of the largest Brazilian enterprises of the early twentieth century — the docks at Santos — attempted to win the concession for Rio's public utilities. The city eventually awarded the contract to Brazilian Traction, Light and Power. While failing in Rio, the Brazilian entrepreneurs established a substantial system of public utility companies, dominating such major cities as Salvador, Bahia and Port Alegre, Rio Grande do Sul. Only in the late 1920s were Guinle and Gaffree induced to sell their companies to the

Bond and Share group because they could not raise sufficient capital from the North American capital markets to modernise and expand their systems.[9]

Thus by 1920, foreign-owned companies generated over half of all electricity.[10] By 1940, the Canadian-owned Brazilian Traction, Light and Power — by far the largest foreign company — produced single-handedly over half of all the country's electricity. All foreign companies were responsible for over 80 per cent of Brazil's electrical output.[11]

The foreign-owned electrical generating giants provided the greatest demand for heavy electrical equipment. The growth rate of the electrical machine industry, both of the equipment supplied to generation and distribution and of final user demand, is seen in the expansion of installed generating capacity. Growth was extremely rapid from 1890 to 1910 — over tenfold in both decades. After 1910, generating capacity doubled about every decade except during the war years (Table 3.1). Overall, this capacity expansion indicates an eightyfold increase in the industry between 1900 and 1930 (Baer, 1965).

Table 3.1: Expansion of Installed Electric Capacity (kilowatts)

Year	Thermal	Hydraulic	Total
1883	52	—	52
1890	1,017	250	1,267
1900	5,093	5,283	10,376
1910	32,729	124,672	157,401
1920	66,072	300,946	367,018
1930	148,752	630,050	778,802
1940	234,531	1,009,346	1,243,877
1945	261,806	1,079,827	1,341,633
1950	346,830	1,535,670	1,882,500
1955	667,318	2,481,171	3,148,489
1960	1,158,057	3,642,025	4,800,082
1961	1,136,000	3,809,000	5,205,000
1962	1,603,000	4,126,000	5,729,000
1963	1,876,000	4,476,000	6,355,000
1964	1,946,000	4,894,000	6,840,000
1965	2,020,000	5,391,000	7,411,000
1966	2,040,000	5,524,000	7,556,000
1967	2,255,000	5,787,000	8,042,000
1968	2,372,000	6,183,000	8,555,000
1969	2,405,000	7,857,000	10,262,000
1970	2,405,000	8,828,000	11,233,000
1971	2,426,000	10,244,000	12,670,000
1972	2,736,000	10,979,000	13,715,000
1973	3,067,000	12,765,000	15,032,000

Source: Werner Baer, *Industrialization and Economic Development in Brazil* (Richard Irwin, Homewood, Ill., 1965), pp. 265, 266 for years 1883-1960. For years 1961 to 1973, Brazilian National Committee of the World Energy Conference, *Estatistica Brasiliera de Energia* (Rio de Janeiro, 1974), p. 35.

The foreign firms who built the new generating capacity satisfied their demand for equipment in the pre-Depression years primarily through imports. Imports of the new industry rose sixfold between 1902 and 1912, more rapidly than all other Brazilian industries (Villela and Suzigan, 1975). Virtually no electrical products were produced locally. Indeed, the 1907 Industrial Census reports only one electrical establishment with 33 employees. Even by 1920, there was almost no recorded electrical machinery production. In fact, fewer than 40 electrical firms existed in Brazil.[12] Thus, by 1920, after two decades of consumption and a 3,000 per cent increase in generation, domestic production of electrical equipment in Brazil remained virtually nonexistent.

The Coming of the Equipment Suppliers. The early suppliers of electrical equipment were also predominantly foreign. The old predecessor to General Electric, the Thomson-Houston Company, had established an unincorporated sales subsidiary in Rio de Janeiro prior to 1890 (Banas, 1962). Siemens of Germany was the first international electric firm to incorporate an electrical subsidiary in Brazil in 1905. Prior to the turn of the century, Siemens had built the Vila Isabel railway and founded the Cia. Telefonica do Rio de Janeiro, partly to promote their own equipment sales (Ruiz, 1974). AEG, Ericsson of Sweden, Philips of the Netherlands, Standard Electric (ITT) and Pirelli soon followed these examples.

The history of General Electric in Brazil illuminates how one member of the international oligopoly established control over prices and development of the domestic market. In 1921, at about the same time it renewed licensing arrangements with the principal European producers, GE began assembling incandescent bulbs in Brazil. In 1925, the parent company established (or probably renewed) a licensing arrangement with its Brazilian affiliate. In most of the international agreements, Brazil was defined as a 'nonexclusive territory'. This meant that the European cross-licensees, in most of whom GE owned a substantial equity share, could sell lamps in Brazil using GE technology, but only at 'prices that are not more favourable to the producers than those of the General Electric Company' (FTC, 1928, p. 140).

The European licensees were prevented by contract from manufacturing in Brazil using GE technology. Of the major European lamp manufacturers, only Philips of Holland set up early operations in Brazil incorporating a sales subsidiary in 1925 (Banas, 1961). GE owned about 18.7 per cent of Philips in Holland and was its principal licensor.

The patent exchange contracts stipulated that GE could set all prices in Brazil (Stocking and Watkins, 1946). All Philips lamps were supplied by GE's plant in Rio, though they were marketed under the Philips' name. In short, this non-manufacturing Brazilian subsidiary shared GE's lamp monopoly instead of threatening it. Philips did not begin manufacturing light bulbs domestically until after 1949. Neither of these firms engaged in export production, even to nearby countries in Latin America, until the 1960s (Banas, 1962).

The First World War had created partial and temporary protection from imports for both Brazilian and foreign electrical firms. However, the industry appears to have stagnated while other domestic manufacturing accelerated with growth rates of over 25 per cent per year from 1914 to 1919 (Bergsman, 1970). Electrical imports fell from an index (1902 = 100) of 634 in 1912 to 182 in 1914, and then remained below 150 until 1919 when importation resumed (Villela and Suzigan, 1975). But local production did not develop. Growth in generating capacity slowed; while it had grown 150 per cent in the five years before 1914, in the war years the increase was only 20 per cent (Recenseamento, 1920). The cut-off of imports during the First World War simply stifled growth because those with the technology — the foreign corporations — had no capability to produce locally, while Brazilian firms without access to technology could not enter the industry. Importation resumed after the First World War and lasted until 1930 (Villela and Suzigan, 1975).

To review the development of the industry to 1930, then, is to see a picture of rapid domestic demand satisfied by mainly imported electrical products. Foreign companies built or soon acquired most of the electrical generating capacity in Brazil, and these companies bought foreign equipment often from financially related suppliers at home. Local subsidiaries imported from abroad to satisfy equipment buyers and local consumers. The Depression brought about massive changes in the international economy.

The Origins of the Contemporary Industry: 1930-45

With the collapse of the international economy in 1930, the scarcity of foreign exchange created temporary but substantial protection for Brazilian manufacturing in light consumer products. With idle plants at home and depleted treasuries from stagnant demand, MNCs could not readily undertake manufacturing activities in countries like Brazil. One or two companies already in the market, such as GE, could and did expand using domestically generated funds. As foreign exchange became expensive, GE opened a parts factory for its lamp operations, and by 1937 production amounted to 4 million bulbs per year. The company began assembling electricity meters, small transformers and radio receivers in the late 1930s. For the most part, however, components were imported (Banas, 1962). Few other MNCs followed GE's example.

Because the Depression removed temporarily the threat of foreign competition in imported consumer products, Brazilian firms could at last enter the industry in the low-technology end of the market. They often purchased technology for comparatively simple consumer products from firms in the developed countries, which could not now reach the Brazilian market. Brazilians also undertook production by simply copying the design of products previously imported.

In effect, barriers to entry were lowered at the same time protection was increased for consumer electrical goods. Significantly, of the 100 largest firms in 1960, 38 enterprises were established during the 1931 to 1950 period, and at least 80 per cent of these were Brazilian-owned (Newfarmer, forthcoming). Most of these entrants were electrical wire and small parts producers and light electrical appliance producers. For example, Arno was founded during this period and later became one of the largest domestically owned firms in Brazil (Banas, 1962).

Only after the Second World War did MNCs begin to manufacture appreciable quantities of electrical machinery in Brazil. General Electric, for example, began producing some light induction motors in its San Andre plant, beginning in 1949. These powered light household appliances and small industrial machines. GE began refrigerator production in 1951 and fans in 1958. It was not until 1962 with the opening of the Campinas plant that General Electric began producing heavy electrical equipment such as large motors, generators and transformers (Banas, 1962).

The history of General Electric was repeated by the other early transnational producers. AEG and Siemens, for example, did not begin manufacturing until after the Second World War, and the same generally held true for other producers (Table 3.2).

Growth of local electrical manufacturing was noteworthy. While overall manufacturing production doubled between 1939 and 1949, the electrical industry grew even more rapidly. In fact, the electrical industry has been a leading industrial sector from 1939 to the present. Its share of manufacturing value added rose from 1.2 per cent in 1939 to 5.7 per cent in 1972 (Table 3.3). While growth rates of the industry were impressive, its economic impact was still relatively small because of a small initial base. The 'take-off' of the industry really occurred after 1949, in the period of import substitution and rapid expansion of the multinational corporations in Brazil.

Table 3.2: Pre-1939 Selected MNCs: Pattern of Establishing Productive Activities

Firm	Began Direct Selling in Brazil	Incorporations of Sales Subsidiary	Some Manufacturing or Assembly Activity	Capital Goods Manufacture[d]
Siemens	Pre-1900	1905	1958[b]	Late 1960s[c]
AEG	Turn of the century	1913	Mid-1950s	Mid-1950s
GE	Pre-1900	1914	1921	1949
Ericsson	Pre-1900	1924	1955	1955
Philips	Early 1920s	1925	1949	Not applicable
Standard Electric ITT	Pre-1908	1926	1942	Post-war
Pirelli	Unknown	1929	1923[a]	1948
Electrolux	1924	1926	1950	Not applicable

Notes: [a]Pirelli entered the market by buying CONAC, a São Paulo firm founded by Roberto Simonsen in 1923, which made electrical connectors. In 1930 Pirelli engaged in some wire-stretching and packaging, but all cable and conductors integration was not complete until after the Second World War. The 1929 firm was acquired as a joint venture with GE International, whose share was sold within 5 years. Pirelli controlled the international patents on its cable products.

[b]In 1957 Siemens acquired Icotron of Porto Alegre, its sales representative since 1954.

[c]Entered the heavy transformers market in joint venture with AEG.

[d]Using at least one-fifth local material inputs by value.

Source: Banas, 1961, 1962; interviews.

In review, the electrical machinery industry remained relatively stagnant and devoid of Brazilian producers until the coming of the Depression, despite the rapid growth of generating capacity and final demand for electrical goods. After the Depression, the effective barriers to imports created a fortuitous environment for import-substituting domestic entrants into local production relatively free of foreign competition. Thus after 1939, local participation in the industry was high, and growth rates were more rapid than the average for all Brazilian manufacturing.

Table 3.3: Industrial Value Added by Industry (per cent, selected years)

	1919	1939	1949	1959	1969	1973
Electrical equipment	—	1.2	1.7	3.9	5.4	5.7
Metals	4.3	7.7	7.4	11.9	11.6	11.9
Machinery	2.0	4.0	2.2	3.5	7.1	8.7
Transportation	—	0.6	2.3	7.5	8.0	7.6
Rubber products	0.2	0.7	2.1	2.3	2.0	1.8
Chemical & pharm.	6.0	10.4	9.4	13.4	16.9	17.4
Non-metalic minerals	4.7	5.3	7.4	6.6	5.9	5.0
Wood	5.8	5.1	3.4	3.2	2.5	3.2
Furniture	2.0		2.2	2.2	2.1	2.0
Paper & allied	1.5	1.4	2.1	3.0	2.6	3.0
Leather	2.4	1.7	1.3	1.1	0.7	0.7
Textiles	28.6	22.7	20.1	12.0	7.3	9.3
Apparel	8.6	4.7	4.3	3.6	3.4	3.6
Food	22.2	22.9	19.6	16.9	13.4	11.6
Beverages	5.9	4.5	4.3	2.9	2.4	2.1
Tobacco	3.9	2.2	1.6	1.3	1.3	1.2
Printing & publishing	—	3.6	4.2	3.0	3.7	3.2
Miscellaneous	1.9	1.1	1.9	1.6	2.1	2.0
	100.0	100.0	100.0	100.0	100.0	100.0

Sources: For 1919-1959, Werner Baer, *Industrialization and Economic Development in Brazil* (Richard D. Irwin, Homewood, Ill., 1965), p. 269. For 1969, IBGE, *Census Industrial*. For 1973, IBGE, *Pesquisa Industrial* (1973).

Oligopolistic Rivalry and Dependent Development

Speaking to Moran's first dependency proposition, the historical evidence suggests that the rapid erosion of the monopolistic advantage of the MNCs predicted by the product cycle model did not occur during the first six and a half decades of the industry's history. Instead of evolving rapidly from a highly concentrated industry through oligopoly into a workably competitive industry, the industry went through a cycle of initial competition and then consolidation in domestic markets to international informal and formal cartelisation. The consequences of these international oligopolistic practices for interactions in the bilateral monopoly situation were to give MNCs considerable market power over the entire period and thus give them an unfair share of the gains.

The early restrictive practices of the dominant MNCs succeeded in reducing competition in the world markets for electrical products and electrical technology. Territorial divisions of world markets reduced competition and undoubtedly resulted in above-normal profits. Collusive pricing in world trade in cables, heavy electrical equipment and many consumer goods had the effect of raising price above marginal costs, penalising consumers. The patent pools raised the prices of goods sold in the covered territories by eliminating competition and the joint ventures institutionalised the shared monopoly.[13]

There were, of course, economic benefits of international trade and investment accruing to both MNCs and consumers in Brazil. However, because of their international market power, MNCs were able to benefit to a far greater extent than if competition had prevailed. In the markets for technology, the case is even clearer: the large firms in effect traded technology in return for pledges not to compete and not to sell the technology to unrelated parties. The agreements generally prohibited foreign investment in manufacturing using the shared technology. In those occasional cases when manufacturing was permitted, overseas markets, such as Brazil's lamp industry, were clearly non-competitive. Brazilian lamp consumers faced a tightly organised shared monopoly of local producers.

The distributional consequence of these concerted actions of the MNCs was to increase returns to the owners of capital and technology located in the advanced countries and their managers at the expense of consumers in the developing countries. If the present is any guide,[14] consumers paid a non-competitive premium money for MNC products. In other words, the concentrated structure of international production and the restrictive practices it facilitated served to shift investible surplus from the developing periphery to the industrial centre, much as the first dependency proposition posits.

The long-run structural ramifications of MNC behaviour were perhaps even more important because they had implications for the 'control' element of economic returns.

'Control' and MNCs' Role in Impeding Development

Moran's second dependency proposition is that MNCs create 'distortions' in the local economy. This case study suggests such distortions were more subtle than those presented by Moran. The study indicates that MNC market power did produce a symbiotic structural tie between the domestic and international industry that favoured foreign corporations by leaving them in 'control' of the industry, contrary to what occurred in the industrialised countries. Similarly, the important political interaction in this process, discussed under Moran's third dependency proposition, did not involve 'perversion' or 'subversion' by MNCs, but rather the gradual formation of alliances between foreign and domestic groups.

This research points out that the roots of the present foreign control over the Brazilian industry and its contemporary structurally 'dependent' position can be traced to a complex interaction between the evolution of class relationships in the political economy of Brazil after 1889 as well as the exercise of MNC economic power in international markets. The first set of reasons can be referred to as institutional factors and the second set as factors of international market structure.

Institutional Factors

The absence of a class of industrialists unrelated to the export agricultural economy was crucially different from the situation in the developed countries. In the Western European world, industrialists were able to break into the early technology monopoly of Edison by developing their own technology, pirating inventions and using home governments to seek favourable tariff and legal treatment. In Germany, for example, the Siemens brothers had the technological capability to move from the railway business into electrical equipment production, and General Electric had no success in controlling the German market. The same could be said for Japan.

In Brazil, by contrast, coffee and other export interests wanted electricity regardless of who supplied it or its equipment. Although they often built the first municipal utilities to supply electricity, Brazilians later sold these to foreign investors. This was not because of direct foreign competition but rather because of high opportunity costs in increased investment in export crops and other local industries, or because of difficulty in raising capital abroad. Local industrialists did demand preferential tariff treatment, but these were mainly for food and textiles, not for electrical products which all groups wanted at the lowest costs, and which hence received duty exemptions.

Moreover, Brazilians did not perceive a natural conflict between themselves and foreigners. Long accustomed to liberalism and a belief in the need for foreign capital and labour to tap Brazil's tremendous riches, most Brazilians believed that foreigners and foreign companies established within Brazil were in fact Brazilian, even if their headquarters and stockholders were abroad. Nationalism almost never focused on foreign industries that actually brought capital into the country. Foreign capital created much of the infrastructure necessary to develop the country's export sector. Hence, Brazilians tended to view it as complementary to, rather than competitive with, their own interests.[15]

Even Brazilian manufacturers did not oppose the establishment of foreign-owned industries within Brazil, and, indeed, became associated with it. The country's largest industrial organisation, the Centro Industrial, welcomed companies headquartered abroad as members because they 'nationalised' production (and decreased imports) even if they did not nationalise dividends.[16] Indeed, Brazilian industrialists often cooperated closely with foreigners. Guilhermo Guinle, while losing his battle with Light for the Rio concession, maintained close relations with São Paulo Light and later became President of two companies allied with Light investors. He also owned a General Electric concession for importing electrical machinery. After he sold his companies to the American and Foreign Power Company, he became President of one of its subsidiaries.[17]

Consequently, there emerged at a very early stage a perhaps unfortunate fusion of contented interests and a division of production responsibilities between Brazilian and foreign producers. The Brazilian producing groups reaped the benefits (until 1930) of comparative advantage in coffee and in local production of light consumer items of low technology. Foreign exchange purchased high-technology goods from foreign electrical companies. Foreigners also provided bond and equity capital as well as management of utilities. Contrary to the situation in the developed countries, this arrangement produced little incentive to challenge the shared monopoly of technology enjoyed by world's largest enterprises.

The Depression and war years did trigger growth (though growth rates were much higher after the war). New entrance into manufacturing came primarily from Brazilian entrepreneurs. However, they were linked for the most part to the pre-1930 class of producers. Brazilian entrepreneurs often kept one foot on the coffee plantation or in the mercantile house as they shifted the other to manufacturing in the city. They were linked to foreigners as suppliers and buyers of their technology. Both because of their structurally dependent position and because of their small size as a group, Brazilian manufacturers made no effective demands on the national government for preferential treatment over foreigners in the national market. As a consequence, the Brazilian state, unlike the German and later the Japanese state, lacked the 'political will' — to use Moran's term — to bargain with the MNCs.

Market Structural Factors

The electrical industry failed to develop in Brazil not only because of institutional factors, but also because of the structure of the international industry. Foreign companies based in the industrialised world controlled four determinant aspects of the industry that foreclosed most industrial growth in Brazil prior to 1940 — and allowed growth only on their own, dependent terms after that time. They controlled the supply of products, production technology, international finance and domestic Brazilian demand for heavy equipment.

The major international producers exercised control of product supply and production technology through international cross-licensing agreements among themselves. The central purpose of these agreements was to restrict diffusion of technology to precisely such countries as Brazil. Contracts included limitations on manufacturing in the designated territories.

The effects on manufacturing in Brazil were twofold. First, foreign electrical firms agreed not to manufacture in Brazil, reserving the non-exclusive areas as export markets only. While production costs probably favoured production in the home countries for most products, there were no microeconomic incentives with foreign ownership to try to develop comparative advantages in local production. Horst (1974) has shown why, given large fixed investments at home, MNCs may delay or avoid opening new plants abroad, even in industries where the marginal cost advantage lies overseas. Thus, General Electric did not begin producing large motors in Brazil until 1962 — motors that it produced at home before 1900 (Banas, 1962).

Second, the international agreements raised virtually insurmountable barriers to entry to any Brazilian firms that may have wanted to enter these lucrative markets. Undoubtedly, there were Brazilians disposed and technologically capable of entering. Brazilian firms had greater success in almost all other industries. For example, in both 'traditional' industries such as textiles and 'dynamic' industries such as non-electrical machinery Brazilian entrepreneurs showed themselves capable of efficient production. Only when the Depression removed the threat of foreign competition were entry barriers sufficiently low so that domestic firms could begin production in the light consumer goods end of the industry. In electrical machinery, however, technological barriers impeded Brazilian entry into production. In an accentuated pattern that persists until the present day in the industry, Brazilian firms were relegated to technology-dependent or marginal supplier positions in the market-place. Potential Brazilian producers confronted a tightly organised, international oligopoly.

This problem was compounded by the structure of equipment demand. Also, again unlike the industrialised countries, the demand side for electrical equipment was, or soon became, largely foreign-controlled. Because of their privileged access to capital markets in the industrialised world and their utility-operating experience, foreign investors quickly bought up and expanded local utilities. The utilities owned by the Brazilian Traction, Light and Power Company and the Electric Bond and Share Company came to be the source of demand for equipment in generation, transmission and distribution of electricity. Their preference was undoubtedly for imported equipment; indeed, if the patterns established among Bond and Share utilities in the United States held for Brazil, agreements probably evolved to purchase equipment from its parent (until 1924) General Electric (see FTC, 1928). Foreign-controlled demand for equipment in the incipient stages of the industry's development raised a barrier to domestic entry exactly where in the industrialising world, such as Germany and Japan, nationally controlled demand had provided an incentive to national industrialists.

Access to foreign financing was crucial to the success of the foreign-owned utilities. Local financing for investment purposes, including utilities, was available, but it generally went into coffee and other products controlled by Brazilians. While coffee growers had little interest in managing utilities, foreign electrical firms had initially established the bond-holding companies to invest their burgeoning coffers at home and expand demand for their equipment. Foreign financing continued to flow to utilities because that was the area of foreign experience and expertise at home. Rates of return in utilities, though higher than discount rates at home, probably were initially lower than those in Brazilian-controlled investment areas. Thus, while it could not be argued that a 'monopoly of finance' in the world metropolis retarded Brazilian participation, it is clear that access to the capital market of the industrialising world facilitated foreign control of utilities in Brazil and, hence, control of a significant segment of demand for electrical equipment.

In sum, the retarding factors in the development of the Brazilian electrical industry are traceable to a dynamic interaction between institutional forces and market structural factors. Had Brazil experienced greater industrialisation independent of coffee and primary exports, industrialists might have had the technological and political capabilities to break the early technology monopoly of the fledgling giants abroad.

That said, the international oligopolists' control of the supply of products and technology and, to a lesser extent, foreign control of demand within Brazil curtailed technology and manufacturing diffusion. In combination with other historical forces the international oligopoly effectively impeded the rise of an independent Brazilian-owned industry, and, perhaps inadvertently, set the stage for subsequent multinational corporate expansion.

As an epilogue to this story, events after 1945 bear out the success of MNC strategies to maintain market control. The dominant firms that had exported to Brazil through the cartel and cross-licensing arrangements expanded their local manufacturing operations or jumped tariff walls to maintain their position. At the same time, many of the Brazilian-owned firms established in the 1930-45 period were driven from the market or acquired by existing or entering multinationals. By 1960, the industry was 66 per cent foreign-controlled and by 1974 MNCs controlled 77 per cent of the industry. Virtually all of the increase in the foreign share after 1960 was due to MNCs' acquisitions (Newfarmer, 1978). Partly because of this take-over activity, market concentration has not appreciably diminished, and in most product classes the dominant firms produce over half of production. Lamps, for example, continue to be the privileged domain of General Electric and Philips, as it has been since the 1920s (see Newfarmer, forthcoming).

Conclusions

The historical study of the international electrical industry and its development in Brazil points to the great value in pursuing Moran's 'dialogue' in the study of dependency questions and multinational corporations. We have shown how economists and other social scientists can use the tools of industrial organisation to shed light on dependency hypotheses, particularly the consequences of MNC market power for the international distribution of gains. In the electrical industry, MNCs have been fairly successful – at least through the first two-thirds of the industry's life traced here – in capturing an unequal share of gains from their international activity and controlling industrial development. In this sense, the study lends support to the first two dependency propositions as formulated by Moran.

The study also suggests that more historical and contemporary industrial case studies are needed before it can be concluded that international competition is increasing and the share of gains to developing countries with it. The product cycle model, for all its utility, must be embedded in a larger theory of international industrial organisation that explains increasing denationalisation, the persistence of concentrated industrial structures around the world, and the structural and behavioural sources of the MNCs' economic power.

Finally, the history of the international electrical industry calls attention to a weakness in the bilateral monopoly approach. As Moran himself notes, the formulation assumes that national governments have the 'political will' to bargain with MNCs. Although he attempts to treat this issue in his third proposition, he overlooks exactly the kind of structural symbiosis or fusion of class interests that cannot properly be termed 'cooptation', 'subversion' or 'perversion'. Social scientists using the bilateral monopoly approach must look behind the 'state' and see which groups influence policy and for whose benefit. Perhaps communities of interest between MNCs and those influential groups shaping public policy are more important in determining bargaining outcomes than are antagonisms.

The research agenda provoked by the 'dialogue' is indeed formidable.

Notes

1. At the lower limit, the price must be sufficient to induce the MNC to supply the needed factor or product; at the upper limit, the price cannot be so high that the host country would forgo purchasing it or, in the case of technology, re-invent it (Kindleberger, 1965; see also Vaitsos, 1974b).

2. Although GE retained and even increased its shareholdings in British Thomson-Houston and AEG, it appears not to have exerted significant managerial control. None the less, GE continued its policy of investing in its licensees abroad. Its total foreign investment grew from $530,743 in 1893 to $4,423,294 in 1906 (see Federal Trade Commission, 1928). George Westinghouse had lost effective management of British Westinghouse control by 1909 (see Jones and Marriott, 1970) and later sold British Westinghouse to Vickers (see The Monopolies Commission, 1957; and also Epstein, 1971). In the United States market, the Siemens brothers sold their Chicago affiliate to General Electric in 1900 (see Passer, 1953).

3. The cross-licensing system is intended to permit firms which own related patents covering aspects of the same product to combine their patented knowledge and bring the new product into the market. The cross-licensing system is subject to abuse since licences may contain clauses that restrict the licensee to certain markets or pricing policies, impeding competitive forces.

4. The era of comprehensive cartelisation had several important antecedents. The domestic electrical groups that were formed in Britain, Germany and elsewhere throughout Europe after the turn of the century comprised an important building block for subsequent international cartels (The Monopolies Commission, 1957).

Second, the international lamp cartel formed in 1924 under the leadership of General Electric was another important precedent. It brought together for the first time the world's majors in a tightly organised group of concerted action (Monopolies and Restrictive Practices Commission, *Report on Electric Lamps* (HMSO, London, 1952)).These behaviour patterns and the co-operation during the early cross-licensing years set the stage of comprehensive cartelisation of the industry.

5. These were included: steam turbines (Section A); steam turbine driver alternators (Section B); compressors and blowers (Section C); water turbine driven alternators (Section E); rotating condensers (Section F); switchgear (Section G); transformers (Section H); rotating converting plant (Section J); rectifiers (Section K); electric traction (Section L); electrical equipment for hoists (Section N); electrical equipment for rolling mills (Section P); water turbine (Section W); and electrical porcelain (Section Z). Other sections were added later (see Federal Trade Commission, 1948).

6. Brasil, Departmento Nacional de Industria e Comercio, *Sociedades mercantis autorizadas a funcionar no Brasil, 1808-1945* (Imprensa Nacional, Rio, 1947), pp. 101-50; Brasil, *Leis do Brasil*, 1890-1915, *passim*; Brasil, *Diario Oficial*, 1915-1930, *passim*; *Brazilian Business* (September 1923), p. 57.

7. See Dean, 1969; Diegues Junior, 1964. Members of the Brazilian elite frequently exercised multiple economic roles so that Gabriel Osorio e Almeida, Vice-President of the Centro Industrial de Brasil, also headed the federally owned Central de Brasil railway and was a planter in the state of Rio (*Defeza Nacional*, no. 3 (1915), p. 180). So close were the relations between commerce and industry that the President of the Centro Industrial also served as President of the Associacao Comercial (Associacao Commercial do Rio de Janeiro, *Commissao de revisao de tarifa aduaneira* (Typ. Jornal do Comercio, Rio, 1903) while in São Paulo the major trade organisation represented both sectors: the Associacao de Comercio e Industria.

8. *Wileman's Brazilian Review*, 29 May 1930, p. 719; Brasil, *Diario Oficial*, 30 May, 1924, pp. 10829-32; *Moody's Public Utilities* (1954) (Moody's Investment Service, New York, 1954), pp. 1472-3; also Wilkins, 1974.

9. In both Belo Horizonte, Minas Gerais and Porto Alegre, Rio Grande do Sul, the cities leased their own public utility companies to American and Foreign Companies, *Wileman's Brazilian Review*, 3 October 1929, p. 1130 and *O Combate*, Rio, 25 October, 1959, p. 5; *Brazilian Review*, 26 November 1907, p. 1345; Gauld, 1964.

10. Brasil, *Recenseamento de 1920*, V, pt. 3, p. 77; although in 1920 the majority of lighting companies in Brazil were municipally owned, almost all companies that produced electrical lighting were private.

11. Swiatowslaw Sirke *et al.*, *Energia eletrica, pioneirismo e desenvolvimento na regiao Rio-Sao Paulo* (Edicoes Cruzeiro, Rio, 1966), p. 114; *Moody's Public Utilities Manual* (1954), pp. 1472-3.

12. Brasil, *Recenseamento de Brasil*, V: Industria (Typo. da Estatistica, Rio, 1927), pp. xvi-xxii. The Centro Industrial do Brasil, when it took its industrial census in 1907 (*O Brasil, suas riquezas naturais*, II: *Industria fabril* (Orosco, Rio, 1907-8), p. 150).

13. These conclusions can be found in all the major government investigations into the various restrictive practices. For example, the US Federal Trade Commission investigation of the patent pools concluded as early as 1923:

There is no question that pooling of all the patents pertaining to vacuum tubes has resulted in giving the Radio Corp. [RCA] and its affiliated companies a monopoly in manufactures, sale and use thereof. With such a monopoly, the

Radio Corporation apparently has the power to stifle competition in the manufacture and sale of receiving sets, and prevent all radio apparatus from being used for commercial radio communication purposes (FTC, 1923).

Likewise, investigating the cross-licensing arrangements, the FTC cóncluded in 1928:

Under these circumstances [of high concentration in each country's electrical industry], if the General Electric Co. and the Westinghouse Co. each has one or two contracts with the largest interests in each important foreign industrial country, the effect upon competition in the United States in the way of eliminating potential foreign competition is obviously great . . . Not only is direct foreign competition in the United States eliminated but so is the possibility that other American manufacturers will obtain the right to use important foreign patents, trade secrets, and manufacturing information . . .

It therefore appears that the General Electric Co.'s score or more contracts and the Westinghouse Co.'s seven contracts reserving the American market as their exclusive territories effectually close the door to a large number of otherwise potential competitors (FTC, 1928, p. 145, p. 146).

In a similar vein in 1947, the United Kingdom's Board of Fair Trade analysed the effects of the cross-licences:

The general effect of these [territorial exclusions] is to reserve North America and to some extent South for International General Electric Corporation [and] Northern Europe and to some extent the non-manufacturing countries of the rest of Europe to AEG . . . (UKBT, 1947, p. 46).

The fact that prices would be higher to US consumers was the basis for the consent decree in 1947 that enjoined American producers from participating in the international cartel.

The rationale for all anti-trust law — in the US, EEC and abroad generally — is that concentration of economic power leads to its abuse, and thus the collecting of monopoly rents from consumers. The great body of evidence in the industrial organisation literature by and large confirms this. For example, in the case of the electrical industry, Stocking and Watkins find, on the basis of their study of the international lamp cartel, that 'the cartel has made prices higher than they would have been under free competition' (1946, p. 343). Epstein (1971) reaches similar conclusions in her study of the modern electrical cartel.

14. Since the advent of the computer, sophisticated statistical techniques have permitted quantification of the degree of overcharge. Almost all of the major studies conclude that there is a strong and positive relation between the degree of concentration in the market and the rate of profit. See, for example, Weiss's (1974) review of these. More recently, Connor and Mueller (1977) find a clear association between degree of concentration, relative market shares of MNCs and their advertising rates and the rate of profitability of MNC subsidiaries in Brazil and Mexico.

15. For more on Brazilian attitudes to foreign investment see Steven Topik, 'Economic Nationalism and the State in an Underdeveloped Country: Brazil, 1889-1930', PhD dissertation, University of Texas at Austin, 1978.

16. See Centro Industrial do Brasil, *Relatorio* (1912), p. 4; *Boletim* (1905), p. 258 and (1915), p. 48.

17. *Brazilian Review*, 26 November 1907; *Diario Oficial*, 24 May 1930, pp. 10829-32; Gould, 1964.

4 THE INTER-REGIONAL DISTRIBUTION OF WEST GERMAN MULTINATIONALS IN THE UNITED KINGDOM

H.D. Watts

Introduction

It is probable that in early 1980 over one million UK manufacturing workers were employed in plants owned by multinational enterprises based outside the United Kingdom. The latest available data from the Business Statistics Office indicate that the number of such workers rose from 821,576 in 1973 to 925,689 in 1975. Although the US-based multinationals are dominant within the United Kingdom, an important subgroup is made up of EEC-based multinationals for whom employment rose from 107,000 to 118,000 over the same two-year period. Of course, these increases do not necessarily represent additions to the UK manufacturing work-force, as they are due partly to transfers of ownership from the indigenous to the foreign-owned sectors. Earlier analyses of UK employment data have examined the overall pattern of employment in foreign-owned plants (Dicken and Lloyd, 1976; McDermott, 1977; Watts, 1979 and 1980b) as well as investigating the location of European-owned plants (Watts, 1980a). This chapter develops from this earlier work and focuses upon the spatial patterns created within the United Kingdom by multinationals based in the German Federal Republic.

The selection of West German multinationals reflects a number of reasons. It enables research to break away from the current emphasis on the behaviour of United States and United-Kingdom-based multinationals and has the more practical value that, within the United Kingdom, industrial development associations have been looking towards West Germany for new inward investment. Moreover, since the developments date mainly from the 1960s onwards, it means that in dealing with cross-sectional data for the 1970s the problem of a historical inheritance of earlier periods is less than that with, for example, Dutch- or French-owned activities, which date back to the 1930s (Watts, 1980b).

The study of West German investment in UK manufacturing activity poses a number of questions. To what extent do West-German-owned activities reflect changes taking place in the West German economy? Why do West German firms select a UK location in preference to locations in other West European countries or the Third World? What is the inter-regional distribution of West German investment in the United Kingdom? Only the third question is discussed here and investment is measured mainly in terms of the inter-regional distribution of West-German-owned plants or the inter-regional distribution of employment in those plants.

Methodologically, two approaches are adopted. The majority of the chapter is concerned with macro-level analysis of aggregate data, but since almost half the employment is controlled by one major firm, this firm is subject to a detailed examination within the tradition of the geography of enterprise. These two approaches are used to achieve the primary aim of the chapter, which is to chart the development and present pattern of the inter-regional distribution of West German manufacturing activities in the United Kingdom. In its emphasis on the whole of the United Kingdom it differs from those studies which attempt to elucidate intra-regional patterns. This emphasis is deliberate. It is vital that these national scale studies are undertaken to allow students of specific regions to place their work in a carefully researched national context. The background sketch of the national setting of a region's activities is no longer adequate with large multi-regional, multinational enterprises increasing the interdependence between regional systems.

Overall, this chapter is empirical in content and descriptive in nature. This is not the place to rehearse the arguments for and against foreign investment, nor to provide a lengthy review of overseas expansion paths of multinationals. The discussion does not attempt to make any general contribution to a theory of the spatial behaviour of multinational enterprise, but it does perhaps have a wider relevance in that much of the analysis does present some evidence which can contribute to the debate on the role of multinationals in contributing to regional disequilibria within developed countries. It has something to say to the Third World too, in that it stresses that the location of an investment within a country may, in the long run, be as important a decision as that to establish production activities in the country.

The discussion is in five parts. The first places employment in West-German-owned plants in context by considering UK employment in plants owned by all foreign and EEC-based firms. The second reviews the published data on West German investment in the United Kingdom and previous studies of West German plants in Ireland and the

Netherlands. A discussion of the overall distribution of West-German-owned plants in the United Kingdom forms the third section, while the final sections look at two important subsets of the data: the new entrants to UK manufacturing in the 1970s and the activities owned by the principal West German employer in the United Kingdom.

Inter-regional Variations in Foreign Ownership

All Foreign-owned Operations

Figure 4.1 shows the inter-regional variations in the importance of employment in foreign-owned plants in 1975. Foreign-*owned* is the term used throughout this chapter in preference to foreign-*controlled*. There is no evidence available as to the degree of control foreign firms exert over the plants they own. These Census of Production data relate to employment in manufacturing industry, excluding merchanting, transport and warehouse activities, but including head offices engaged mainly in the administration of production units. Further, the data relate to all manufacturing enterprises, including estimates for smaller enterprises excluded from the Census, non-respondents and unsatisfactory returns.

In 1975 925,689 jobs in UK manufacturing were in plants owned by firms based outside the country. High levels of foreign ownership occurred in East Anglia and the South-East, where 18.6 per cent and 18.3 per cent of the manufacturing employment was in foreign-owned plants. In addition, the peripheral regions of Northern Ireland, Wales and Scotland had relatively high levels of foreign ownership (21.1 per cent, 15.2 per cent and 15.8 per cent respectively). All these regions were well over the national average of 12.4 per cent. With the exception of the North-West (11.7 per cent), all other regions had between 6 and 8 per cent of their employment in plants owned by firms based overseas. The general picture that emerges is that while central and peripheral regions have attracted or have been sought out by foreign firms, the regions located between the centre and periphery have failed to attract either new foreign plants or acquisition of their indigenous firms by foreign-based concerns.

Such cross-sectional data tell little of current behaviour and the limited Census data available permit comparisons to be made only with 1963 and 1971. Watts (1979) shows that for the earlier period (1963-71) 45 per cent of the increase of employment in foreign-owned

Figure 4.1: Inter-regional Variations in Foreign Ownership, 1975

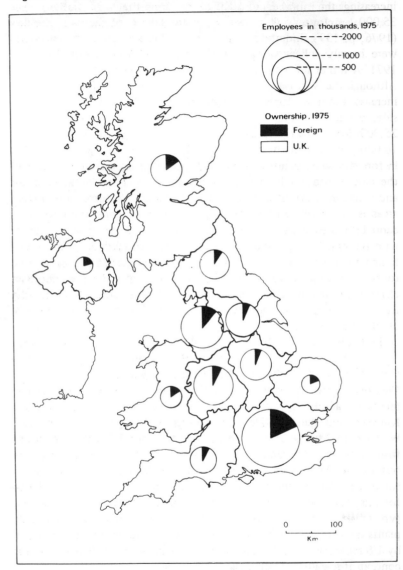

Source: Business Statistics Office, *Report of the Censuses of Production 1974 and 1975. Summary Tables: Enterprise Analysis* (HMSO, London, 1979).

plants went to the North-West, the South-East and Scotland, the latter increasing the number of jobs in foreign-owned plants by almost 35,000 employees. This kind of pattern is confirmed by Keeble's (1976, p. 139) finding that the first UK plants of foreign companies were heavily concentrated in the peripheral areas between 1966 and 1971. A rather different picture emerges for 1971 to 1975 (Table 4.1). Although the North-West and South-East account for 34 per cent of the increase, the most important single region was Yorkshire and Humberside, where the number employed in foreign-owned plants rose by 25,000 jobs. The Northern region too experienced an increase of 16,000 jobs and in these two regions the percentage increase in jobs in foreign-owned plants was over four times the percentage increase in the nation as a whole. The small degree of change in Wales, Scotland and Northern Ireland suggests that the interest of foreign firms in these areas is not as active as it once was. If any general pattern can be discerned it is a trend away from the 'far' periphery to the 'near' periphery with the two Midland regions between the south and the periphery still failing to obtain significant amounts of new foreign investment. The four-year period (1971 to 1975) is rather short, with the result that changes created by one or two decisions may unduly influence the figures, and minor changes may well lie within the measurement errors of the Census. Nevertheless, this period does give an indication of current behaviour.

EEC-owned Operations

Figure 4.1 and Table 4.1 have indicated the broad outlines of the location of employment in foreign-owned plants in the United Kingdom, but they provide only a very general setting for the study of West German firms. This is because of the dominant role of US-owned firms in establishing this pattern. It is, therefore, important to separate out the influence of the United States firms. Fortunately access to some unpublished tabulations prepared by the Business Statistics Office for this study makes this possible. Analysis of an earlier data set of this type (Watts, 1980a) has illustrated that the location of employment in plants owned by EEC-based firms does differ from that in plants owned by US-based firms, and West German investment should be seen in the context of the former rather than the latter.

The US dominance is illustrated quite clearly in Figure 4.2, but most interest here centres upon the relative importance of employment in EEC-owned plants in the different UK regions. EEC employment is particularly well represented in Northern Ireland, where just over a quarter of foreign employment is linked to other EEC countries. This is true also of East Anglia, where 29.2 per cent of foreign employment

Table 4.1: Employment Change in Foreign-owned Plants, 1971-5

Region	1971	1975	Absolute Change (thousands)	Per Cent Change
South-East	327.5	347.9	+20.4	6.2
East Anglia	31.1	36.8	+ 5.7	18.3
South-West	20.9	31.3	+10.4	49.8
West Midlands	72.8	77.0	+ 4.2	5.8
East Midlands	27.1	34.0	+ 6.9	25.5
Yorkshire & Humberside	27.0	51.9	+24.9	92.2
North-West	100.8	122.9	+22.1	21.9
North	25.6	41.9	+16.3	63.7
Wales	41.5	48.5	+ 7.0	16.9
Scotland	95.5	101.2	+ 5.7	6.0
Northern Ireland	34.2	32.3	− 1.9	− 5.6
Total	804.0	925.7	121.7	15.1

Sources: Business Statistics Office, *Business Monitor PA 1002 Report on the Census of Production, 1971* (HMSO, London, 1976); Business Statistics Office, *Business Monitor PA 1002 Report on the Censuses of Production 1974 and 1975* (HMSO, London, 1979).

is in plants owned by EEC-based firms. In contrast, Wales and the East Midlands have been conspicuously unsuccessful in attracting the interests of such firms, while Scotland, Yorkshire and Humberside and the Northern region are well below the national average too. The lack of success of these regions in attracting EEC investment is surprising, as some have strong trading links with Europe.

Table 4.2 indicates (by a location quotient greater than 1.00) those regions where the share of employment in EEC-owned plants is in excess of the share of employment in UK-owned plants. Over-representation is found both in the south and east (the South-East and East Anglia regions) and in Northern Ireland. The North-West is the only other region in which any marked over-representation occurs; indeed in comparison with the 1973 data (in 1971, of course, the EEC excluded Ireland and Denmark as well as the United Kingdom) the North-West recorded an increase of 7,000 jobs in plants owned by firms based elsewhere in the EEC. This finding should be interpreted cautiously because of the data problems discussed earlier, but it does seem that in the mid-1970s the North-West was particularly attractive to EEC-based firms. Why this should be so has yet to be investigated.

This general description of the overall distribution of employment owned by all foreign or EEC-based firms can give only a crude indication of the locational preferences of overseas investors. The pattern could, for example, reflect the distribution of those industries in which

Figure 4.2: Inter-regional Variations in Nationality of Foreign-owned Operations, 1975

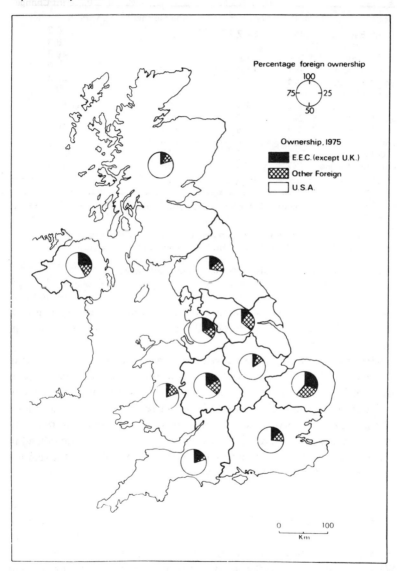

Source: Business Statistics Office, unpublished tabulations.

Table 4.2: Regional Distribution of Employment in EEC-owned Plants, 1975

Region	Total	Per Cent	Location Quotient[a]	Location Quotient[b]
South-East	37,442	31.7	1.34	0.94
East Anglia	10,751	9.1	3.64	3.16
South-West	4,559	3.9	0.66	0.80
West Midlands	13,457	11.4	0.79	1.04
East Midlands	1,424	1.2	0.14	0.23
Yorkshire & Humberside	3,988	3.4	0.33	0.70
North-West	23,274	19.7	1.39	1.23
North	5,347	4.5	0.71	0.51
Wales	1,597	1.4	0.34	0.31
Scotland	7,859	6.7	0.82	0.96
Northern Ireland	8,227	7.0	3.89	5.69
Total	117,925	100.0		

Notes: [a]Comparing the distribution of employment in EEC-owned and UK-owned plants.

[b]Comparing the distribution of employment in EEC-owned plants with *all* employment in Orders V and IX of the UK Standard Industrial Classification.

Source: Business Statistics Office, unpublished tabulations.

overseas investment was concentrated, as indeed is probably the case in South-East England. Watts (1980a) showed that EEC employment tended to be concentrated in chemicals and electrical engineering and if EEC employment is compared with all employment in Orders V and IX of the UK Standard Industrial Classification then only East Anglia and Northern Ireland show a marked over-representation and even this is due in part to the effect of small base values in the location quotient (Table 4.2). The North-West still appears as having an important if not marked over-representation. It is therefore possible to conclude that while structural features account for over-representation in the South-East, this is not true of the other regions.

West German Multinationals

In late 1979 a guesstimate would place the number of employees of West German firms in the United Kingdom at about 30,000. Many of these employees were in non-manufacturing activity and the latest information on manufacturing activities relates to 1975. The data from the 1975 Census of Production allow the identification of some important structural features of West German manufacturing activity. A summary of EEC operations as a whole has been provided elsewhere (Watts, 1980a). Firms based in West Germany, France and the Netherlands owned approximately similar numbers of UK enterprises in 1975 (53, 49 and 42 respectively), while West German firms came second in number of plants owned (94) and third in number of employees (13,000). Overall, in 1975 the mean size of West German firms was smaller than that of all EEC-owned firms in the United Kingdom (245 compared with 630 employees) and the plants were smaller too (138 compared with 331 employees).

The evolution of these characteristics is difficult to trace in official sources. Until 1968 there was no accurate quantitative assessment of West German operations in the United Kingdom. The data relating to West Germany in the 1963 Census of Production must be discounted as they appear to be erroneous. The majority of developments have occurred in the 1970s and predominantly since the UK's entry to the EEC. This is well illustrated by Davies and Thomas's (1977) estimate that of the 13 West German firms in Wales at the end of 1974, only 5 pre-dated 1968, and no less than 5 had been established in 1974. Table 4.3 summarises national changes between 1968 and 1975. Although there are some minor differences of definition, it can be seen that the numbers employed and the number of firms rose threefold, and the number of plants increased fourfold. The West German share of the employment in plants owned by Denmark, France, the Irish Republic, the Netherlands and West Germany rose from 5 to 11 per cent. This faster than average rate of growth contributed to the increasing significance of West German firms in the United Kingdom. Indeed, from 1973 to 1975 the actual employment added to West German operations in the United Kingdom was at least twice that of their nearest rival among EEC countries, and was exceeded only by firms headquartered in the Netherlands.

Estimates of post-1975 growth have to rely on unofficial estimates. Feddersen (1978) suggests that the number of West German subsidiary companies with manufacturing facilities in the United Kingdom rose from 111 in 1976 to 149 in 1978. These data, while indicative of the rate of change, are not directly comparable with the data in Table 4.3 for reasons discussed later.

While published data allow the construction of some summary characteristics of West German investment in the United Kingdom, detailed locational information is absent on a national scale. Admittedly some limited data are available in some regions for specific years

— for example, West-German-owned plants accounted for 2.7 per cent of employment in Wales at the end of 1974 and 3.1 per cent in the North West in mid-1975 (Welsh Office, 1978; North-West Economic Planning Council, 1978). Before examining some new research material on the spatial pattern of West-German-owned plants, it is pertinent to examine studies of the location of West-German-owned plants in other areas.

Table 4.3: West German Industrial Activity in the United Kingdom, 1968-75

	Employment	Enterprises	Establishments
1968[a]	3,900	19	22
1975[b]	13,000	53	94

Notes: [a]Private sector enterprises with industrial activities in the United Kingdom, employment data including estimates for establishments employing fewer than 25 persons.

[b]United Kingdom private sector enterprises in manufacturing. Data include estimates for establishments not making satisfactory returns, non-response and establishments employing less than 20 persons.

Sources: Department of Industry, Business Statistics Office, *Report on the Census of Production 1968*, Pt. 158 (HMSO, London, 1975), p. 116.

It is likely that two major processes will contribute to the changing pattern of West-German-owned plants in any area; these processes are acquisition of existing plants and establishment of new ones. Intuitively one might expect acquisitions to be associated with rapid-growth indigenous firms in the centre of the space economy while new plants might be associated with peripheral regions receiving government aid. Some evidence to support the latter contention is shown in Figures 4.3(a) and 4.3(b).

These figures summarise data collected by Blackbourn (1972) and de Smidt (1966). The former study examined foreign factories established from 1955 to 1969, and found that West German plants tended to be small, to have a high propensity to locate in the designated (i.e. Assisted) Areas and to prefer locations in small remote towns. In the Netherlands, the small size of the West German plants established between 1945 and 1963 was again apparent, and as can be seen in Figure 4.3(b) they preferred to locate not in the most industrialised and urbanised part of the Netherlands, but in a narrow strip of land along the West German frontier. It has already been shown that in plant size characteristics the West German firms in the UK do tend to be smaller than the EEC average, thus confirming at least one of the general features shown in both the Netherlands and Eire. It would be unwise to draw too much from this evidence, especially as the new UK plants might be aimed at the UK market, while those in the Netherlands and Ireland might be primarily export-oriented. Nevertheless the locational patterns of new plants support the expectation.

The Spatial Pattern of West-German-owned Plants

Sources

It is fortunate that for a number of years the German Chamber of Commerce in London has published a directory of UK firms in which West German firms have a holding of 50 per cent or more (Feddersen, 1974, 1976, 1978). A small minority of these firms may in fact be West German subsidiaries of multinationals based outside that country. It does not seem unreasonable to assume that if they are listed as West German firms in the directory then decisions involving investment in the United Kingdom will be taken in West Germany. The scope and availability of the directory have improved since the first edition, and although a number of inaccuracies appear in detail, the broad outline is thought to be reasonably correct (personal communication, German Chamber of Commerce, 10 January 1980).

It is likely that the directory overestimates the number of West German firms with manufacturing subsidiaries in the United Kingdom. There are three reasons for this. First, information was collected from the West German parent and respondents in West Germany may have had little knowledge of the details of the UK operation. They may have assumed manufacturing facilities in the United Kingdom when such facilities did not exist.

Second, among manufacturers the term manufacturing is perhaps used more widely than it is understood in the Standard Industrial Classification. In particular, warehouses where machines are checked over after transit may have been classed as manufacturers. Third, although specifically focused on firms in which the German shareholding was 50 per cent or more, the exact share was not always known and in a number of cases, although there was a West German investment, it did not meet the 50 per cent criteria.

Cross-checking by a telephone survey (described in detail later) the

Figure 4.3: (a) Factories Established in the Republic of Ireland by West
German Firms, 1955-69 (b) Factories Established in the
Netherlands by West German Firms, 1945-63

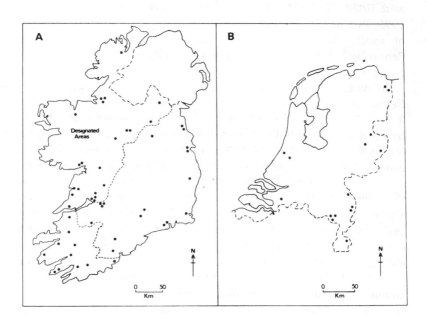

Sources:
(a). A. Blackbourn, 'The Location of Foreign-owned Manufacturing Plants in the
Republic of Ireland', *Tijdschrift voor Economische en Sociale Geografie*, 63
(1972), p. 440.
(b). M. de Smidt, 'Foreign Industrial Establishments Located in the Netherlands',
Tijdschrift voor Economische en Sociale Geografie, 57 (1966), p. 10.

firms appearing for the first time as manufacturers in 1978 showed that
8 (20 per cent) did not have UK manufacturing facilities, and of the 31

manufacturing firms 5 (16 per cent) did not meet the 50 per cent holding criteria. Admittedly some of these differences might reflect changes in circumstances between early 1978 and late 1979. A surprising feature was a number of firms denying any West German links, although alternative sources (for example, *Who owns Whom*) confirmed West German ownership. Overall, in 1976, 112 manufacturing firms were listed, compared with a Census of Production estimate of 53 in 1975. Part of this difference is probably due to the fact that a number of smaller West-German-owned firms are probably missed by the Census, and also that the Census counts joint operations (with a 50 per cent UK/50 per cent West Germany holding) as UK-owned activities.

In sum, this listing probably overestimates the number of West-German-owned manufacturing operations in the United Kingdom, but it provides a useful base from which to work. For all but the very largest manufacturing firm directory evidence (for example, *Kompass*) was used to identify the manufacturing sites; for the largest firm direct contact was made to establish its UK corporate structure.

Industrial Structure

The industrial structure is described in Tables 4.4, 4.5 and 4.6. The data used in Tables 4.4 and 4.6 have been compiled directly from directory sources and have not been adjusted to allow for the discrepancies highlighted in survey work with some of the firms. Further, it should be noted that in Table 4.4 the structure is assessed in terms of the number of firms and not by relative importance in output or employment. Where a firm was allocated to two industries a score of one half was allocated to each industry. The industrial classification is based on that used in the directory. The most interesting feature of Table 4.4 is the concentration on the machinery and components industry, and if the engineering and chemical groups are taken together they account for 76 per cent of all the firms, the remainder being spread over 17 different industrial categories.

Table 4.4: Industrial Mix of West German Firms in the United Kingdom, 1978

Industry	Number	Per Cent
Metal machinery and components	58	38.9
Pharmaceutical and chemical products	17	11.4
Electrical equipment, computer	15	10.1
Instruments	13	8.7
Plastics	10	6.7
Next largest industry	4	2.7

Source: Based on Feddersen, 1978.

Comparable data on industrial structure measured by employment are not available elsewhere, but data on the net assets of West German firms in the United Kingdom provide important supplementary material. Table 4.5 summarises the industrial structure at the end of 1974. In these investment terms the dominance of the chemicals and rubber industry stands out clearly, while the engineering group of industries (mechanical and instrument engineering, electrical engineering and motor vehicle manufacture) accounts for a further 24 per cent. Measuring structure in this way over-stresses the role of the capital-intensive chemical industry, and were employment data available, the engineering sector would play a more important and probably dominant role.

Table 4.5: Industrial Structure of West German Investment in the UK, End 1974

Industry	Net Assets £ million	Per Cent
Food, drink & tobacco	0.2	0.2
Chemicals & allied industries, rubber	50.8	60.5
Metal manufacture	1.3	1.5
Mechanical engineering and instrument engineering	13.2	15.7
Electrical engineering	2.9	3.5
Motor vehicle manufacture	3.7	4.4
Textiles, leather, clothing &footwear	6.8	8.1
Paper, printing & publishing	1.4	1.7
Other manufacturing industries	3.7	4.4

Source: Business Statistics Office, *Census of Overseas Assets, 1974* (HMSO, London, 1978).

Of course, the firm size structure shown in Table 4.6 is partly a reflection of the industries in which the firms operate, but one particularly important feature does emerge from the table. Half the firms have fifty employees or less, and about 40 per cent have more than a hundred employees. This remarkable bipolarisation of firm size may reflect the distinction between the entirely new plant and the acquisition of larger well established UK firms.

Spatial Patterns

The bipolarisation in firm sizes suggests that there is both a qualitative and quantitative distinction between the larger and smaller firms, and thus the analysis of spatial patterns concentrates only on those firms with over 100 employees and on their manufacturing operations which employ more than 100 workers on one site. By concentrating on these larger-scale operations the danger of including sales offices rather than manufacturing operations is reduced. The 1978 distribution of West-German-owned plants is shown in Figure 4.4. The map is based on the sources discussed earlier and has *not* been corrected for errors which are known to exist in regions for which other data sources were available. These regions were primarily in the Assisted Areas (for example, Wales and Scotland) and correction there would bias the observations in favour of the Assisted Areas, as similar checks were not available for the non-Assisted Areas.

Table 4.6: Size Distribution of West-German-owned Firms, 1978

Number of Employees		Number of Firms	Per Cent
1 - 20		30	20.1
21 - 50		45	30.3
51 - 100		16	10.7
>100		58	38.9
	Total	149	

Source: After Feddersen, 1978.

The number of sites displayed in Figure 4.4 totals 71. A dispersed pattern can be seen, but with a concentration in Northern Ireland. Indeed the West German operations in Northern Ireland are largely responsible for the over-representation of EEC-owned plants in that region. If the United Kingdom is divided into two areas separated by the dotted line in Figure 4.4 (broadly the Assisted and non-Assisted Areas) the proportion of West German plants with over 100 employees in each area differs little from that which would be expected from the distribution of all UK plants with over 100 employees.

It is perhaps more interesting to compare the West German distribution with the distribution of plants with over 100 employees in the four industries (chemicals and mechanical, electrical and instrument engineering) in which the West German activities are concentrated. This is done in Table 4.7 and it shows a slight tendency ($p < 0.10$) for the plants to favour the Assisted Areas. However, it seems reasonable to exclude those plants whose locations are influenced strongly by the structure of the major West German enterprise. Repeating the exercise excluding these plants indicates clearly that if the remaining plants are treated as a sample of all West German plants they are significantly

Figure 4.4: West-German-owned Plants with Over 100 Employees, 1978

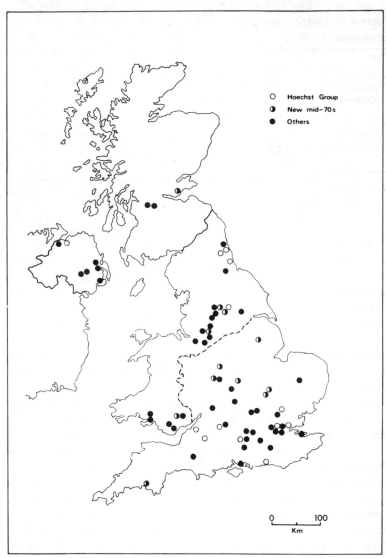

Sources: Feddersen (1978) and various directories.

over-represented (p < 0.05) in the Assisted Areas.

Table 4.7: Distribution of West-German-owned Plants with Over 100
Employees, 1978

		Assisted Areas	Non-Assisted Areas
A All Plants			
Expected[a]		26.5	44.5
Observed		34.0	37.0
	$x^2 = 3.39$		
B All Plants less Hoechst			
Expected[a]		21.6	36.4
Observed		29.0	29.0
	$x^2 = 4.04*$		

Note: [a]Based on the proportion of all UK plants with over 100 employees operating in Orders V, VII, VIII and IX in 1975.

An earlier study of the 1976 distribution (Watts, 1980a) identified
an over-representation in the South-East which did not appear in the
1978 data. In part this reflects the fact that in the earlier analysis no
adjustments were made for industrial structure and the plants of the
dominant large enterprise were treated as part of the data set. However,
some of the increased dispersion outside the South-East results from
the growth of plants from the less than 100 category to the more than
100 category and from the wider spread of recent acquisitions. It is to
the new entrants, of which acquisitions form a part, to which attention
is now turned.

New Entrants

The preceding analysis of cross-sectional data did not allow for variations in the patterns created by acquisitions and by new plants set up
by firms establishing their first UK manufacturing operations. For such
a distinction to be made survey work was necessary and this was
focused upon new entrants to the manufacturing sector in the 1970s.
They were identified by selecting firms appearing as manufacturing
concerns in the 1978 directory, but not in the 1976 directory. Basic
data on ownership, employment and manufacturing characteristics
were checked by a telephone survey over a three-week period in late
1979. It was not possible to establish a contact prepared to release the
information in 8 cases out of the 48 firms. Out of the remaining 40

firms one had ceased operation and, as was described earlier, 8, despite the directory evidence, did not operate manufacturing sites in the UK.

In all some 31 firms provided information. All but three of the firms were able to provide the year in which manufacturing operations began in the United Kingdom. Of those responding, almost three-quarters began their UK manufacturing operations from 1974 to 1978 inclusive, and the majority of the remainder began manufacturing operations in the United Kingdom in the 1970s. It does not seem unreasonable to treat these data as indicative of the behaviour of West German multinationals in the United Kingdom in the 1970s.

The 31 plants which had links with West German firms in the mid-1970s were linked in one of three ways: by being an associate of a West German firm (with a West German holding of more than 10 per cent and less than 50 per cent), by being part of a joint operation (a 50 per cent West German holding), or by being a subsidiary (a firm with a West German holding of more than 50 per cent). In each case the link could have been established with an existing plant or the UK and German partners could have established the associate/joint/subsidiary manufacturing operations on a new site.

These new entrants of the mid-1970s had much in common with earlier firms, their interests being spread widely over 11 industrial categories but with almost half of the firms concerned with mechanical and electrical engineering. The main difference was the lack of any marked emphasis on chemicals which, as was shown earlier, is a predominant feature of West-German-owned operations as a whole. Table 4.8 summarises the plant-size data and reveals the small number of plants in the 50-99 category indicating that plants, like firms, tend to be small (50 employees) or large (100 or more employees), with few plants in an intermediate category. The largest of the new plants had just 200 employees.

Table 4.8: Size of Plants Acquired or Newly Established by West German Multinationals, Mid-1970s

Number of Employees	Number	Plants Per Cent
< 25	5	20.8
25 - 49	5	20.8
50 - 99	3	12.5
100 - 149	8	33.4
150 - 199	2	8.3
≥ 200	1	4.2
Total[a]	24	

Note: [a]Includes one plant for which entry path information was not available, and excludes joint operations and associate firms.

Source: Survey.

The preferred modes of entry into UK manufacturing operations in the mid-1970s are shown in Table 4.9. It indicates clearly that the preferred modes were either acquisition or establishment of a new plant. The mean number of employees at the acquired firms was 101, in contrast to a mean of 64 in firms that had recently begun manufacturing operations. This figure for the new operations may be unduly high as the result of the inclusion of previously existing sales activities.

Table 4.9: Mode of Entry to Manufacturing Operations, Mid-1970s

Entry Path	Firms		Employment	
	Number	Per Cent	Number	Per Cent
Subsidiaries				
Acquisitions	12	38.7	1,213	51.2
New Plants	11	35.5	707	29.8
Associates	5	16.1	345[a]	14.6
Joint	3	9.7	105	4.4
Total	31		2,370	

Note: [a]Includes estimates for two firms.

Source: Telephone survey.

Joint operations appear insignificant as a mode of entry, and it is difficult to generalise about the associates. The directory listing did not aim to include associates and those identified here are those listed as subsidiaries but which in the telephone survey did not have a sufficient West German holding to be treated as an acquisition or joint operation. With so few and biased observations on associate activities it is difficult to generalise, but two types of associate firm could be picked out; that using West German expertise (for example in pharmaceuticals) and that which used the multinational to provide financial backing for the early operations. An example of the latter is a small West Midlands firm which turned to West Germany when it was unable to obtain the backing it required in the United Kingdom. Initially the West German firm took a 48 per cent interest, dropping back to 33 per cent as the UK operation grew.

Figure 4.5 depicts the spatial pattern of the new and acquired plants and their different patterns make clear this is an important distinction to make. The spatial pattern of the acquired plants is widely dispersed and does not seem to show any particular spatial preferences. The new plants appear to show a preference for sites south of the Wash; whereas half the acquired plants were north of this line, only one-tenth of the

Figure 4.5: Newly Acquired or Established West-German-owned Plants, Mid-1970s

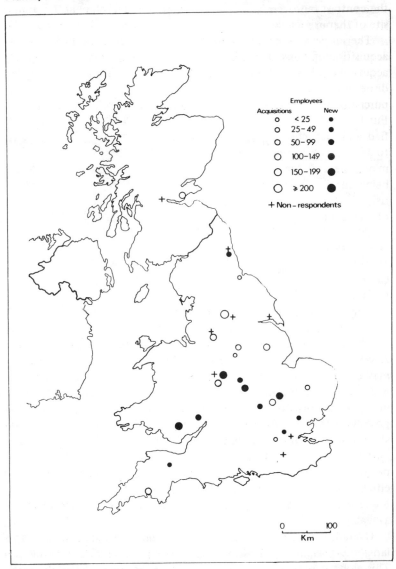

Source: Telephone survey.

new plants were so located. Impressionistic evidence suggests also that the majority of non-respondents were acquired plants: this would make the contrast more marked. The general pattern is, of course, the opposite of that expected.

The dispersed pattern of the acquisitions is due entirely to the acquisition of single-plant firms, so none of the dispersion is due to the acquisition of multi-plant firms based in the South-East. Nor is the dispersion due to indirect acquisition by, for example, West German purchase of a French firm which had UK manufacturing operations. Further, only one case of post-acquisition locational change was identified and that involved the transfer of production from the South-East to Wales. The distinct spatial preference of new plants for the south may reflect an orientation to UK markets; entry to the UK market being encouraged by the increasing strength of the Deutschmark and rising labour costs in West Germany. In the long run a wider dispersion of plants might be expected as the scale of operations grows.

These data, of course, relate only to the mid-1970s (some large new plants were established in peripheral areas at an earlier stage) and exclude, for example, new plants set up or acquired by the major West German firm operating in the United Kingdom. Furthermore, acquisitions perhaps played a more important role in post-1975 behaviour than they did in the late 1960s and early 1970s.

Entry Paths

A number of writers suggest that the usual entry path to an overseas market is to proceed from selling to manufacturing. More formally, it is possible to identify a three-stage process of agency selling, the setting up of a sales organisation and a final stage of manufacturing. It was possible with these mid-1970s data to establish the validity of the last stage of moving from sales to manufacturing.

To assess the role of prior selling organisations the West German parents of the 31 firms in the sample were sought in the 1976 directory either under their British or West German names. Two firms had interests in two subsidiaries, so the number of firms for which data are available is 29.

Overall, in just over half the newly established manufacturing subsidiaries their parent firms had *no* prior sales office in the United Kingdom. This alone raises the need to question the established view. Sales offices preceded manufacturing activities in only 50 per cent of the cases.

Locationally, an interesting feature is the extent to which the pre-existing sales office and new manufacturing site coincide. In most cases they do so (although this may in part reflect changes in classification from sales to manufacturing as a result of an erroneous sales only entry in the earlier directory). One not unexpected movement tendency may however be discerned: sales offices in the South-East and Midlands spawned manufacturing units elsewhere. One sales unit in Chalfont St Giles (near London) was followed by a plant in Newcastle; one in Northamptonshire by a plant in Yorkshire and Humberside.

Where sales offices did not exist prior to manufacturing operations it is likely that sales were handled by an agency agreement. There is no strong evidence to support this contention, but it seems unlikely that a firm would establish UK market-oriented manufacturing activities before testing the market in some way. Anecdotal information also suggests that acquisition was more frequently preceded by an agency arrangement than was the setting up of a new plant. In several cases the firm acting as the UK selling agent was the firm acquired.

This discussion of cross-sectional data of the overall spatial pattern of West German plants and the more detailed analysis of new entrants has adopted an essentially aggregate approach. The next stage is to identify and assess the effects of the one large industrial enterprise which dominates the employment structure of West-German-owned operations in the United Kingdom.

Hoechst AG

Most of the major West German enterprises have some manufacturing activities in the United Kingdom including August Thyssen-Hütte AG, Mannesmann AG, Siemens AG and Bayer AG, but the largest in terms of its UK manufacturing employees is Hoechst AG. Indeed, the number employed in manufacturing plants in which Hoechst or its subsidiaries have a share of 50 per cent or more is exceeded, among EEC-head-quartered firms, only by Philips (Watts, 1980a) and Michelin. Within the United Kingdom Hoechst UK ranked 139th by turnover in *The Times 1000*, 1978-9 and it is estimated that the group's UK employees probably represent about 5 per cent of its world total. To establish the salient features of the operations of Hoechst in the United Kingdom the discussion establishes the current corporate structure, examines the associated spatial structure and considers the evolution of the corporate activity pattern within UK space.

The corporate structure of manufacturing activities in late 1979 is illustrated in Figure 4.6. Two firms are owned directly by Hoechst AG

Figure 4.6: Hoechst in the United Kingdom: Corporate Structure

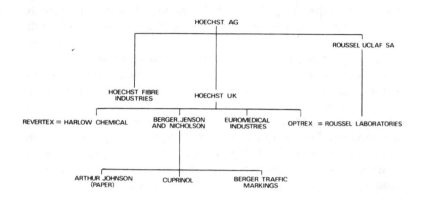

Source: Corporate Data

(Hoechst Fibre Industries and Hoechst UK), and of these Hoechst UK is the controlling group for most of the UK activities. A third firm (Roussel Laboratories) is a subsidiary of one of Hoechst's operations based in France (Roussel Uclaf SA). Below this level Hoechst UK controls Euromedical Industries and the Berger group, has a joint interest in Optrex with Roussel, and with Revertex (a UK concern) has a 50 per cent share in Harlow Chemical. The Berger group, in turn, owns Arthur Johnson, Cuprinol and Berger Traffic Markings.

It is likely that it is on this group of manufacturing firms that the policies of Hoechst AG may have a major influence. If anything, Figure 4.6 may underplay Hoechst's role by excluding associate firms in which Hoechst has a less than 50 per cent share. It must also be stressed that Hoechst has a number of other important UK activities which are engaged primarily in marketing, selling and distribution and which do not undertake manufacturing in the United Kingdom.

In 1979 these manufacturing concerns employed around 5,000 employees, and they were engaged primarily in the chemical industry as defined in Order V, and within that order most of their activities would be classified to MLH 272 (pharmaceutical chemicals and preparations) and MLH 274 (paint).

The overall pattern of plants owned by Hoechst AG is shown in

Figure 4.7. It depicts an orientation towards the southern parts of Britain, and the majority of plants lie outside the regions which for most of the 1970s comprised the Assisted Areas. This orientation is emphasised further if employment figures are taken into account, as almost 70 per cent of the employees were in the South-East and South-West regions.

A breakdown of this overall pattern gives an indication of the range of Hoechst's activities. The one joint operation with a firm outside the Hoechst group (Harlow Chemical) produces synthetic resins and polyvinyl alcohol, primarily at Harlow (174 employees), but with a smaller-scale operation at Stallingborough. The joint operations with Roussel are responsible for the 115 employees at Basingstoke, manufacturing primarily pharmaceuticals and proprietary health care products, while Roussel's main manufacturing plant with over 500 employees is in Swindon. This latter plant manufactures pharmaceuticals and fine chemicals.

The directly owned operations include the Limavady plant in Northern Ireland, whose 450 employees produce Trevira Polyester filaments while Hoescht UK's sales, research and manufacturing activities employ directly around 1,250 employees. This firm appears to manufacture under its own name at only three sites — one at Wisbech for the manufacture of pesticides for agricultural and horticultural use, one at Milton Keynes for the manufacture of veterinary products for farmers and vets and a third at Halifax. The Euromedical subsidiary producing disposable hospital supply products at Worthing employs only 170, whereas the Berger group with 3,108 employees on manufacturing sites is responsible for over half of Hoechst's UK manufacturing employment.

Berger and its subsidiaries operate some ten plants in the United Kingdom (Figure 4.7) and these are concerned primarily with the manufacture of paint, although one on Tyneside concentrates upon the production of surface coatings for a variety of products in the automotive and marine industries. Of the sites in the South-West, one produces road markings together with reflective road studs and high-visibility safety garments, while the other produces various types of wood treatment and preservatives. The northern sites at Peterlee and Guiseley manufacture wall coverings, although the latter site also produces polystyrene and waxed paper wrappers for the bread industry.

This descriptive material provides an indication of the variety of activities taking place within Hoechst's corporate spatial structure. It does not, however, provide any understanding or explanation of the

Figure 4.7: Employment at Manufacturing Sites Owned by Hoechst AG, End 1979

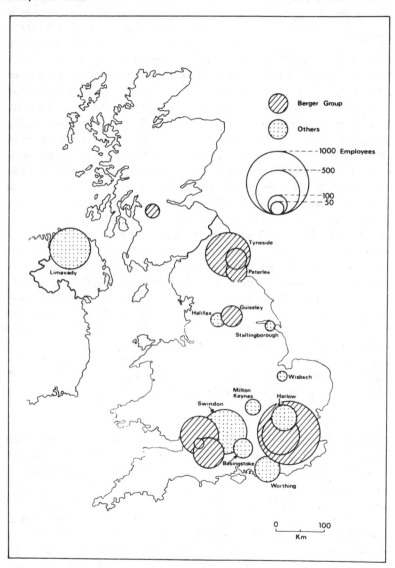

Source: Corporate data.

structure as it appears in Figure 4.7. A historical or genetic explanation of this pattern can be ordered around two time periods; pre-1970 and the last decade.

Pre-1970

Until 1970 Hoechst had only limited manufacturing in the United Kingdom, and in this it reflects the general pattern of West German interest in this country noted earlier. Hoechst UK was registered as Lawfer Chemicals in 1947, changed its name to Hoechst Chemicals in 1955 and to its present title in 1965. Its first major manufacturing operation appears to have been the setting up of Harlow Chemical in 1963. Clearly, its site must have been influenced strongly by the location of Revertex, the joint owner. A rather different approach was taken in 1968 when the fibre operation was begun in Northern Ireland; here too it was a new operation, but it was owned and set up by Hoechst AG, the parent company. It is still run independently of Hoechst UK. In the same year Roussel Laboratories became part of the Hoechst group (Corina, 1970) and thus through the French parent another manufacturing site was added to the Hoechst spatial structure. If this latter operation is discounted (as it was a by-product of changes in France) Hoechst's main entry to UK manufacturing activities was through new plants, either independently or in conjunction with a British firm. Locationally there was a marked contrast, as one plant is perhaps in the most peripheral of UK regions and the second in a London new town. All the operations within the Hoechst group, both manufacturing and non-manufacturing, probably employed just over 1,000 persons in 1969, Hoechst UK having only 509 employees.

The Last Decade

Figure 4.8 illustrates the dramatic increase in Hoechst UK's operations after 1969, and the general upward trend in employment over the period 1970-8. These figures relate only to Hoechst UK and appear to exclude joint operations as well as those in Northern Ireland. The post-1969 growth raised Hoechst from near the bottom of the UK top 500 firms to a position between around 140th to 150th. The group is seen in its publicity literature as employing 8,000 people in the UK.

The major change came in 1970 with Hoechst's acquisition of the Berger group of companies. The group had been built up through the merger of four of Britain's leading paint makers and at the time of acquisition by Hoechst post-merger integration of activities was still incomplete (*The Economist*, 1969c). The group had shown quite marked growth in the three years prior to acquisition, moving from 239th to 186th in the *Times 1000*. One of the major reasons for Hoechst's interest in the group appears to have been Hoechst's aim to widen the UK outlets for its pigment production (*The Economist*, 1969b). Hoechst's original aim was to set up a joint UK/West German operation and it planned to give the UK Reed (paper) group an option to take a half-share in the equity of Berger exercisable up to three months after the bid had gone through (Lumsden and Corina, 1969).

Figure 4.8: Hoechst UK: Employment Growth

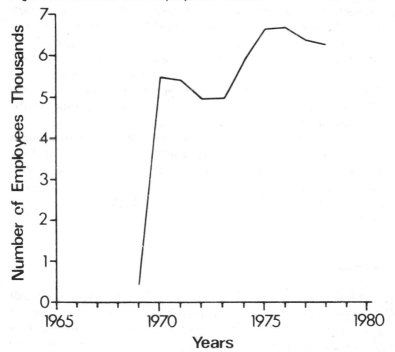

Source: Extel Statistical Services.

Acquisition was not straightforward. Berger did not like the Hoechst-Reed link, primarily as this implied there might be further rationalisation of the Berger and Reed paint operations (*The Economist*, 1969a). A counter-bid was launched by Sherwin-Williams from the US, as Sherwin Williams had owned Berger until 1911 and still had a market share agreement with them. This rival bid raised the price Hoechst had to pay for entry to the UK market; the initial price rose from £0.50 to £0.65 per share, and the total price of £26.1 million was the fourth largest acquisition in the fiscal year 1969-70 (*Times 1000*, 1970-1). The rival bid was defeated, the plans for joint operations with Reed did not materialise and the acquisition added some 10 production sites to Hoechst's spatial structure. As Corina (1970) observed, this brought 'Hoechst into Britain with a bang, to consolidate a bridgehead established only a few years ago'.

Subsequent developments were more gradual, with new plants at Swindon (Roussel) and Worthing (Euromedical Industries) in 1971, a vaccine plant at Milton Keynes in 1974 and agricultural products at Wisbech in 1979. Two acquisitions were made in the mid-1970s, a plant in Halifax and the plant of Optrex at Basingstoke. No new joint operations were begun, but Harlow Chemicals opened a branch plant at Stallingborough in 1978. With the exception of Limavady, the wholly owned new plant operations have all been established in the South-East or East Anglia. Only in acquisitions were plants acquired mainly outside the South, but the majority were a by-product of the acquisition of the Berger group headquartered in the South-East.

This examination of the behaviour of Hoechst illustrates the growth of just one large industrial enterprise, and generalisation to other large West German enterprises in the United Kingdom would be unwise. However, the operations of both Thyssen and Bayer would probably merit closer investigation, especially as during 1979 Bayer made some important acquisitions.

Conclusion

This chapter has illustrated the way in which both aggregate analysis and the geography of enterprise approach may be used to complement one another. The first has been used to analyse the behaviour of a multiplicity of subsidiary firms, while the second was able to focus on the behaviour of the predominant large industrial enterprise.

In the 1970s it has been shown that all foreign firms were showing a preference for the near periphery with much less emphasis on Scotland and Northern Ireland than was the case previously. The regions between the south and periphery are still failing to attract major interest from foreign firms. Within this general framework employment in EEC-owned plants was shown to focus upon either the South-East/ East Anglia or North-West/Northern Ireland, although the South-East concentration was shown to be mainly a reflection of the industrial structure of EEC investment.

West German firms were growing more rapidly in employment in the United Kingdom than the average for firms owned by other EEC countries and were concentrated in the engineering and chemical sectors. In the distribution of plants with over 100 employees in 1978 there was a bias towards the Assisted Areas, even when the plants of the principal enterprise were omitted from the analysis. An interesting distinction was identified in the new manufacturing operations of the 1970s in that the greenfield sites showed a predominantly southern location, whereas the acquisitions indicated a more dispersed pattern. These new operations as a whole were preceded by sales offices in only half the cases, and there are hints that acquisitions may be preceded by agency agreements.

The growth of Hoechst's operations followed primarily the acquisition route, and its own spatial patterns are similar to those created in aggregate by the smaller firms. New plants are primarily within the southern half of the country, while acquired plants show a wider spread. However, there is an important difference in that this wider spread reflects not acquisition of Northern firms but the dispersed pattern of plants owned by Berger at the time it was acquired.

In their overall distribution West German plants do seem to favour the Assisted Areas, but in their new plants in the mid-1970s this facet of behaviour does not appear. New job creation in new plants does seem to be primarily in Southern England. More difficult to isolate are the consequences for job creation or loss of the acquisition of firms. There is no measure of what would have happened if the acquisition had not occurred, nor are data available as to employment levels at the time of acquisition. The national employment consequences of acquisition of indigenous firms have yet to be explored.

Acknowledgements

The University of Sheffield Research Fund made a generous contribution to the funding of this research. The author is also indebted to Alf Thwaites and Ian Smith of the Centre for Urban and Regional Development Studies at the University of Newcastle-upon-Tyne for some helpful comments on an earlier version of this chapter.

5 THE CHANGING INTERNATIONAL DIVISION OF LABOUR WITHIN ICI

I.M. Clarke

Introduction

Current research in industrial geography seems unable to explain a number of related spatial phenomena. This failing is evident in a recent review of the field by Wood (1980) which catalogues some of the main foci of research: measures of regional economic change; prediction and policy evaluation; 'components of change' studies; the growing dependency of regional economies on outside control and the implications of multinational activity for regional policy. Although these areas of study are valuable in their own right, no adequate link has been forged between them. Hamilton and Linge's (1979) systems framework and Massey and Meegan's (1979) structural analysis are only partial aids to uncovering this link (Taylor and Thrift, 1979).

Many studies in industrial geography demonstrate this lack of any comprehensive alternative framework — particularly those based on a regional perspective. These regional studies provide only a partial picture of the effects of industrial change on employment, owing to the multinational dimension of most large organisations' operations. In fact, a complete explanation can only be cast at the international level. This is especially the case from the late 1960s onwards, for several reasons, including developments in manufacturing technology and communications, the formation of trading blocs (such as the EEC and ASEAN) and the opening up of financial, resource and labour markets on a world scale. As a direct result of these trends, the opportunities for large corporations to spread their geographical production networks have increased dramatically. A useful indicator of this trend is the sudden increase in the level of foreign investment in manufacturing production in the 1970s, which grew by 82 per cent between 1971 and 1976 (UNESCO, 1978). Most of this growth was controlled by slightly more than 400 large multinational corporations operating at a global level (Stopford, Dunning and Haberich, 1980). Indeed, the growth of internationalised production — superimposed on earlier developments in the global circulation of commodities and then capital (Palloix, 1975; Forbes, 1982) — has through the medium of the multinational corporation, succeeded in dividing and using labour on an international scale. This is the 'new' international division of labour (Fröbel, Heinrichs and Kreye, 1980). In many developed countries such as the UK, it is only now beginning to be realised that deindustrialisation and rising unemployment are an integral part of the new global trends in production.

The following discussion is a preliminary attempt to redress the imbalance caused by the over-emphasis in industrial geography on regional-level analyses. The first section of this chapter demonstrates some of the limitations of these studies in explaining job losses, and then proceeds to an alternative avenue for investigation − examining job losses world-wide within single multinational corporations. The subsequent two sections provide a detailed investigation of the changes taking place in the international division of labour within one UK-based multinational company − Imperial Chemical Industries Ltd (ICI). Changes in the number and geographical distribution of ICI's work-force are assessed for the ten-year period from 1970 to 1980. The conclusion reached is that in order to develop any knowledge of the dynamics of global production, individual corporate acts of restructuring need to be understood. An analysis of the restructuring initiatives taken within ICI in 1980 shows the reinforcement of the long-term trends evident within the company in the previous decade. The study concludes with an evaluation of the international division of labour emerging within ICI, as a response to changes taking place in the production environment of the company.

UK Job Losses in an International Corporate Framework

In a recent article, Townsend (1981) has made an attempt to explain recent major job losses in the UK by concentrating on the process of deindustrialisation. He noted that:

> Large private corporations with a multiplicity of plants of different ages and an equal variety of products are also streamlining their activities nationally: bankruptcies, at their highest for several years, are closing many smaller companies; a great range of industries and places are involved, supply as well as market-oriented industries (p. 33).

Corporations have a variety of effects on particular localities ranging from the economic stability (McAleese and Counahan, 1979) or instability (Smith, 1979) induced by the plants of multinational corporations (Firn, 1975; Dicken and Lloyd, 1976), to longer-term effects on employment and industrial structure related to the types of technology introduced (Ashcroft and Ingham, 1979). The effects of the recession in the UK have been felt particularly strongly in the areas most affected by deindustrialisation, especially in the inner cities with their concentrations of declining industry and ageing infrastructure (Gripaios, 1977a, 1977b; McLoughlin, 1978; Thrift, 1979).

Corporate restructuring of production can also have wider implications than those indicated simply by direct job losses. When a particular plant is closed, in the North-East of England for example, organisational linkages with more local firms, both small and large, are severed. Such a change can act as a reverse multiplier or 'contraction pole' (Rabey, 1977; Van den Bulcke *et al.*, 1979). Thus, international structural changes in production can produce both direct and indirect effects on employment trends in the UK, even in the smaller towns and rural areas. Two recent studies, one in the United States (Walker and Storper, 1981) and another in the UK (Massey and Meegan, 1979) have correctly stressed the linkages between spatial and aspatial forces and outcomes in production; but only within the context of the national economic situation. Both studies therefore reveal themselves as based on the traditional approach to industrial change. They fail to consider the degree to which unemployment trends are a product of international firms reacting to international forces. Thus many of the direct job losses listed by Townsend stem from the decisions of large multinational corporations — several of them with headquarters in the UK — to rationalise and restructure production on a global scale. These corporations include ICI, ITT, Courtaulds, National Cash Register and Singer, for example.

The exact number of such jobs lost still remains a matter of conjecture and job losses in the UK only tell part of the story. No adequate understanding can be gained without also considering the growth of multinational manufacturing industry in many so-called Third World countries such as Hong Kong, Singapore, Mexico, Brazil and Argentina (Landsberg, 1979). The difficulty in such a comprehensive approach lies in relating the position of industrial plants in the UK to overall adjustments in the world-wide operations of individual corporations (Chapman, 1974). Product changes are not the only structural adjustments multinational corporations can make. They can also change production processes (Carmichael, 1977) and shift location (Rees,

1972). What needs to be asked, therefore, is not only why jobs are being lost in the UK, but also *where* production is going to, and in what *form*.

The strategy adopted in this chapter is to examine the role of the multinational corporation in the creation of a new international division of labour and then to proceed to an understanding of major job losses in the UK as part and parcel of a process affecting numerous national economies — caused through their mutual dependence on the *same* multinational companies. The work of Krümme (1981) and Teulings (1981) shows the way. Krümme's research on the Volkswagen company's operations in North America and the 'unspoken' competition for manufacturing plants both between and within the United States and West Germany represents, despite its many attractive features, an establishment-based approach viewing the corporation from the 'bottom upwards'. Teulings' work on the Dutch group, Philips, on the other hand, is both simpler and more revealing. The study examines movements of capital between the main Continental divisions of the company, as reflected in inter-divisional employment changes — demonstrating the relative ease with which multinational corporations compared to smaller national corporations can restructure their production.

Teulings' results suggest that in the last decade multinational corporations have concentrated their expansion movements outside the home country, whereas rationalisation and replacement investments have tended to affect the home base. The organisational structure of the multinational corporation makes it an efficient vehicle for capital movement compared to other institutions,[1] but of equal importance has been the strengthening of relationships with international financial institutions. Within the multinational corporation, the nature of multi-plant operation allows the 'fixed' capital of individual plants to be checked against each other, and against more profitable investments elsewhere (Bluestone and Harrison, 1980; Perrons, 1981; Teulings, 1981).[2]

The following two sections demonstrate this process of restructuring of production on a world-wide scale by one multinational corporation, ICI Ltd.

The Changing International Division of Labour within ICI World-wide, 1970-80

ICI is a multinational, multiproduct company, formed in 1926 by the

merger of four companies: Nobel Industries Ltd, a powerful explosives firm; Brunner, Mond and Company Ltd, a large alkali company;
British Dyestuffs Corporation and the United Alkali Company Ltd
(Reader, 1970). A large number of products are produced and marketed
by the corporation under nine main business classifications — agriculture, fibres, general chemicals, organic chemicals, industrial explosives,
paints, petrochemicals, pharmaceuticals and plastics. ICI's geographical
base is as broad as its product range. With factories in more than forty
countries and selling organisations in more than sixty, ICI is not only a
multinational but also a 'global' company in the true sense of the word.
The distribution of all ICI's factories and offices world-wide in 1980 is
shown in Figure 5.1.

In the decade 1970-80, employment within ICI underwent a significant process of restructuring, so that it has even been dubbed 'International Chemical Industries Ltd' (*The Economist*, 1980a). By implication, global restructuring of production within ICI in the last decade
has produced a vastly different form of the division of labour. The new
international division of labour which is emerging within the company
is in a state of flux. The objective of this and the subsequent section is
simply to describe the underlying elements of this process. There is no
finite form to the spatial (or aspatial) division of labour, so the
emphasis on *process* is intentional. The key elements which are brought
out are the changing *magnitude* and *form* of manufacturing production,
and shifts in its *geographical structure*. Each of these three elements of
the division of labour interact to give the new international division of
labour a complex spatial and aspatial format.

A divisional breakdown of employment within ICI for the period is
given in Table 5.1 and illustrated in Figure 5.2. The most apparent
feature is that in terms of the size or magnitude of employment, there
has been a substantial decrease. Employment in ICI rose from 190,000
in 1970-1 to 201,000 in 1973-4, and then fell off gradually to 192,000
in 1975-6. Only after this date did employment decrease rapidly to
143,200 in 1979-80. Over the period as a whole, ICI has, therefore,
shed 29 per cent of its 1970 work-force. This is the first and most ele-
mentary feature of ICI's newly emerging international division of
labour; a declining world-wide labour force.

A second feature is the drop in employment within the UK. This
trend becomes sharper after 1975-6 when the number in the corporate
labour force dropped by 37,000 in one year. Over the decade, ICI's
employment in the UK fell by as much as 38.5 per cent. It is important
to note that of the 52,700 jobs lost from ICI in the UK between 1970

Figure 5.1: The World-wide Distribution of ICI's Factories and Offices, 1980

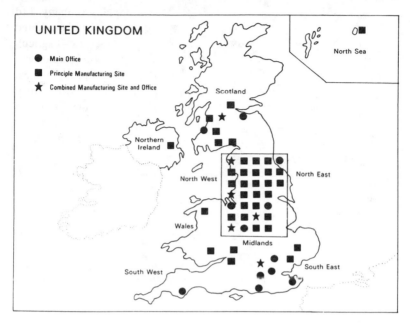

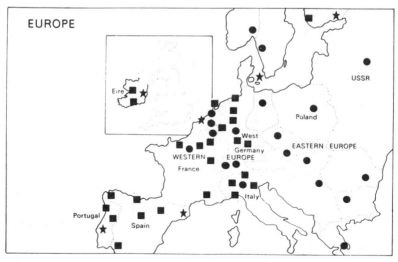

Source: ICI (1981).

Figure 5.1 (cont'd)

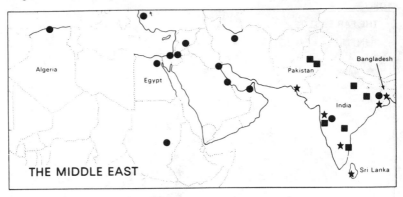

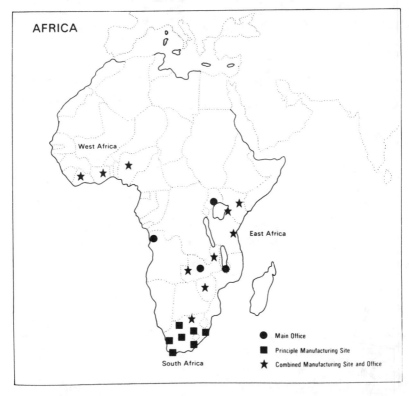

Figure 5.1 (cont'd)

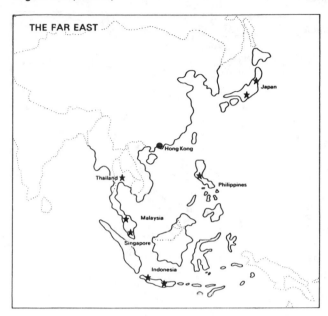

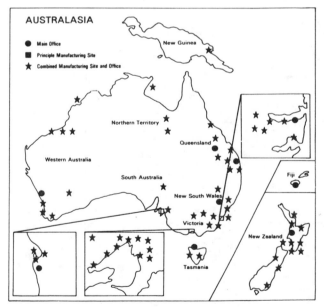

Figure 5.1 (cont'd)

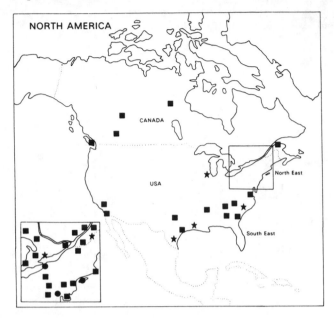

Table 5.1: Employment in ICI Divisions World-wide, 1970-1 to 1979-80 (thousands of employees)

Division	1970-1	1971-2	1972-3	1973-4	1974-5	1975-6	1976-7	1977-8	1978-9	1979-80
United Kingdom	137,000	132,000	130,000	132,000	129,000	132,000	95,000	92,500	89,400	84,300
Continental Western Europe					16,000	11,800	11,000	10,700	10,700	10,800
The Americas					23,000	19,700	19,900	19,500	20,200	19,900
Australasia & the Far East	53,000	67,000	69,000	69,000	13,000	12,900	12,400	15,700	15,500	15,700
Indian Sub-continent					1C,000	10,800	10,800	11,000	10,500	10,600
Other Countries					5,000	4,800	4,900	1,800	1,900	1,900
Total	190,000	199,000	199,000	201,000	196,000	192,000	154,000	151,200	148,200	143,200

Source: Various annual reports.

Figure 5.2: The Divisional Breakdown of Employment in ICI

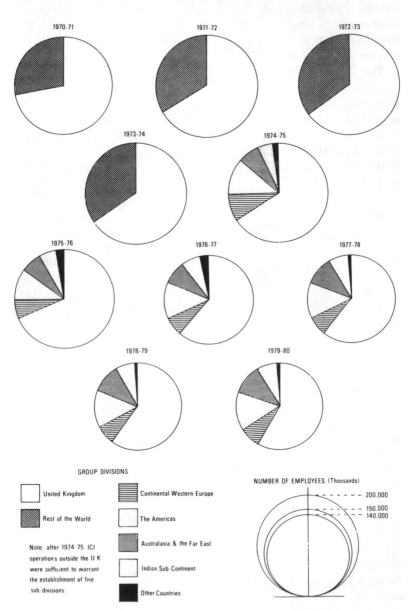

Source: Various annual reports.

and 1980, only 5,900 were effectively 'transferred' to other ICI regional divisions outside the UK. Clearly, then, by far the greatest number of jobs (46,800) have been rationalised and lost altogether. It is interesting to investigate in what form and by what mechanism these jobs are lost and transferred in ICI.

The year 1973-4 represents a significant watershed in the development of ICI. After this date, ICI operations outside the UK were of sufficient significance to warrant the division of the 'rest of the world' in company reports into five separate regional categories (Figure 5.2). Examining these divisions as a whole reveals a third important trend, which is that although employment increased within the divisions taken together (not including the UK) from 53,000 in 1970-1 to 69,000 in 1973-4, and then fell to 58,000 in 1979-80, all except two regional divisions recorded an absolute loss in employment. Only the Indian Sub-continent, which has retained an even balance, and Australasia and the Far East actually experienced a growth in employment. Decentralisation of employment from the UK within ICI, therefore, has been spatially selective and uneven.

Geographical diversification of production within ICI deserves more detailed attention (Figure 5.3). The expansion of 3,700 jobs experienced in Australasia and the Far East between 1974 and 1980 demonstrates, to some degree, the 'centre-periphery' movement of production which has been described by a number of authors (Utrecht, 1978; Alford, 1979; Taylor and Thrift, 1981b). But the exact extent to which the growth has concentrated either on Australasia or on the Far East is hard to ascertain because of their amalgamation into one operational division. Figure 5.3 illustrates this movement. It is crucial, at this stage, to recognise the decrease in employment in Continental Western Europe and the Americas — despite ICI's emphasis on expanding production in these two regions. Employment figures alone do not explain how production is still expanding in these two regions, despite the overall decrease in employment. The only answer can be that there is some connection with the changing form of manufacturing production.

A further part of the explanation for this trend would appear to lie in the restructuring of ICI's product divisions over the period. Figure 5.4 illustrates the changing trading profits for each of the individual product divisions. All product divisions in Figure 5.4(c) have experienced growing profits between 1970 and 1980. In particular, the general chemical and agricultural divisions grew rapidly, providing the bulk of profits. Figure 5.4(a), on the other hand, demonstrates that for plastics and petrochemicals profits have been highly attuned to cycli-

Figure 5.3: The Geographical Diversification of Production within ICI

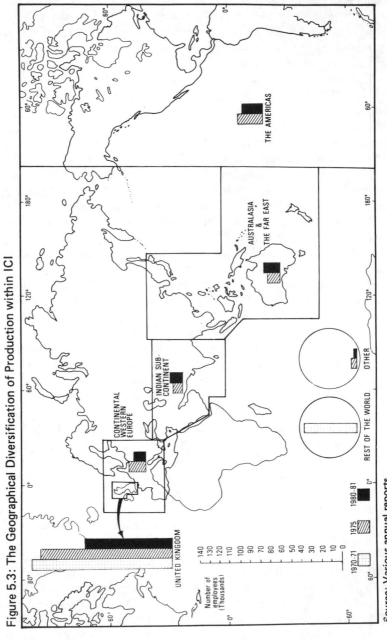

Source: Various annual reports.

Figure 5.4: Divisional Trading Profits, 1970-80

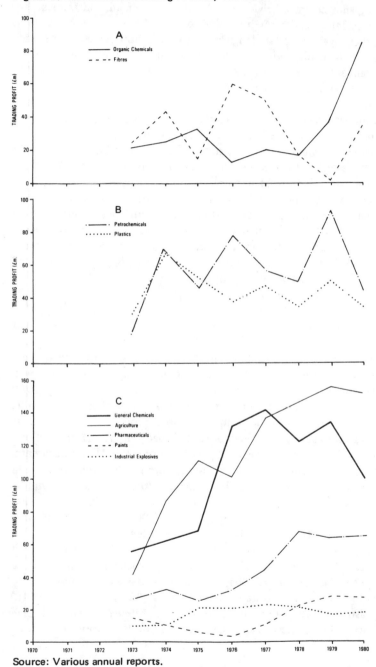

Source: Various annual reports.

cal variations in market demand (*The Economist*, 1981g). The fibres
and organic chemical divisions, on the other hand, illustrate a very
different fate. Profits for both divisions fell between 1974 and 1976
and then again in 1978 (Figure 5.4(b)). In both cases an upswing
in profits coincided with substantial shedding of employment within
the company. After two rounds of job cut-backs in 1979 and 1980,
the fibres and organic chemical divisions have again begun to show
profits.

Although changes in the magnitude, form and geographical spread
of production have been studied separately, it is increasingly difficult
to evaluate changes in the international division of labour within ICI
without referring to how each of these factors interrelates. How, for
instance, can the decrease in employment in the petrochemical division
in the UK and its growth on the Continent be explained? A full
explanation requires the consideration of individual acts of restructuring
of production, such as closures, redundancies and openings, over a
shorter time period. At the same time, it is necessary to relate these
individual activities to the strategic continuity of ICI's policy over the
decade. This is done below for one year, 1980.

Structural Change and Strategic Continuity: a Year in the Life of ICI

The trend towards decentralisation of production within ICI away from
the UK — so evident within the last decade — is reinforced by each
annual initiative. The history of the corporation in the year 1980
illustrates this well. A deepening of the world recession made trading
conditions difficult for a company whose product divisions sell as
much as three-quarters of their output abroad (*Sunday Times*, 1980a).
Profits fell during the year, especially from the UK, Continental
Western Europe and American divisions (*Daily Telegraph*, 1980a). In
tandem with earlier trends, the company forecast a similar annual
round of job losses comparable to 1979 (*The Times*, 1981a). The forecast was not wrong. The company shed 6,000 workers world-wide
in 1980 and the trend looks like continuing in 1981.

The product divisions that were hardest hit were those which formed
over half of ICI's total business: dyestuffs, petrochemicals, plastics and
fibres (*The Economist*, 1980b), so that there was a continuing need to
move towards more profitable commodities (*The Economist*, 1981a)
and also to rationalise operations (ICI, *Annual Report*, 1980).
Obviously, during the decade, ICI's emphasis on these forms of restruc-

turing had a direct bearing on making it become the world's fifth most successful chemical company (*The Economist*, 1981b). But the global spread of ICI factories and a diverse product range allowed the company to weather 1980 by taking a number of initiatives. The primary objective was to cut back on surplus capacity, a situation common to all Europe's nine largest man-made fibres producers (*The Economist*, 1981c). The point which needs to be stressed is the geographical implications of global restructuring of production within ICI. With product divisions interlaced and interlinked between a large number of countries, repercussions were obviously variable. The interaction of the three main strategic alternatives open to the corporation — higher-value and more successful products, new technologies and geographical shifts in production — dictated changes in the structure and pattern of production within ICI. Ironically it was Britain, as a 'geriatric home' of industry (*The Economist*, 1981d) within ICI, which came off worst of all countries in the 'chess game' of 1980. There at least 6 per cent of the manufacturing labour force are employed in chemicals of one form or another. Trouble for a large chemical company such as ICI meant trouble for British workers.

Geographical Changes and the Corporate Context

The intention of this section is to proceed from the structural closures and redundancies of ICI in the UK to an analysis of the overall global trends described in the previous section. Placing these widespread geographical changes in their corporate context enables us to appreciate the results of a move towards a new international division of labour within ICI.

The divisions that were most badly hit — fibres, petrochemicals, plastics and organic chemicals — are closely related in production terms. In each case the UK felt the brunt. The fibres industry continued to come off worst of all. Having employed 25,000 people in 1979, this division had been cut back gradually to 7,500 by 1980, but with an equivalent output to 1971 (*The Times*, 1980). In 1980, two more plants were closed, one at Kilroot (Northern Ireland) where 1,100 jobs were lost, the other at Ardeer (Scotland) where there were 700 redundancies. Carrington Viyella, in which ICI is a major shareholder (49 per cent), also closed four plants and made 2,000 redundancies (*The Economist*, 1980c). Some of ICI's major textile competitors made similar cut-backs: Coats Patons has axed 4,000 jobs since 1979; Tootals closed six plants and made 3,000 workers redundant in 1979; and Courtaulds cut its labour force by 7,000 in the eighteen months from June 1979 to December 1980.

Further job losses were spread across the man-made fibre plants and the petrochemical factories which supplied them. At Pontypool, Doncaster, Radcliffe (Lancashire), Wilton and the divisional headquarters at Harrogate, 20 per cent redundancies were felt. The major plant at Wilton on Teesside became fully loaded only because of these cut-backs and the closure of the Ardeer unit alongside it (*The Economist*, 1980d). In total, 4,000 jobs were axed in the fibres division, a significant proportion of the 6,000 jobs lost within all product divisions of ICI world-wide. The majority of these were lost in the UK.

A decision was also made in the 1980s to merge the plastics and petrochemical divisions and to scale down heavy chemical research (*The Economist*, 1981e). In the UK, 500 workers were therefore made redundant at the Hillhouse plant in Lancashire and 600 more at the soda-ash plant at Northwich in Cheshire (*The Daily Telegraph*, 1980b). One-quarter of the Mond plastics division's work-force, based on Merseyside, Cheshire, Teesside and Derbyshire, faces redundancy over the next three years, expected to total 3,900 jobs. The polythene plant at Stevenage, Hertfordshire, was also ordered to be closed, with the loss expected in 1980 at 340 jobs (*The Times*, 1981b).

The closure of outdated UK plants in ICI has quite frequently been accompanied by a change in the method of production in those remaining plants. Several such cases were reported in 1980. Recession in the textile industry had a profound impact on the organic chemicals division of ICI because of the reduction in the demand for dyes as a number of customers ceased production. Highly automated plants were opened at Huddersfield and Stevenston (Scotland), both of which were to produce industrial biocides (*The Economist*, 1980e). Further modernisation took place in other divisions, including the paints division (Stowmarket) and agricultural division (Billingham's high-protein animal feed plant). One of the most important examples, illustrating ICI's strategy of concentrating on areas in which it has a strong technological and manufacturing ability, has been the move up market in the fibres division. The most obvious case in point is the production of the polyester fibre, Mitrelle, to imitate silk, at Pontypool (*The Economist*, 1981a; *Daily Telegraph*, 1981).

However, plant closures and modernisation of plants in the UK were essentially a precondition of geographical extension of production globally, and it is these movements which are the subject of the next section.

The Geographical Extension of Production

Complementing the closures and modernisation of plants in the UK described above were moves towards geographical extension of production within ICI. For instance, the plastics division's strategy was essentially based on extending the division abroad. The goal was local, market-oriented production and is typified by a series of projects in Europe and North America (*The Economist*, 1980e). In Europe, geographical diversification was centred on the construction of a plant in Wilhelmshaven in West Germany, commissioned in 1980 and opened in 1981. This complex parallels the Teesside plant in the UK, so that ICI now has manufacturing bases for polymers in both the UK and the Continent. Construction of the plant has enabled the group to accelerate the closure of older, less economic units, those in the UK, as part of a programme to reduce operating costs. However, operating costs are not merely a function of labour. In the chemicals industry, energy considerations also form a significant cost factor.

ICI has been worried about increasing energy costs in the UK for a number of years. Electricity amounted to 80 per cent of costs of chlorine production in the Mond plastics division (Northern England). Electricity costs, which are 50 per cent cheaper in West Germany, therefore had a strong bearing on the opening of the plant in Wilhelmshaven to produce chlorine (*The Economist*, 1981h). In this highly modernised plant, ICI employs no more than 40 process workers on any one shift (Richardson, 1981). In the same chlorine and derivatives business in Cheshire and on Teesside, ICI employs 11,500 workers. It takes little to imagine what might happen, should production in the UK become too costly.

One final point needs to be mentioned about the construction of the Wilhelmshaven plant. That is, the plant was aimed at local production for the European market. The dying British car market, for instance, each car of which had traditionally contained around £54 worth of ICI products (including such things as fibres for seat covers, paint for the body, plastics for hoses and soda-ash for glass) (*Sunday Times*, 1980b), forced ICI to look to Europe for alternatives. The Wilhelmshaven plant therefore acted as a 'doorstep' producer to the West German motor company, Volkswagen.

The close ties between the problem of geographical extension of production and energy and resource considerations (Forbes, 1982) are given added weight by the fact that many European chemical companies are now building new capacity in North America and the Middle East. In these two regions, plentiful supply of cheap natural gas provides an attractive alternative to naphtha-based chemicals produced in Europe. In fact the output of these plants is replacing both products and employment that would otherwise have come from European plants (*The Economist*, 1981g). ICI has a $600m petrochemical plant about to come on stream in America, taking the company downstream to sources of ethylene feedstocks for fibres and plastics (*The Economist*, 1980a). In part, this plant again duplicates production of the Wilton plant in the UK.

We have considered, on the one hand, the rationalisation taking place in the UK petrochemical industry and, on the other hand, the opening of new productive capacity in West Germany and North America. These initiatives taken in 1980 seem to suggest a continuity to ICI strategy in the 1970s and 1980s, a trend towards geographical diversification. Whether either of these two new plants will eventually replace productive capacity in the UK, especially in the North-West and North-East, is still a matter for conjecture. But what must be remembered is that large global companies, such as ICI, whilst they have a strategy, do not have a 'grand design'. The international structure of production must, by necessity, remain flexible. The importance of the Wilhelmshaven plant, for example, is not only to gain local market access and cheaper energy supplies, but also to integrate into the overall *global* production network of ICI.

In this sense, it matters very little whether a plant is opened in, for instance, Europe, North America or the Middle East. The *internal* flexibility of these multiproduct sites and the elasticity of their *external* relations – between plants – make global integration less of a problem today. Corporations are now able to take advantage of government incentives, cheap resources and various financial arrangements at both regional and international levels. For instance, various regional development policies operating in the UK have attracted major companies, but because infrastructural and financial incentives are usually offered, the tendency has been to attract capital-intensive industries. Labour-intensive industries have located in the South-East (*The Economist*, 1980f).

Such incentives also apply on an international scale in competition between regions which might be far apart. For example, the UK development areas can compete with the emerging free production zones of the Asian countries. In this light, global companies have a strong hold over national governments. ICI Australia's plan to start a big $500m petrochemical project at Point Wilson near Geelong in Victoria (*The Economist*, 1981f) is a good example of this. The plan has subsequently been shelved, with the blame being put squarely on the shoulders of the Australian Federal government's policies (*The Australian*, 1981). A similar plant has been commissioned in Canada, but its future remains in doubt.

To sum up, the particular initiatives taken in 1980 by ICI served to reinforce the overall corporate strategy in the period 1970 to 1980. It is possible, from the above discussion, to distil five main features of ICI's policy, all aimed at responding to the recession which has hit ICI's main business areas:

(1) rationalisation and closure of plants in the UK;
(2) opening of new, occasionally parallel plants in other divisions such as Continental Western Europe;
(3) interaction between 1 and 2 to produce a shift in the geographical centre of gravity of ICI, and a change in the corporate division of labour;
(4) changes in the products produced;
(5) changes in the process of production and, possibly, changes in the labour process, as geographical restructuring has taken place.

The individual initiatives taken in 1980 combined to reaffirm the continuity of ICI policy of the previous decade, which was a trend towards selective geographical rationalisation and diversification at a global scale. This trend will continue in 1981. The British work-force will be cut to 73,000 as a result of the fibres division being pruned to a few premium fibres, the plastics and petrochemical divisions being merged to cut overheads, and investment being concentrated in a few key profit areas (*The Economist*, 1981). The flexibility of ICI's network of plants is the key to the continued success of the company, even in times of recession. The strategy retains profits for the company, but does little to increase the stability of jobs for individuals in the different countries in which ICI operates. Major job losses within individual national economies, such as the UK, must increasingly be explained at the international level. Redundancies within one part of the world and job creations within other regions are effectively two sides of the same coin. Within the new international division of labour of the corporation described here, individuals, in whatever part of the world they may work, must increasingly come to realise that, in the words of one ICI manager, 'they respond to the divisions, they work with me, but they work for ICI' (Richardson, 1981, p. 87).

Conclusions and Prospects: Towards a Geography of the Labour Process

This study has concentrated on the changing location of employment which is taking place within ICI world-wide, drawing together information on particular plant openings, closures, expansions and contractions in the period from 1970 to 1980. A new international division of labour has been shown to be emerging within ICI. However, like the old international and regional divisions of labour before it, this particular geographical pattern of labour use is historically specific. The pattern will go on changing through time, especially since multinational corporations can 'quickly abandon . . . locations . . ., switching the destination of their next round of investment should the conditions for profitable production change' (Hudson, 1981, p. 26).

However, the study also brings out the limitations of studying changes in international production by reference to employment data alone. Figures on the location of employment depict patterns of change, but they reveal nothing of the causes and methods underlying such developments. Seidman and O'Keefe (1980), for example, have studied the influence of specific companies such as General Electric, General Motors and Ford on the changing new international division of labour between South Africa and the United States, but are unable to make any detailed statements about changes in production which underlie the formation of this new spatial division of labour (Fagan, 1980).

The development of ICI has seen the replacement of old methods of production with more advanced techniques. Quite frequently, these changes were associated with the closure, rationalisation or opening of plants in new locations. The combination of these processes of change alters the fortunes of the labour forces in associated areas, both in terms of the number of workers required and the type of skills these workers will need. The impact of these changes in methods of production on labour requirements is well covered in the literature on the labour process.[3]

The labour process in a capitalist economy takes place in the context of conflict between workers and management. In the struggle to acquire the value created by workers labouring over and above the time required to subsist, management is forced to revise continually the form of the labour process. The location of the workplace between the labour force in a labour market on the one hand (Blackburn and Mann, 1979) and management and the structure of industry on the other

(Walker and Storper, 1981) means that the labour process performs a crucial mediating role in industrial transformation as the pivot of a constant struggle over production in which management obtains the 'consent' (Burawoy, 1979) of workers to co-operate in the pursuit of profit.[4] However, the formation of this 'contractual relationship' (Clark, 1981) is a reflexive process: sometimes profits are lost when management fails to exert control. When this occurs, there is a tendency for management to re-exert control by altering the form of the labour process, so that a certain continuity of change can be expected. The logic behind these transformations in the labour process is illustrated in Table 5.2.[5]

Table 5.2: Form and Transformation in the Labour Process

Phase of Labour Process	Characteristics	Contradiction of Transformation
Manufacture	Simple co-operation of crafts. Division of labour.	Emergence of factory allowed centralised capital investment in machine form (fixed labour)
Machinofacture	Machines introduced. Gradual commodification of labour.	Factory-produced collectivised labour, highlighted need to manage.
Scientific Management	Empirical gathering of knowledge of production process. Dissociation of conception from execution in labour process. Labour appended to machine.	'Efficiency drives' to eliminate labour.
Fordism	Control over the pace of assembly by a semi-automatic assembly line. Institutionalisation of class struggle in collective bargaining.	Inability to divide work tasks evenly in time to co-ordinate with uniform machine pace; problems of human strain and motivation.
Neo-Fordism	Automatic production control. Recomposition of tasks in production.	Superficial worker autonomy produces rising demands for worker participation and democracy in the labour process.

The continuity of the labour process can be demonstrated historically. In the case of Britain (Table 5.3), characteristics of the labour process can be related to labour market conditions. For instance, before the 1840s, the geographically dispersed nature of industry weakened any major national attempts to form worker solidarity (Friedman, 1977a). This compares with the situation from the 1970s onwards, when the *international* dispersal of activities within multinational companies began to have similar effects. Historically, there is strong evidence to suggest that variations in the division of labour have been the only constant cause of conflict over production (Cronin, 1979; Ramsay, 1981), so that the growth of multinational companies can be expected to have profound implications for industrial relations. For instance, the apparent threat of multinationals to relocate tends to have a destabilising effect on industrial relations at the plant level (Morgan and Blanpain, 1977).

Of course, the interdependence of capital and labour still affects the multinational, but the transnational location of many major elements of production (Clegg, 1980) means that the corporation now has the upper hand and can segment production facilities both functionally and spatially, thereby dividing labour groups and isolating contractual negotiations (Clark, 1981). The strategy of conflict within the multinational corporation is a 'zero-sum' game at any point in time (Davis, 1973; Schelling, 1980), but not necessarily in the long run. This is because spatial decentralisation of production and the division of labour can be used by multinationals as an explicit bargaining strategy. Therefore, for any single plant, the ultimate form of the labour process adopted by a multinational corporation does not have to follow a sequential path, but depends on how management perceives the structure of a local labour market and what they see as the most appropriate labour force for the job at that time (Walker and Storper, 1980). In this way, it is possible within a single multinational corporation to have different labour processes, such as Fordism, Scientific Management and Neo-Fordism, each performing a similar production task, but in different locations. Exactly how these spatial variations in the form of the labour process relate to overall corporate strategy is a matter which is relatively untouched in the literature.

The conflict between workers and management does not only alter the form of the labour process at the level of the plant, it can also, with the emergence of the multiplant corporation, lead to the alteration of the spatial structure of the firm. In this interpretation of the corporate restructuring of production, the interaction between changes in the plant labour process and industrial spatial structure is highlighted. Two further dimensions can therefore be added to 'in situ' changes in the labour process. The first is *restructuring by relocation*, as in the case of the closure of plants of the Mond division of ICI on Merseyside and the opening up of a new plant at Wilhelmshaven in West Germany. Second, and less frequently considered, is restructuring of the labour

Table 5.3: Control and Resistance in the Transformation of the Labour Process: the Case of Britain, 1780s to 1980s

Period	Characteristics of Control in Labour Processes	Labour Market Conditions	Characteristics of Worker Resistance	Limiting Factors to Worker Resistance
1780s - 1840s	Growth of factories enabled mechanisation and discipline to be imposed. Basic division of labour was enforced by outlawing unions and fining recalcitrant workers.	Unskilled workers flooding the market — especially women and children.	Strict methods of control led to both individual and collective acts of machine-breaking and riots.	Geographically dispersed industries weakened strike solidarity.
1840s - 1870s	Mechanisation continued, with flexibility being maintained by employing outworkers in boom periods. Craft-labour divisions split the union movement.	Reserve armies drying up so that even the most poorly paid workers (women) won rises.	Split in unions caused a fall in mass demonstrations. Only the groups who bargained hardest won concessions.	Size of unions limited owing to the small size of the production units.
1870s - 1914	Mergers increased stability of industry, but the internalisation of the labour market increased firm overheads, necessitating direct control through new techniques such as Taylorism.	Internalised labour market lessened the influence exerted by the reserve army of labour.	Growth in firm size: (i) spread the union movement (ii) institutionalised bargaining. Non-skilled workers also became organised. Protests made by slackening productivity due to decreased bargaining power based on skill. This led gradually to experiments in new methods of control, particularly Fordism (1914).	Size of firm led to parallel centralisation of union hierarchy, but simultaneously caused it to diverge from the rank and file members.
1914 - 1945	Internalising of labour markets continued.	Decreased power of reserve armies relative to internal supply. Geographical differences in the location of expanding and declining industries led to pressure from the reserve army in selected areas.	Closer union-management collaboration but decreased union membership and hence increase in unofficial resistance (2,427 stoppages 1916-18).	Centralised unionism diverged further from rank and file members.
	Direct control served to increase production.		Methods of direct control exacerbated strike conflict, and growth of the organisation of the less skilled.	
1945 - 1970		Drying up of reserve and active armies early on brought women into the labour force.	Growth of more specialised unions as women, unskilled and immigrants entered the labour market.	
	Barriers constructed to job entry by stipulating qualifications.	Growth of reserve army due to internalising of labour market creating discretion based on qualifications.	Increased integration of production process made it susceptible to official and unofficial resistance.	Growth in reserve army of labour necessitated unofficial types of action for effectiveness.
1970 - ?	Technical and bureaucratic (Neo-Fordist) methods of control are increased to prevent disruption of production by unofficial types of worker resistance.	Opening up of access to labour markets on a world scale.	Pressure for greater union democracy and worker participation.	International dispersal of activities within companies prevents worker solidarity at this new level.

process by altering the relative roles played by individual plants. This might be termed *inter-locational restructuring* as, for example, is illustrated for ICI by the closure of the Ardeer plant in Scotland and the shift of its production task to Wilton on Teesside. This provides a much fuller specification of the relationship between corporate restructuring and the labour process, and would require the complementary use of secondary data (see, for example, Massey and Meegan, 1979; Walker and Storper, 1980) and individual plant studies (for instance the work of Burawoy, 1979; Coriot, 1980; Friedman and Meredeen, 1980; Gallie, 1978; and Nichols and Beynon, 1977). Looked at in this way, the spatial implications of restructuring of the labour process became a logical extension of contractual conflict within production (Massey and Meegan, 1979; Clark, 1981). A multiplant approach allows the labour process and the changes in this process through time to be related to the changing structure of labour markets (Clark, 1982). It also allows the knock-on effects between labour markets to be investigated, linking areas of industrialisation to areas of deindustrialisation.

The perspective advocated here extends the examination of the labour process beyond the level of the individual plant to the global scale of the multinational corporation, and attempts to seek out and explain spatial variations in the labour process as they relate to corporate strategy. Overall, multinational reorganisation has three essential elements. The first of these is the *capital-product strategy* of the firm, which is based on the best options open to the firm for investment. The second element consists of the various *methods of production* open to the firm, including the division of labour and the specific form of the labour process. Finally, the *geography of resources* can be a consideration for the firm. In the case of labour these will include spatial variations in its social structure, cost and industrial record, for example. Conceptually, each of these elements can be represented as a single vector, each contributing to a single component, the direction of which shifts occasionally and thereby transforms the various spatial and aspatial dimensions of production.

Dicken (1977) has summarised this viewpoint of the corporation:

In the most highly developed multinational enterprises an international division of labour is practised in which individual plants specialize in those activities for which their comparative advantage is greatest in relation to other plants within the enterprise. The objective is the attainment of overall corporate goals rather than necessarily maximizing the profitability of individual units. Thus profits of one component unit may be used to cross-subsidize the losses of other component units. Further, new plants may be opened, old ones expanded, contracted, or closed down, or activities shifted between one unit and another as and when corporate strategy deems such adjustments to be necessary (p. 139).

This conclusion reaffirms the need to look at factors other than employment in the new international division of labour. Focusing on the geography of the labour process, which is influenced by all three of the above factors, would go some way towards this goal.

The task created by this approach is not a simple one. The network of plants within ICI world-wide (Figure 5.1), for example, demonstrates the scale of the data collection – a task which led McDermott (1977) to suggest that comparative studies will always have to be used owing to the impracticability of collecting comprehensive data on a large number of regions. However, the adoption of a corporate approach, such as the one outlined in this chapter, simplifies the data problems to a considerable extent – although these should still not be minimised.

There are at least four advantages to this approach. First, it complements work which is presently being done on the new international division of labour. Second, the framework makes the conceptual leap between changes at the level of the plant and changes in the spatial structure of multinational corporations far easier to construct. Third, the emphasis on spatial dynamics as well as structure offers industrial geography a chance to understand how process and space work in tandem (Forer, 1978). The final prospect is of a more practical nature. Through an understanding of both the cause and the nature of changes taking place in multinational production, industrial geographers might be able to offer more constructive policies to cope with the strategies of corporations – both to governments and labour movements – thus providing a useful counterbalance to the seemingly one-sided game of multinational production (Holland, 1976). Forging the link between changes in the spatial distribution of the labour process and the new international division of labour is a first and necessary step in constructing a geography of the labour process.

Acknowledgement

I would like to thank my supervisors, Dr M.J. Taylor and Dr N.J. Thrift, for their help in the preparation of this chapter.

Notes

1. Plasschaert's (1979) work on transfer pricing in multinationals expands on this theme.

2. See Chapter 1, which gives one example of how a multinational – Coats Patons Ltd – solves its labour cost problem.

3. There is a large literature on the labour process, but see especially: Aglietta (1979); Banaji (1977); BLPG (1977); Braverman (1974); Burawoy (1979); Coriot (1980); CSE (1976); Edwards (1979); Friedman (1977a; 1977b); Gallie (1978); Gorz (1976); Merkle (1980); Nichols (1980); Nichols and Beynon (1977); Palloix (1976); Rose (1975); Sohn-Rethel (1976) and Zimbalist (1979).

4. Workers have a number of options open to them including bargaining, working to rule and strikes. Four main options are open to management to enable it to maintain control of the labour process. These principles are extracted from a number of studies (see, for example, Friedman, 1977a; Zimbalist, 1979; Coriot, 1980); and can be summarised as follows:

(a) changes in the *'conditions of work'* in order to make the work environment more conducive to labour. Provision of fringe benefits and staff facilities are good examples;

(b) alterations to the *'rules of work organisation'*. Historically, this might include the gradual shift from a strict 'clocking-in' system to the introduction of work by flexitime;

(c) changes in *'job content'* alter the skills required of labour in individual components of the work process. Experiments in job 'enlargement' and 'rotation' are prime examples. A model of job content has been attempted by Walker and Storper (1980).

(d) the reorganisation of *'job classifications'* is a final alternative to restructure the labour process between workers.

5. The first four phases, from manufacture to Fordism, are generally accepted in the literature; but the evidence for a fifth phase of Neo-Fordism is conjectural and sometimes contradictory. Whether it constitutes a completely new phase in the development of the labour process must remain a matter for further research.

6 THE GEOGRAPHICAL PATTERN OF THE AUSTRALIAN TRADING BANKS' OVERSEAS REPRESENTATION

J. Hirst, M.J. Taylor and N.J. Thrift

Introduction

Australia has six major domestically owned banks (soon to be reduced to four by take-overs). These are the Commonwealth Trading Bank (CTB), which is government-owned, the Bank of New South Wales (BNSW), the Commercial Bank of Australia (CBA), the Commercial Banking Company of Sydney (CBCS), the National Bank and the Australia and New Zealand Banking Group (ANZ).[1] All of these banks are large enough to be of world significance. In 1979, for instance, each of them appeared in the 'Top 300' list published by *The Banker* (see Table 6.1). This chapter has one quite simple aim, which is to investigate the geographical pattern of overseas representation of these six trading banks. The first part therefore considers the form and extent of overseas representation, while the second part considers the impact of regulation on this pattern of representation. Finally, in a brief conclusion, some further directions for research are pointed out.

Table 6.1: Australian Trading Banks in *The Banker* 'Top 300' List of June 1979

Banks	Ranking	Assets Less Contra Accounts ($US millions)
Commonwealth Banking Corporation	86	15,148
Bank of New South Wales	90	14,062
Australia and New Zealand Banking Group	101	11,897
National Bank of Australia	159	7,091
Commercial Bank of Australia	201	5,328
Commercial Banking Corporation of Sydney	246	4,095

Source: *The Banker* (June 1979), pp. 87-101.

The Form and Direction of Overseas Representation by Australian Banks

Each of the Australian trading banks has an extensive overseas direct

117

representation (Table 6.2), as well as a corresponding bank network of representation. In most of the world's main financial centres, with the major exception of those in Europe, most or all of the Australian trading banks have some form of direct representation. In the UK, USA and Japan, for example, all six companies have offices and in Hong Kong, Singapore, Bahrain and the Cayman Islands at least three of the banks are present.

From Table 6.2 it can be deduced that there is a particularly notable Australian banking presence in the Pacific Islands so that when the individual size of the countries is considered, as well as aggregate size and economic importance of the area, the Australian trading banks are significantly over-represented.

Another measure of the trading banks' overseas representation is the total number of overseas offices for each country in which the Australian banks operate. This is set out in Table 6.3. As an index of the importance to the banks of their representation in the individual countries, this measure is obviously crude, for at least two main reasons. First, all the forms of direct representation of the banks are aggregated in the table as if they were of equal importance. This is unreasonable, not only because three different forms of representation are included, but also because an unequal significance may be attached by Head Office to the same form of representation (for example it can be expected that an agency in Kiribati would be of lesser importance to a trading bank than an agency in New York). Second, Table 6.3 excludes, as a form of trading bank overseas representation, any subsidiary companies. But all of the trading banks have overseas subsidiary companies, some of the more notable of which have been included in Table 6.2. Of the overseas subsidiary companies, some are merely shelf companies, some are holding companies; others, while active operating companies are, for the trading banks involved, simply an investment interest in which the bank plays little or no management role. But some companies are a deliberately chosen form of bank representation in a country, a form which is generally forced on the banks concerned by the banking legislation in the host country involved. This has been the case in Hong Kong, for example, where, to circumvent local banking legislation, Australian trading banks have established finance company subsidiaries under the *Hong Kong Deposit-Taking Companies Ordinance* (1976) (Rowley, 1978, p. 56).

Further, it must be noted that a simple geographical distribution of a trading bank's overseas offices is not an effective measure of the areas directly serviced by the bank (as distinct from areas indirectly serviced

Table 6.2: Bank Representation 1979

	ANZ	NSW	CTB	CBA	CBCS	National
New Zealand	151 B 52 A	121 B 33 A	RO (1980/81)	79B 25A	RO ('77)	RO
Japan	RO	RO	RO)(1980)	RO	RO - 	RO
Hong Kong	SBSD (78)	JV (10%)	SBSD)		SBSD (1980)	JV (HK)
Singapore	B (79) agency	B (79) RO prior ISBSD (49%)		RO		RO
Malaysia		ISBSD (49%)				SBSD 9%
Indonesia		RO		JV (15%) '78		RO SBSD 10%
Papua New Guinea	6 B 1 A	15 B 3 S/B 12 A	B JV (1980)			9 B; SBSD
Fiji	4 B 1 A	7 B 11 A				
Kiribati		1 B 1 A				
New Hebrides	1 B −1 B '77 +SBSD (fin services '77)	B		B + Trust Co. −1 B '77		B (off-shore banking only)
Tonga						
Solomons	B	JV Bank	1 B) to be SBSD) JV 1980			
Norfolk Island		B	B			
Western Samoa		JV Bank				
Christmas Island		B				
Bahrain		RO		RO		RO
UK						
London	3 B (−1 '77)	3 B	3 B	2 B	2 B (1 1980)	3 B
Other	1 A					
Channel Is.	1					
US						
New York	A	A	A (78- prior RO)	A (77- prior RO)	A (79- prior RO)	A (77- prior RO)
West Coast	A					A
Cayman Islands	B	B	B (1980)	B (1980)		
Total countries	11	18	8	9	4	10 = 62 = 60

counting West Coast/East Cost separately = 60

B = Branch   A = Agency   RO = Representative Office   SBSD = Subsidiary   ISBSD = Indirect Subsidiary   JV = Joint Venture

Source: Banks' Annual Reports, 1977-80.

by correspondence banks). Thus, as Skully (1980) has shown, a bank's representative office in Japan can also service South Korea, while another office in Hong Kong can service Taiwan and the Philippines, and yet another office in Singapore can service Malaysia and Thailand. The area serviced from a particular financial centre may, therefore, be much more extensive than the immediate surrounds. Jao (1979), for example, has noted the existence of Hong-Kong-based organisations servicing Indonesia, Malaysia, the Philippines, South Korea, Taiwan and Thailand. The need to take into account this multiple country servicing by trading banks becomes particularly relevant when comparisons are made with the distributions of overseas bank representation and other forms of Australian off-shore activity, like foreign trade and overseas manufacturing. In these cases, it is necessary to adjust the country-by-country data, a practice followed in the second part of the chapter, so that the degree of areal representation is more accurately reflected.

Table 6.3: The Overseas Representation of Australian Trading Banks

	Number of Australian Banking Companies Represented	Number of Branches, Agencies, Representative Offices, etc.
New Zealand	3	461
Papua New Guinea	4	45
Fiji	2	23
Kiribati	1	2
New Hebrides	4	4
Tonga	1	1
Solomon Islands	2	2
Norfolk Island	2	2
Western Samoa	1	1
Japan	6	6
Hong Kong	5	7
Singapore	4	4
Indonesia	3	3
United Kingdom	6	17
United States	6	8
Cayman Islands	4	4
Bahrain	3	3

Source: *The Banker's Magazine of Australia Rydges* (April 1979), pp. 26-8.

From Table 6.2 it can be seen that underlying the simple country-by-country distribution of the banks' representation are various different forms of representation in the host countries. The form and nature of a trading bank's overseas involvement depends essentially on two sets of factors: the volume and type of business that the bank foresees is either available or can be generated in the centres in which it plans to establish; and the host country regulations in force at the time of establishment. These factors combine to create a spectrum of overseas representation from unrestricted full banks to tightly constrained representative offices. Obviously the terminology and details of regulation vary from country to country but, for the purposes of the present analysis, three forms of overseas representation can be distinguished.[2]

The form of representation that permits a bank the widest range of functions is the *branch*, a full bank offering a wide range of services to all classes of lender and borrower in the host country. It was by the use of this form of representation that US banks operating in the UK moved into high street operations to deal with the general public, as well as continuing to conduct the merchant banking and inter-bank business for which they had been first set up (*The Economist*, 1979). To this form of representation some more regulated forms of operation might be added; for example, the 'restricted' and 'overseas' banks operating in Singapore. In Singapore, restricted banks cannot accept very small domestic time deposits and they cannot operate savings accounts or open sub-branches in the country. 'Overseas' banks have now come to resemble these 'restricted' banks although, as their title would suggest, they were originally restricted to mainly foreign exchange dealings.

Next in importance in the continuum of representation are *agencies*. The regulation of these agencies varies from country to country. Even within the USA, for example (where Australia's major agency representation is located) regulation differs between states so that in California agencies have the legal power to take deposits whereas those located in New York do not (Skully, 1980). Agencies' prime tasks are asset management and the financing of international trade. They are actively engaged in banking and can earn income in their own right. Further, they can become actively engaged in wholesale banking. Most US agencies appear to have been established by Australian trading banks when the US dollar began to take on greater importance as Australia's trading currency, thereby generating sufficient trade financing for the Australian banks to justify establishment costs for such agencies that are in the order of $US 0.5 million (Skully, 1980).

The most restricted form of overseas bank representation is the *representative office*. This type of establishment fulfils essentially representative functions and is not permitted to conduct banking business as such. Its principal activities revolve around public relations, liaison, trade development services and the supervision of a bank's investments in a particular area. Liaison is a particularly important function of the representative office. It includes liaising with local dealers on foreign exchange prices and availabilities, liaising to facilitate the parent banks' involvement in foreign loan syndication, and keeping a close watch on the reciprocity of correspondent banks. In this way the representative office of an Australian bank will seek to ensure maximum income for its parent in Australia. Unlike an agency, however, it cannot be directly involved in banking activities, either retail or wholesale, and so can generate no income of its own (Skully, 1979).

The distinction has therefore been made between the various forms of bank representation in terms of their spread of functions. A branch which can participate in a full range of banking activity can be seen to have a greater range of functions than an agency or a representative office. But it is necessary to restrict this statement further. In most cases branch representation allows retail banking, and perhaps relief from some restrictions on wholesale banking, over and above the more restricted merchant banking activities that have been associated with agency banking. But in many cases, branch representation indicates a primary, and in some cases a sole, involvement in retail banking. The associated 'agencies' then bear more resemblance to 'sub-branches' than to merchant banks.

From Table 6.3, it can be seen that many of the Australian trading banks' overseas *branch* representation is in areas of traditional involvement, viz. the South-East Pacific including New Zealand, the 'ex-colony' of Papua New Guinea and the UK (in itself the ex-colonial power). Most of this involvement is probably more correctly interpreted as off-shore retail banking involvement than the ultimate form of foreign bank representation. From the changes indicated in Table 6.2, it can be deduced that there has been some relatively recent reconsideration of this activity. In particular, an increasing concentration of London banking on wholesale banking has led to rationalisation and closure of some branches in that centre (Skully, 1981a), and the role of the New Hebrides' representation has changed from a mixed one with definite retail interests involved to almost exclusively off-shore banking activities.

The Issue of Regulation

To a major extent the different regional forms of Australian trading bank involvement can be explained in terms of the *timing* and *regulation* of the establishment of foreign banks in different countries — the 'ex-colonial overhang' is only one example. For the present study there are two aspects to this issue of regulation; the restrictions imposed on the establishment of foreign banks in Australia itself, which create major problems of reciprocity, and the diversity of regulations confronting Australian banks wishing to establish in foreign countries.

Australia's regulation of foreign banks is particularly severe. It is in some ways curious that in the post-war years when a greater need for overseas bank representation has arisen from more equal commercial relations Australia has legislatively denied access to domestic markets to foreign banks by means of the *Australian Bank (Shareholdings) Act* of 1945 (Campbell Committee, p. 356).[3] There are now only two foreign banks with licences to operate in Australia,[4] although many banks have representative offices (often sharing representatives).[5] Until foreign investment legislation was introduced in 1975, foreign banks were, however, able to gain access to the Australian financial market by establishing wholly or partly owned merchant banks or finance companies. In this capacity they have made notable incursions into the domestic financial market (for example, it has been estimated that at June 1978 non-residents owned 62 per cent of the assets of money market corporations and 34 per cent of those of finance companies (Campbell Committee, 1980, p.185)), and although the operations of the Foreign Investment Review Board have, since its inception, virtually halted any new foreign ventures in the financial sector, commentators have not unreasonably been able to refer to the operations of the multinational banks in Australia as an invasion (Stilwell, 1980; Crough, 1979). Nevertheless, the existing legislation still creates problems of reciprocity and affects the ability of Australian banks to set up in other countries. Certainly reciprocity has, in recent years, been a problem with New Zealand (although it has not been stated officially as such). In Hong Kong and the USA reciprocity is even built into legislation affecting bank entry (Jao, 1979; Skully, 1980). Therefore Australian banks' overseas branches are mainly located in the South-West Pacific and London, and originated at a time of less regulation in the colonial period when reciprocity was not a major issue.

The multinational development of Australian banking beyond the Pacific is both hindered and helped by existing regulations, although these are constantly changing. Thus legislation in Japan, the USA and

New Zealand, for example, currently hinders or at least fails to expedite development, while in Singapore and Hong Kong a somewhat more permissive situation exists as these two city states vie to become Asia's principal financial centres.

Technically, the entry of foreign banks into Japan is unrestricted, with the banking sector being subject to only the normal regulations and restrictions imposed by MITI on any foreign investment. This freedom is, however, illusory. There are restrictions on the opening of branches and there are limits on the amount of foreign currency that can be converted to yen. This last constraint clearly limits the extent of foreign bank activity, notwithstanding the 15 per cent increase in this limit in 1979. Equally, certain types of borrowing from the short-term money market are discouraged, although controls on the gathering of ordinary deposits have recently been lifted (*The Banker*, 1979; Gregory, 1979). The mainstay of foreign banking in Japan has been the impact loan — a loan in foreign currency made to a Japanese borrower. In the past, Japanese domestic banks have provided guarantees to their customers to cover these loans from foreign banks. But since the late 1970s the domestic banks have been reluctant to give such guarantees. This has obviously reduced foreign bank business. A further reduction in business has taken place as a result of Japanese banks encouraging their customers to liquidate their foreign currency loans and refinance in yen, and by other changes in legislation which have removed the advantage to Japanese borrowers of impact loans as a hedge against currency fluctuations which was the prime incentive for them to contract for such loans (Bronte, 1981). The result has been a major drop in impact loans (15 per cent between 1977 and 1979), a decrease exacerbated by lower interest rates being offered on loans in yen (Gregory, 1979). Margins on impact loans have been seriously squeezed and world banking leaders such as Citicorp and Bank of America have started to report losses.

In 1979, 137 foreign banks had offices in Tokyo. Of these offices, 57 were branches and 80 were representative offices. Wisely, perhaps, Australian trading banks have chosen not to become involved in wholesale banking in Japan and all operate only through representative offices.

In the United States, restrictions on the operations of foreign banks have, until recently, been applied on a state-by-state basis (under recent legislation foreign banks, in particular, can be licensed under Federal law, thereby by-passing State restrictions) (Skully, 1980). The majority of States did not previously permit any foreign banking involvement.

Of those that did, the most active markets for foreign banks were the New York, Chicago and California markets. But even between these regulations differ and foreign banks are not entirely without restriction. For example, to operate fully in the Californian money market, foreign banks have had to set up State chartered banks. Branches could not operate in the State as they could not obtain deposit insurance, with the only alternative being the establishment of an agency (Skully, 1980). The situation was, therefore, either one of feast or one of famine.

Australian representation in the United States currently takes the form of eight agencies. At the time of their establishment, there was no alternative to State government licensing and most State legislation had reciprocity requirements written in, in particular for branching (Skully, 1980). The agencies were established when the US dollar began to undermine the hegemony of sterling as Australia's trading currency. Now, approximately 70 to 80 per cent of Australia's trade is transacted in US dollars. The profits to be made by the banks from their own trade financing became too good to miss (Skully, 1980). Since 1980, new US banking legislation has offered the alternative of Federal as opposed to State branch licensing, and this new legislation does not have a reciprocity requirement. But it remains to be seen whether Australian banks will upgrade their representation in the United States now that this option is available to them. However, coming under the umbrella of the Federal Reserve (which is not the case for the Australian bank agencies) provides both advantages in the form of guarantees, and costs in terms of reserve requirements, which the banks must carefully weigh up.

The entry of foreign banks into New Zealand is now under the restrictive control of the *Overseas Investment Act* of 1973. However, of the five trading banks in New Zealand, three are Australian-owned, the most recent entrant to the market (Australian or local) having been the Australian CBA in 1912. Recent regulation has therefore essentially served to protect the existing foreign-owned banks (four in all) from further possible entrants to the market.

The Philippines is a final example of a country where restrictive legislation has prevented foreign bank entry. A ban on foreign bank branches was first imposed after the Second World War and remained in force until 1970. Since that time there has been gradual liberalisation of banking regulations which has eased foreign bank entry, but by no means completely (*The Banker* (1978), pp. 61-5). However, since Australia's trade and manufacturing involvement in the Philippines is not particularly substantial at present, it can be more than adequately served from Hong Kong.

In contrast with these highly regulated situations, Hong Kong and Singapore have actually attempted to develop as major regional financial centres, but by two very different routes. Singapore consciously and actively promoted itself as a financial centre after independence in 1965 by offering concessions and incentives. Hong Kong adopted merely a permissive and accommodating posture. Singapore has become the home of the Asian dollar market since it abolished withholding interest tax on off-shore deposits. Hong Kong has not (Jao, 1979). In Singapore there are few direct barriers to the entry of foreign banks. There is, however, a plethora of regulation and control which inhibits the free operation of both domestic and foreign banks. Contrasting Singapore with Hong Kong, a commentator in *The Banker* (December 1978, p. 47) has gone so far as to compare 'the laissez-faire atmosphere of Hong Kong' with the 'dirigist way in which affairs are managed in Singapore'. Since 1978, however, there has been much greater liberalisation of bank regulation in Singapore with, for example, the complete removal of exchange controls.

Hong Kong is a far larger financial centre than Singapore and now ranks third in the world. It is a rapidly growing country (an 8.2 per cent growth rate per annum from 1966 to 1976) in a rapidly industrialising region. Of particular financial significance are its relatively low taxes and simple tax structure but, most importantly, Hong Kong has a free exchange market. These advantages are coupled with a stable and liberal government which does not believe in intervention. There is no Central Bank as such, and the government's budget consistently shows a surplus.[6] Hong Kong's growth as a financial centre was rapid until 1966 when a moratorium, stimulated by the fear that Hong Kong was becoming over-banked, was imposed on the granting of licences to foreign banks. Liberalisation again occurred in 1976 when deposit-taking companies (DTCs) were allowed to set up, and 239 were established in the two years to 1978. In 1978 Hong Kong allowed foreign banks to open branches freely if certain criteria were met. These included reciprocal rights of bank entry into the parent country and that the parent bank was subject to central bank control, so that Hong Kong could at least indirectly acquire some central bank control.

Given these characteristics of the Singapore and Hong Kong financial centres, it is not surprising that they are the most significant foci of Australian trading bank operations in Asia. Only in Singapore do these banks have full branches and in this centre they operate a total of six offices. In Hong Kong, however, Australian banks have ten offices but because of the timing of the investments and the reciprocity requirement, five branches are joint ventures or subsidiaries; the other five are no more than representative offices.

There are, therefore, major institutional factors that influence both the form and location of the banks' overseas representations. But still a bank must, in the first instance, decide to operate overseas offices on the expectation of known market opportunities. It can be expected that the known off-shore market for banks would in the first instance be generated by their domestic customers — in particular through their customers' international economic relations, viz. foreign trading and off-shore investing and manufacture.

To examine the links between trading patterns and the overseas manufacturing activities of domestic companies and the pattern of representation of Australia's trading banks, Tables 6.4 and 6.5 respectively present information on the dollar value of Australia's international trading links and the world-wide distribution of branches on Australian-domiciled manufacturing companies. The overwhelming importance of Japan, the US and the UK as trading partners is evident in Table 6.4, as too is the relative significance of New Zealand. Individual Asian countries, such as Singapore and Hong Kong, are also important trading partners but, with the exception of Papua New Guinea, the newly independent Pacific Island nations are of only minor importance.

The pattern of Australia's overseas manufacturing activities has been estimated for 1977 from an unpublished list of 207 Australian-domiciled manufacturing enterprises with overseas operations which had been prepared in answer to a question asked in the Australian Parliament. As many as possible of these enterprises were traced through a range of directory sources (including *Jobson's Directory*, *Kompass* and *Who owns Whom in the Pacific and Far East*) to identify the countries in which they operated (Table 6.5). Again, New Zealand, Papua New Guinea, Fiji, Hong Kong and the ASEAN nations figure prominently in the spatial pattern together with the United States and United Kingdom. However, since almost one-third of the list of companies was at least partly foreign-owned, the spatial distribution of the operations of these companies has been separated from that of the wholly Australia-owned companies. In general, the two distributions are very similar except that while foreign-owned companies have a stronger representation in New Zealand and the Philippines, the genuinely Australian-owned companies are more attracted to Malaysia.

Table 6.4: Total Australian Trading Relationships (imports and exports), 1977

		Value of Imports and Exports $A m	Per Cent
New Zealand		945	4.05
Pacific Islands:			
Papua New Guinea		311	
Fiji		88	
Kiribati		18	
New Hebrides		10	
Tonga		4	
Solomons		10	
Norfolk Island		3	
Western Samoa		8	
	Total	452	1.91
Asia:			
Japan		6,088	
Hong Kong		481	
Singapore		503	
Malaysia		335	
Indonesia		281	
Korea		387	
	Total	8,075	34.58
Rest of the world:			
USA		3,611	
UK		1,761	
Other		8,509	
	Total	13,881	59.44

Source: Australian Bureau of Statistics, 1980.

However, as pointed out above, a more realistic comparison of the distribution of overseas bank representation with foreign trade statistics and overseas manufacturing activity is achieved if the country-by-country data in Tables 6.1, 6.2 and 6.3 are amalgamated. The amalgamation undertaken for the purposes of the present analysis distinguishes six regions and nations, each with at least 4 per cent of the Australian trading banks' overseas offices, no matter what their nature or function (Table 6.6).

When the distribution of the overseas operations of banks is compared with the pattern of Australia's trade flows, it is clear from Table 6.6 that Australia's trading banks are heavily over-represented in New Zealand, Papua New Guinea and throughout the Pacific Islands.

Table 6.5: The Overseas Presence of Australian Manufacturing Companies

	Total	Per Cent	Number of Companies Represented Foreign-controlled	Per Cent	Australian-controlled	Per Cent
New Zealand	93	18.2	43	24.1	50	15.0
Pacific Islands:						
Fiji	25		9		16	
Papua New Guinea	34		13		21	
Nauru	1		1		0	
Solomons	1		1		0	
Western Samoa	2		0		2	
New Hebrides	4		1		3	
Nieue	1		0		1	
Cook Islands	1		0		1	
Tonga	2		0		2	
Tahiti	1		0		1	
Norfolk Island	1		0		1	
Honolulu	1		0		1	
Total	74	14.5	25	14.0	49	14.7
Asia:						
Malaysia	37		8		29	
Singapore	43		17		26	
Hong Kong	35		11		24	
Philippines	14		8		6	
Indonesia	22		10		12	
Sarawak	1		1		0	
Japan	10		5		5	
Thailand	11		4		7	
Total	173	33.9	64	36.0	109	32.7
Rest of the World:						
USA	19		8		11	
UK	35		11		24	
Canada	10		3		7	
EEC (excl. UK)	36		11		25	
Other	71		13		58	
Total	171	33.4	46	25.8	125	37.5

Source: Directory information.

This conclusion is only to be expected, and the use of a Chi-square Test, for instance, is meaningless because the aggregate population size (the number of the banks overseas operations) is so heavily dominated by the banks' retail-banking branch networks in these locations (Table 6.7). In particular, in New Zealand the three Australian trading banks which operate there have a total branch network of 461 offices. This compares with a total world representation of the six Australian trading banks of 593. Something over 75 per cent of Australia's overseas banking representation is therefore located in New Zealand.

Table 6.6: Australia's Overseas Bank Representation and its Relationship to Overseas Manufacturing and Trade

	Bank Establishments No.	Total Trade Percentage of Trade Value	Overseas Manufacturing Percentage of Firms
New Zealand	461	4.0	18.2
Papua New Guinea	49	1.3	6.7
Fiji	23	0.4	4.9
Rest of Pacific Islands	11	0.2	2.9
Asia	28	34.6	33.9
Rest of World	31	59.4	33.4

	Expected Bank Representation from Trade Relations	Difference	Expected Bank Representation from Manufacturing Base	Difference
New Zealand	24	+437	110	+351
Papua New Guinea	8	+ 41	40	+ 9
Fiji	2	+ 21	30	− 7
Rest of Pacific Islands	1	+ 10	18	− 7
Asia	209	−181	204	−176
Rest of World	358	−327	201	−170

Source: Directory data and Australian Bureau of Statistics, 1980.

Given that retail banking activity (which may not be expected to be very closely determined by current trade links) is associated with a proliferation of banking outlets, and that commercial banking (which can be expected to be more closely correlated with other commercial links between countries) is 'by and large' not a multi-outlet form of banking, then it is always to be expected that when considering the share of total world banking activity the centres of retail banking will be over-represented, and the areas of commercial banking (in this case Asia and the rest of the world) will be correspondingly under-represented.

The distribution of overseas operations of banks in relation to the pattern of overseas manufacturing activity is, however, by no means as diverse. Again, banks are over-represented in New Zealand, but in this instance over-representation is comparatively minor in Papua New Guinea. Through the rest of the Pacific Islands there is an equivalent minor under-representation of Australian banks, with under-representa-

Table 6.7: The Type of Overseas Representation of Australian Trading Banks

	Type of Representation											
	Branches			Subsidiaries and Joint Ventures			Agencies			Representative Offices		
	A^a	E^b	A-E	A^a	E^b	A-E	A^a	E^b	A-E	A^a	E^b	A-E
New Zealand	351	324	+27	0	11	−11	110	112	−2	0	14	−14
Papua New Guinea	34	34	−	2	1	+ 1	13	12	+1	0	1	− 1
Fiji	11	16	+ 5	0	1	− 1	12	5	+7	0	1	− 1
Pacific Islands	7	8	− 1	3	0	+ 3	1	3	−2	0	0	−
Asia	2	20	−18	10	1	+ 9	1	7	−6	15	1	+14
Rest of the world	19	22	− 3	0	1	− 1	9	7	+2	3	1	+ 2

Notes: [a] Actual number of offices.

[b] Expected number of offices based on total office representation (as in Table 6.1, column 2).

tion again being greatest through Asia and the rest of the world. In comparison with the patterns of trade and overseas manufacturing activity, Australian trading banks are, therefore, predisposed to locate in the Pacific Islands, including both Papua New Guinea and New Zealand. One explanation for this lower level of over-representation with investment links is that the factors which favour the establishment of retail banking, namely close historical, cultural and colonial links, are also important indirect factors in fostering investment links.

The causes of this predisposition amongst Australian trading banks to locate their overseas operations in the Pacific Islands are, of course, largely historical in nature. New Zealand, for example, has always been strongly associated with Australia, first as a British colony, then as a Dominion and now as a member of the Commonwealth. Moreover, until relatively recently, the entry of banks into New Zealand was legislatively unimpeded. By the time restriction was imposed, over 50 per cent of the market had come to be controlled by Australian and UK banks, and this situation has persisted to the present. However, the close relationship between the two countries is still supported by trade agreement (NAFTA), the absence until this year of passport controls and the use by multinationals of Australia as a base from which to control their New Zealand operations (Keegan, 1974). A similar historical relationship exists between Australia and Fiji, one now bolstered by tourism, for example (Britton, 1980). However, perhaps the strongest tie exists between Australia and Papua New Guinea, which was virtually an Australian colony until independence in the mid-1960s and which is still heavily dependent on Australia for budgetary support. For the remaining Pacific Island states, relationships with Australia have been largely exploitative. Many are ex-British colonies or condominiums which were administered from Australia. Their populations are tiny and their economies are barely viable (Ward and Proctor, 1980). Under these circumstances some islands have adopted the Australian currency and, in some cases, the Australian trading banks operate virtually as these countries' central banks.

However, the Australian banking presence in the Pacific appears to have been contracting in recent years, partly in deference to local nationalist feelings (for example Nauru) and partly through bank rationalisation (for example the withdrawal from retail banking in the New Hebrides). In Australian terms the smaller island states are becoming as peripheral in terms of banking operations as they are in terms of many other economic ties.

In seeking, therefore, to establish what links, if any, exist between the strength of Australian banks' overseas representation and trade and investment links, it is necessary to choose a statistical technique which abstracts from the inherent bias in the total population towards the more numerous retail banking outlets and the distortions that this factor introduces. A measure of rank correlation is one such technique. Because of the restricted number of observations[6] that it is possible to make from the aggregated data, it is preferable to apply this technique to the total population of all the individual overseas countries where the Australian banks are represented (17 in all). Two methods can be used for ranking this country by country data. First, the number of representative offices can be used. However, the employment of this method means that the measure is still biased to the countries with large retail branch networks. The alternative is to use the number of banks represented. This provides a crude method of eliminating most of the retail banking sector dominance (Table 6.8).

Table 6.8: Rank Correlation Coefficients

	Trade Data	Manufacturing Data
No of representative offices	.663 (.631)	.735 (.716)
No. of representative banks	.613 (.663)	.308 (. 48)

From Table 6.8 it can be seen that, using the representative office measure, there is a higher rank correlation with manufacturing activity than with trading activity; this is a similar result to that derived above when comparing the expected with the actual representation. But using numbers of representative banks as a measure of the importance of banks representation, trade appears to be a more important determinant than manufacturing activity. (The values in brackets are obtained when the mid-rank method is used to compute rank correlation rather than the bracket method.) The greater variation found for the 'number of representative banks' has arisen because there are a greater number of occurrences for a given frequency that may be expected to have occurred when the maximum extent of bank representation is reduced to 6 (i.e. the total number of banks). The correlation is still very high, especially since the essentially ex-colonial retail banking activity in the small Pacific Island states has not been eliminated by this method, and still achieves a degree of prominence. In addition, banking activity in off-shore banking centres like the New Hebrides and the Cayman

Islands cannot be expected to be directly trade- or investment-based, and these observations must also be expected to reduce the fit of the correlation.

To summarise, the bulk of Australia's overseas banking representation is located in close geographical proximity to Australia, in an area with strong historical and colonial links. This area is not currently dominant in terms of Australia's trading patterns, although it retains a surprising importance in terms of investment patterns. But the important Australian banking links are now more geographically distant and these are more closely related to trade.

Conclusion

The Australian trading banks are few in number. The patterns of their overseas representation are remarkably uniform and extend into the international market the competition through duplication of services that is so characteristic of their oligopolistic behaviour in the domestic market.

One explanation that may be suggested to explain the relative degree of uniformity in this pattern of overseas representation is that the trading banks have all been subject to the same major influences in determining the extent and location of their overseas activities. In this chapter, a first examination of the subject, two influences appear to be of the greatest significance — the pattern of trade financing and the presence of areas of traditional involvement from an earlier, 'colonial' era.

If these are indeed the major determining influences on the trading banks' overseas representation, then this would suggest that, at least until recent times, this pattern of representation has been essentially an extension of the banks' domestic activities, aimed at providing a better service to existing customers as they extend their activities, or to ensure services for an area which has been considered by the banks to be their rightful territory.

This chapter is a very preliminary investigation of the spatial aspects of the Australian trading banks' overseas representation. Many questions have been left unanswered. These include the extent to which patterns of representation are changing and have changed under the influence of changing determinants of investment and, more particularly, to what extent, if any, the banks are becoming more international in their overseas activities, rather than simply extending their domestic business. The trading banks are, for instance, becoming more actively involved in Eurocurrency transactions. These questions await further study.

Finally, the impact of an expected extension in the internationalisation of the domestic banking market has already foreshadowed consequences in terms of the structure of the domestically owned banking sector (through merger and take-over). This reorganisation may well have feed-through effects to the international activities of Australian trading banks as well. This will also be an area of future interest.

Notes

1. In a technical sense, the ANZ is a recent addition to this list since, until the late 1970s, it was domiciled in the UK. The head office and main share register have only recently been transferred to Australia.

2. Subsidiary companies have not been included, as it is difficult, in practice, to distinguish those which are a form of representation and those which are an investment interest or enabling device.

3. 'The Banks (Shareholdings) Act limits individual or associated holdings in an Australian bank — whether by foreign or Australian interests — to less than 10% of the bank's voting shares. The Government had indicated that it would also be opposed to acquisitions by overseas interests short of 10% where the intention was to exercise influence over the bank concerned' (Campbell Committee, 1980, p. 356).

4. The Bank of New Zealand and the Banque Nationale de Paris are known as prescribed banks and operate under licences which are conditional in that they specify the places at which the respective banks may operate their business (Campbell Committee, 1980, p. 245).

5. The Campbell Committee (1980, p. 246) puts the number of overseas banks that have obtained permission from the government to establish representative offices in Australia at 86.

6. Some central banking functions are carried out by a consortium of large local banks.

PART TWO:

THE GEOGRAPHICAL RAMIFICATIONS OF
MULTINATIONAL CORPORATIONS

7 INTRODUCTION

M.J. Taylor and N.J. Thrift

The impacts of multinational and, latterly, global corporations manifest themselves at the behavioural and global scales in a number of ways:

(1) the form which investment takes — its degree of transience, its unequal, asymmetric competition with domestic enterprise and its relations with the operation of both home and host governments, for example;
(2) the spatial form which this investment assumes, bringing with it uneven regional consequences;
(3) the transformation of national and regional labour markets through such processes as migration, deskilling, dualism and the reorientation of managerial loyalties away from the state and towards the company;
(4) cultural realignment towards mass consumption and the accompanying modification of family life and personal goals and motivations, and even the health problems caused by modification of diet.

There has been a strong tendency to explain spatial forms of multinational development in terms of historically specific, risk-minimising strategies, product cycle strategies and follow-the-leader behaviour under conditions of oligopolistic competition. In short, the geographical expansion and the spatial ramifications of multinational corporations have been seen as a series of waves caused by corporate pebbles being thrown into a global pool.

But, with the emergence of the global corporation, risk-minimising is no longer a full and adequate explanation of corporate spatial expansion. The global corporation already possesses a world-wide information system of either grid or matrix form. Spatial change thus becomes no more than a rearrangement of existing parts or the incorporation of newly acquired parts into this established framework. Even the operations of mineral and mining corporations can be viewed in these terms, notwithstanding the location-specific nature of non-renewable mineral resources. The surge in mineral exploration in the past two decades, in part to circumvent the monopsony powers of primary product cartels has, in fact, demonstrated the relative ubiquity of many minerals. For the global mining corporation, production can be shifted from one location to another with 'surplus' operations being placed on 'care and maintenance'. Under these conditions, as Australian miners are coming to realise, jobs may be more ephemeral than the life of the ore body that is being worked.

The integration of industrial and banking capital in the operations of such global corporations has also brought a new emphasis on the purely financial aspects of these enterprises. Thus, the currency shift has become an important source of profits (see for example Tugendhat's (1976) example of the Ford Motor Company in the UK), and corporations now seek the most cost-rational investments in the lowest cost locations. Coats Patons' scheme for locational selection based upon only labour costs and exchange rates is a clear trend (Chapter 1). It is hardly surprising, therefore, that acquisition has become an important, if not the most important, avenue for corporate expansion sectorally and geographically, twinned with rationalisation as a major vehicle for spatial adjustment. Recession in particular will see the greatest divergence between the value of a company and what its management is willing to accept. To highly liquid multinationals, therefore, there are at these times more global opportunities to expand through acquisition. Thus commentators can now write of a purely financial rationale for merger. However, recession would also appear to encourage a search for real assets by firms set on acquisition, and this tendency has been identified in the massive take-overs and take-over bids that have occurred in the US in 1981 (*The Economist*, 1981).

As financial motives have come to the fore under 'global' capitalism, so corporate commitment to a venture in any one location has also become more transitory. National and regional subsidies by governments, together with legislation to facilitate the financial secrecy of corporations (UN, 1979), only make these investments increasingly ephemeral. This, then, is a major contradiction in governments' relationships with multinationals. It is paralleled by a second. Since many large multinationals depend on governments as some of their principal customers, cuts in public expenditure which have occurred in countries such as the US, UK and France in areas other than defence tend to encourage these corporations to leave.

Acquisition, however, has not been the exclusive preserve of multinational industrial capital. Banking capital and especially the financial institutions have also become embroiled. Initially, these institutions created financial instruments, principally international bonds, to facilitate multinational investment. The institutions themselves have subsequently expanded beyond their national frames of reference and are now being radically restructured through take-over and merger in order not only to keep abreast of but also to manage this demand for funds (Stetson, 1980, *The Economist*, 1981f; Davis, 1981). Furthermore, while industrial organisations are taking on financial functions, financial institutions are taking on industrial functions (Taylor and Thrift, 1980). The sum of these trends is an increase in the mobility of capital in the new phase of global capitalism, growing ephemerality in investment and yet also a concealment of this very mobile condition. But the development of multinationals, and their expansion into global corporations with a financial rather than an industrial or production emphasis, holds important implications for the North-South debate, country-to-country relations and the crippling inequalities that exist in all aspects of life between the developed and less developed countries. Within this debate, the less developed countries (LDCs) are envisaged as being in direct competition with the developed nations. In other words, the whole issue of inequality is seen as *country-to-country* competition which is, by definition, *location-specific*.

Such a specification of competition may only be partial (Pettman, 1979). If the aim of the international monetary system is to redistribute some nations' surpluses to finance others' debts, then the ability of global corporations and multinationals to divert these flows and open up massive lines of credit must also be taken into account in this debate. Indeed, the competition for funds between North and South is perhaps best seen as a three-cornered conflict between developed countries, LDCs and multinationals. What is more important from the geographical perspective is that while countries are locationally and spatially *constrained* corporations are, in the light of the preceding discussion, locationally *fickle*. Corporations would, in fact, seem to be more able to raise finance than many Third World countries and this is clearly illustrated in data on corporate borrowings to finance mergers to borrowings by Third World countries for the 1980-1 period (Table 7.1). Many LDCs are more properly seen as being in *country-to-company* competition as well as *country-to-country* competition.

The problem confronting LDCs is their inability to overcome the risks they are perceived to present to institutional lenders. Assessing country risk is, in fact, a complex problem for the financial institutions which has been attacked through the doubtful impartiality of statistical methods (Frank and Cline, 1971; Fisk and Rimlinger, 1979). Even though many aspects of this issue are not properly quantifiable, scoring systems are widely used which lay emphasis on political and legal considerations. In the scheme outlined by Robinson (1981), for example, which has been suggested as being representative of the methods used by many banks, ås many as 41 of a possible 100 points are devoted to legal and political considerations and the power of a government to effect economic change (Table 7.2). Because of these rating schemes, high interest rates and the world's poorest nations' pessimism about their credit ratings, some LDCs have been deterred from raising the loans they so desperately need.

Table 7.1: Borrowing to Finance Mergers versus Borrowing by Third World Nations, March 1980 to March 1981 (US$ billion)

Mexico	11.3
Brazil	6.8
Mobil Oil	6.0
Gulf Oil	6.0
Argentina	5.6
Texaco	5.5
Marathon Oil	5.0
DuPont	4.0
Seagrams	3.9
Venezuela	3.6
South Korea	3.2
Cities Services	3.0
Allied Corporation	3.0
Conoco	3.0
Panama	2.7
Elf Aquitaine	2.7
Chile	2.5
Pennzoil	2.5
Taiwan	1.2
Philippines	1.1
Egypt	1.0
Philips Petroleum	1.0
Nigeria	0.9
Ivory Coast	0.6

Source: *South* (October 1981), p. 70.

Nevertheless, banks in particular are anxious to make loans to increase the visibility of their own institution, to give the impression of corporate success and to boost their positions on such things as the Eurobond 'league table' (Mattle, 1981). Massive lines of credit have been opened to allow multinationals to finance take-overs and mergers (*South* (1981b), pp. 30-71) and the banking community has actively sought to lend money to the more prosperous LDCs such as Mexico and

Table 7.2: A Scheme for the Assessment of Country Risk

			Approximate Weighting
A.	Legal considerations — The operation and efficiency of courts, and prejudice towards foreigners for example		10
B.	Political considerations — Type of political system; the basis and breadth of government's support; likelihood of refusing to honour previous government's debts; distribution of income and wealth		25
C.	Economic considerations — Power of the government (e.g. a Danish-type minority government which finds it difficult to introduce unpopular measures compared with a British first-past-the-post system)		6
	— Assessment of current plans for the economy Feasibility of development plans, main bottlenecks, etc. Resource base — natural and human resources, etc.		15
	— Recent events and present state of the economy		
	GNP growth	0.3	
	Rate of inflation	0.6	
	Government budget position	0.6	
	Money supply growth	0.3	
	Current account balance of payments	0.3	
	Unemployment	0.6	
	Level of external debt	1.2	
	Debt service ratio	1.2	
	Latest date of published statistics	0.9	6
	— Future prospects for the economy in present trends and policies continue		
	GNP growth	0.7	
	Rate of inflation	1.3	
	Government budget position	2.0	
	Money supply growth	0.7	
	Current account balance of payments	2.0	
	Unemployment	1.3	
	Level of external debt	2.5	
	Debt service ratio	2.5	13
	— Ability of the country to correct adverse implications of present trends and to withstand unforeseen shocks (vulnerability)		
	Imports as a proportion of GDP	0.7	
	Exports as a proportion of GDP	0.7	
	Diversification of imports by category and by geographical area	4.6	
	Diversification of exports by category and geographical area	4.6	
	Compressibility of imports (i.e. extent to which imports consist of non-essentials)	6.4	
	Vulnerability of the economy of changing prices of main exports and imports		
	Energy dependence	8.0	25
			100

Source: Robinson, 1981, p. 74.

Brazil (Killick, 1981). There is now acute over-competition between lenders in the Eurocurrency markets and the potential exists for the creation of a massive squeeze on funds which can only be to the disadvantage of the LDCs. In short, company-to-country competition means that LDC loans are stymied by lines of corporate credit. A recent study by the UN Economic and Social Council, reported in *South* (1981, p. 73), also shows that multinationals exacerbate the balance of payments problems of Third World countries, with imbalances in international intra-firm trade being far from offset by imports of capital into these economically precarious nations. Indeed, Killick (1981) has suggested that 'the credit criteria of the Euromarket have in effect resulted in a transfer of funds from the poorest to the richest LDCs' (p. 20). This transfer is demonstrated in Table 7.3 and can be ascribed to the activities of multinationals compounded by the lending preferences of developed country financial institutions.

Table 7.3: Developing Country Assets and Liabilities with the Eurocurrency Market (US$ billions, March 1980)

Developing Country Groupings[a]	Assets	Liabilities	Net Balance[b]
Upper-income LDCs	60.5	119.7	−59.2
Middle-income LDCs	26.1	43.2	−17.1
Lower-income LDCs	7.9	4.4	+ 3.5

Notes: [a] Defined on 1978 *per capita* incomes;
        upper-income = above $1,000
        middle-income = $300 - $1,000
        lower-income = below $300

  [b] Negative sign indicates net borrowings from Eurocurrency market; positive sign indicates net deposits and other assets.

Source: Killick, 1981, p. 20.

It is also important to remember that traded services (finance and investment, insurance, tourism, etc.) play an important, if neglected, role in the world economy in themselves. Reliable data on traded services are hard to find. However, in 1976 traded services formed 27.7 and 24.0 per cent respectively of total receipts and payments on traded goods. If payments for tourism are regarded as final services, 17.6 of the total was for foreign travel payments, a figure representing 4 per cent of total payments on current account (Tucker, 1981). Studies of invivsble trade suggest that traded services are of growing importance for both developed and developing countries. However, payments for traded services by developing countries (as a share of total payments) exceed, on average, those for advanced countries; a conclusion which suggests that developing countries are still largely dependent upon the supply of intermediate services from developed countries. This is just one other facet of the problem of dependence faced by the LDCs, a problem that is most serious for those LDCs that are heavily dependent upon tourism. These countries include the Bahamas, which relies on tourism for 72.5 per cent of its foreign earnings, Jordan (37.0 per cent), Fiji (25.0 per cent), Morocco (24.0 per cent) and Tunisia (19.5 per cent) (*South*, 1981). Multinational corporations involved in the tourist industry have such economies firmly in their grip. In their hands tourist flow can readily be redirected to alternative destinations, illustrating once again the vulnerability born of volatility that is characteristic of many Third World economies.

International tourism is also a vital aspect of the more general spatial impact of multinational corporations on the development of culture and consciousness (Peet, 1980). This is, of course, a notoriously difficult area (Williams, 1976, 1981). The most coherent attempts to grapple with the problem have been located within the context of Marxist theories of imperialism (cf. Brewer, 1980; Warren 1980). Certainly there is little doubt that internationalisation of the economic system through the agency of multinational corporations has brought with it a degree of political and cultural domination. However, it is important to guard against functionalism in explaining this domination, a trap that too many commentators fall into.

The Chapters

The types of impact discussed above are illustrated in a variety of national and supranational contexts in the six chapters in the second section of this volume. The chapters by *Blackbourn* and *Abumere* illustrate the geographical implications of the historically specific forms of corporate expansion related to the adoption by multinationals of risk-minimising, product cycle and follow-the-leader strategies. While Blackbourn addresses the developed nation context, Abumere explores the underdeveloped context through the specific example of Nigeria. *Rogerson* also addresses this issue but in a third geographical circumstance — the semi-peripheral, dominion capitalist context of Southern Africa — demonstrating the locational preferences within South Africa of multinationals of different national origins. In addition, Rogerson explores some aspects of country-to-country competition through an examination of multinational investment in Southern Africa. South Africa, Botswana, Lesotho, Swaziland, Zimbabwe, Zambia and Namibia are seen as competing to attract foreign multinational investment. However, historically, multinationals have favoured South Africa as the base for their investment in other Southern Africa states, just as Australia is being used as a way-station for multinational investment in the Pacific (Taylor and Thrift, 1981b).

The changing investment strategies of multinationals and global corporations are shown graphically in *Smith's* chapter on foreign investment in the United Kingdom. The shift from greenfield to acquisition investment strategies in the mid-1970s is shown to have had considerable geographical consequences in the UK for, while greenfield investment favoured peripheral 'development area' locations, acquisition investment brought a reorientation to core area locations, especially the South-East. This chapter also raises fundamental questions concerning the ability of government-collected statistics to identify adequately trends and changes in, and the spatial implications of, multinationals' investment strategies. However, the message is plain. Through the adoption of acquisition strategies, and owing to the inadequacies of national statistics, the locational activity of multinational and global corporations is becoming more and more concealed.

The chapter by *Britton* demonstrates some of the problems of company-to-country competition confronting the world's LDCs in the context of the international tourist industry in Fiji. Approximately a dozen multinational transport operators, retail and wholesale organisations, tour companies and hoteliers have monopolised this vital sector of the Fijian economy. With tourist patronage in the hands of these organisations Fiji's foreign earnings are made extremely vulnerable.

Finally, *Peet's* analysis focuses on the impact of multinationals as institutional elements of the more general internationalisation of capitalism. Accompanying this geographical extension and penetration of capitalism is a gradual homogenisation of world culture that raises false consciousness to the level of 'ultra-culture'.

8 THE IMPACT OF MULTINATIONAL CORPORATIONS ON THE SPATIAL ORGANISATION OF DEVELOPED NATIONS: A REVIEW

A. Blackbourn

Introduction

Multinational corporations (MNCs) are distinguished by their large size and by their foreign identity in most of the host countries in which they operate. In the United States, Japan, the United Kingdom and the Netherlands the 200 largest companies (almost all of which are MNCs) have a turnover exceeding 40 per cent of Gross Domestic Product (Robinson, 1979). Between 1971 and 1988 MNCs' share of Gross World Product is expected to grow from 20 per cent to 40 per cent (Jazairy *et al.*, 1976). Their impact on industrial location is even greater than their large size and their large share of Gross World Product would suggest. Since many MNCs are assembly operations, they attract numbers of suppliers and services to the locations they select, thus stimulating local development indirectly as well as directly.

The steady replacement of the traditional single-plant firm typical of nineteenth-century industry by MNC branches and the plants dependent on them can be expected to influence the geography of manufacturing. Because MNCs are both large and foreign the factors influencing their locational decisions may differ from the location factors important for small locally owned firms. Moreover, because they are large, their impact on the development of the host regions' economy will be considerable. This chapter reviews the literature on the location of MNCs and their impact on their host regions to determine the extent to which the growth of manufacturing MNCs can be expected to influence industrial geography.

The Locational Preferences of MNCs

Multinational corporations were rarely established as large enterprises operating in many countries (Wilkins, 1974a). Most MNCs started as small single-plant, single-product companies and expanded to become multiproduct, multiplant corporations with branches in many lands. In order to expand in local, national and international markets, the companies had to develop business strategies which enabled them to prosper. Successful strategies could differ greatly even in the same industry and nation. In the US automobile industry, Ford developed a standard product (the Model T) which was produced in regional assembly plants all over the United States and in overseas countries with no modifications to suit local conditions unless changes were unavoidable (Wilkins and Hill, 1964). The corporation that eventually replaced Ford as the United States' largest automobile producer, General Motors, expanded at home and abroad by purchasing existing companies and improving their existing products (Sloan, 1964). However, even though they differ in many respects, they are both products of the American business system. Both corporations developed regional assembly operations with centralised administration and research and development. Both in the formative years of the American automobile industry and at the present time, senior executives move from one company to another and despite the multinational nature of operations are almost always American..

Executives of European and Japanese corporations are products of very different business environments (Chandler and Daems, 1974). Regional assembly plants are rarely needed within the nation in which they are based. Government relationships with businesses are generally closer than in the United States. Several European base nations invested heavily in overseas colonial territories and some nations experienced heavy loss of overseas investments due to expropriation (Wilkins, 1974b). Schollhammer's study of MNCs' locational strategies revealed significant differences between American, British, French and German companies' assessment of factors considered important in the decision to invest in a host country (Schollhammer, 1974). It is argued here that not only do MNCs differ according to national base in their assessment of a host country business environment, as Schollhammer suggested, but that they also differ in their preferences for particular regions of a host country.

National Borders

Border orientation is the most obvious type of distortion of the pattern of industrial location in a host country which foreign investment creates. Border orientation was incorporated into an interaction model of location of American subsidiaries in Ontario, Canada, by Ray (Ray,

1965; 1971). Although there is some evidence that border orientation has decreased in importance as a location factor in Ontario since the early twentieth century, border concentrations of American-owned plants are still important (Blackbourn, 1968).

Border orientation is an important factor in location of MNC branches in other countries, notably the Netherlands and France (de Smidt, 1966; DATAR, 1974). Examination of DATAR data for France in 1971 shows that German investment is concentrated in Alsace, close to the German border, Belgian investment is concentrated in the Nord and Lorraine close to the Belgian border, and Swiss investment in Rhône-Alpes and Alsace close to the Swiss border. The German concentration in Alsace has been explained in cultural terms, since German-owned plants are concentrated in the regions with a population that is ethnically German (Martin, 1973). Industrial promotion efforts directed at Swiss and German manufacturers by Alsatian communities may be another explanation of the concentration in that border region (SADE, 1968). Border orientation is also present in the Netherlands but is less apparent because of that nation's small size.

Despite the evidence of border orientation for MNCs in Ontario, the Netherlands and France, such locational preferences are sometimes lacking. Canadian firms in the US are more likely to locate in the South than in the manufacturing belt (Arpan and Ricks, 1975). Canadian-owned plants along the St Lawrence in upper New York state are examples of border orientation, but they are not numerous enough to influence the pattern of Canadian preference for the South. Dutch companies in France are another exception, since they locate not along the Belgian border to be as close as possible to the Netherlands, but in the Paris region.

Although the evidence on border orientation is rather limited since suitable studies exist only for Canada, France, the Netherlands and the US, it seems safe to conclude that MNC branches will normally be attracted to border regions. There are exceptions to this rule which can perhaps best be understood by reference to the peculiarities of industrial location in a particular nation. For example, Canadian preference for the southern USA is more easily understood if the labour cost figures presented by Britton for Ontario, the North-East and the South are examined (Britton, 1977).

Economic Core Regions

Core region orientation has been predicted for some MNC facilities by Hymer and observed in six of seven nations for which adequate data were available (Hymer, 1972; Blackbourn, 1978). Economic core regions are attractive to companies producing consumer goods. Schollhammer's study shows that market factors are the third most important location factor for both Europe and American MNCs (Schollhammer, 1974). Firms concerned with market access will be attracted to economic core regions. Core regions usually have the best scheduled air service in a nation and access to a major airport can be a great attraction for some MNCs, as Hoare's study of London airport shows (Hoare, 1975). Even airports outside a core region can attract many MNC branches, as the success of Shannon Industrial Estate in Eire in attracting American plants illustrates.

Core region orientation may be lacking because of political pressures. Dunning's 1958 study of Britain discusses the preference of American companies for locations in the South-East, close to the large London market (Dunning, 1958). However, Keeble's 1976 map of foreign manufacturing firms, many of which were American, established in Britain between 1966 and 1971, shows a strong preference for the peripheral assisted areas (Keeble, 1976). The main reason for the change may be the introduction of a strict industrial location policy by the British government which forces foreign companies wishing to enter the British market to locate in regions of high unemployment.

McConnell's study of foreign investment in a country which lacks an industrial location policy, the USA, between 1974 and 1978 shows a growing preference for locations in the peripheral Sun Belt states (McConnell, 1980). The manufacturing belt of the North-East still attracts the largest share of foreign investment, but foreign MNCs are beginning to follow domestic corporations moving to the South and West. McConnell explains the delayed shift of foreign corporations by arguing that they have only recently acquired sufficient experience in the US market to risk locating outside the 'safe' heartland region. Questions of risk avoidance in MNC decision-making are important, but must be studied on an individual plant basis. Consequently the literature on locational patterns of foreign investment tends to avoid the topic.

Government and Industrial Location

Political influences on the location of MNC branches are becoming increasingly important as governments assume a greater responsibility for the economic well-being of their nations. MNCs and government-owned national enterprises are almost the only organisations which can provide large numbers of jobs in the depressed regions which politicians must help if they are to remain in power. Consequently, great pressure is put on MNCs to establish plants in depressed regions. Most governments rely on some mixture of controls and subsidies to influence industrial location. An examination of one large, highly visible MNC's recent plant locations illustrates the importance of this factor. In the sixties, Ford established large automobile plants at Saarlouis, the main city of West Germany's isolated and depressed Saar coalfield and at Genk on Belgium's Kempen coalfield. Subsidies were obtained for both plants. In 1970, Ford obtained grants to locate a new transmission plant at Bordeaux in South-Western France. Doubtless, M. Chaban-Delmas, the Prime Minister at the time and a former mayor of Bordeaux, was delighted to help his home region attract such a large and important new plant (Ardagh, 1977). Ford's most recent plants have been engine plants established at Windsor, Ontario and Bridgend in former British Prime Minister Callaghan's political power base of South Wales. Both were heavily subsidised. In the case of Bridgend, Ford's unions were also allowed to breach the wage and price guidelines in force at the time the plant was announced.

Ford is not the only MNC to secure political concessions for locating plants in depressed regions. Michelin first obtained large subsidies for their tyre plants in Nova Scotia and then proceeded to induce the province to change its labour relations code to make it very difficult for unions to organise Michelin plants in Nova Scotia (*Globe and Mail*, 1979). In the United Kingdom, Hitachi obtained strong support for their proposed television factory to be located in Washington New Town in the depressed North-East (*Financial Times*, 17 December 1977). In this case, pressure from northern interests was insufficient to overcome the objections of British television manufacturers to the proposed plant.

Sometimes MNCs can use their influence to locate facilities in core regions where such developments would not normally be encouraged. IBM's research, administrative and production complex at Hursley and Havant on the south coast of England is one example of an MNC having sufficient influence to locate in a core region. Libby's were encouraged to establish a cannery in Languedoc at a time when American investment was generally unwelcome because their plant would stir the archaic French canning industry to modernise itself (Ardagh, 1977). The power of MNCs over host country governments has often been discussed (Vernon, 1972). MNCs have been able to use that power to obtain favourable terms for locating plants which provide much-needed employment in the host region.

National Locational Preferences

Local influences on the location of MNCs are important to some regions: German MNCs, accustomed to labour shortages in the industrial cities of their homeland, prefer to locate in small towns. In Eire, German plants were concentrated in the small towns of the South-West (Blackbourn, 1972). In the US, Faith has claimed that German companies prefer the small towns of the South-East, but his statements are supported by quotations from industrial commissioners and factory managers rather than by statistics (Faith, 1972). Arpan and Ricks' statistics show some concentration of German plants in the South-East, but also a much larger German concentration in the Middle Atlantic (Arpan and Ricks, 1975). In France, the German-owned plants in Alsace are almost all located in small towns where labour is readily available. The regional capital, Strasbourg, has a reputation for labour shortages and only one of the fourteen German-owned plants in Alsace is located there (DATAR, 1974). However, four of the nine American-owned plants in Alsace are located in Strasbourg, the regional capital.

Since other regional capitals in France had several American-owned plants and few plants controlled from other nations, the percentages of American-owned plants and plants controlled from other nations in Ireland and France, the two countries for which data were available, were examined. In France, the regional centres of Bordeaux, Lille, Lyon, Marseilles, Nantes, Nice and Toulouse accounted for only 23 of the 256 American-owned plants, while 21 of the 246 plants controlled from other nations were located in regional centres (DATAR, 1974). Although 24 of the 57 American-owned plants in the Irish Republic were located in Cork, Galway, Limerick-Shannon and Waterford, compared with only 40 of the 204 plants controlled from other countries, the American concentration in regional centres is explained by the Limerick-Shannon Airport concentration of 15 American plants (Blackbourn, 1972). Although foreign investment in some of France's regional centres was dominated by American MNCs, no general preference for regional centres in either France or Ireland was observed.

However, in Ireland, a strong preference by American corporations for the Shannon Industrial Estate suggests industrial parks are of importance in the location of American MNCs. Dunning's study of Britain revealed a preference for locations in the early industrial estates at Trafford Park, Manchester, and Slough, near London (Dunning, 1958). Since Mingret observed a similar preference for industrial estates in Belgium, this may be a distinctive American locational preference (Mingret, 1970). Since the studies referred to above cover a total of four industrial parks — Shannon, Trafford Park, Slough and Haute-Sarts — it would be dangerous to generalise, but the role of industrial parks in attracting MNC branches to a region seems worthy of further investigation.

The locational preferences of MNCs need further investigation. The only general statements that can be made are that border orientation is common, and that if land borders with the investing company's homeland are absent, a location in the economic core is likely unless political influences lead the MNC to prefer a peripheral region.

The Impact of MNCs in their Host Regions

Regional policy in many countries sometimes seems to consist largely of efforts to attract MNCs to depressed regions. The political benefits of attracting a well known MNC to locate a plant in a city experiencing high unemployment are obvious. However, the economic benefits to the host city or region have been questioned in some studies.

Labour

The obvious benefit of providing large numbers of jobs at wages that are often above the regional average cannot be denied. However, Salt's study of Ford and General Motors plants on Merseyside suggested that there was a cost to the host region as well as a benefit (Salt, 1967). The new MNCs attract the best workers from existing enterprises, and in some cases a shortage of skilled labour may force local companies to close or to move elsewhere. If the MNC remains in the region and buys parts locally, the stimulus to small business in the region may outweigh problems of labour poaching. However, low-wage industries may eventually disappear if a high-wage MNC enters a region. Since most local workers prefer to work ·for large MNCs, job creation must be considered a net benefit.

In some environments, MNCs may influence labour relations. Ardagh suggests that American team methods may help solve some French labour problems (Ardagh, 1977). British financial papers have commented on the success of Japanese and German systems of labour relations at British subsidiaries of MNCs based in those countries (*Financial Times*, 25 November 1977; 16 December 1977; 6 March 1978). However, other studies suggest that the remote-control labour relations practised by some MNCs have a disastrous effect (Young and Hood, 1977).

Linkages

Canadian studies of the local linkages of American MNCs and Canadian firms in the same region suggest that linkages both to parts suppliers and suppliers of professional services are lower for MNCs than for local companies (Britton, 1976; Bater and Walker, 1974). Caloren has shown that the centralised purchasing systems used by American automobile producers under the Canadian-American automotive free trade agreement have favoured purchases from other MNCs rather than from local producers (Caloren, 1978). The World Automotive Council of the International Metalworkers Federation claims that American automobile companies in Europe use multinational sourcing for parts (International Metalworkers' Federation, n.d.). Extensive use of multinational sourcing reduces the bargaining power of unions organised on a national rather than international basis. The Scottish electronics complex is sometimes regarded as an example of a region developing a new industrial base because of linkages between plants and between producers and research establishments, but McDermott's study suggests that local linkages are not of less importance to MNCs than to locally based firms (McDermott, 1976).

Studies of linkages between MNCs and local industry in countries other than Canada and Britain are needed. MNC branches are part of an international system of production, so one would expect them to have more extra-regional linkages and consequently fewer local linkages than locally based firms (Stewart, 1976). This independence of local linkages may be an advantage, since at least in theory it makes it easier to attract MNCs to regions with poor local industrial structures. However, once MNCs are located in an area, their impact on local businesses can be quite small.

Technology Transfer

One attraction of MNCs for host-country governments has been that they provide access to the latest technology. Even though MNCs often transfer obsolete machinery and designs from advanced countries to less developed countries, the technology transferred may be better than that currently used locally. Moreover, in developed countries, the time-lag between the introduction of new technology in the national base and in the host country may be too short to be significant.

Recent Canadian studies have suggested that technology transfer by MNCs leads to a truncated industrial system and high royalty and licence fees (Britton and Gilmour, 1978). MNCs maintain assembly plants using imported technology providing jobs on the assembly line for blue-collar workers, but creating unemployment among scientists and engineers by substituting technology imported, often at high cost, for locally developed technology. Chossoudovsky found that Ford of Canada conducted no research and development and did not employ a single scientist with a doctorate (Chossoudovsky, 1978). McDermott's study of the Scottish electronics industry tends to confirm the Canadian findings (McDermott, 1976).

Stability

One of the great advantages of attracting an MNC branch to a region is that few MNCs go bankrupt. Really large corporations like Chrysler, Citroen, Lancia, Leyland, Lockheed or Rolls-Royce are not allowed to fail, but are instead supported by government actions of various types. Not only are MNCs protected by home country governments, but very few of them ever get into serious trouble. Thus an MNC branch is unlikely to be closed because the parent company goes bankrupt. However, MNCs can and do close down plants in unprofitable areas. In the late seventies, British financial papers carried frequent stories on the deindustrialisation of Merseyside (*Financial Times*, 13 April 1978). Several British-owned MNCs, including state-owned British Leyland, closed branch plants in this region, which had one of the poorest productivity records in Britain.

MNCs may not go bankrupt, but they do have considerable locational flexibility and can shift production from troublesome plants to more productive areas. Caloren's study of plant closures in Canada shows that even profitable plants may be closed if corporate strategy changes and the plant becomes redundant (Caloren, 1978). Although high productivity normally provides protection against closure, there are exceptions where profitable plants have closed or been moved to locations where even greater profits are expected.

Conclusions

Any conclusions relating to such a large and rapidly changing topic as the relationships between MNCs and their environments must be tentative. The literature reviewed here refers primarily to MNCs established to serve national markets protected by tariff or distance barriers. Many MNCs are changing to a global system of production using central administrative and design facilities and production of part of or all of their product in low-wage export platforms (Barnett and Muller,

1974). The problems of impact on local regions, i.e. labour problems, linkage problems and technology transfer problems, may be more serious in globally organised MNCs than in MNCs organised to serve separate national markets. Predictions of future problems associated with MNCs will probably have to consider developments in the rapidly industrialising nations of Asia which were excluded from this survey of MNCs activities in the developed world.

The tentative conclusions that can be drawn from this study are:

(1) that MNC branches tend to concentrate in regions of a host country that have a land border with the country in which the MNC is based;

(2) that MNCs have in the past preferred to locate in the economic core region of the host country;

(3) that the location of MNC branches is no longer a strictly economic decision but is increasingly becoming a political decision of great importance to the host country;

(4) that MNCs retain national identities and attitudes that influence their locational behaviour;

(5) although MNC branches are valuable providers of employment in depressed areas their activities can upset the local labour market in the host region;

(6) that links to other parts of the multinational system will often be more important than links to local industry;

(7) that technology transfer by MNCs may be very limited and of little benefit to the host country;

(8) that although MNCs themselves are unlikely to go bankrupt, their branch plants are far less stable and may fall victim to changing corporate strategies.

Although some of the studies referred to offer some scientific proof for these assertions, most of them are based on observations of a very limited number of cases, often with inadequate access to necessary data (particularly recent data — it is a good deal easier to discuss Henry Ford's decisions in the twenties than those of the current directors of Michelin). With a few notable exceptions, theoretical studies of the locational dynamics of MNCs are lacking (Yannopoulos and Dunning, 1976).

The MNC is unlikely to go away, because it provides a valuable service increasing the efficiency of production in the world economic system. Indeed the multinational status of the state oil companies of

Britain, France and Italy and the increasing use of co-production agreements between European MNCs and East European Communist states suggest that even state ownership will not greatly slow the growth of MNCs. This study has focused on some of the side-effects of their growth. Both MNCs and host-country governments must pay some attention to these problems if the MNCs are not to become an increasingly familiar scapegoat for the ills of the international economic system.

9 MULTINATIONALS AND INDUSTRIALISATION IN A DEVELOPING ECONOMY: THE CASE OF NIGERIA

S.I. Abumere

Introduction

Most less developed countries (LDCs) are now committed to the objectives of rapid economic development and higher living standards for their population. This concern may have arisen from demonstration effects arising from contact with the developed countries (DCs). To achieve these objectives, the LDCs have often turned to experts in the DCs and to the economic development literature. The economic development literature itself is replete with suggestions to the LDCs on how to achieve these goals. Probably the most crucial and frequently mentioned factor in the development process is capital. Indeed, Nukse (1953) has argued that a low investment ratio is both a cause and an effect of poverty in the LDCs. In order to break out of this vicious circle of poverty, most LDCs have therefore sought massive injections of foreign capital which often involve not just capital alone, but also management and know-how, all in one package. It is therefore important to examine some of the impacts and consequences of decades of massive inflows of foreign capital in such LDCs.

Nigeria, because of her natural resources and her open-door industrial policy, has always been very attractive for the investment of multinationals. It is therefore surprising that, to date, no serious attempt has been made to study the socio-economic consequences of such investment in Nigeria, which Kilby (1969) has described as an 'open economy'. According to Kilby, characterising Nigeria as an open economy summarises many important features about the economy. First, 'by following a conservative monetary policy and avoiding foreign exchange restrictions, Nigeria has remained open to international trade to an unusual degree'. Second, 'free entry to foreign capital, foreign entrepreneurship and foreign technical skills has been of central importance to industrial development. So too has the absence of extensive state intervention contributed to an open, market-oriented economy'.

158

Last, 'a similar openness and mobility based on achievement has obtained in the modernized segments of Nigerian society. Whether in politics, commerce, administration or the professions, all careers have been open to talent with few impediments to upward progress' (Kilby, 1969, pp. 1-2). [All these aspects of openness have served to make Nigeria very attractive to foreign investors, as has the fact that there is no national policy to guide investment by multinationals.] As Hakam (1966, p. 51) has observed, 'aside from broad recommendations and a few requirements for those seeking pioneer status, the foreign industrial investor was left free to invest wherever he desired and whatever he wished'. Pioneer status gave a new investment a tax-free holiday of up to five years to enable it to take off. This chapter will therefore examine the sectoral and spatial consequences of multinational industrial investment in the open Nigerian economy. In this discussion, the term foreign private investment will be used synonymously with investment by multinationals since they both amount to the same thing in the Nigerian context.

The Beginning of Multinational Activities in Nigeria

It is important to point out that multinational activities predated colonial rule in Nigeria. According to Dike (1956), between 1450 and 1800 several European companies set up stores along the coast of Nigeria engaging in the oil palm trade. McPhee (1926) has stressed that this 'trader's period' was marked by the commercial penetration of the interior, mainly through the help of African middlemen serving as agents of European firms on the coast. It was these middlemen 'who established stores in the interior on the basis of credit goods advanced to them by their European principles on the coast' (Mabogunje, 1968, p. 36). Between 1800 and 1900, the most important of these trading companies was British, the Royal Niger Company. During the Berlin Conference of 1885, when African countries were assigned to separate European nations on the basis of their having 'effective control' in the areas, Nigeria was assigned to the British on the basis of the effective presence established by the Royal Niger Company. Thus colonial rule in Nigeria was foreshadowed by the operations of multinational companies.

In the 1920s, Nigeria came to be dominated by a relatively small number of large and highly integrated multinational companies. These included the United Africa Company (a Unilever affiliate formed from the Royal Niger Company in 1879), John Holt, Paterson Zochonis, the Union Trading Company and so on. There can be no doubt that the colonial administration policy from 1900, which placed great emphasis on export and import trade, led to the proliferation of these companies in Nigeria, many of which were quite large by the standard of the time. Indeed, Kilby (1969) reckons that by 1949, the largest three of these companies accounted for some 49 per cent of all traded commodities in Nigeria. With the discovery of oil in Nigeria in the 1960s, several multinational oil companies (Shell, BP, Mobil, Gulf, Agip, Esso, etc.) began to invest in Nigeria. It can be argued that the volume of investments as well as the profits of these multinational oil companies far exceed those of the multinationals established at an earlier date.

Most multinationals at first devoted all their investment to the export and import trade. However, after Nigeria's political independence in 1960, several of these companies switched from the general import trade to three more specific areas; the distribution of specialised imported merchandise, the setting up of import substitution manufacturing industries and the exploitation of forest and mineral resources. Indeed, according to Onimode (1978), multinational activities now span almost all sectors of the Nigerian economy — petroleum, mining, manufacturing, banking and insurance, construction, distribution, transport and agriculture.

The remaining sections of this chapter will be devoted to an examination of the sectoral and spatial patterns of these multinational industrial investments in Nigeria. The important questions to ask include: which industries and areas receive the bulk of multinational investments in Nigeria? Are the locational preferences of the multinationals different from those of indigenous enterprises? What are the sectoral and regional development problems posed by the pattern of multinational investments? What are the possible solutions to these problems?

The Sectoral Preferences of Multinationals in Nigeria

Foreign private investors have always been free to invest in whatever industry they liked in Nigeria. Under such circumstances, personal interests tend to guide investors in their decision-making. At first sight, it is tempting to hypothesise that multinational firms will invest mainly in profitable or export-only industries, as their interests are more strongly oriented to returns on investments than humanitarian considerations.

The first thing to note is that multinational firms represent the front through which expatriates channel their investment capital into Nigeria. They also constitute the agency through which foreign managerial and technological abilities are brought to Nigeria. There can be little doubt that multinationals dominate industrialisation in Nigeria. Table 9.1 shows the extent of this domination. Until about 1970, more than 70 per cent of shares in companies with paid-up capital of over £N20,000 were held by foreign-owned multinationals. In contrast, Nigerian investors concentrated their holdings of shares in companies with paid-up capitals in the £N1,000 to £N5,000 range. The implications of having the industrial sector dominated by foreign firms have only recently attracted the attention of the Nigerian government, which has now adopted an indigenisation policy. This policy lists some 357 enterprises (mainly small-scale industries) in which Nigerians must control 100 per cent of the shares and another 593 enterprises (medium to large industrial concerns) in which Nigerians must own approximately 40 per cent of the shares. Needless to say, this policy has not altered the situation drastically, since expatriates have never invested significantly in small-scale industries even before the establishment of the policy. Besides, as Onimode (1978) has argued, even if the indigenisation policy were to offer equity participation, it would not guarantee control over management and technology in the industries concerned.

Table 9.1: Expatriate Concentration of Shares in Nigerian Companies

Shareholders	Number			Per Cent		
Value of Shares Held (in $N)	Nigerian	Expatriate	Total	Nigerian	Expatriate	Total
1	146	113	259	56.4	43.6	100.0
1 - 1,000	267	418	685	39.0	61.1	100.0
1,000 - 5,000	182	193	375	48.5	51.5	100.0
5,001 - 10,000	62	124	186	33.3	66.7	100.0
10,001 - 20,000	46	82	128	35.9	64.1	100.0
20,001 - 50,000	47	128	175	27.9	73.2	100.0
50,001 - 100,000	28	80	108	25.9	74.1	100.0
Above 100,000	43	120	163	26.4	73.6	100.0

Source: O. Teriba, E.C. Edozien and M.O. Kayode, Some Aspects of Ownership and Control Structure of Business Enterprise in a Developing Economy: the Nigerian Case', *Nigerian Journal of Economic and Social Studies*, vol. 14, no. 1 (1972), p. 8.

Table 9.2: Distribution of Investments in Nigeria by Source, 1963

	Private Nigerian	Private Non-Nigerian Govts.	Fed. & State	Total Private 1+2	Grand Total 1+2+3	Private Non-Nigerian as % of Total Private	Private Non-Nigerian as % of all Total
	1	2	3	1+2	1+2+3	6	7
1. Meat products	40	160	60	200	260	80.0	61.5
2. Dairy products	2	202	—	103	103	98.0	98.0
3. Fruit canning	31	—	258	31	298	—	—
4. Grain mill products	27	520	60	547	1,107	95.0	47.0
5. Bakery products	236	224	20	460	480	48.7	46.7
6. Sugar confectionery	6	304	70	310	380	98.0	80.0
7. Misc. food preparations	384	5,526	750	2,910	6,700	93.5	82.5
8. Manufacture of beer	224	2,256	7	2,480	2,487	91.0	90.7
9. Soft drinks	150	215	736	356	1,101	57.5	19.1
10. Manufacture of textiles	173	2,809	1,456	2,982	4,435	94.2	63.8
11. Footwear	98	144	—	242	290	59.5	49.7
12. Wearing apparel	40	41	—	81	81	50.6	50.9
13. Made up textile goods	139	159	—	298	298	53.4	53.4
14. Saw milling	1,181	1,578	369	2,759	3,128	57.2	50.5
15. Other wood products	0.4	—	—	—	—	—	—
16. Furniture and textiles	104	275	95	379	474	72.6	58.0
17. Paper products	6	45	169	51	220	88.2	20.5
18. Printing	417	584	1,572	1,001	2,573	58.3	22.7
19. Tanning	17	138	86	155	241	89.0	57.3
20. Travel goods	3	13	—	16	16	81.3	81.3
21. Rubber products	267	2,956	2,262	3,223	5,685	91.7	52.0
22. Basic industrial chem.	—	203	77	280	280	72.5	72.5
23. Vegetable oil milling	59	1,804	71	1,863	1,934	96.8	93.3
24. Paints	—	504	30	504	534	100.0	94.4
25. Misc. chemical prod.	80	1,628	—	1,708	1,708	95.5	95.5
26. Bricks & textiles	6	284	—	290	290	97.9	97.9
27. Pottery & glass products	8	50	67	58	125	86.2	40.0
28. Cement	1,078	889	3,282	1,968	5,250	45.1	16.9
29. Concrete products	71	754	245	825	1,076	91.4	70.4
30. Basic metals	97	366	175	463	638	79.0	57.4
31. Metal products	267	3,559	369	3,826	4,193	93.0	91.2
32. Electrical equipment	34	194	20	228	248	85.0	74.2
33. Boat building & rep.	—	250	60	250	310	100.0	100.0
34. Motor vehicle & bic. ass.	2	6,075	—	6,077	6,077	100.0	100.0
35. Motor vehicle repairs	279	3,511	64	3,790	3,854	92.6	91.1
36. Misc. manufactured prod.	15	291	32	306	338	95.1	86.0
Total	5,541	38,511	12,462	41,020	57,212	87.3	79.9

Source: E.C. Edozien 'Linkages, Direct Foreign Investment and Nigeria's *Economic Development', Nigerian Journal of Economic and Social Studies,* vol. 10, no. 2 (1968), p. 204.

The volume of multinational investment in Nigeria is very large, in some cases outstripping national effort. Table 9.2 shows that multinational investments in Nigeria in 1963 represented 87.3 per cent of all private investment and 79.9 per cent of total investment in Nigeria. For Bendel State in Nigeria (Table 9.3) the figure is 82.8 per cent for all investment in the state. As a result of this very high involvement of multinational capital in the industrialisation of Nigeria, it is also important to appreciate the sectors and industries in which a preference for investment is shown. For the present study, this sectoral analysis is undertaken for two of the most important sections of the Nigerian economy, the export valorisation and the import substitution industries.

Table 9.3: Distribution of Investment in Bendel State by Source and Nature of Activity, 1963-9

Nature of Activity	Private Nigerian	Capital Investments (%) by Source Private Non-Nigerian	Fed. Govt.	State Govt.	Others	Percentage of Grand Total
1. Petroleum & nat. gas	—	100.0	—	—	—	56.1
2. Palm products	4.0	46.5	—	8.1	41.4	4.1
3. Grain mill products	93.7	—	—	—	6.3	0.01
4. Bakery, soft drinks & carbonated water	94.5	—	—	0.06	5.4	0.02
5. Manufacture of wearing apparels	90.0	—	—	—	100.0	0.02
6. Manufacture & repair of footwear	72.4	15.3	—	—	12.3	0.6
7. Sawmill & manufacture of cork	14.1	84.4	0.6	0.6	0.4	3.3
8. Carpentry & woodwork	74.1	—	17.6	—	8.3	0.05
9. Printing & publishing	88.6	—	—	0.7	10.7	0.09
10. Tyre retreading, rubber products & plastic chem.	22.6	41.6	—	25.2	10.6	7.3
11. Cement	0.1	10.0	—	89.9	—	5.6
12. Welding & iron works	58.9	31.8	—	—	9.3	0.02
13. Electrical industries	1.2	98.7	—	—	0.1	3.1
14. Motor vehicle repairs	16.2	83.7	—	—	0.2	4.9
15. Building & construction	42.1	50.7	0.9	1.1	5.2	0.6
16. Retailing	8.7	90.0	—	0.7	0.6	8.9
17. Catering	76.3	14.6	—	—	9.1	0.2
18. Transport	28.1	56.2	—	0.5	15.2	4.7
19. Insurance	93.2	—	—	—	6.8	0.02
Percentage of Grand Total	6.4	82.7	0.03	7.4	3.4	100.0

Source: *Bendel State of Nigeria Industrial Surveys*, vol. 1 (1966), p. 10; vol. II (1966), p. 7; vol. III (1970), p. 18 (Ministry of Economic Development, Benin City, Nigeria).

Multinational Investment in Export Valorisation Industries

Valorisation of exports represents the oldest area of industrial development in Nigeria. This involves preliminary processing of primary
products prior to their export. Until the 1950s, almost all multinational
investment in Nigeria went into this area of industrialisation. However,
after attaining political independence, Nigeria removed the processing
and export of several cash crops (cocoa, palm oil and kernel and
rubber) from the multinationals and transferred these functions to
Marketing Boards. This has probably reduced the investment by multinationals in this area of industrialisation.

From Tables 9.2 and 9.3 it is possible to gauge the extent of multinational investment in the area of export valorisation. This includes
investment (Table 9.2) in saw-milling, rubber products, basic metals,
metal products and palm products (Table 9.3). If export valorisation
industries are extended to include all industries producing and processing primary items for export, then textiles, furniture, carpentry and
woodwork should also be included. Oil and natural gas also belong in
this group although, in many respects, this industry is unique on
account of its overwhelming importance for the Nigerian economy. No
less than 60 per cent of all multinational investment in Nigeria is now
in the oil and natural gas industry and it can be argued that, although
the number of export valorisation industries now invested in Nigeria is
small, this area of industrialisation is still important, as it continues to
command the highest proportion of multinational investment in terms
of the amount of money invested owing to the interest of multinational
corporations in exportable items. The recent surge in multinational
investment in South-East Asia (South Korea, Hong Kong, etc.) may also
be seen in this light.

It is to be expected that multinational investment in export valorisation industries will probably decline with time. As nationalism grows
and the Nigerian nation becomes more confident, it will probably
reduce the role played by multinationals in the areas of mining, processing and export of primary production. In that case, the loss in this
area will probably bring increased multinational investment in import
substitution industries.

Multinational Investment in Import Substitution Industries

Import substitution has now become a very attractive area for investment by multinationals in Nigeria. It has not always been so. For a long time, most of the multinationals in Nigeria were interested in either the export and import trade (export of primary products and import of manufactured goods for distribution within Nigeria) or the export valorisation industries. Interest in import substitution industries, designed to make in Nigeria goods that had previously featured prominently on the import bills, has grown recently. Following Nigeria's political independence, several factors have led to a change in the operations of the multinational companies. First, the establishment of the Marketing Boards largely removed from these multinationals the role of export agents for primary produce. Second, the role of these companies as importers and distributors was threatened by three main developments:

(1) the arrival of new multinationals after the Second World War increased competition for the more established enterprises forcing major changes in the operational strategies;

(2) many foreign-owned manufacturing multinationals (ICI, Tate & Lyle, for example) entered the Nigerian market undermining the importing role that the established multinationals had performed (Kilby, 1969);

(3) competition in the import and distribution trades was emerging from indigenous concerns.

As a result of these changes, many multinationals operating in Nigeria switched their operations from the general import trade to two areas, the distribution of specialised, imported merchandise and the setting up of import substitution industries. Table 9.2 shows the extent of multinational involvement in these import substitute industries in Nigeria. The sectors involved include such industries as textiles, footwear, dairy products, vegetable oil, paints and electrical goods. Indeed, apart from the few industries mentioned under export valorisation above, almost all the other industries listed in Tables 9.2 and 9.3 come under the heading of import substitution. With regard to the amounts actually invested, it is easy to identify the import substitution industries of most interest to the multinationals. These include food processing, brewing, textiles, vegetable oil, chemical products and motor vehicle assembly. It is important to note that almost all these industries are producing consumer rather than capital goods. This bias probably derives from the fact that the pattern of demand for imported goods before the 1960s largely determined what import-replacing industries could be set up.

The few capital goods industries in Tables 9.2 and 9.3, like the cement industry, have been largely financed by indigenous capital and the government.

On the whole, it can be said that the multinationals have provided needed capital, technology and managerial skills for Nigerian industrialisation. There are also obvious income and employment effects from their investments. However, a number of criticisms have recently been made of their role in Nigeria. The first relates to technology. Mabogunje (1978) noted that because of the overwhelming importance of making a profit, multinational corporations invariably import technology into the country that is at too advanced a level of sophistication. Such technology has little chance of being internalised. At the same time, the import of technology has largely put a stop to indigenous technological development by eliminating markets. The case of the virtual disappearance of Nigerian blacksmiths, iron-smelters, brass workers and weavers is often cited (Onimode, 1978). It is also often noted that most multinationals bring into Nigeria only capital-intensive technology, whereas what the country probably needs is more labour-intensive technology (Onimode, 1978). Second, multinational corporations have been accused of tying the import of the raw materials and intermediate goods needed for domestic production to sources of supply within the corporate structure, thereby frustrating the very principle of import substitution, since backward growth is effectively blocked (Mabogunje, 1978, p. 17). Third, multinationals have been accused of investing heavily in industries like beer and tobacco, which yield quick and high profits, but which are unrelated to the development priorities of Nigeria. Last, the issue of profit repatriation is often mentioned. As far back as 1963, the profits made by the multinational oil companies alone exceeded £N1 billion (Onimode, 1978). The use of transfer pricing, which allows multinational companies to inflate their costs and so evade tax, serves to increase even the real level of these profits. The other criticisms of multinational operations have been exhaustively discussed elsewhere (Mabogunje, 1978; Onimode, 1978) and so should not delay the discussion any longer. What has not received enough attention is the locational consequences of the multinational investments. This will be discussed below but, first, the spatial pattern of multinational investments in Nigeria must be investigated.

Spatial Preferences of Multinational Investments in Nigeria

Perhaps the most important factor in the explanation of the spatial distribution of multinational investments in Nigeria is historical. The initial advantage which the coastal areas gained during the traders' period of the nineteenth century has been cumulative. During this traders' period, stores and other basic facilities were established in coastal areas. Later, the British Colonial administration's emphasis on the export and import trade gave coastal areas in Nigeria additional advantages. Ports were established which served as collecting centres for exports and imports. Basic infrastructure to facilitate this flow of trade was established. When the multinational firms switched their major role from trading to manufacturing, their investments were located in the areas they knew very well and these were usually the coastal areas.

Historically, internal transport was also very poorly developed in Nigeria. It would therefore be expected that multinational companies will, in locating their enterprises, be biased towards areas that have an advantageous location with respect to transport, especially areas of easy entry into and exit from the country. For a long time in Nigeria such areas were the coastal ports. Also, foreign companies, in the absence of required equipment and machinery within Nigeria, have often had to import such equipment and machinery by sea from more advanced countries. Since transportation into the interior is poor, location not far from the sea port is generally favoured. In addition, many multinational companies in Nigeria invest in export valorisation and other enterprises (for instance raw materials, oil and natural gas) for which coastal sites are necessary. The discovery and production of oil and natural gas in the coastal areas of Nigeria since the 1960s has merely served to intensify the coastal concentrations.

The influence of the location of amenities and basic infrastructure such as water supply, electricity, health facilities and schools is also important. There is enough evidence in Nigeria to show that there was a bias for coastal areas in the location of these items during the colonial period. For instance, in 1917 the colonial administration created three categories of towns: first-class, second-class and third-class (Mabogunje, 1968). Nearly all the first- and second-class towns were along the coast or the railway lines. The classification of these towns was not based on their population size or on their traditional importance, but on their ability to support the export and import trade. The fact is that during this period the colonial administration was interested only in areas that produced the major export crops. These export crops included oil palm and kernels, rubber and timber. These crops are mainly found in the south of Nigeria. The distribution of amenities and infrastructure during the colonial era was, of course, influenced by this township classification. The distribution of schools had the same pattern. For a long time, Christian missions were mainly responsible for founding schools. They also showed a bias towards coastal areas. This factor is largely responsible for the well known fact that education declines from the coast inland in Nigeria. With time, all these factors have led to a concentration of amenities, infrastructure, manpower and effective demand in the south of Nigeria, all of which are very attractive to multinational investments. There are signs that the situation is changing, but it is certainly not changing fast enough.

Since independence, no real locational guidelines have been formulated in Nigeria to control the location of multinational enterprises. According to Aboyade (1968):

> The only long locational programme available is the one called sundry assistance. The most crucial instrument on which government has long relied is the set of fiscal concessions known in official circles as 'industrial incentives'. They consist mainly of import duty relief, income tax relief for plants declared as pioneer industries and high initial capital allowance. Location policy as a means of achieving a higher level and a rationally distributed pattern of industrial activity was ignored.

It can be argued that in the absence of such a location policy, multinationals are free to locate their enterprises where they like. This probably means the selection of locations in areas that will ensure least cost and maximum profits. According to Hakam (1966) and Kilby (1969), the factors that guided multinationals in the location of their manufacturing plants in Nigeria were knowledge of the local market and the economic environment, the existing distribution network and the cost of gathering information. In effect, multinational manufacturing plants were located in areas which the merchant firms already knew well and within which they had established distribution networks. The areas which the multinationals know very well in Nigeria are the coastal areas which had been crucial for the export and import trade of an earlier period. It is logical, therefore, to hypothesise that multinational investment in Nigeria will show a bias to coastal locations.

It is easy to argue that the evidence in support of this hypothesis can be found in Nigeria. For instance, by 1969, well over 50 per cent of all investment by multinationals in Nigeria was in industries located in Lagos. If we add the other coastal towns of Sapele, Warri, Port Harcourt and Calabar (Figure 9.1), the figure quickly jumps to about 70 per cent. Indeed, according to Hakam (1966), about 57 per cent of all multinational investment in Nigeria is located in just two of the principal coastal ports.

Figure 9.1: The Subdivision of Nigeria into 19 States in 1975

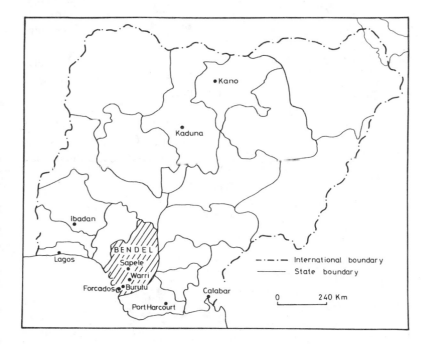

However, no detailed area breakdown of multinational investment is available for Nigeria as a whole. However, such data are available for the Bendel State region of Nigeria (Figure 9.2). Bendel State may be regarded as sharing some of the essential characteristics of Nigeria as a whole necessary for testing the hypothesis at hand. For instance, the state has a coastal south and a northern hinterland. The state yields more than half of all the oil and gas produced in Nigeria. The spatial pattern of multinational investments in Bendel State can therefore be considered

Figure 9.2: Geographical Subdivisions of Bendel State, Nigeria

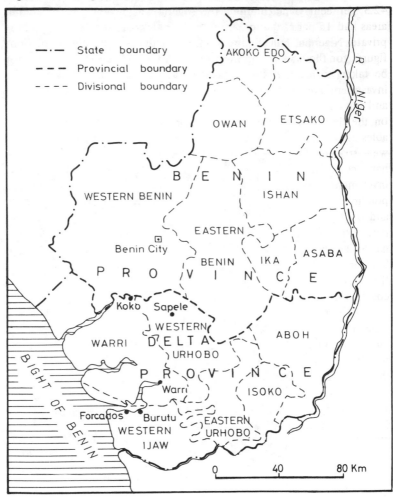

to reflect that of Nigeria as a whole.

Examination of the Spatial Pattern of Multinational Investments in Bendel State of Nigeria

Table 9.4 shows the spatial distribution of multinational investments in the Bendel State region of Nigeria. From the table, it is evident that whereas about 91.5 per cent of the total investment in the coastal areas was accounted for by multinationals, the hinterland area received only 42.3 per cent of such investment. However, whereas the hinterland areas had 15 per cent and 38.5 per cent of investment accounted for by private Nigerian and State government respectively, the equivalent figures for the coastal areas are 3.7 per cent and 1.7 per cent. This can be taken to mean that the areas preferred by the multinationals for investment are different from those preferred by indigenous concerns and state government. Indeed, a set of correlation analyses carried out on the data confirm this hypothesis (Abumere, 1978). The two variables used to measure distance from the coast in the correlation analysis were straight line (Euclidean) and road distance. These were found to have correlation coefficients of -0.62 and -0.63 with multinational investments respectively for the 1965 period compared with corresponding coefficients of -0.30 and -0.37 with indigenous investments and 0.77 and 0.85 with State government investments. For the 1969 period, the correlation coefficients were -0.76 and -0.81 with multinational investments, -0.47 and -0.58 with indigenous investments and 0.83 and 0.94 with State government investments. These figures show that whereas multinational investments decline significantly from the coast, indigenous investments only decline moderately and generally insignificantly from the coast and State government investments generally increase with distance from the coast. These results might be taken to mean that the solutions found by the multinationals to the traditional Weberian locational problem are somewhat different from those of indigenous firms and State government.

Table 9.4: Distribution of Investments in Bendel State by Source and Geographical Division, 1963-9

	Capital Investment (%) by Source					
Provinces and Divisions	Private Nigerian	Private Non-Nigerian	Fed. Govt.	State Govt.	Others	Per Cent of Grand Total
(1) Benin Province (Hinterland)	15.0	42.3	0.2	38.5	3.9	21.00
Afenmai	0.2	9.9	—	89.7	0.1	4.5
Akoko-Edo	100.0	—	—	—	—	0.002
Asaba	1.7	9.2	—	83.0	6.2	2.8
Benin	22.3	60.4	0.2	12.4	4.7	13.5
Ishan	63.1	—	17.1	16.4	3.3	0.1
(2) Delta Province (Coastal Areas)	3.7	91.5	0.04	1.7	3.0	79.0
Agboh	15.0	47.3	—	37.3	0.4	0.8
Urhobo	12.2	71.7	—	10.3	5.8	9.4
Warri	2.0	92.4	0.09	2.9	5.2	10.3
Western Ijaw	2.6	95.8	0.03	—	1.6	48.4
Per Cent of Grand Total	6.4	82.7	0.03	7.4	3.4	100.0

Source: *Bendel State Industrial Surveys*, vol. 1 (1964), p. 9; vol. II (1960), p. 9; vol. III (1970), p. 20.

Perhaps it is more rewarding to examine the spatial pattern formed by multinational investments by computing location quotients.

Table 9.5: Location Quotients for Multinational Investment in Bendel State, 1963, 1965 and 1969

Provinces & Division	1963 A	B	C	1965 A	B	C	1969 A	B	C
1. Benin Province									
(Hinterland)	0.579	0.105	0.099	0.556	0.249	0.235	0.522	0.129	0.122
Akoko-Edo	—	—	—	—	—	—	—	—	—
Asaba	—	—	—	0.125	0.113	0.151	—	—	—
Benin East	—	—	—	—	—	—	0.034	0.007	0.005
Benin West	0.659	0.55	0.340	0.903	1.180	0.728	0.771	0.650	0.401
Etsako	0.209	0.002	0.001	0.153	0.132	0.101	0.113	0.075	0.058
Ika	—	—	—	—	—	—	—	—	—
Ishan	—	—	—	—	—	—	—	—	—
Owan	—	—	—	—	—	—	—	—	—
2. Delta Province									
(Coastal Areas)	1.077	1.217	1.309	1.222	1.260	1.356	1.088	1.742	1.875
Aboh	0.804	0.207	0.257	0.667	0.040	0.034	0.567	0.043	0.034
Isoko	—	—	—	—	—	—	—	—	—
Urhobo East	—	—	—	—	—	—	—	—	—
Urhobo West	1.318	2.048	4.868	0.833	0.563	1.340	0.884	0.349	0.830
Warri	1.318	1.474	0.785	1.333	7.333	3.907	0.964	1.368	5.931
Western Ijaw	0.836	2.275	1.784	1.236	1.044	0.819	1.122	7.560	5.931

Quotients in columns A, B and C were derived with multinational investments, population and real sizes respectively as bases (see text for computational formula).

Sources: As for Table 9.4.

The location quotients computed here (Table 9.5) are simply devices for comparing an area's share of multinational investment with its share of some basic aggregate such as population and areal size. The equations for obtaining the quotients in columns A, B and C in Table 9.5 are given as:

$$A = \frac{S_i/S}{N_i/N} \qquad \dots\dots\dots\dots (1)$$

$$B = \frac{S_i/N_i}{P_i/P} \qquad \dots\dots\dots\dots (2)$$

$$C = \frac{S_i N_i}{A_i/A} \qquad \dots\dots\dots\dots (3)$$

S_i = value of multinational investment in Division i
S = value of all investment in the Division
N_i = value of all multinational investment in Bendel State
N = value of all investment in the State
P_i = population of Division i
P = population of Bendel State
A_i = areal size in sq. kms. of Division i
A = area of Bendel State

From Table 9.5, column A, it is obvious that the coastal areas taken together have done rather better (quotients greater than 1) with regard to multinational investment than is suggested by the level of multinational investment in Bendel as a whole, but that the hinterland areas have done badly, receiving less than their share (quotient less than 1) of multinational investments. Column B also shows that the coastal areas have received a far higher share of multinational investment than is suggested by their share of the total population of Bendel. The same is true of column C, which shows that the coastal areas have done far better with respect to multinational investment than their areal size might suggest. The conclusion that may be drawn here is that coastal locations are highly favoured for the location of multinational investment. This conclusion is also true of Nigeria as a whole.

Implications of the Spatial Pattern of Multinational Investments in Nigeria

As has been shown, the distribution of multinational investment in Bendel State favours coastal locations. This pattern clearly has income, employment and political implications. These three factors are elaborated upon in turn.

Perhaps the most important consequence of this pattern is that it tends to divide the nation and therefore makes the problem of national unity and integration that much more difficult to solve. The current difference between the north (hinterland) and south (coastal states) in Nigeria with respect to level of development is traceable, in part, to the activities of multinationals. Nigeria is a multi-ethnic country. The regional inequalities of development partially created by multinational investment follow ethnic boundaries, since specific ethnic groups may be identified with the coastal and hinterland states. This creates ethnic tension in Nigeria and is a major worry to many Nigerians.

Then there are the income and employment implications. Lagos, along with five other coastal States (Nigeria now has 19 States), commands nearly 65 per cent of the industrial employment in Nigeria (Ayeni, 1979), leaving the remaining 35 per cent to be shared by the remaining 13 hinterland states. The same coastal States were responsible, in 1975, for about 71 per cent of all incomes from industrial activities in Nigeria (Ayeni, 1979). The picture is even clearer when we examine the Bendel State case in Table 9.6. In this table, regional relativities based on multinational investment, employment and income in Bendel have been computed. The relativities were obtained using the formula:

$$RR = \frac{S_i/P_i}{N_i P} \times 100 \qquad \ldots\ldots\ldots\ldots (4)$$

where RR is the regional relativity and other terms are defined as before. The regional relativities provide the means for direct comparisons of the changes in multinational investments, income and employment of a Division relative to the changes in that investment in Bendel State as a whole. Figure 9.2 shows all the Divisions of Bendel State recognised in the analysis. In Table 9.6, any Division scoring more than the State figure of 100 has done better than the average performance of the State, while any Division scoring less than 100 has done worse. The coastal areas, taken together, generally have relativities above 100 with respect to employment and income. Most of the individual Divisions making up the coastal areas have relativities above 100. The picture is entirely different with respect to the hinterland areas where the relativities based on income and employment are generally less than 100.

The relativities in Table 9.6 also make it possible to determine whether the regional inequality in the distribution of multinational investment, employment and income in Bendel State is increasing or decreasing over time. Since the Bendel State relativity is 100, a trend towards convergence on the figure 100 by the divisional relativities, over time, will indicate that inequality is decreasing, while the reverse will show that it is increasing. Convergence could come about either by a rise, over the period, of the relativities for the hinterland areas towards 100 and/or a decline of the relativities for the coastal areas towards 100. Table 9.6 shows that there is no evidence of such convergence.

It may be argued that since the spatial pattern of multinational investment has serious political and regional development consequences, the Nigerian government ought to consider policies that will guide the location of multinational investment in Nigeria. Such policies ought to be able to provide locational principles for the multinationals in order that their investments can conform with national needs and aspirations.

Table 9.6: Regional Relativities Based on Multinational Investment, Employment and Income in Bendel State

Provinces and Divisions	Multinational Investment			Employment Relativities[a]			Income Relativities[a]		
	1963	1965	1969	1963	1965	1969	1963	1965	1969
1. Benin Province	15.6	32.3	13.8	65.2	76.0	69.4	93.4	68.7	85.4
Akoko Edo	—	—	2.0	2.0	—	—	170.6	—	—
Asaba	—	15.6	15.5	42.9	66.6	21.4	51.0	49.5	75.3
Benin East	—	—	0.8	—	—	101.6	—	—	92.6
Benin West	124.6	229.8	103.3	433.9	514.5	366.0	83.2	77.3	79.4
Etsako	0.3	12.7	6.2	6.0	12.1	7.7	92.9	92.1	143.9
Ika	—	—	—	—	—	15.3	—	—	40.5
Ishan	—	—	—	37.3	14.8	42.6	69.4	55.8	80.5
Owan	—	—	—	—	—	—	—	—	—
2. Delta Province (Coastal Areas)	212.5	190.3	215.0	146.3	132.1	140.9	94.7	124.7	228.7
Aboh	40.2	6.0	4.2	65.2	43.9	35.1	59.0	58.0	62.9
Isoko	—	—	—	—	—	—	—	—	—
Urhobo East	—	—	—	—	—	12.8	—	—	—
Urhobo West	580.8	138.6	70.2	609.2	523.7	470.3	122.1	95.7	99.5
Warri	189.0	813.5	123.2	123.6	150.4	306.4	91.5	220.0	91.2
Western Ijaw	465.0	183.9	1092.1	80.0	74.4	20.5	106.0	125.1	830.8
Bendel State	100.0	100.0	100.0	100.0	100.0	100.0	100.0	100.0	100.0

Note: [a]Employment and income arising from the investments in Table 9.4.

Sources: For multinational investments, as for Table 9.4; for income and employment, *Bendel State Industrial Surveys*, vols. I, II and III.

The Nigerian Response to the Sectoral and Spatial Patterns of Multinational Investment

There is no doubt that as far as Nigeria is concerned, multinationals are playing a useful role in the industrialisation of the country. However, the industries and areas they invest in may, in some cases, run counter to national needs and aspirations. It is therefore necessary for the government to evolve policies to guide multinational investment so that they conform with these national objectives. Attention is focused here mainly on policies to achieve a more equitable spatial distribution of multinational investment.

The geographic literature is full of positive and negative policy instruments for directing investment to desired areas. The positive inducements include capital grants and concessions to foreign firms which locate in less favourable areas (for instance the hinterland areas of Nigeria, away from the coast), while the negative inducements consist of controls and penalties (higher taxes, legal restrictions and so on) for foreign firms attempting to locate their investments in certain congested and attractive areas (for instance some of the coastal areas of Nigeria). There are two reasons why these policy instruments may not be as effective in Nigeria as they have sometimes been in some other countries. First, multinational companies that have a considerable proportion of their investment tied up in Nigeria are in a strong bargaining position, since they can always threaten to take their investments to other countries. This is especially true for investment in import substitution industries. The threat will not apply in the case of investment in oil and natural gas, since these items are not ubiquitous. The Nigerian government, because of its drive for economic development through industrialisation, wants these multinational investments, but then finds it difficult to regulate the locational preferences of the multinationals. This is probably why Nigeria, to date, has not been able to evolve any meaningful location policies for such investments.

Second, there is the point made by Harvey (1973) that there appears to be a built-in tendency for the capitalist market system to counteract any attempt to divert funds from the most profitable areas. However, in spite of the difficulties these policy instruments should not be discarded. They should be tried. There are signs that with the flow of oil money and a growing market, Nigeria can now more confidently attempt the application of such policies.

Perhaps the best and easiest policy at this stage of development in Nigeria is the so-called 'infrastructure instrument'. Logan (1972) has argued that a way of achieving some measure of redistribution of investments is for governments to invest heavily in infrastructure in the less attractive areas, for instance in most of the hinterland areas of Nigeria. This infrastructure programme would have to include the provision of roads, water supply, electricity or even industrial estates with all these facilities provided as a package. One of the major locational constraints in the developing countries is the non-availability, in most areas, of the basic infrastructure necessary for the location of industry. This usually means that private investment goes to the few areas where such facilities exist, a situation which soon leads to a concentration of investment in these few areas and an intensification of regional inequality. If basic infrastructure is available in the deprived areas, multinational investments may be more mobile. There will soon be an opportunity to test the effectiveness of this infrastructure thesis in Nigeria. In 1975 the Nigerian government embarked upon a policy of dispersing developmental infrastructure through the creation of States (12 States were created from the existing 4 in 1967. The number was again increased to 19 in 1975, see Figure 9.1), and through direct Federal government participation in infrastructure development in all parts of Nigeria. In the next few years, it should be possible to test whether investment in Nigeria is tending towards dispersal following the dispersal of infrastructure.

Conclusion

Multinational corporations will continue to have an important role to play in the process of industrialisation in Nigeria. The capital, technology and managerial skills which they provide still continue to be crucial. In certain sectors such as the petroleum and natural gas industry, it is doubtful if much can be achieved without the co-operation of the multinational corporations. However, because of self-interest, especially the profit motive, multinationals may invest in sectors or areas that are against national interests and aspirations. There can be little doubt that the concentration of multinational investment in certain areas of Nigeria is increasing regional inequality. This regional inequality itself has the potential to work against national unity and integration. There is therefore an obvious need for government to evolve some kind of locational policy for potential investors before the situation gets out of hand.

10 MULTINATIONAL CORPORATIONS IN SOUTHERN AFRICA: A SPATIAL PERSPECTIVE

C.M. Rogerson

'The Republic of South Africa has always been regarded by foreign investors as a gold mine, one of those rare and refreshing places where profits are great and problems are small' — *Fortune*, 1972.

'It is essential for Botswana's development that we should retain foreign investment and attract much more such investment' — President Seretse Khama, Botswana, 1975.

'There is no better location from which an industrialist can operate in his effort to capture the vast market of the whole African continent than Lesotho' — Hon. M.V. Molapo, Minister of Commerce and Industry, Lesotho, 1979.

'For my part I have always recognised that external capital and skills play a very important part in the development of the country's substantial natural resources; and I am confident that the entrepreneur will find in Swaziland promising opportunities and a highly satisfactory climate for investment' — King Sobhuza II, Swaziland, 1976.

'We look ahead . . . Regardless of what experts and scientists think or say, the African masses, like any human being, urgently need work, shelter, food, education, clothing, health and freedom. If they have these they are easy to please and difficult to corrupt' — First National Development Corporation of South West Africa, Namibia, 1979.

Introduction

In the post-Second World War era and especially since 1960, Africa has become the locus of extensive activity by multinational corporations

179

(MNCs) (Widstrand, 1975; Seidman, 1977; Lanning and Mueller, 1979). The winds of change that swept across the continent, culminating in the attainment of political independence for nearly fifty African nations, radically reshaped the macro-environment confronting the MNC. Advantage could be taken by MNCs of the newly acquired independence of African states to penetrate British and French spheres of influence from which they had previously been excluded by colonial rule (Seidman, 1970).

Africa began to experience two competitive scrambles of equal intensity. The first was a scramble amongst MNCs, each struggling to increase their rate of capital accumulation, initially through the acquisition of low-cost raw materials and markets for manufactured goods (Seidman, 1977). But with the emergence of a 'new international division of labour', increasingly MNCs are competing in Africa also to secure supplies of cheap and disciplined labour for relocated production from the industrialised countries (Fröbel, Heinrichs and Kreye, 1977; Hancock and Lloyd, 1980). Throughout Africa the traditional geographical domains of British and French MNCs were challenged aggressively by corporations based in the United States, West Germany, Japan and several other nations. The second competitive scramble in Africa took place between African nations, as governments vied with each other to foster the most hospitable investment climate to attract the MNC. As neo-colonialism superseded colonialism as the primary form of imperialist domination in Africa, in the majority of the newly independent states the emergent bureaucratic bourgeois classes accepted conventional Western economic wisdom that foreign investment and production for export were the keys to overcoming poverty and underdevelopment.

The sub-continent of Southern Africa has been the major area of attraction for MNC investment in Africa. Reflecting the unprecedented spread of MNCs into the region, there are burgeoning popular and scholarly debates concerning their implications for development and underdevelopment. Particularly controversial are those arguments surrounding the relationship of MNCs to the South African government's policies of apartheid. Questions of 'constructive engagement', divestment or withdrawal hinge on whether MNCs are (or can become) progressive forces towards the elimination of racial discrimination and oppression in South Africa. All these are matters of intense and vital debate both inside and outside South Africa (Harvey, 1974; Blausten, 1976; Legassick and Hemson, 1976; Lipton, 1976; Legassick and Innes, 1977; Litvak, De Grasse and McTigue, 1978; Ashford, 1979; Seidman,

1979; Sullivan, 1980; Whisson, 1980). Notwithstanding this plethora of discussion, the historical penetration and spatial behaviour of MNCs in Southern Africa has largely been a neglected field of research. Indeed, with certain notable exceptions (Abumere, 1978; Rogerson, 1978, 1981a; Van der Wees, 1981), Africa as a whole has been bypassed in the empirical advances of the past decade in studies of the geography of enterprise.

Figure 10.1: Southern Africa: Location Map

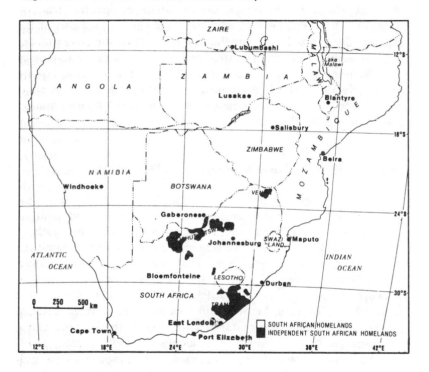

It is the intention in this chapter to redress this situation of neglect through examining the nature and spatial consequences of the competition for MNC investment as manifested between the states of Southern Africa. The arena of study is defined here as consisting of the Republic of South Africa, including the three so-called 'independent' Homelands of Bophuthatswana, Transkei and Venda; the three former British colonies of Botswana, Lesotho and Swaziland; and the politically disputed territory of Namibia (Figure 10.1). The discussion falls into three major sections. First, explanation of the geography of MNCs must be set in the context of a world-systems perspective (Taylor and Thrift, 1979) which acknowledges the macro-environment in which corporations operate. The major facets of the macro-environment of Southern Africa are therefore presented. Second, an investigation is undertaken of the differential expansion and patterns of MNC investment between the several states of Southern Africa. At the international level the search for raw materials has scattered MNCs throughout the sub-continent. But only South Africa emerges as a centre of substantive MNC manufacturing investment, despite intense competition from, in particular, Botswana, Lesotho and Swaziland. In the final part of the chapter, the focus shifts from the international to the intra-national scale of analysis. Attention centres upon the locational behaviour of manufacturing MNCs within the Republic of South Africa and, more particularly, in light of government exhortations that foreign firms become spearheads in the programmes of industrial decentralisation and Homelands development.

Southern Africa: the Macro-environment for Penetration

The twentieth century, and more specifically the period since 1945, has witnessed considerable changes in the economic and political circumstances within which MNCs have sought to penetrate Southern Africa. Three facets of the changing macro-environment of Southern Africa are of particular significance. First, the transformation of South Africa from 'a peripheral part of the world economic system to a developed sub-metropole' (Legassick, 1977, p. 175). Second, the transition of Botswana, Lesotho and Swaziland from British colonial rule to a neo-colonial path of dependent capitalist development. Third, the persistence of the 'political economy of theft' (Green, 1979, 1980) in Namibia and of heightening political struggles for independence in the territory. Beginning in the middle 1960s, after political independence for Botswana, Lesotho and Swaziland, the MNC confronts an increasingly competitive struggle between the states of Southern Africa to attract investment.

South Africa: From Periphery to Semi-periphery in the World System

Until as late as 1930 South Africa occupied a peripheral position in the capitalist world system. In the classic mould of a colonial economy the country exported raw materials, primarily gold, and imported consumer manufactures. Domestic industry remaind stunted and undeveloped, the result of imperial domination by Britain (Innes, 1980). Although the temporary rupture of 'free trade' during the First World War gave local manufacturing an opportunity to expand, it was during the inter-war period that there occurred a series of economic and political changes which facilitated an industrial transformation in South Africa. The country began to break out of a vicious cycle of underdevelopment and to embark on a path of independent capitalist development, an economic metamorphosis which underpinned South Africa's rise from periphery to semi-periphery (Frank, 1979b; Milkman, 1979; Wallerstein, 1979) within the world economy. As Bozzoli argues:

> whereas before the first World War, the South African economic and social system was under imperial domination of a far-reaching and complex kind, by the 1930s economists of a Rostowian bent could apply to the South African economy terms such as 'take off'; and by the end of the Second World War the South African system was set on a path of capitalist development, albeit of a peripheral sort (Bozzoli, 1978, p. 42).

At the root of this economic transformation there were changes both internal and external to South Africa. Externally, there emerged a changed imperial relationship with the waning world economic power of Britain (Innes, 1980). But the changing balance of the imperial relationship with Britain afforded only an opportunity, not a guarantee, for industrial expansion in South Africa. Of equal importance for substantive industrialisation to occur was the existence of local markets, the provision of disciplined labour and the organisation of an infrastructure. In this context, it is imperative to recognise the internal change in the nature of the South African state which took place in the inter-war period (see Davies *et al.* 1976; Kaplan, 1977; Bozzoli, 1978). There crystallised an increasingly strong 'national' state which began to restructure some of the central features of South Africa's imperial social formation (Bozzoli, 1978).

During the 1930s and 1940s the state increasingly sought to stimulate a local manufacturing base. The structures of racial domination, early established in the industrial colour bar legislation, served to place whites on the favourable side of South Africa's unfolding dynamic of development and underdevelopment, creating a relatively high-income group which furnished a market for local manufactures (Ehrensaft, 1976; Seidman and Seidman, 1977; Rogerson, 1981a). The state vigorously pursued industrialisation directly through participation in production, infrastructure support and finance and indirectly through encouraging the large mining and finance houses to move beyond their initial narrow interests and to diversify into local manufacturing (Phillips, 1974; Weiss, 1975; Rogerson, 1981a). Most importantly, the state established and ensured the social conditions for the greater exploitation of black labour by capital. The institutions of cheap labour in South Africa, forged in mining (Wolpe, 1972; Legassick, 1977; Magubane, 1979), progressively began to be consolidated, extended and elaborated for the conditions of an industrialising society. South Africa's road to industrialisation was paved by the 'modernisation' of a racist system in which the black majority participates only as cheap labour. The essential basis of the country's 'forced labour economy' (Legassick, 1977) is the system of migratory labour. This system enables capital in South Africa to secure labour power at a rate set at less than the bare minimum advocated by Marx as essential under capitalism, namely the socially necessary wage required to support the worker and his family (Wolpe, 1972; Legassick, 1974; Magubane, 1979). By allowing only the black male migrant into the areas of capitalist production and by forcing his family to eke out an existence in the rural reserves, industrial South Africa is spared, in large measure, the welfare costs of housing, pensions, social facilities and amenities for the black majority of the work-force (Legassick, 1977; Seidman and Seidman, 1977).

Upon the advantages of cheap labour the objectives of industrialisation and an independent path of capitalist development were vigorously pursued in South Africa after 1948 with the electoral victory of the National Party (Rogerson, 1980, 1981a). The gradual introduction, from this time, of policies and programmes which are subsumed under the rubric of apartheid are to be understood as 'the attempt by the capitalist class to meet the expanding demand for cheap African labour in the era of industrial manufacturing capital' (Wolpe, 1972, p. 427). Modernising the institutions of racial domination in post-war South Africa centred around the strengthening of migratory labour and the creation of a series of 'independent' Homelands, such as Bophuthatswana, Transkei and Venda (Figure 10.1). Such policies serve to ensure that the black majority is forced into reservoirs of low-skilled labour from which economic avenues of escape are few. Legassick and Wolpe (1976) maintain that the Homelands constitute the essential means whereby South Africa's industrial reserve army is dispersed around the geographical periphery where social control is easy and from where it can be mobilised, when required, through the agency of migrant labour.

The several government-sponsored programmes, introduced since 1960, for the 'development' of these areas — initially through a policy of industrial decentralisation to border areas appending Homelands and later to growth points within the Homelands themselves — represent no fundamental challenge to their essential role in the contemporary political economy of South Africa (see Rogerson and Pirie, 1979; Rogerson, 1981a).

Towards attaining the goal of constructing an increasingly self-reliant, self-centred and industrially based economy, throughout the post-Second World War period government in South Africa sought to harness the potential of MNC investment (Legassick, 1974, 1977). The Viljoen Commission in 1958 urged that the state 'encourage industries in the Union by publicising overseas the advantages of the country in regard to industrial development and by actively encouraging foreign firms voluntarily to establish themselves in the Union' (South Africa, 1958, cited in Good and Williams, 1976). During the 1960s, alarmed by the international reaction to the Sharpeville massacre and by threats of sanctions, the state intensified its endeavours to attract MNCs into participating in the construction of key strategic sectors of local industry (Legassick, 1974). Yet, by direct state investment in foreign enterprises, by requiring sales of stock locally, by forcing or encouraging MNCs to accept increasing degrees of local participation and control, and by forcing industrialisation through regulations demanding increased local content in products assembled in South Africa (especially of motor vehicles) the state sharply defined the terms of MNC investment in the country (Grundy, 1976).

It was officially reiterated in 1970 that South Africa 'welcomes foreign investment and in formulating economic policy will also endeavour to retain a favourable investment climate for foreign-controlled enterprise' (South Africa, 1970, para. 963). Increasingly, at this time, MNCs were being urged not merely to invest in South Africa but to participate in the programmes for border area and Homelands industrial development, which were backed by substantial packages of investment allowances and tax incentives. Throughout the 1970s, however, there strengthened an international campaign against MNC involvement in apartheid South Africa. The reaction of South Africa to mounting international pressure on MNCs' investors and to the growing competitive struggle of contiguous states in Southern Africa also seeking to attract MNCs (see below), is a major effort to make the country 'more attractive' to the potential international investor. The much-heralded (largely cosmetic) 'improvements' in South Africa's labour legislation, including the removal of the industrial colour bar, may be interpreted as part of government's strategy to recapture the country's former appeal to MNC investors (Davies, 1979; Shafer, 1979). Moreover, they point to South Africa's resolve to win the competitive international scramble within Southern Africa to attract the MNC.

Botswana, Lesotho and Swaziland: from Colonial to Neo-colonial Development

Throughout the period of colonial rule Britain did little to restrain the forces of South African economic expansionism or 'sub-imperialism' (Coles and Cohen, 1975; Nyathi, 1975; Frank, 1979b) in Botswana, Lesotho and Swaziland (Winai-Ström, 1978; Crush, 1979; Colclough and McCarthy, 1980). At the close of the colonial era these territories functioned in terms of the Southern African social formation primarily as stagnant labour reserves, a structural situation little different from that of the Homelands of South Africa (Palmer and Parsons, 1977; Fransman, 1977; Winter, 1978; Leys, 1979).

At independence, during the middle 1960s, the new governing classes of Botswana, Lesotho and Swaziland were committed to a path of dependent capitalist development, which involves a more intensive participation as peripheral producers in the world economy (Wallerstein, 1979). The post-colonial states in each of the newly independent nations were strongly representative of the interests of foreign capital (Cooper, 1976-7; Winai-Ström, 1978; Winter, 1978; Crush, 1979). Accordingly, under the banner of promoting economic development an openly solicitous attitude was adopted towards the MNC. The 'open-door' policies of these countries in relation to foreign investment found concrete expression in the national development plans. The Second National Development Plan for Lesotho states:

> We look to private enterprise for initiative, technical know-how, industrial training and commitment to the national development effort. We repeat once more that foreign investment is very welcome (Lesotho, 1975, p. xvii).

In essence, the post-independence development strategies of Botswana, Lesotho and Swaziland have centred around the arranging of package deals with foreign entrepreneurs and companies. All three countries guarantee foreign investors against expropriation, permit unfettered profit repatriation, afford assistance through local development banks and corporations, and often grant certain monopoly rights and tax incentives (Winai-Ström, 1975; Gurr, 1977; Baffoe, 1978).

Investment by MNCs in Botswana, Lesotho and Swaziland was encouraged in primary resource development, but more particularly in the sphere of manufacturing activity. Industrialisation is being pursued by all three countries as one panacea to the problem of accelerating locally available productive employment opportunities as alternatives to migrant labour in South Africa. For example, Prime Minister Leabua Jonathan declared that Lesotho's 'salvation lies in developing labour intensive industries vigorously' (Jonathan, 1977, p. 6). The major advantages offered by these peripheral economies for manufacturing activity are those of duty-free access to the South African market through membership of a Common Customs Union (Ettinger, 1973; Baffoe, 1978; Mosley, 1978) and to the EEC markets through accession to the Lomé Convention. In addition, the growing international sentiments and pressures against MNC investment in apartheid South Africa offer further opportunities for the industrial promotion of these countries. Typically, the Manager of Lesotho National Development Corporation writes:

> In the face of growing political pressure on transnational corporations to eliminate expansion within the Republic of South Africa, Lesotho offers a solution to TNCs who want to expand and still maintain their market position in South Africa. Relocation in Lesotho overcomes problems like job restriction and eliminates tireless hassles at shareholders' meetings about increasing investments in South Africa (Gurr, 1977, p. 257).

To support materially this drive for industrial progress and to attract MNCs in the face of strong South African competition, the three countries offer an extensive package of tax inducements (Matsebula, 1979). Moreover, these countries also advertise their attraction of cheap and disciplined labour and wage levels comparable even to the low levels pertaining in South Africa (Gurr, 1977; Winter, 1978). Notwithstanding that the governments of Botswana, Lesotho and Swaziland are committed to reducing their dependency relationships with South Africa, at the same time all three countries warmly welcome and even court the South-African-based MNC.

Namibia: the Political Economy of Theft

The territory of Namibia is not a formal colony of South Africa in the sense that Botswana, Lesotho and Swaziland were British colonial possessions. None the less, Namibia has effectively constituted a South African colony since 1919, when the territory was mandated to South Africa by the League of Nations. During the succeeding six decades Namibia evolved economically and politically as a dependency of South Africa. The unique colonial history of Namibia is aptly captured by Green (1979, 1980) as that of 'the political economy of theft' — theft of land, labour, resources and residence rights.

Under South African control Namibia initially experienced a period of economic stagnation (Innes, 1978). Beginning in 1948, however, the colony increasingly became the focus of South African capitalist exploitation as the essential structures of the apartheid system were transferred to Namibia. The post-war transition from stagnation to capitalist penetration centred upon an intensified Namibian dependence upon South Africa and of the establishment of conditions for the increased exploitation of labour (Innes, 1978, 1980). There emerged a form of economic growth in Namibia well suited to South African interests, but one which inevitably engendered mounting opposition from exploited classes. Ultimately this opposition crystallised in the formation of the South-West African Peoples' Organization (SWAPO) which launched an anti-colonial struggle in the territory (Cronje and Cronje, 1979). The South African state's response to this threat was twofold: the repression of SWAPO's activities and initiation of a programme to further catalyse economic growth in Namibia within the existing economic and political structures (Innes, 1978). Against the opposition of South Africa the mandate of the territory was revoked in 1966. In the context of both an increasing internal and international opposition to South African occupation of Namibia, the state deliberately sought to involve North-American and Western-European-based MNCs in Namibia in an effort to create greater geopolitical support for continuing South African rule (Green, 1979). The attractions of Namibia for the MNC were almost exclusively raw material riches rather than, as was the situation in Botswana, Lesotho and Swaziland, a potential for manufacturing.

Throughout the 1970s the political struggle for the territory intensified. SWAPO became transformed into an anti-imperialist movement committed to the goals of national liberation in Namibia (Kiljunen, 1980), whereas South Africa has sought to ensure the success of a neo-colonial transition in the territory. The nature of Namibia's post-independence development path is vital for MNCs (Green, 1979). A path of national liberation would offer only limited possibilities for continuing the present levels of exploitation of Namibian labour and resources. By contrast, a neo-colonial transition would add Namibia to that list of Southern African nations committed to welcoming (and possibly even competing for) MNC investments.

Multinational Corporations in Southern Africa

The penetration and international location choices of MNCs in Southern Africa are best presented through a descriptive historical survey. Two broad periods of MNC involvement in the sub-continent are distinguished. The first phase, which extends until 1945, witnesses the initial establishment of MNCs in Southern Africa. The second phase of MNC penetration is the story of the major expansion and involvement of MNCs within South Africa's 'military-industrial complex' (Seidman and Makgetla, 1978) and of the growing interest and participation of MNCs — including South-African-based corporations — in primary resource developments and nascent industrialisation in Botswana, Lesotho and Swaziland. For Namibia the period is one characterised by the steady expansion of MNC operations in mineral developments in the politically disputed territory.

Early Penetration

Historically, the primary focus for overseas capital in Southern Africa was the vast mineral wealth — specifically gold and diamonds — of South Africa. But the bulk of this investment, which overwhelmingly derived from the United Kingdom, took the form of share purchases in South Africa's several large mining finance houses (see Seidman and Seidman, 1977; Lanning and Mueller, 1979). The vanguard of the modern MNC began to establish in South Africa to supply the local markets for manufactured goods which were generated directly by mining and indirectly through expanding consumer markets. As early as the beginning years of this century 'a few foreign-owned companies were establishing plants locally to supply the market' (Innes, 1980, p. 351). Typical of these initial foreign ventures was the expansion of Lever Brothers (a part of the Unilever Group) in South Africa, the genesis and growth of which is well documented in a recent study (Fieldhouse, 1978). Foreign manufacturing investment in South Africa continued to expand, albeit slowly, in the period between 1900 and 1930. After 1933, however, there began a surge of new MNCs establishing industrial facilities in South Africa coinciding with the state's renewed efforts to stimulate national industrialisation. Included amongst this new tide of MNCs seeking access to the South African market were the earliest American and West European concerns such as Nestlé, Ford, Siemens, General Motors, Davy Ashmore, Firestone and General Electric (Legassick, 1974). In addition, at this time, other foreign enterprises already operating in South Africa, like ICI and Lever Brothers, experienced a period of considerable growth (see Fieldhouse, 1978; Innes, 1980). Yet, by 1939, despite this new influx of MNCs into manufacturing, the volume of overseas capital invested indirectly in South African mining exceeded severalfold the total foreign investment in manufacturing (First, Steele and Gurney, 1972).

Throughout the period until the Second World War MNCs evinced little interest in any involvement in Botswana, Lesotho or Swaziland. Reflecting an assumption that these territories eventually would be incorporated into South Africa, the colonising power – the United Kingdom – made almost no effort to develop these areas (see Fair, Murdoch and Jones, 1969; Winai-Ström, 1978; Colclough and McCarthy, 1980). Equally, the transference of Namibia from German to (*de facto*) South African colonial rule saw no new developments taking place before 1945. Indeed, after gaining monopoly control over Namibia's rich diamond resources in 1920, the South-African-based Anglo-American Group, for short periods, halted production at these labour-intensive mines in order to increase the world diamond price (Innes, 1978, 1980).

Extension and Geographical Spread

In the post-Second World War period Southern Africa has been the theatre of a deepening penetration and extension in terms of the operation of MNCs in South Africa. In addition, there has occurred a geographical spread of MNCs within the region, attracted initially by the possibilities of resource extraction and more recently by the industrial potential of the peripheral states of Southern Africa.

MNCs and South Africa's Post-war Development. The richness of South Africa's mineral resources continued to attract considerable foreign investment in the post-war period. Much of this investment now came in the form of direct participation in the ownership and opening of new mines in the Republic. Prominent amongst the leading investors are several British and North American-based MNCs, including Lonrho, Rio Tinto Zinc, Phelps Dodge, American Metals Climax and Newmont Mining (Lanning and Mueller, 1979; Lanning, 1979). None the less the archetypal form of overseas investment in South Africa since the

Second World War 'has been direct investment in manufacturing industry by the major British, American and, to a lesser extent, Western European corporations' (First, Steele and Gurney, 1972, p. 126). Through involvement in local production, the provision of technology, know-how and finance, MNCs assumed a key role in building up and maintaining what Seidman and Makgetla (1978) style as 'South Africa's military-industrial complex' (see Figure 10.2). As Legassick argues:

For South Africa the advantages have been not so much quantitative as qualitative. If there is debate on the precise significance of foreign capital in South Africa for rate of economic growth or balance of payments, its contribution to industrial sophistication is undoubted. South African industrialization has depended on employment of more and more capital-intensive and 'modern' methods in a succession of industrial sectors. And in each case, it would appear, it has been foreign capital which has financed the purchasing of the requisite machinery, and it has been foreign firms which have imported the expertise to initiate the handling of such machines (Legassick, 1977, p. 189).

In the course of expanding the strategically important sectors of local industry a milestone in the history of foreign investment was passed in the mid-1960s when direct investment in manufacturing finally surpassed even that of portfolio investment in South African mining (First, Steele and Gurney, 1972).

The post-war wave of new investment was spearheaded by United Kingdom engineering firms during the 1940s and 1950s. Also, at this time, several British firms went into partnership with the South African state in the establishment of a modern textiles industry. Further significant areas of United Kingdom involvement occurred in South African chemicals, food processing and canning. Although it remains that 'no country is tied to South Africa by closer economic links than Britain' (First, Steele and Gurney, 1972, p. 23), since 1960 the proportional share of the United Kingdom in total MNC investments in South Africa progressively has fallen. United States and West-European-based MNCs in particular expanded their manufacturing commitments in South Africa in the 1960s and 1970s (Seidman and Makgetla, 1978). No longer was Africa seen as an internationally 'remote location' (Vernon, 1971, p. 68) as United States and EEC enterprises collaborated closely with the South African state in initiating new ventures

Figure 10.2: Multinational Corporations in South Africa's Military-industrial Complex

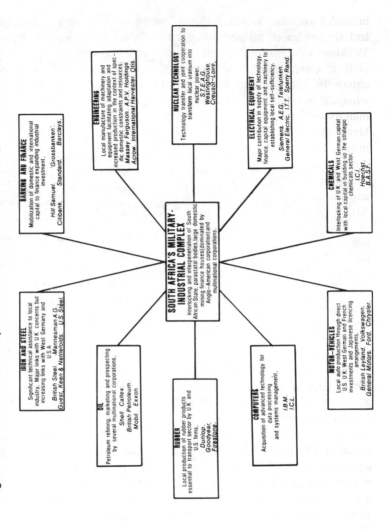

SOUTH AFRICA'S MILITARY-INDUSTRIAL COMPLEX
Interlocking and interpenetration of South African State, parastatal bodies, large domestic mining finance houses (dominated by Anglo-American corporation) and multinational corporations.

BANKING AND FINANCE
Mobilization of domestic and international capital to finance expanding industrial investment.
Hill Samuel. 'Grossbanken'. Citibank. Standard. Barclays.

ENGINEERING
Local manufacture of machinery and equipment facilitating adaptation and increased production in the context of specific domestic constraints and resources.
Massey Ferguson. A.P.V. Holdings. Acrow. International Harvester. Otis.

NUCLEAR TECHNOLOGY
Technology transfer and joint cooperation to transform local uranium into nuclear power.
S.T.E.A.G. Westinghouse. Creusot-Loire.

ELECTRICAL EQUIPMENT
Major contribution in supply of technology, finance, capital equipment and machinery to establishing local self-sufficiency.
Siemens. A.E.G. Telefunken. General Electric. I.T.T. Sperry Rand.

CHEMICALS
Interlocking of U.K. and West German capital with local capital in building up the strategic chemicals sector.
I.C.I. Hoechst. B.A.S.F.

IRON AND STEEL
Significant technical assistance to local industry. Major links with U.K. concerns but increasing links with West Germany and U.S.A.
British Steel. Mannesman A.G. Guest, Keen & Nettlefolds. U.S. Steel.

OIL
Petroleum refining, marketing and prospecting by several multinational corporations.
Shell. Caltex. British Petroleum. Mobil. Exxon.

RUBBER
Local production of rubber products essential to transport sector by U.K. and U.S. firms.
Dunlop. Goodyear. Firestone.

COMPUTERS
Acquisition of advanced technology for data processing and systems management.
I.B.M. I.C.L.

MOTOR-VEHICLES
Local auto production through direct U.S. U.K. West German and French investments and Japanese licencing arrangements.
British Leyland. Volkswagen. General Motors. Ford. Chrysler.

in motor vehicles, auto accessories, oil refining, chemicals, computers and electronics (Seidman and Seidman, 1977; Seidman and Makgetla, 1978).

It is clear that South Africa is the prime international location choice for MNC operations both in Southern Africa and Africa as a whole. It is estimated that almost three-quarters of all United Kingdom manufacturing investments in Africa are in the Republic (Seidman and Makgetla, 1978), and for the key sector of machinery manufacture the proportion rises to over 90 per cent. Likewise, four out of every five US dollars invested in African manufacturing are in South Africa and in the manufacture of machinery the share reaches 96.8 per cent (Seidman and Makgetla, 1978). In sharp contrast to the situation in the rest of Africa, where MNCs have invested only in last-stage assembly and processing, in South Africa MNCs have helped to build an 'integrated industrial complex characterised by an increasing degree of technological self-sufficiency' (Seidman, 1977, p. 413). Moreover, as Seidman maintains, 'Foreign investment and technology have played a primary role in building up the South African military-industrial complex as the most significant regional sub-center at the expense of the neighbouring underdeveloped political economies and peoples in the entire Southern African peripheral region' (Seidman, 1977, p. 412). Despite the competitive endeavours of other African nations, not least those of Botswana, Lesotho and Swaziland, to attract foreign capital South Africa appears to have offered MNCs the internationally most 'hospitable investment climate'. The locational attractions of South Africa for manufacturing MNCs have been several; a high rate of return on investment above world averages, a well established infrastructure, a cheap and largely disciplined labour force, extensive tax benefits and, above all, an expanding market (Seidman and Makgetla, 1978). Indeed, notwithstanding the inducements of South Africa's cheap 'labour-coerced economy' (Legassick, 1977), most MNCs have been set up so as to capture the local rather than an export market (Kaplan, 1979). The world market industry (Fröbel, Heinrichs and Kreye, 1977; Wheelwright, 1980), using South Africa's cheap labour to establish an international export platform, presently is the exceptional case.

MNCs and the Southern African Periphery. The large-scale penetration of the Southern African periphery by MNCs is a post- Second World War phenomenon. The initial spread of MNCs into Botswana, Lesotho and Swaziland occurred against a backdrop of the colonial power's belated acknowledgement of a responsibility towards the economic advancement of these areas. In Namibia penetration was closely associated with the extension of the structures of apartheid to the territory, creating conditions 'for the enhanced exploitation of labour' (Innes, 1978, p. 51).

The global search for new sources of low-cost raw materials drew MNCs into the Southern African periphery. In sharp contrast to the characteristic patterns of investment in South African industry, the bulk of MNC activity in the four peripheral states of the sub-continent takes place in primary resources (Figure 10.3). Not surprisingly, a survey of the motivations of MNC investors in Swaziland concluded that the major foreign companies came to the country to exploit local natural resources (on the whole) for sale to the highly industrialised countries (Fransman, 1977). Only in a minority of cases did foreign firms produce for the domestic market (Fransman, 1977). Although an asbestos mine was the first major MNC involvement in Swaziland (Fair, Murdoch and Jones, 1969), the country is somewhat unique within Southern Africa. The primary focus of MNC involvement in Swaziland is that of agribusiness, specifically the production of sugar, pineapples and forest products (Crush, 1977; Fransman, 1977; Crush, 1979). In the rest of the sub-continent mineral resources are the magnet for MNCs: copper, nickel and diamonds in Botswana (Lewis, 1975; Cooper, 1976-7; Lanning and Mueller, 1979); diamonds in Lesotho (Winai-Ström, 1975; Ngwenya, 1977; Winai-Ström, 1978); and copper, lead, silver, zinc, diamonds and (most recently) uranium in Namibia (Innes, 1978; Thomas, 1978; Green, 1979, 1980). It is striking that MNCs continued to invest in Namibian mining even after the revocation of South Africa's mandate in the Territory and a 1971 World Court ruling which declared that all new developments constitute mines with no lawful mineral rights and are − quite literally − grand larceny (Green, 1980, p. 73; see also Commonwealth Secretariat, 1978). Finally, one further recent area of MNC-dominated 'resource' development in Botswana, Lesotho and Swaziland is that of tourism. Both the Holiday Inn and Hilton chains are engaged in notable hotel/casino developments in these countries, seeking to capitalise on the severity of South Africa's gambling legislation and racial restrictions (Winai-Ström, 1975; Crush, 1977; Ngwenya, 1977).

In all countries of the Southern African periphery there occurs a close interpenetration of European, North American and South African capital straddling the 'commanding heights' of these economies (Johns, 1973; Winai-Ström, 1978; Winter, 1978; Crush, 1979; Green, 1979, 1980). As Arrighi and Saul (1973) aver, 'the penetration of the Southern

Figure 10.3: Major Resource Developments in Southern Africa by Multinational Corporations

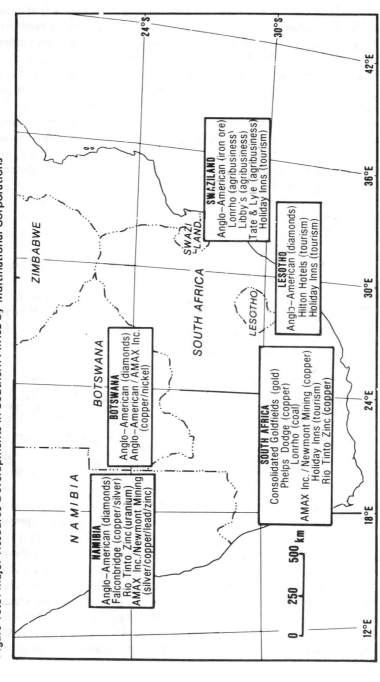

NAMIBIA
Anglo–American (diamonds)
Falconbridge (copper/silver)
Rio Tinto Zinc (uranium)
AMAX Inc./Newmont Mining
(silver/copper/lead/zinc)

BOTSWANA
Anglo–American (diamonds)
Anglo–American AMAX Inc.
(copper/nickel)

SOUTH AFRICA
Consolidated Goldfields (gold)
Phelps Dodge (copper)
Lonrho (coal)
AMAX Inc./ Newmont Mining (copper)
Holiday Inns (tourism)
Rio Tinto Zinc (copper)

SWAZILAND
Anglo–American (iron ore)
Lonrho (agribusiness)
Libby's (agribusiness)
Tate & Lye (agribusiness)
Holiday Inns (tourism)

LESOTHO
Anglo–American (diamonds)
Hilton Hotels (tourism)
Holiday Inns (tourism)

NAMIBIA

ZIMBABWE

BOTSWANA

SOUTH AFRICA

SWAZI-
LAND

LESOTHO

LESOTHO

0   250   500 km

12°E   18°E   24°E   30°E   36°E   42°E

24°S

30°S

African complex on the part of European and American corporations has been matched by the outward expansion of South African corporations and a growing interconnection between the two.' Productive activity in Namibia is, for example, dominated by the 'gang of five', which comprises four MNCs — originating variously from South Africa, Canada, United Kingdom and United States — and the South African state (Green, 1979, 1980). Indeed, of increasing significance in the context of these peripheral economies is the emergence of South Africa as the national base for several geographically expansive corporations.

Figure 10.4: The Organisation of the Anglo-American Group in Central and Southern Africa

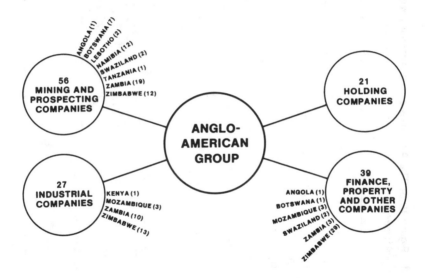

Outstandingly, the most important of these is the Anglo-American Group which is involved in many of the key resource developments presently occurring throughout the sub-continent (see Figure 10.3). The Anglo-American Corporation represents a classic case of a diversified conglomerate. It is engaged in a wide range of economic activities not only in Central and Southern Africa, but reaching out also across much of the capitalist world from its power base in the South African economy (Innes, 1980). The widespread nature of the Group in Southern Africa is revealed in Figures 10.4 and 10.5. In 1976 Anglo-American controlled at least 140 different companies in Southern

Figure 10.5: The Activities of the Anglo-American Group in Central and Southern Africa

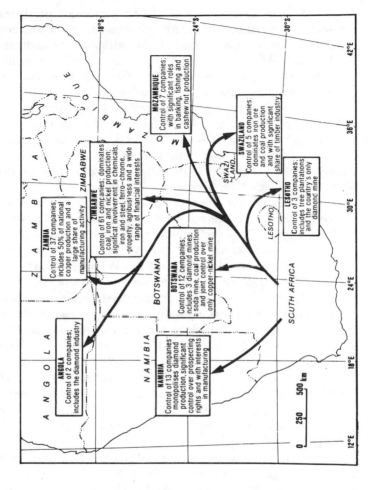

ANGOLA
Control of 2 companies; includes the diamond industry

ZAMBIA
Control of 37 companies; includes 50% of national copper production and a large share of manufacturing activity

ZIMBABWE
Control of 61 companies; dominates coal, iron and nickel production; significant involvement in chemicals, iron and steel, ferro-chrome, property, agribusiness and a wide range of financial interests

MOZAMBIQUE
Control of 7 companies; with significant roles in banking, fishing and cashew nut production

SWAZILAND
Control of 5 companies; dominates iron ore and coal production and with significant share of timber industry

LESOTHO
Control of 3 companies; includes tree plantations and the country's only diamond mine

BOTSWANA
Control of 12 companies; includes 3 diamond mines, a soda mine, coal production and joint control over only copper-nickel mine

NAMIBIA
Control of 13 companies; monopolises diamond production; significant control over prospecting rights and with interests in manufacturing

0   250   500 km

Africa and surrounding states, included amongst which was the control over sectors of strategic importance to the generation of wealth in the countries concerned (see Figure 10.5). Although the roots of this South African MNC are located in mining, which still remains its most important activity, the operations of the modern Anglo-American Group encompass industry in Zimbabwe, Zambia, Namibia and Swaziland, finance and property throughout the sub-continent, timber plantations in Lesotho and Swaziland and even fish processing and karakul pelt production in Namibia (Figure 10.5; Innes, 1980). With these, and many other, interests added to its key position in mining throughout the sub-continent, the Anglo-American Corporation is by far the leading single MNC operating in the region.

In parallel with the experiences of foreign penetration in raw materials extraction in the rest of Africa (Seidman, 1970; Widstrand, 1975; Seidman, 1977; Lanning and Mueller, 1979), MNCs engaged in resource developments in Southern Africa have contributed only marginally (South Africa excepted) to industrialisation or, more generally, to large-scale employment creation in these countries. The pattern is typically one of 'export enclave development' with associated manufacturing, if present at all, confined to simple raw material processing. No substantive backward or forward linkages are present within the host peripheral economies of Southern Africa. A study, for example, of the multiplier impact of MNCs in Swaziland concluded that local linkages were minimal (Fransman, 1977). And in Botswana the output of the key copper-nickel mine is shipped out of the country for further processing (Lewis, 1975; Cooper, 1976-7), a pattern replicated in mineral developments elsewhere in the region (Crush, 1977; Green, 1979, 1980).

The post-independence efforts of Botswana, Lesotho and Swaziland to attract foreign investors, by offering a range of incentives to industrialists for the establishment of export platforms, have enjoyed only limited success (Rogerson, 1981a). The reluctance of most MNCs to invest in manufacturing facilities outside South Africa is partly explained in terms of economic factors (Selwyn, 1975), but is also inseparable from the institutional context of industrialisation in the sub-continent. Several MNCs already operating in the Republic are under political pressure or sometimes explicit obligations to confine their expansions to South Africa (Mosley, 1978). Equally significant in constraining industrial development in these peripheral economies is the intervention of the South African state, on several occasions, to subvert incipient industrial ventures in surrounding countries which might threaten existing vested interests in the Republic (Rogerson, 1981a). Opposition from Pretoria, for example, prevented Honda from initiating a motor assembly plant in Lesotho in 1971 and, more recently, thwarted proposals for the establishment of television assembly operations in both Swaziland and Lesotho (Rogerson, 1978). The 'beggar-thy-neighbour' international competition engaged in by Botswana, Lesotho and Swaziland to attract mobile industry is made more invidious by the incentive programmes offered by the South African government in order to attract manufacturers to decentralised areas or Homelands locations. As a consequence of these several factors, the tax incentives offered by the governments of Botswana, Lesotho and Swaziland have done little to affect MNC location decisions (Matsebula, 1979). Of greater importance in accounting for the modest flow of industrialists establishing in these countries has been the new export possibilities offered by membership of the Lomé Convention. Current evidence, however, suggests that it is predominantly South-African-based corporations which are locating in these countries in order to open new export markets in the European Economic Community.

The Geography of Multinational Corporations in South Africa

The axis of discussion is shifted now away from the international to the intra-national scale of analysis. In the previous section attention was centred on the international patterns, geographical and sectoral, of MNC investments between the countries of Southern Africa. The bulk of such investments, it was emphasised, have occurred in manufacturing industry in South Africa. The focus is narrowed here to examine the specific location patterns of manufacturing MNCs within the Republic. The following investigation of the geography of MNCs in South Africa, to a large extent, parallels other studies of the intra-national location patterns of foreign enterprises (e.g. de Smidt, 1966; Blackbourn, 1972; Dicken and Lloyd, 1976; Watts, 1980a, 1980b). But whereas in Europe and North America this topic has generated a substantial corpus of empirical work, in Africa research into the geography of MNCs is as yet in its infancy. For South Africa, in particular, there exist only two previous studies which have dealt with the spatial dimensions of foreign investment (Rogerson, 1974, 1981b).

Data Base

Despite a voluminous literature discussing the operations of MNCs in apartheid South Africa, there is remarkably little concrete statistical information concerning the degree of foreign penetration, the specific industrial structure, its organisation or spatial patterns. In large measure, the dearth of reliable statistics reflects the veil of secrecy which shrouds the activities of MNCs in South Africa. The official Census of Foreign Investment, for example, incorporates data for Namibia with that for the Republic, a practice which is repeated also in data made available by the leading investor nations. Moreover, the Census provides no clear indication of the national source of investment other than by broad (and not particularly helpful) classifications of EEC, North and South America, Rest of Europe, Africa and Oceania. It is striking also that the South African Reserve Bank discontinued its statistical series on the national origins of capital inflows in order, as the *Financial Mail* commented, 'to avoid possible political embarrassment' (*Financial Mail*, 15 April 1976).

In the absence of official data the present analysis is based on a data bank specially compiled to allow exploration of the extent, industrial type and spatial distribution of MNCs in South Africa. The first stage in the preparation of this data base necessitated the compilation of a list of foreign-controlled enterprises. The preparation of such a list was facilitated by information and listings made available variously by the commercial or trade sections of embassies, the South African Institute of Race Relations and several anti-apartheid organisations, the most useful being those published through the offices of the United Nations Centre Against Apartheid (Seidman and Makgetla, 1978). Nevertheless the most valuable source of information detailing names of foreign-controlled enterprises in South Africa is the series of *Who Owns Whom* publications of Dun and Bradstreet (1978/9). Examination of various international editions of *Who Owns Whom* permitted the extraction of the names of enterprises in South Africa which are either subsidiaries or associates of MNCs. The cross-checking of these several sources of information allowed the compilation of a comprehensive list of what are considered here as 'foreign-controlled' enterprises. The second stage in the preparation of the data bank demanded the further cross-checking of this listing with information contained in the Bureau of Market Research's Industrial Register of South Africa. The unpublished Register provides information for 1978 on the location of all industrial establishments in South Africa, their size as measured by an index of employment and industrial classification by SIC grouping. The data bank used in this study thus includes the national origin, size, location and industrial classification of all foreign-controlled enterprises in South Africa. The data are analysed in terms, first, of the structural characteristics and, second, of the spatial patterns of foreign-controlled enterprises in South Africa.

Structural Characteristics of Foreign-controlled Enterprises

In total, the study disclosed 930 foreign-controlled enterprises with manufacturing facilities in South Africa. Together these enterprises operate 1,284 plants which employ nearly 400,000 workers. Relative to the most recent national industrial census (South Africa, 1978), this finding suggests that at least one in four of all industrial jobs in the Republic is in a foreign-controlled enterprise. The actual degree of foreign penetration in manufacturing is estimated as 28 per cent, a figure which on international comparisons would place South Africa behind Canada (57 per cent) and Australia (36 per cent) and on a par with New Zealand (30 per cent) in terms of the extent of foreign control (Wheelwright, 1980). Table 10.1 records the leading investor nations in South Africa as indexed by numbers of enterprises, plants and employees. The United Kingdom and United States clearly emerge as the first and second sources of MNC investment. Indeed, as a proportion of all foreign-controlled manufacturing the United Kingdom and United States together account for 83 per cent of all enterprises and plants and 81 per cent of employment. West Germany is the third most important investor nation, accounting for approximately 7 per cent of enterprises, plants and employment. The organisational fabric of foreign enterprises is presented in Table 10.2. Almost 80 per cent of the 930 enterprises are single-plant operations. But amongst the remaining 20 per cent of multiplant enterprises are numbered some of the largest and most well known foreign-controlled concerns in South Africa. These include, for example, African Explosives and Chemical Industries, Cadbury-Schweppes, Dunlop, Firestone, Unilever, Siemens and Nestlé. The last-mentioned two enterprises are amongst that select group of MNCs operating more than six plants in South Africa.

The average-sized foreign-controlled enterprise in South Africa employs 405 persons. Between enterprises of different national origins there occur only minor differences (cf. Watts, 1980a, 1980b); respectively, the mean sizes of enterprises for the United Kingdom, United States and West Germany are 381, 420 and 387 employees. The mean plant size is 294 employees, three times larger than the average-sized

South African plant which employs 88 workers. Again, United States plants (average 315 employees) are slightly larger than those under United Kingdom (average 274 employees) or West German (average 288 employees) control. Irrespective of national origin, these findings illustrate that, measured by employment, foreign-controlled enterprises and plants are substantially larger than those under indigenous control.

Table 10.1: Foreign-controlled Enterprises in South Africa, by Country of Origin, 1978

	Enterprises		Plants		Employment	
	No.	Per Cent	No.	Per Cent	No.	Per Cent
United Kingdom	551	59.2	767	59.7	210,186	55.7
United States	228	24.5	304	23.7	95,818	25.4
West Germany	67	7.2	90	7.0	25,932	6.9
Switzerland	21	2.3	36	2.8	9,583	2.5
France	18	1.9	24	1.9	7,575	2.0
Netherlands	15	1.6	21	1.6	10,409	2.8
Others	30	3.2	42	3.3	17,596	4.7
Total — All foreign	930	100.0	1,284	100.0	377,099	100.0

Source: Author's data bank.

These statistics of averages, however, conceal considerable variations in the spectrum of size distributions of both foreign-controlled enterprises and plants. The data presented in Table 10.3 reveal that the smallest foreign enterprises, those employing less than 250 workers, account for 59 per cent of all enterprises but provide only 12 per cent of total employment. Medium-sized enterprises, in the range 250-999 employees, contain one-third of enterprises and 36 per cent of employment. The greatest proportion of foreign-controlled employment occurs in the top 9 per cent, or largest enterprises, those employing over 1,000 workers. Collectively the large enterprises, the majority of which are multiplant, account for over half of all foreign-controlled employment. The size distribution of plants is presented in Table 10.4. The numerically dominant small plants (less than 250 workers) constitute 63 per cent of all plants but record only 16 per cent of employment. Most employment falls in plants in the medium-size range (between 250 and 999 employees) which account for 31 per cent of plants and 47 per cent of employment. Only just over 5 per cent of foreign plants engage more than 1,000 workers but these still account for 36 per cent of employment. Tables 10.3 and 10.4 record a remarkable degree of

Table 10.2: The Organisation of Foreign-controlled Enterprises in South Africa, 1978

Country of Origin	Organisation of Enterprise												
	1 Plant		2 Plants		3 Plants		4 Plants		5 Plants		6 Plants		>6 Plants	
	No.	Per Cent	No.	Per Cent	No.	Per Cent	No.	Per Cent	No.	Per Cent	No.	Per Cent	No.	Per Cent
United Kingdom	438	79.5	65	12.0	24	4.3	12	2.2	5	0.9	2	0.3	5	0.9
United States	179	78.5	32	14.0	9	3.9	6	2.6	2	0.9	–	–	–	–
West Germany	58	86.6	4	6.0	1	1.5	1	1.5	2	3.0	–	–	1	1.5
Others	66	78.6	11	13.1	3	3.6	2	2.4	–	–	1	1.2	1	1.2
Totals	741	79.7	112	12.0	37	4.0	21	2.3	9	1.0	3	0.3	7	0.7

Source: Author's data bank.

Table 10.3: The Size Distribution of Foreign-controlled Enterprises in South Africa, 1978

Size Categories

Country of Origin	<50 Plants	<50 Empl.	50-99 Plants	50-99 Empl.	100-249 Plants	100-249 Empl.	250-499 Plants	250-499 Empl.	500-999 Plants	500-999 Empl.	1,000-2,499 Plants	1,000-2,499 Empl.	2,500-4,999 Plants	2,500-4,999 Empl.	5,000+ Plants	5,000+ Empl.
United Kingdom	137	3,842	83	6,412	106	15,162	116	39,216	63	43,785	34	54,039	9	27,550	3	20,180
Per cent	24.9	1.8	15.1	3.1	19.2	7.2	21.1	18.7	11.4	20.8	6.2	25.7	1.6	13.1	0.5	9.6
United States	50	1,289	25	1,792	59	8,673	53	18,129	20	13,380	13	22,034	6	19,121	2	11,400
Per cent	22.0	1.3	11.0	1.9	25.9	9.1	23.2	18.9	8.8	13.9	5.7	23.0	2.6	20.0	0.9	11.9
West Germany	18	411	16	1,224	16	3,083	5	1,800	5	3,679	5	7,305	1	3,430	1	5,000
Per cent	26.9	1.6	23.9	4.7	23.9	11.9	7.5	6.9	7.5	14.2	7.5	28.2	1.5	13.2	1.5	19.3
Others	14	440	13	960	9	1,488	20	6,425	15	9,745	12	23,580	1	2,525	—	—
Per cent	16.7	1.0	15.5	2.1	10.7	3.3	23.8	14.2	17.9	21.6	14.3	52.2	1.2	5.6	—	—
Total	219	5,982	137	10,388	190	28,406	194	65,570	103	70,589	64	106,958	17	52,626	6	36,580
Per cent	23.5	1.6	14.7	2.8	20.4	7.5	20.9	17.4	11.1	18.7	6.9	28.4	1.8	14.0	0.6	9.7

Source: Author's data bank.

Table 10.4: The Size Distribution of Foreign-controlled Plants in South Africa, 1978

Country of Origin	Size Categories													
	< 50		50 - 99		100 - 249		250 - 499		500 - 999		1,000 - 2,499		2,500 +	
	Plants	Empl.	Plants	Empl.	Plants	Empl.	Plants	Empl.	Plants	Empl.	Plants	Empl.	Plants	Empl.
United Kingdom	201	4,986	138	10,100	142	20,400	175	56,950	79	55,550	29	50,200	3	12,000
Per cent	26.2	2.4	18.0	4.8	18.5	9.7	22.8	27.1	10.3	26.4	3.8	23.9	0.4	5.7
United States	81	2,261	46	3,379	68	9,592	66	22,538	24	16,812	15	25,220	4	16,016
Per cent	26.6	2.4	15.1	3.5	22.4	10.0	21.7	23.5	7.9	17.6	4.9	26.3	1.3	16.7
West Germany	28	607	23	1,680	20	3,625	7	2,750	7	5,270	4	7,000	1	5,000
Per cent	31.1	2.3	25.6	6.5	22.2	14.0	7.8	10.6	7.8	20.3	4.4	27.0	1.1	19.2
Others	22	578	21	1,535	20	3,100	35	11,200	13	7,750	12	21,000	–	–
Per cent	17.9	1.3	17.1	3.4	16.3	6.9	28.5	24.8	10.6	17.2	9.8	46.5	–	–
Total	332	8,432	228	16,694	250	36,717	283	93,438	123	85,382	60	103,420	8	33,016
Per cent	25.9	2.2	17.8	4.4	19.5	9.7	22.0	24.8	9.6	22.8	4.7	27.4	0.6	8.8

Source: Author's data bank.

consistency in the size distributions of plants and enterprises of differing national origin; in particular the patterns of small-, medium- and large-sized United Kingdom and United States enterprises and plants are very similar. The most distinct category is the 'Others' group — dominated by Dutch-, French- and Swiss-controlled enterprises (see Table 10.1) — in which there is a higher proportion of both plants and enterprises in the medium- and large-size groupings.

The industrial composition of foreign investment, as shown in Table 10.5, reveals a notably uneven pattern of sectoral participation. Foreign-controlled enterprises are predominantly concentrated in the fabricated metals, machinery and equipment group, which accounts for nearly 170,000 jobs or approximately 45 per cent of all employment. This is followed respectively by the sectors of chemicals, rubber and plastics (18.6 per cent), food, beverages and tobacco (11.3 per cent) and textiles, clothing and leather (8.8 per cent). Relative to the overall patterns of indigenous South-African-controlled enterprises (Rogerson, 1981c) foreign enterprises are over-represented in only two industry groups: the strategically significant areas of fabricated metals, machinery and equipment and chemicals, rubber and plastics. In all other industrial groupings there is a relative 'under-representation' of MNC investment.

Some striking differences emerge from Table 10.5 in the patterns of investment originating in particular countries. Although the fabricated metals, machinery and equipment group is the leading focus of investment for all countries, the proportion of West German investment in this sector is 68 per cent, marking a strong concentration in this particular sector. In addition, relative to the total pattern of foreign investment, United Kingdom enterprises are concentrated in chemicals, food and base metals, United States enterprises in chemicals, fabricated metals, paper and non-metallic minerals,West German enterprises in textiles and clothing; and the Others category in textiles, clothing and wood products. The finding that enterprises of particular foreign countries tend to specialise in characteristic industrial groups in South Africa mirrors the results of similar studies in Europe and North America (see Watts, 1980a, 1980b).

In terms of their structural characteristics, therefore, it is apparent that foreign-controlled enterprises in South Africa exhibit a number of recognisable features. Foreign enterprises are significantly larger than indigenous concerns, many of them are multiplant in their organisation, and the largest of these enterprises account for the greatest share of all employment. In addition, foreign enterprises show a marked concentra-

Table 10.5: The Industrial Composition of Foreign-controlled Employment in South Africa, 1978

SIC Group	United Kingdom			United States			Nationality West Germany			Others			All Foreign	
	Plants	Empl.	Per cent	Plants	Empl.	Per cent	Plants	Empl.	Per cent	Plants	Empl.	Per cent	Plants	Empl.	Per cent
Food, beverages and tobacco	110	32,124	15.6	25	5,645	5.9	–	–	–	16	4,268	9.5	151	42,637	11.3
Textiles, clothing and leather	55	14,239	6.8	10	3,437	3.6	9	2,998	11.6	18	12,418	27.5	92	33,092	8.8
Wood and wood products	7	953	0.5	1	250	0.3	–	–	–	10	4,265	9.4	18	5,468	1.5
Paper and paper products	45	8,822	4.2	18	7,368	7.7	1	90	0.3	1	18	–	65	16,298	4.3
Chemicals, rubber and plastics	147	40,510	19.3	99	23,049	24.1	17	3,865	14.9	21	2,676	5.9	284	70,100	18.6
Non-metallic minerals	35	7,660	3.6	12	8,950	9.3	3	1,000	3.9	11	2,960	6.6	61	20,570	5.5
Basic metals	32	12,026	5.7	12	3,602	3.8	2	145	0.6	5	2,490	5.5	51	18,263	4.8
Fabricated metal, machinery and equipment	329	92,547	44.0	123	43,057	45.0	57	17,709	68.3	39	15,763	34.9	548	169,076	44.8
Other manufacturing	7	705	0.3	4	460	0.5	1	125	0.5	2	305	0.7	14	1,595	0.4
Totals	767	210,186	100.0	304	95,818	100.0	90	25,932	100.0	123	45,163	100.0	1,284	377,099	100.0

Source: Author's data bank.

tion in a narrow range of industrial activities of which the broad engineering category is the most important. Certain variations exist, however, in the patterns of industrial investment deriving from particular countries. These identifiable structural characteristics clearly will be significant influences in shaping the overall geography of foreign investment in South Africa.

The Location of Foreign Manufacturing in South Africa

The overall spatial distribution of foreign-controlled manufacturing employment is represented in Figure 10.6, which records employment data on the basis of 61 economic regions in South Africa. The greatest absolute concentration occurs in the national core area, the Pretoria-Witwatersrand-Vereeniging (P-W-V) complex. Whereas the P-W-V accounts for 44 per cent of all South African industrial employment (Rogerson, 1980), it contains over half of all foreign-controlled jobs.

Figure 10.6: The Location of Employment in Foreign-controlled Enterprises in South Africa, 1978

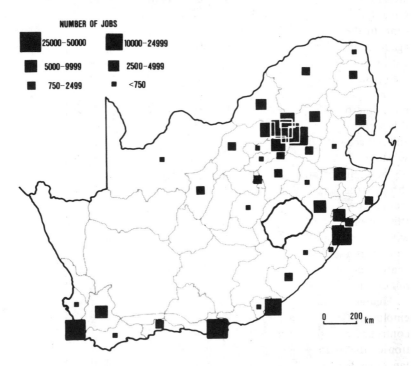

Secondary nodes of concentration emerge in the Metropolitan Cape Town, Durban and Port Elizabeth regions which share a further one-third of all employment. Together these four metropolitan areas of South Africa contain exactly 83 per cent of all foreign-controlled employment, a considerably higher proportion than their share of all South African industry. The remaining 17 per cent of foreign-controlled jobs are widely dispersed throughout South Africa, including a small number in the Homelands. Essentially the broad geographical pattern of foreign manufacturing employment reflects the particular structural characteristics of foreign enterprises as described above. This is best illustrated by a series of maps which portray the spatial distribution of employment in the four leading industrial sectors and in the three major investor nations.

Figures 10.7 to 10.10 record the geographical patterns of employment in the major industrial sectors (see Table 10.5). The distribution of employment in fabricated metals, machinery and equipment (Figure 10.7) denotes a major concentration of activity in the metropolitan areas; the P-W-V alone accounts for 57 per cent of employment, while Cape Town, Durban and Port Elizabeth together add a further 30 per cent. In the chemicals, rubber and plastics group (Figure 10.8) there is again represented a strong metropolitan focus with employment peaking in the P-W-V, which records 46 per cent of the sector's employment. But, in this particular industry group, Durban emerges as a strong secondary node of activity with 25 per cent of employment. The four major metropolitan areas in total share 88 per cent of employment in this sector. In the third most important group, namely food, beverages and tobacco (Figure 10.9), the primacy of the metropolitan loci is substantially reduced; the four major metropolitan areas account for 56 per cent of employment, the remainder being widely distributed through the rest of South Africa. Finally, in the textiles, clothing and leather group (Figure 10.10), the particular locational requirements of this sector in South Africa are reflected in a pattern of employment in which Metropolitan Durban (24 per cent) and Cape Town (23 per cent) emerge as the dominant loci, Port Elizabeth (13 per cent) is the third centre and the P-W-V (11 per cent) is relegated to only a relatively minor role in this sector.

Figures 10.11 to 10.13 represent the specific distributions of employment in United-Kingdom-, United-States- and West-German-controlled enterprises. In all cases there is manifest the primary attraction of the national core region and secondarily of the other metropolitan areas for MNC investment. The proportion of total employment

Figure 10.7: The Location of Employment in Foreign-controlled Enterprises Operating in the Fabricated Metals, Machinery and Equipment Sector in South Africa, 1978

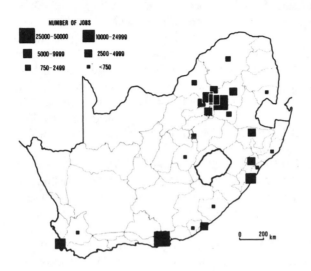

Figure 10.8: The Location of Employment in Foreign-controlled Enterprises Operating in the Chemicals, Rubber and Plastics Sector in South Africa, 1978

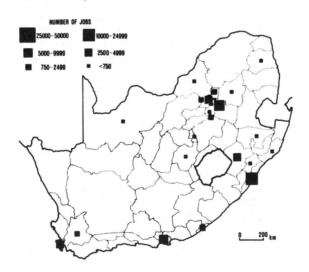

Figure 10.9: The Location of Employment in Foreign-controlled
Enterprises Operating in the Food, Beverages and Tobacco Sector in
South Africa, 1978

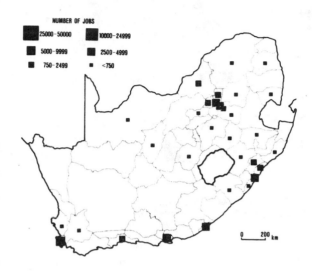

Figure 10.10: The Location of Employment in Foreign-controlled
Enterprises Operating in the Textiles, Clothing and Leather Sector in
South Africa, 1978

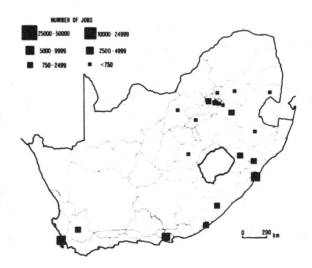

Figure 10.11: The Location of Employment in United-Kingdom-controlled Enterprises in South Africa, 1978

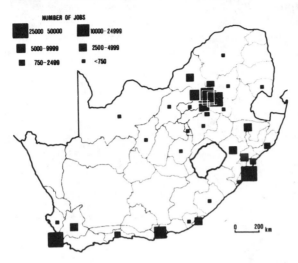

Figure 10.12: The Location of Employment in United-States-controlled Enterprises in South Africa, 1978

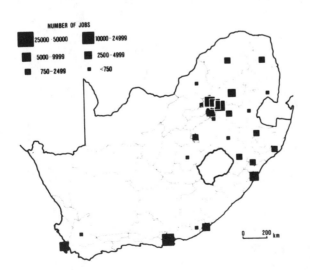

which is located in the four metropolitan areas is 85 per cent for United Kingdom, 80 per cent for United States and 83 per cent for West German enterprises. Only in terms of the distribution of employment between these metropolitan areas are there notable differences in the spatial patterns of different nations. Whereas in all three cases the P-W-V is the major node of concentration, accounting for between 46 and 52 per cent of employment, the relative importance of the secondary metropolitan areas varies considerably for different national enterprises. For United Kingdom enterprises, Durban and Cape Town enjoy 28 per cent of total employment, a situation which contrasts with their much-diminished roles in terms of United States and West German investment. Taken together, Durban and Cape Town account now respectively for only 14 and 9 per cent of employment. Similarly, in the case of Port Elizabeth, the share of total United Kingdom employment is a mere 6 per cent. But, for both United States and West German enterprises, Port Elizabeth is the second most important centre of investment, accounting for 20 and 23 per cent of total employment. These differentials primarily reflect the concentrations of different national enterprises in differing industry groups. Illustratively, the importance of Port Elizabeth for United States and West German investment is explicable simply in terms of the location of the motor-vehicle industry in this region and of the South African plants of Ford, General Motors and Volkswagen.

As there exists a wealth of evidence from empirical studies of the geography of MNCs in Western Europe (see, for example, de Smidt, 1966; Blackbourn, 1972; Watts, 1979, 1980b) which suggests that 'foreign firms with differing national origins react to national space in different ways' (Watts, 1980a, p. 80), relationships between national groups in South Africa and, in turn, of these to South-African-controlled employment were examined in detail. Different locational preferences of differing foreign enterprises might be hypothesised from the results of studies concerning the various management patterns of MNCs operating in South Africa. Surveys have shown, for example, that a high proportion of both West German and United States investment in South African manufacturing is accompanied by direct control (First, Steele and Gurney, 1972; Seidman and Makgetla, 1978). By contrast, United Kingdom MNCs 'have tended to merge their interests with the South African firms, holding a significant proportion in the form of minority shares' (Seidman and Makgetla, 1978, p. 17). Following on the methods adopted by previous researchers (Dicken and Lloyd, 1976; Watts, 1979, 1980a, 1980b), the analysis was undertaken through the use of a non-parametric test of association (Spearman's R) and location quotients. The unit of spatial disaggregation was the economic region.

Figure 10.13: The Location of Employment in West-German-controlled Enterprises in South Africa, 1978

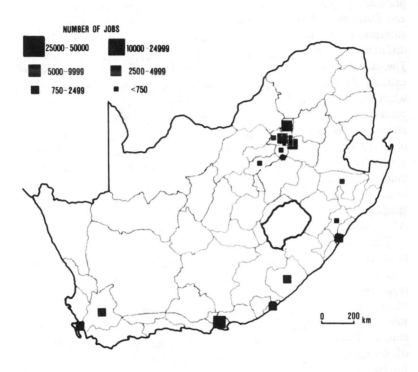

Overall, the patterns of foreign employment as measured by a Spearman's rank correlation coefficient display a relatively high and positive association with the patterns of employment in indigenous South-African-controlled enterprises (R_s = + 0.87, p < 0.01). As United Kingdom enterprises comprise over half of all the category of foreign enterprises, it is therefore not surprising that their distribution is also highly correlated (R_s = + 0.84, p < 0.01) with that of indigenous South African enterprises (Rogerson, 1981b). More surprising, perhaps, is the finding that the patterns of employment in United States enterprises also reveal a relatively high and significant positive correlation with employment in South African enterprises (R_s = + 0.79, p < 0.01). In addition, a comparison of the patterns of United Kingdom and United States employment in South Africa further shows a positive and significant correlation (R_s = + 0.70, p < 0.01). Taken together, these results offer scant support to the hypothesis that foreign firms of different national origin will display markedly varying locational preferences. Neither do they support the contention of Yannopoulos and Dunning (1976, p. 389) that 'the choice of sites of foreign-based enterprises will be dominated by locational considerations that are different from those affecting similar choices of national enterprises'. The caveat must be added that it is not possible on the basis of the existing data bank to compensate adequately for industrial structure when comparing spatial patterns (see Watts, 1980a). None the less the consistently positive and significant associations of the various data sets suggest the conclusion that in South Africa the key explanation for observed spatial distributions lies in the structural variations between foreign enterprises of differing national origin and between these and indigenous South African enterprises. At this macro-scale of industrial location it appears that the internal national forces shaping both the geographical patterns of indigenous and foreign enterprises in South Africa have been similar.

The spatial pattern of over- and under-representation of foreign-controlled enterprises is indexed by location quotients and mapped in Figure 10.14. It is clear that there are only a small number of economic regions in South Africa in which there occurs an 'over-representation' of foreign employment. Significantly, the highest location quotient values are recorded in two regions (namely the Brits/Rustenburg area and the Ladysmith region) with decentralised areas offering a package of location incentives. Further notable areas of concentration of foreign employment appear in parts of the P-W-V complex, Port Elizabeth and the decentralised area of East London. Figures 10.15 and 10.16 evidence certain contrasts but many commonalities in the patterns of concentration of specifically United Kingdom and United States employment. In both cases there are several economic regions recording high location quotients, which reflect the number-base problem. For example, in Northern Natal the high location quotient for United Kingdom employment (Figure 10.15) is accounted for by the presence of isolated large sugar-milling concerns. In terms of the employment patterns of both United Kingdom and United States enterprises high location quotients are strikingly recorded in the major

Transvaal and Natal decentralised areas. Also in the case of United Kingdom employment concentration occurs in the metropolitan areas of Durban, East London and in parts of the P-W-V. By contrast, in the pattern of United States employment (Figure 10.16) Port Elizabeth emerges as a significant node of over-concentration. Finally, it should be noted that in all cases the Metropolitan Cape Town region, rural Cape Province and the entire Orange Free State emerge as zones of relative under-representation for foreign investment in South Africa.

Figure 10.14: The Relative Concentration of Foreign-controlled Employment in South Africa, 1978

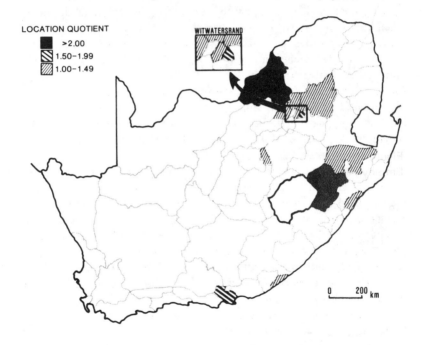

From the foregoing discussion it is apparent that only glacial progress has been made so far by the South African government in luring MNCs into the Homelands. As argued earlier, MNCs have readily taken advantage of the package of location concessions offered at several decentralised areas (for example Rosslyn near Pretoria, East London, Brits, Rustenburg, Pietersburg and Ladysmith) and may even be described as having 'spearheaded decentralization policy' (Legassick and

Figure 10.15: The Relative Concentration of United-Kingdom-controlled Employment in South Africa, 1978

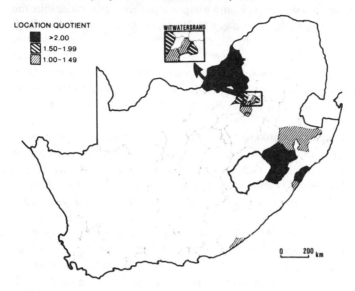

Figure 10.16: The Relative Concentration of United-States-controlled Employment in South Africa, 1978

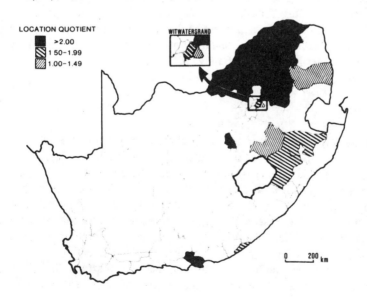

Hemson, 1976, p. 8). None the less there has been a marked reluctance by MNCs to invest directly in the Homelands themselves. This is notwithstanding an intense government-sponsored promotional campaign specifically designed to encourage MNCs to invest in these areas. Typical of the blandishments is the following:

> Stop pussyfooting around. If you want a nice, fat, highly profitable overseas operation, invest in South Africa. But make sure you build your factory in a Black area (*Financial Mail*, 11 October 1974).

By 1978 it appears unlikely that there were in excess of 2,000 manufacturing jobs in foreign-controlled enterprises in all the Homeland areas. The majority of this employment is focused in Transkei and typically occurs in textile enterprises originating in Western Europe. As Transkei is the showcase for South Africa's Bantustan scheme, further intense efforts are being made to encourage a semblance of industrial growth in order to refute those critics who aver that the Homelands are simply labour reserves. Towards achieving this goal it is interesting that South Africa is now looking to Taiwan for investment which might succour Transkei's industrial advancement. Bailey (1977) attributes the general reluctance of MNCs to invest in the Homelands to the political uncertainties of locating in these areas. These uncertainties were highlighted with the passage of a United Nations resolution, two days after Transkeian 'independence', that member states should take effective measures to prohibit corporations under their jurisdiction from having any dealings with 'the so-called independent Transkei or other Bantustans' (Bailey, 1977, p. 237).

Conclusion

At a time when some observers are beginning to question the value of continuing empirical studies in the geography of enterprise (Taylor and Thrift, 1979) it is imperative to stress that the advances of the past decade are confined almost exclusively to work conducted in highly developed economies. In the underdeveloped world as a whole and in Africa in particular, research on the increasing penetration of large firms or of the implications of the emergent new international division of labour (Fröbel, Heinrichs and Kreye, 1977) scarcely has begun. Studies in the geography of multinational corporations in Africa comparable to those substantive works undertaken both in Europe and

North America (cf. Watts, 1980a) simply do not exist. The present chapter sought to address this empirical vacuum in the setting of Southern Africa through investigating the spatial outcomes, at both the international and intra-national levels of resolution, of the attempts to attract MNC investment by the several states of the sub-continent.

In seeking to understand the spatial patterns of MNC investment the changing economic and political milieu confronting the MNC in making a location choice initially was presented. Shifting imperial relationships with Britain, South Africa's emergence as a semi-peripheral industrial power, political independence for Botswana, Lesotho and Swaziland and intensifying struggles over the character of Namibian independence are all events with considerable ramifications in terms of the changing macro-environment of Southern Africa. At the international location level, the Republic of South Africa emerges overwhelmingly as the primary focus of MNC investment, not only in Southern Africa but also in Africa as a whole. Notwithstanding the attractions of the country's mineral wealth and of the apartheid cheap labour system, it has been predominantly South Africa's industrial market opportunities which have polarised international location patterns of MNC investment. Under the umbrella of the South African state, MNCs variously have been wooed, prompted and even, at times, hectored into multiplying their investments in the country. In particular, since 1960, MNCs have participated in the establishment of several strategic industrial sectors which have forged the most advanced, vertically integrated manufacturing system on the African continent (Seidman, 1977). By contrast, in the peripheral countries of Southern Africa MNCs are engaged only in primary resource extraction and simple last-stage assembly or processing operations. The success of Botswana, Lesotho and Swaziland's recent endeavours to reverse this pattern of investment, through encouraging the establishment of export platform manufactures, is militated against by the strict parameters set by their subordination to South African sub-imperialism. Indeed, it is striking that throughout the Southern African periphery an increasingly prominent role is played by South-African-based MNCs led by the Anglo-American Group. That said, the overall geography of MNCs in South Africa is dominated by the location decisions of European and North American-based MNCs in South African manufacturing.

The examination of the detailed intra-national location patterns of MNCs engaged in South African manufacturing produces some sugges-tive findings. Overall there emerges a marked concentration of MNCs within the national core region and, more generally, in the metropolitan areas as a whole. Nevertheless certain variations appear in the geography of MNCs of different national origin. In previous studies it was suggested that such differences reflect fundamentally differing reactions to national space. The South African study lends no credence to this view. Rather it points to the imperatives of identifying structural variations in the industrial composition of enterprises of different national origin. The caveat must be added, however, that research in Southern Africa has yet to penetrate behind the spatial patterns and explore the several processes shaping the geographical fabric. One striking finding that does emerge here is that MNCs have responded to South African government incentives, showing a marked relative 'overrepresentation' at several decentralised areas in the national periphery. The outstanding exception to this pattern is the meagre response of MNCs to intensive state efforts to encourage industrial progress in the Homelands areas. Thus, whereas the South African state is manifestly the winner in the international competitive scramble in Southern Africa to attract the MNCs, internally it is losing the battle to influence their location behaviour in favour of some deflection towards the Homelands.

Acknowledgement

Mr Philip Stickler is thanked for the preparation of the diagrams which accompany this chapter.

11 THE ROLE OF ACQUISITION IN THE SPATIAL DISTRIBUTION OF THE FOREIGN MANUFACTURING SECTOR IN THE UNITED KINGDOM

I.J. Smith

Introduction

Recent studies of direct inward investment in the United Kingdom have had little to say about the relative significance of the main processes in the growth of the foreign sector. The paucity of substantive research in this field is surprising in view of the fundamental differences between new and acquisition investment, and their quite different implications for national and regional economic development policies.

This neglect stems not so much from a lack of appreciation of the problem as from the unsatisfactory nature of official statistics on direct inward investment in the UK. For example, although manufacturing employment in overseas-owned plants increased by over 70 per cent between 1963 and 1975, the contribution of new jobs as opposed to existing jobs reclassified through take-over remains unknown (Dicken and Lloyd, 1980). It is also impossible to gauge adequately the level of either foreign take-over or greenfield investment in the UK owing mainly to the way in which foreign investment is defined in official statistics. Thus, an analysis of changes in the spatial distribution of foreign manufacturing employment is severely handicapped at the outset because disaggregating the major components of change involves an unavoidable element of conjecture.

Recently published figures for 1975 on regional changes in foreign manufacturing employment in the UK (*Business Monitor*, PA 1002, 1979) show that trends evident in the 1960s have not continued into the 1970s for, while foreign manufacturing employment increased at a faster rate in the development areas[1] in the 1960s, the same did not hold true in the 1970s. Such a reversal of trends can obviously be explained in a number of ways, and it is these possible explanations which are investigated in this chapter by means of a components of change analysis. For example, does overseas investment no longer show a preference for development area locations? The raising of the Indus-

221

trial Development Certificate control threshold to 10,000 square feet and the greater geographical coverage of the assisted areas after the 1972 Industrial Act makes a shortening of the average distance of moves of foreign-owned plants from the South-East a distinct possibility. Alternatively, has the absolute importance of new foreign manufacturing investment declined during the recession of 1971 and 1972 and is greenfield investment being replaced by acquisition investment? It has been shown elsewhere that domestic acquisition activity is heavily concentrated in the more developed regions (Goddard and Smith, 1978); and it would seem reasonable to suggest that the same be true for inward investment mergers. Should this be correct, it would provide an explanation of the major increases in foreign manufacturing employment in the South-East and other non-assisted regions in the UK between 1971 and 1975. Finally, there is the possibility that either foreign-owned manufacturing plants in the development areas have increased their employment at a relatively slower rate than elsewhere, or a relatively higher proportion of foreign-owned plants in development areas have failed to survive the recession.

In spite of their deficiencies, existing official statistics can shed some light on each of these questions. The *Business Monitor* (M4) *Overseas Transactions* provides a time series of the value of net inward investment[2] in the UK since 1960. In Figure 11.1 these annual values have been deflated to 1962 prices using the *Financial Times Actuaries 500 Ordinary Share Index*. The resulting trend can best be described as one of slow growth during the 1960s followed by a sharp increase in the value of net inward investment during the early 1970s. After the 1974 peak, the decline was to a much higher level than existed during the 1960s. The trend in new inward acquisition investment[3] closely parallels that of total inward investment and on this evidence it seems that the absolute significance of this component also increased during the early 1970s, although declining substantially after 1974. The *Business Monitor* (PA 1002) also provides more intermittent data on the value of net capital expenditure[4] by foreign *manufacturing* companies in the UK on new investments. These are only available for four years: 1963, 1971, 1973 and 1975. Their deflated values are also shown in Figure 11.1. Again the trend closely parallels that of total new inward investment. However, there is one major difference from the trend for net inward acquisition investment: during the recession years of 1971 and 1972 there was a marginal fall in the absolute value of expenditure by foreign companies on new fixed assets, although the amount accelerated again between 1973 and 1975. The aggregate data therefore tenta-

Figure 11.1: Temporal Variations in the Value of Domestic and Foreign Acquisitions in the UK, 1963-77

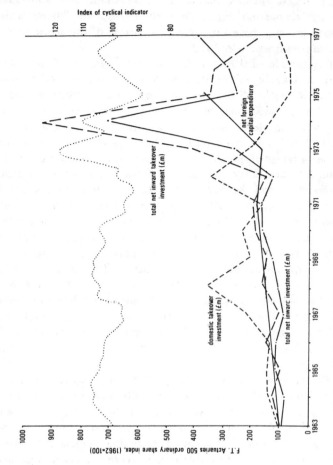

Index of cyclical indicator

F.T. Actuaries 500 ordinary share index, (1962=100)

total net inward takeover investment (£m)

net foreign capital expenditure

domestic takeover investment (£m)

total net inward investment (£m)

Sources: *Business Monitor, M4 (1977); Business Monitor M7 (1976)*

tively suggest a relative increase in the importance of inward investment through acquisition during the early 1970s, and that net acquisition investment may have been the major cause of the accelerated rate of inward investment after 1972.

Explanation of these trends in inward investment is, however, more difficult because of the wide variety of possible influences at work during the early 1970s. The major question to answer is: why should the level of inward investment through acquisition have increased at a time when the level of domestic acquisition investment was declining rapidly? It has been established that acquisition investment tends to assume a larger proportion of total domestic investment when business conditions are fairly buoyant and finance more freely available (e.g. Aaronovitch and Sawyer, 1975; Hannah, 1976; Meeks, 1977). For example, during the peak merger year of 1968, Hannah calculates that almost half of the total investment expenditure of UK quoted companies was on take-overs. In contrast, during the recession year of 1971, expenditure on acquisitions formed only 14 per cent of the total investment expenditure of these companies. Thus, a marked characteristic of domestic acquisition expenditure is that it is highly volatile, fluctuating widely with the level of business confidence and the relative buoyancy of the stock market. This is shown in Figure 11.1, where the deflated value of domestic take-over activity rises and falls with peaks and troughs in the business cycle as shown by the *Coincident Cyclical Indicator*.

The same degree of variability does not, however, appear to have been characteristic of net inward acquisition investment, although there are slight falls in the recession years of 1967 and 1972 and a marked increase in 1974 coincident with a temporary upturn. Interestingly Stewart (1977) in his analysis of Australian mergers in the 1960s also found that inward investment through take-overs was much less influenced by prevailing business conditions than domestic take-over activity. Thus, during the recession years of the mid-1960s, the ratio of the number and value of domestic to foreign take-overs was much lower than during cyclical upturns. Stewart also provides some explanations of this phenomenon which are equally applicable to the UK situation. First, tighter controls on the availability of investment capital during recession have the effect of reducing the net present value, and hence the selling price, of indigenous companies to potential foreign buyers. Second, the distributed profits of private overseas companies are taxed on the same basis as public indigenous companies. This encourages foreign firms to maximise retained profits, thus increasing their liquidity and stimulating acquisition during recession. Third, foreign acquirers are generally much larger companies than domestic acquirers and are therefore less financially constrained.

The fact that foreign companies tend to be larger and more liquid than their indigenous counterparts does not of course explain why they should favour acquisition investment during recession, for retained profits could equally well be invested in new or existing assets. However, the fact that relatively more bargains are available at these times in the form of underpriced domestic companies with good expansion prospects may well strengthen foreign companies' preferences for acquisition. In such circumstances potential victims would also be more inclined to sell out owing to their own liquidity problems during recession. Gort's (1969) economic disturbance theory of mergers may be relevant in this context, as it provides a plausible explanation of why the level of international merger activity is maintained during a recession. At such times there is likely to be a greater discrepancy between the valuation placed on a potential acquirer by its existing management and the valuation placed on it by the management of a large foreign or domestic multinational company.

Table 11.1: Number and Value of Inward Investment Mergers as a Proportion of All UK Acquisition Activity, 1969-78

Time Period	All Overseas Sources				EEC Sources			
	Acquired		Value		Acquired		Value	
	N	Per Cent[a]	£m	Per Cent[a]	N	Per Cent[b]	£m	Per Cent[b]
1969-73	97	2.0	247.5	3.6	7	7.2	11.0	4.4
1974-8	53	2.4	429.3	13.4	14	26.4	32.1	7.4
1969-78	150	2.1	676.8	6.7	21	14.0	43.1	6.4

Notes: [a]Percentage of the number and value of all UK take-overs.

[b]Percentage of the number and value of all inward investment mergers.

Source: *Business Monitor*, M7, Tables 1 and 5.

Inward investment through take-overs may, however, have been preferred for other reasons during the early 1970s. For example, the UK's entry into the EEC in 1973 is likely to have been a major spur to net inward acquisition investment in 1974. Acquisition had the undoubted advantage over greenfield investment of speed of entry into the UK market for United States companies faced with the prospect of an EEC tariff barrier. Indeed, Table 11.1[5] shows that most of the absolute increases in the value of foreign take-overs in the United Kingdom between 1974 and 1978 were not attributable to EEC sources, which still only accounted for just over 7 per cent of the value of foreign take-overs during this period. It is likely that most of the remaining activity is attributable to US companies. The effect of Common Market tariff barriers may also have been reinforced by the flotation of the pound in June 1972 and its rapid devaluation during 1973. This again would have the effect of making UK companies more attractive to foreign purchasers based in countries with relatively stronger currencies.

Whatever the underlying reasons, two reasonably firm conclusions can be reached from this discussion: first, the absolute value of direct inward investment increased substantially during the 1970s; second, acquisition played a major if not dominant role in this increase. These findings have important spatial implications since, in contrast to new foreign investment, take-over investment is less likely to favour the assisted areas. Holland (1971) has noted that foreign take-overs have generally involved UK companies with a high share of the domestic market and good growth prospects. The above-average size of inward investment mergers is confirmed in Table 11.1, where foreign take-overs, occurring between 1969 and 1978, are shown to have accounted for only 2 per cent of the number of all UK take-overs during this period, but almost 7 per cent of their value. Such firms are much more likely to be based in the more developed regions, particularly the South-East, where the majority of the UK's fast-growing, larger companies are headquartered. To the extent that these firms also have most of their manufacturing capacity in the same region or in the same part of the UK as their headquarters, an increase in the relative importance of acquisition can be expected to lead to a shift of foreign investment away from the assisted areas. This, therefore, would provide a very plausible explanation of why foreign manufacturing employment grew relatively more quickly outside the development areas between 1971 and 1975. The major problem involved in fully accepting this thesis is that thus far the discussion has concerned *all* inward acquisition investment in the UK. Official statistics do not, however, indicate how much of this acquisition investment was in the manufacturing sector, although the *Business Monitor* (M4) does show that the proportion of all inward investment in the manufacturing sector declined between 1972 and 1975. It is highly probable that a large percentage of foreign acquisition of non-manufacturing companies would also involve substantial interests in the manufacturing sector, especially since financial conglomerates were heavily involved in this take-over activity (Graham, 1979).

The possibility that closures of foreign-owned manufacturing plant have become relatively more concentrated in the development areas during the most recent recession cannot be discounted as an important influence on the inter-regional convergence of foreign employment growth rates after 1971. Henderson (1979), for example, has shown that the closure rates of new manufacturing plants of varying origin (inter-regional moves, intra-regional moves and enterprises new to manufacturing) have been consistently higher in Scotland than elsewhere, and that they became relatively higher during the 1970s. In view of the relatively large complement of US-owned plants in Scotland, it appeared likely that foreign-owned plants would have made some contribution to these higher closure rates. Young and Hood (1977) have recently provided evidence that larger US companies (represented in the *Fortune* list of the leading 500 US corporations) with affiliates in Scotland instituted large-scale reorganisation and rationalisation strategies during the recession years 1974/5 which had a significant negative impact upon employment growth. In the case of US affiliates represented in the *Times 1000* lists between 1968 and 1975 with Scottish manufacturing plants, they stress declining profitability during the recession as a contributory factor. Where a foreign-owned manufacturing plant based in the development areas produced primarily for the EEC market, however, the UK's entry in 1973 may have encouraged some foreign companies to centralise production in either the South-East or on the Continent. There are therefore some grounds for expecting higher closure rates in the development areas than elsewhere in the UK which could have contributed to a slowing down of foreign manufacturing growth in the country as a whole after 1971.

A final possible explanation of the post-1971 employment trends is that new foreign investment was to some extent diverted from the development areas by changes in regional policy. For example, the availability of financial assistance in the intermediate areas after 1969 and the upgrading of several intermediate areas to development area status between 1969 and 1974 may have attracted potential new foreign investment away from the development areas. The considerable reduction in the absolute level of assistance[6] available after 1970 is also likely to have had an effect on the proportion of inter-regional movement with development area destinations. Nunn (1980) has provided evidence of the impact of these policy changes by demonstrating that there was a marked increase in the share of employment generated by inter-regional moves locating in the Intermediate Areas between 1972 and 1975. At the same time there was a 10 per cent reduction in the share of employment in inter-regional moves locating in the development[7] and special development areas. It is not certain to what extent this shift represents a diversion of employment from the development and special development areas and to what extent it reflects an increase in the coverage of areas with intermediate status. Accepting that the former explanation is more probable, to what extent were moves originating abroad involved? Nunn, for example, also notes that Scotland attracted a considerably higher proportion of 'oil-related' moves with overseas origins during the early 1970s, so that there were obviously countervailing forces also at work. Large foreign multinationals may also be expected to be less influenced in their location decisions by marginal policy changes than smaller indigenous firms (Holland, 1976).

The major objective of the analysis which follows is therefore to assess the extent to which changes in the prevalent type of inward investment are reflected spatially in a shift of foreign manufacturing employment towards or away from the UK periphery. In this instance, the 'UK periphery' is strictly defined as consisting of the four development areas of Scotland, Wales, Northern Ireland and the North. In order partly to overcome the problem of the multiregional operation of acquired companies, the analysis is conducted at a highly aggregated level by comparing the development areas with the South-East and with the rest of the UK (comprising all other planning regions). It is necessary first, however, to discuss the limitations of official statistics relating to inward investment as these must necessarily place caveats on the conclusions that can be drawn.

Data Sources

The recent publication of aggregate figures for the foreign manufacturing sector for 1975 permits for the first time a comparison of inward investment trends during the 1960s and early 1970s. The *Business Monitor* data are now available for 1963, 1971, 1973 and 1975, so that the 1963-71 period has been used in this analysis to represent an expansionary phase of the business cycle, and the 1971 to 1975 period the recent recessionary phase. Unfortunately, data relating to new foreign investment in manufacturing plants do not precisely correspond with these time periods. The main source, the Department of Industry's

Record of Openings and Closures (ROC), which is a continuation of the movement data published in the *Howard Report*, is available for the periods 1966-71 and 1972-5.[8] The correspondence is close enough, however, to validate its use in attempting to determine the components of change of foreign manufacturing employment.

It is important, however, to bear in mind that the level of inward manufacturing investment is considerably understated by official data sources. Both the *ROC*, which monitors greenfield investment, and the *Business Monitor Section* (M7), which monitors acquisition investment, are unsatisfactory sources because of the way in which foreign investment is defined. Thus, for a new manufacturing plant to be regarded as a move originating abroad, there must be no pre-existing plant under the same ownership elsewhere in the UK; otherwise the origin is regarded as being the other UK-based plant. Similarly, acquisition through the medium of an existing UK subsidiary is not classified as a foreign take-over by the Department of Industry. Therefore, it is likely that the level of both foreign greenfield and acquisition investment will become increasingly understated over time as more foreign companies establish new branches and subsidiaries in the United Kingdom.

What is more, the *Inventory of Takeovers and Mergers (ITM)* upon which the *Business Monitor* returns are based, contains some surprising omissions of large inward investment mergers which can be identified from other sources. For example, eight of the ten largest take-overs involving foreign acquirers listed in the *Times 1000* for 1977/8 were not included in the *ITM* at all. The value of these eight take-overs alone was more than double the total value of foreign take-overs shown in the *Business Monitor* for 1977. Fortunately, other sources are available to supplement the foreign acquisition data of the *ITM*. As well as the *Times 1000* already mentioned, Dun and Bradstreet publish a quarterly list of take-overs for inclusion in *Who Owns Whom*. More important, however, are the unpublished lists of *proposed* inward investment mergers provided by the Office of Fair Trading (OFT) covering the period 1965 to 1978.[9] After editing out trade investments, acquisitions of minority holdings and uncompleted take-overs, this list proved to be the most comprehensive source available. Obviously, mergers in which the Office of Fair Trading is interested involve fairly large UK companies with substantial market shares. This may have had the effect of imparting a bias to the sample of inward investment mergers used in this analysis towards locations in the South-East because of the size distribution of the companies involved. This may not, however, be too serious in view of the tendency for foreign-acquired companies to be much larger than the average domestic acquisition (*Business Monitor*, M7).

Components of Foreign Manufacturing Employment Change

The net change in employment in foreign-owned manufacturing plants in the United Kingdom over any particular time period is the aggregate result of the effects of three main components: net new investment (employment gained through openings minus employment lost in closures), net acquisition investment (employment gained through take-overs minus employment lost through divestments), and net 'in situ' growth (employment gained through expansions minus employment lost through contractions). Only for net new investment are data available for the UK as a whole, although their usefulness is somewhat limited. This limitation is particularly severe for closures because the *ROC* only indicates the *number* of non-surviving plants and not the *employment* lost through closures. Nevertheless, with some idea of the degree of understatement[10] of foreign plant openings and closures inherent in this source and the realisation that this is likely to increase over time and not vary spatially, the *ROC* does provide a useful index of new foreign manufacturing investment.

It is only possible to disaggregate the relative contributions of the net acquisition and net 'in situ' change components to aggregate foreign employment change from existing regional establishment-based data banks. In this case the *Establishment Data Base* (*EDB*) for the Northern region of the Centre for Urban and Regional Development Studies is used to illustrate the changing significance of the components over time. The problem is, of course, that it is dangerous to extrapolate from the situation in one development area to that in the nation as a whole, although useful comparisons are available from components of change analyses for Merseyside and Greater Manchester (Dicken and Lloyd, 1979). Some indication of spatial variation in the significance of the net acquisition component is provided in this analysis by the acquisition data contained in the *ITM* and OFT lists. The headquarters locations of foreign-acquired *companies* are assumed to be a reasonable index of the location of the *majority* of manufacturing *plants* of these companies. Some evidence is provided that this assumption may not be too unrealistic at the highly aggregated spatial scale at which the present analysis is conducted.

Aggregate Changes in Foreign Manufacturing Employment

Recently published data in the *Business Monitor* series (PA 1002) have helped to clarify the regional allocation of inward manufacturing investment. Dicken and Lloyd (1979) have shown that, during the decade 1963 to 1973, there was a pronounced trend towards a more even distribution of employment in foreign-owned manufacturing plants in the UK. Although the South-East remained by far the most important region, with 39 per cent of foreign manufacturing employment in 1973, this represented a decline from a 51 per cent share in 1963. The relative shift of overseas manufacturing investment during the decade was predominantly towards the development areas, with only marginal increases in other regions outside the South-East (Watts, 1979). However, Dicken and Lloyd also noted that this redistribution was taking place against a background of steadily falling absolute levels of greenfield manufacturing investment after 1972 as indicated by the Department of Industry's *Record of Openings and Closures*. It is therefore probable that the marked decline in the number of new overseas-based openings in the post-1972 period would have a significant impact on the regional distribution of foreign manufacturing employment. The most recently published aggregate regional data (1975) provide some confirmation of this suggestion.

Table 11.2 compares the increase of employment in foreign-owned plants which took place between 1963 and 1971 with that which took place between 1971 and 1975 in the development areas, the South-East and the rest of the UK (all other regions). During the 1960s the absolute increase in the development areas was almost equal to and the relative increase double that of the rest of the United Kingdom. During this period of overall expansion and high mobility, the South-East also registered a relatively modest 10 per cent increase in employment in foreign-owned plants. Outside the development areas, only the South-West region (parts of which also had development area status) substantially increased the size of its foreign manufacturing sector between 1963 and 1971. Applying the national rate of increase between 1963 and 1971 to the base year employment in each UK subdivision gives an expected end-year employment. The difference between this expected total and the actual total can be regarded as an index of whether a region has performed better or worse than the national average. Table 11.2 shows that the development areas attracted over 50,000 more foreign jobs during the 1960s than would have been expected on the basis of their 1963 share of foreign employment. In contrast, during the same period the South-East received only about one-quarter of the

Table 11.2: The Contribution of Employment Created through Moves to Net Change in Foreign Manufacturing Employment 1963-71 and 1971-5, by Major UK Subdivisions

UK Subdivision	Net Change in Foreign Manufacturing Employment 1963-71				Employment Created Through Moves 1960-71			Net Change in Foreign Manufacturing Employment 1971-5				Employment Created Through Moves 1972-5		
	Actual Change 000	Expected Change (a) 000	Per Cent Change	Annual Average Rate of Change 000	Total 000	Annual Average 000	Per Cent Annual[b] Contribution of Moves to Total Employment Change	Actual Change 000	Expected Change[a] 000	Per Cent Change	Annual Average Rate of Change 000	Total 000	Annual Average 000	Per Cent Annual[b] Contribution of Moves to Total Employment Change
South-East	27.2	104.1	9.8	3.4	4.8	0.4	11.8	42.7	75.2	14.0	8.5	1.8	0.5	5.9
Development Areas	86.2	32.0	100.8	10.8	25.9	2.2	20.4	52.1	42.3	30.4	10.5	7.6	1.9	18.1
Rest of UK	88.8	66.3	50.2	11.1	7.6	0.6	5.4	88.2	65.5	33.2	17.6	0.9	0.2	1.1
United Kingdom	202.4	202.4	37.5	25.3	38.3	3.2	12.6	183.0	183.0	24.6	36.6	10.3	2.6	7.1

Notes: [a] Expected change for each subdivision is calculated on the basis of employment change at the national rate of increase during each period.

[b] The average annual contribution of employment in moves to total employment change in each period (i.e. columns 6 and 13 expressed as a percentage of columns 4 and 11 respectively).

Source: *Business Monitor*, PA 1002, 1963, 1971, 1975; *BOT Record of Movement, 1960-6*; *DI Record of Openings and Closures, 1967-75*.

jobs that would have been expected on the basis of its 1963 share of employment in foreign-owned plants.

Since 1971, a substantial change has occurred in the distribution of inward manufacturing investment. The absolute increase in employment in foreign-owned plants in the development areas between 1971 and 1975 was well below that of the rest of the United Kingdom. In relative terms also, the rest of the United Kingdom experienced an increase slightly above that of the four development areas. To some extent, this shift away from the development areas is attributable to the political situation in Northern Ireland, which increased its foreign-owned manufacturing sector by fewer than 3,000 jobs between 1971 and 1975. However, the situation in this region cannot entirely explain the magnitude of the shift because the exclusion of Northern Ireland still produces a relative increase in the remaining development areas of only 34 per cent, i.e. almost exactly the same as in the rest of the United Kingdom during the later period. Although the development areas still received almost 10,000 more jobs than their 1971 share would have suggested, this represents a considerable diminution of the 1965-71 rate of increase. In contrast, the rest of the United Kingdom's rate of increase on this basis was unaltered, with 30,000 more jobs than expected in both periods.

Although the rate of increase in the South-East rose by only 4 per cent after 1971, this represented an increase of over 40,000 jobs in foreign -owned plants in this region in a period of economic recession. Table 11.2 shows that this was a substantially larger absolute increase than occurred in the South-East during the longer 1963-71 period. The actual increase in the South-East between 1971 and 1975 was also well over half the expected increase, a doubling of the rate of growth between 1963 and 1971. There were also major increases in the foreign-owned manufacturing sector of Yorkshire-Humberside and the East Midlands after 1971, which suggests that overseas companies were no longer ignoring regions where they have traditionally been weakly represented.

Greenfield Investment

Yannopoulos and Dunning (1976) have shown that for the period 1945 to 1965 foreign greenfield investment was more likely to go to development area locations than investment originating elsewhere in the United Kingdom. Thus the development areas received 54.7 per cent of overseas moves compared to 48.8 per cent of moves from elsewhere in the United Kingdom during the period covered by the *Record of Movement*

(Table 11.3). The more recent *Record of Openings and Closures* shows that this differential continued in the period from 1966 to 1975, although the development areas received a reduced share of all inter-regional movement, with 48.5 per cent of moves originating abroad and 41.7 per cent of moves originating in other UK regions. However, a very similar proportion of employment generated by these moves went to the development areas as in the earlier period, which suggests that foreign plants locating in the development areas became relatively larger after 1965. In the latest sub-period for which data are available (1972-5), the share of all indigenous movement terminating in the development areas fell substantially to 36.6 per cent, whereas there was an increase in the proportion of overseas moves with development area destinations to 54.6 per cent. Furthermore, almost 75 per cent of employment generated by foreign greenfield investment during this recessionary phase was in plants locating in the development areas, compared to only 40.6 per cent of employment generated in indigenous moves. It would seem therefore that the redirection of greenfield investment has not been a significant factor in the aggregate shift of foreign manufacturing investment away from the development areas after 1971.

Table 11.3: Share of Plants and Employment Originating Abroad and in the Rest of the UK Locating in the Development Areas, 1945-75

| | Originating Abroad | | | | Originating in Rest of UK | | | |
| | Plants | | Employment | | Plants | | Employment | |
	N	Per Cent	000	Per Cent	N	Per Cent	000	Per Cent
1945-65	141	54.7	69.4	64.0	743	48.8	248.4	53.3
1966-75	150	48.5	21.2	64.2	794	41.7	88.3	52.5
1945-75	291	51.3	90.6	64.0	1537	44.8	336.7	53.1
1972-5	61	54.6	7.6	74.2	237	36.6	17.5	40.6

Sources: Yannopoulos and Dunning (1976); *Record of Openings and Closures,* 1966-75; *Record of Movement,* 1945-65.

Table 11.2 attempts to give an indication of the contribution of employment generated in moves to the aggregate growth of the overseas sector in each UK subdivision for the periods 1963 to 1971 and 1971 to 1975. It is obvious that the degree of understatement of the contribution of new investment will be most pronounced during this later period, when the movement data cover only the years 1972 to 1975. Therefore, in order to ease comparison between the two periods, annual averages have been calculated for both the absolute increase in foreign employment and the number of jobs created in new plants. The annual average contribution of greenfield investment to total employment change during each period is shown in columns 7 and 14 of the table. On this basis, new plants made a much more substantial contribution during the earlier period than in the later period. Only 7 per cent of the average annual national increase between 1971 and 1975 can be attributed to moves originating abroad, compared to 12.6 per cent for the 1963 to 1971 periods. In the development areas, however, the annual average contribution of greenfield investment to net employment growth declined by only two percentage points during the later period and the decreases were much more marked in the rest of the United Kingdom (4 per cent) and the South-East (6 per cent). In fact, at a more disaggregated level, in regions such as the North-West and Yorkshire-Humberside, where there was a marked net increase in employment in foreign-owned plants between 1971 and 1975, the contribution of openings as indicated by the *ROC* data appears to have been negligible.

It must be stressed again, however, that the degree of understatement of foreign openings in the *ROC* data is likely to be considerable and increasing over time. The difference between the contribution of openings to the aggregate increase between 1966 and 1971 and between 1972 and 1975 is likely to be exaggerated for the same reason. The degree of understatement can only be gauged from the Northern region situation where only one-third of the foreign-owned openings between 1966 and 1971 were classified as having an origin abroad. If this was the case nationally, then new investment must have accounted for between 50 and 60 per cent of the aggregate increase in foreign manufacturing employment during the 1960s. Assuming a greater degree of understatement during the early 1970s, the contribution of openings is likely to have fallen to approximately 30 per cent.[11] There is, however, no reason to expect any spatial variation in the level of understatement so that the principal conclusions of this section of the analysis seem reasonably firm.

The substantial net increases in foreign manufacturing employment between 1971 and 1975 in regions such as Yorkshire-Humberside are still unlikely to have come about through new investment. They must therefore be attributed to either 'in situ' expansion of plants already in foreign ownership in 1971 or to the extension of overseas interests through acquisition. Without access to regional establishment data banks it is not possible to determine the relative significance of these other processes, although each is likely to have played an important role in the growth of employment in overseas-owned plants after 1971.

For example, the scale of movement into the development areas during the late 1960s would suggest the existence of immature branch plants with scope for expansion during the early 1970s. Conversely, the considerable increase in the value of net foreign acquisition investment between 1972 and 1974 suggests that take-overs may have been significant. In the following section some evidence is presented to support this latter contention.

The Significance of Acquisition

Section M4 (*Overseas Transactions*) and M7 (*Acquisitions and Mergers of Commercial and Industrial Companies*) of the *Business Monitor* provide some evidence that inward investment through acquisition has not shown the same tendency to decline as foreign greenfield investment during the recent recession. Bearing in mind the understatement inherent in the M7 figures, Table 11.1 suggests that the *value* of inward investment mergers occurring between 1974 and 1978 was almost double that for the period 1969 to 1973, even though the actual *number* of take-overs is shown to have fallen. The table also shows that as the level of indigenous take-over activity fell away after 1973, inward investment mergers came to provide a much larger share of the value of all UK take-overs. Only a small part of this relative increase can be directly attributed to Britain's entry into the EEC as this source still only accounted for just over 7 per cent of the value of overseas take-overs between 1974 and 1978. However, as mentioned in the introduction to this chapter, EEC membership may have had an important indirect effect on the level of take-over activity originating from non-EEC sources. The advantages of acquiring production facilities inside the Community's tariff walls may have been a factor in maintaining the level of foreign acquisition activity after 1973.

Although the M7 figures provide an indication that the level of inward investment through take-over has been recently maintained, they do not show whether acquisition investment has recently formed a larger proportion of *all* inward direct investment in the United Kingdom. Table 11.4, which is derived from the financial data of M4, does provide some confirmation of an increase in the relative importance of acquisition between 1972 and 1975, although these figures must be interpreted with extreme caution. The table breaks down the value of total net inward investment[12] in the UK into three major components: profits retained for re-investment, net acquisition of the share and loan capital of UK companies and the net flow of funds from the overseas parent on the inter-company account. It can be seen that the mean annual value of net inward investment increased from £170 million in the 1960-5 period to £623 million in the 1972-5 period, although these figures take no account of inflation. This increase is attributable almost entirely to the retained profits and net acquisition components of net inward investment, with the net inflow of funds from overseas showing only a slight tendency to increase after 1971.

Table 11.4: Total Net Inward Investment by Major Components, 1960-75

Time Period	UK Subsidiaries and Associates				UK Subsidiaries and Branches			
	Mean Annual Retained Profits		Mean Annual Net Acquisition		Mean Annual Inflow from Parent		Mean Annual Net Investment	
	£m	Per Cent	£m	Per Cent	£m	Per Cent	£m	Per Cent
1960-5	75.0	44.2	70.6	41.5	24.4	14.3	170.0	100.0
1966-71	143.2	48.9	107.4	36.7	42.3	14.5	292.9	100.0
1972-5	280.6	45.0	295.3	47.4	47.2	7.6	623.1	100.0
1960-75	152.0	46.1	140.6	42.7	36.8	11.2	329.4	100.0

Source: *Business Monitor*, M4, Overseas Transactions, 1977.

Between 1972 and 1975 net acquisition investment (including minority holding investments) became the most important component of net inward investment, accounting for almost half of the total compared to just over one-third in the preceding 1966-71 period. Retained profits would, however, be expected to fall during a recession so that they would inevitably contribute less and acquisition investment would contribute more to the value of total net investment between 1972 and 1975. Nevertheless, the substantial increase in the absolute value of net inward acquisition investment and the increase in the proportion of total net investment attributable to acquisition between 1972 and 1975 provides some support for the contention that take-overs may have played a relatively more significant role in foreign investment in the UK during the recent recession. It must be stressed, however, that the figures in Table 11.4 apply to *all* inward investment and it is not possible to assess the contribution of acquisition to foreign manufacturing investment alone. The *Business Monitor* (M4) does indicate that a much lower proportion of net inward investment was in the manufacturing sector between 1972 and 1975 (57 per cent) than between 1966 and 1971 (75 per cent). Much of the absolute increase in net acquisition investment during the later period may therefore be attributable to non-manufacturing activities.

Table 11.5: Distribution of Inward Investment Take-overs in the Manufacturing Sector by Major UK Subdivisions

UK Sub-division	Headquarters Location of Foreign-acquired Firms 1972-8		Headquarters Location of Domestic Externally Acquired Firms[a] 1978		Location Quotient = column 2/ column 4
	N	Per Cent	N	Per Cent	
GLC	42	35.9	23	13.2	2.72
Rest of South-East	20	17.1	33	19.0	0.90
Development Areas	10	8.5	28	16.1	0.53
Rest of UK	45	38.5	90	51.7	0.74
Total	117	100.0	174	100.0	1.00

Note: [a] i.e. firms acquired by UK companies based outside the region in which their headquarters are located.

Sources: *DI Inventory of Acquisitions and Mergers*, 1978; OFT list of inward investment mergers, 1972-8.

It can much more readily be established that acquisition investment in the UK manufacturing sector by foreign companies has mainly concentrated upon firms based in the more developed parts of the UK space economy, particularly the South-East. Table 11.5 shows the headquarters locations of all foreign-acquired UK manufacturing companies (including subsidiaries) contained in the *ITM* and OFT lists for the period 1972 to 1978. It can be seen that over half of these firms (53 per cent) were headquartered in the South-East and less than 10 per cent in the development areas. To determine whether this pattern represents a greater concentration of foreign acquisition activity in the South-East than elsewhere, a control group of companies acquired by other UK firms headquartered outside their particular planning region has been drawn from the *ITM* for 1978. Such inter-regional domestic take-overs probably represent the closest parallel to foreign acquisitions in terms of size and spatial distribution, although there may be some bias towards larger acquisitions in the foreign sample owing to the inclusion of take-overs from the OFT list. With this proviso in mind, it does appear that foreign manufacturing take-overs have been relatively more concentrated in the South-East than domestic inter-regional acquisitions. The location quotients in the final column of Table 11.5 show a distinct core-periphery effect in the relative frequency of foreign manufacturing take-overs with the Greater London Council (GLC) area having almost three times as many as would have been expected on the basis of its share of national take-overs, and the development areas having only half their expected share. At a finer level of disaggregation only the West Midlands (quotient 1.22) and North-West (quotient 1.02) outside the South-East appear to have attracted as much overseas as national acquisition investment during this period.

This evidence does tend to suggest therefore that, in contrast to new overseas investment, the extension of foreign interests through acquisition has mainly been focused upon the more prosperous regions of the United Kingdom, at least since 1972. If this trend has been typical of the whole post-war period, one must conclude that take-overs have been a major mechanism promoting the high degree of concentration of foreign headquarters in the South East-region (Crum and Gudgin, 1977). Of course, since many of the acquired companies operate on a multiregional basis, this does not imply that manufacturing employment in foreign-owned plants is correspondingly increased in the more developed regions. However, in so far as the production facilities of acquired companies are mainly concentrated in one planning region or in one of the major subdivisions of the United Kingdom used for this analysis, there should be a reasonably strong relationship between the level of foreign take-over activity and increases in foreign manufacturing employment shown in Table 11.2. The development areas are most likely to be an exception to this general statement in that a high proportion of foreign manufacturing employment increase in these regions is likely to arise from the acquisition of branch plants of companies based elsewhere in the UK. In the case of the Northern region, for example, 65 per cent of the foreign employment increase through take-overs between 1963 and 1973 can be accounted for in this fashion. Nevertheless, the majority of foreign-acquired manufacturing plants (53 per cent) were controlled from within the Northern region at the time of acquisition. Where there are higher levels of indigenous control, it seems reasonable to assume that a much higher proportion of manufacturing plants and therefore employment will be located in the same region as the headquarters of the acquired company. The high level of spatial aggregation at which this analysis is conducted further increases confidence in the validity of this assumption.

Components of Change in the Northern Region

To assess the contributions of 'in situ' growth and growth through take-over to the aggregate change in foreign-controlled manufacturing employment in the UK only evidence from a small number of regional and sub-regional establishment data banks is available. For example, Dicken and Lloyd (1979) found that 'in situ' expansion accounted for about 75 per cent of the increase in the foreign manufacturing sector on Merseyside between 1966 and 1975, and that acquisition made a relatively minor contribution of only 20 per cent. In contrast, increase in this sector in Greater Manchester arose mainly through acquisition, which accounted for 70 per cent of the aggregate increase, while 'in situ' expansion was of negligible importance (7 per cent). Dicken and Lloyd attributed those differences mainly to the development area status of Merseyside, which attracted a large number of foreign-owned plants during the late 1960s, bringing with them the capacity for in situ growth in the early 1970s. Conversely, Greater Manchester retained a relatively large indigenous sector dominated by small to medium-sized companies, which proved attractive to overseas as well as domestic acquirers.

In theory, therefore, the Northern region situation should be closer to that of Merseyside than Greater Manchester, and one would expect the differential growth of overseas branch plants to be a major factor in the increase of employment in the foreign-owned sector. Like Merseyside, the region is characteristically weak in small to medium-sized indigenous companies, and is dominated by large branches of externally owned companies (Smith, 1978). *The Establishment Data Base* (*EDB*) for the Northern region only covers the period 1963 to 1973 and can therefore only provide evidence for the earlier expansionary phase of inward investment. The poor coverage in the *EDB* of plants with fewer than fifty workers is not likely to be a severe limitation in this instance as the majority of overseas-owned plants in the region are likely to be above this employment threshold.

The 'components of change' equation for the foreign manufacturing sector of the Northern region are shown in Table 11.6. Greenfield investment was the most significant component during the decade, accounting for over half the increase in foreign employment. Acquisition investment accounted for most of the remaining increase and the contribution of 'in situ' expansion was relatively limited (9 per cent), reflecting the small number of foreign-owned plants in the region in 1963. At the same time, foreign-owned plants were less liable to close than plants controlled from elsewhere in the UK, with only 5 per cent of 1963 employment having been lost in this manner. The growth rate of surviving foreign-owned plants was also well above the regional average during the decade, representing an increase of over one-third on 1963 employment.

Table 11.6: Components of Change in the Growth of the Foreign and Externally Owned Manufacturing Sectors in the Northern Region, 1963-73

	1963	Closures	Openings	Net 'in situ' Change	Net Change Due to Take-overs	1973
Foreign-owned						
Plants (N)	33	− 4	+ 58	(29)	+ 34 =	121
Employment (000)	9.2	− 0.5	+ 20.0	+ 3.3	+ 13.8 =	45.8
Per Cent of aggregate change		1.3	54.6	9.0	37.7	
Other Externally Owned						
Plants (N)[a]	305	− 76	+ 140	(229)	+ 79 =	448
Employment (000)	192.3	− 31.1	+ 46.5	+ 17.8	+ 18.0 =	243.5
Per Cent of aggregate change		60.7	90.8	34.8	35.2	

Note: [a] Excludes nationalised steel plants and plants employing less than 50 workers.

Source: *Establishment Data Base*, Centre for Urban and Regional Development Studies.

It is interesting to compare the employment performance of the overseas-owned sector with that of other externally-owned plants. In fact, greenfield investment made a relatively larger contribution to employment growth in the case of externally owned UK plants, where it accounted for over 90 per cent of the aggregate employment growth as compared to 55 per cent for foreign-owned plants. Against this pattern must be set a much higher closure rate in externally owned UK plants, with over 16 per cent of 1963 employment having been lost through closures. Most interestingly, and perhaps most surprisingly, the contribution of take-overs[13] to the expansion of employment in establishments owned by companies overseas and elsewhere in the UK was almost identical (37 per cent in the foreign-owned sector, 35 per cent in the external UK sector). The figure for the foreign-owned sector, however, includes both take-overs of plants owned by independent

Northern region companies (18) and of branch plants of other UK companies (16). Although the majority of acquired plants were controlled from within the region, only 35 per cent of the employment increase through take-overs is accounted for in this way. In other words, as on Merseyside, the increase in employment in foreign-owned plants in the 1960s has mainly come about indirectly through the acquisition of externally owned branch plants of major national companies.

Table 11.7: Components of Change in the Growth of the Foreign Manufacturing Sector in the Northern Region, 1971-5

	1971	Closures	Openings	'In situ' Change	Net Takeovers	1975
Plants (N)	103 −	10 +	21	(93) +	14 =	128
Employment (000)	24.4[a] −	1.8[b] +	2.4[b] +	6.5[c] +	9.4[b] =	41.9[a]
Per cent of aggregate increase		10.2	19.4	37.1	53.7	

Sources:
a. *Business Monitor*, PA 1002 (1971, 1975).
b. *Establishment Data Base*.
c. Calculated as a residual.

However, the situation in the early 1970s was very different. Notwithstanding data problems, an attempt has been made in Table 11.7 to assess the relative significance of both acquisition and greenfield investment during the period 1971 to 1975. The use of *Business Monitor* data to construct components of change for employment in foreign-owned plants in 1971 and 1975 involves a considerable degree of understatement of the true position. Nevertheless it is the magnitude of the increase during this period which is important and this may be accurate enough to permit an estimation of 'in situ' growth on a residual basis. The other three components in Table 11.7 are derived from the *EDB*[14] and are known to be reasonably accurate. It is obvious that if the underestimation of 1971 foreign employment is greater than that of 1975, as seems likely, then the residual 'in situ' component will be exaggerated. The figures relating to the numbers of plants in the top row of the table are also from the *EDB* and exclude establishments with fewer than 50 workers in 1973.

The table provides some confirmation of the increasing importance of the net acquisition component during the recession of the early 1970s. Over half of the aggregate increase in foreign employment between 1971 and 1975 appears to have been attributable to take-overs, the most significant of which took place during the boom acqui-sition year of 1972. Some caution is needed here, however, because only three large acquisitions (Corning/James A. Jobling; Allen Bradley Electronics/Morganite Resistors; American Safety Corporation/Kangol) accounted for over two-thirds of the increase. Nevertheless this was the major explanation of the continued expansion of the foreign sector at an accelerated rate in the region after 1971, although there is also some suggestion that *in situ* expansion of plants which moved into the region during the late 1960s was also an important factor, accounting for over a third of the increase. In contrast to the 1960s, new invest-ment during the early 1970s accounted for less than one-fifth of the aggregate increase in employment in foreign-owned plants. The annual average contribution of openings fell from 2,000 jobs per annum during the decade 1963-73 to 680 jobs per annum between 1971 and 1975. The number of openings per annum during the 1970s however was only slightly less than during the 1960s so that the difference must be mainly attributed to the smaller average size of foreign plants moving into the region after 1971 or their greater degree of capital intensity (Nunn, 1980). Finally, it is also apparent that the significance of foreign plant closures has also slightly inreased, with over 7 per cent of 1971 employment lost in closures over a shorter five-year period. It is important to emphasise, however, that the incidence of foreign plant closures was still markedly lower than that of UK-owned plants after 1971.

The Contribution of Closures

The observation that overseas-owned plants have been less prone to closure than plants controlled from elsewhere in the UK, particularly between 1963 and 1973, must be qualified on several counts. A 'com-ponents of change' analysis does not allow for the effects of owner-ship changes between the base and end years. For example, several plants owned by UK interests in 1963 had been acquired by foreign companies before the closure occurred. Nor does this type of analysis pick up the large number of 'short-life' plants, i.e. plants which open up and close down between the start and end of the period. In total, 13 foreign-owned plants employing approximately 2,500 workers closed down in the Northern region between 1963 and 1973. This figure represents a job loss of over a quarter of the total manufacturing employment in foreign-owned plants in the region in 1963 although in strict terms, as Table 11.6 indicates, only 5 per cent of 1963 employment was lost in closures. It is in the period since 1973, however, that closures of foreign-owned plants began to escalate, with 23 closures involving the loss of approximately 3,500 jobs occurring between 1974 and 1979.

A similar pattern of change has also occurred in Scotland, where the escalating scale of foreign-owned plant closures has started to cause concern (Perman, 1979). The Scottish Economic Planning Council (1980) has drawn attention to the fact that substantial contractions and closures of foreign-owned plants since 1975 have been responsible for the loss of some 16,000 jobs and that the 7 per cent decline in foreign manufacturing employment in Scotland after 1975 exceeded the 4 per cent fall in total manufacturing employment. It is tempting to suggest that there may have been some relationship between the switch from predominantly greenfield investment to acquisition investment in the development areas and this recent escalation of closure rates. Certainly in the Northern region over half the closures which occurred after 1973 involved acquisition investment, with the possibility that post-merger rationalisation strategies have had a significant impact.

Fortunately, existing *ROC* data serve to set these closures in their true context by providing a comparative picture of the number of manufacturing plant closures for long-distance movers (inter-regional) and plants originating abroad. Between 1966 and 1971 and between 1972 and 1975, the *ROC* records both the number of moves and the number of survivors at each end year. It is therefore possible to assess closure rates for plants of varying origin during each time period[15] (Henderson, 1979). Table 11.8 summarises the results of this analysis for the three major subdivisions of the UK used in the present analysis by the use of a closure quotient, expressing closure losses in each region as a proportion of total UK losses. Plants with an overseas origin appear to have survived better than indigenous, inter-regional movers throughout the period (Table 11.8), although the difference between these two groups narrowed appreciably between 1972 and 1975. Thus less than 10 per cent of foreign-owned moves failed to survive between 1966 and 1975, compared to almost 15 per cent of UK-owned moves. It must be remembered, however, that the way in which foreign movers are classified in these data could well have affected this result. Moves originating from a foreign company which already has a manufacturing establishment elsewhere in the UK would be classified as indigenous by the Department of Industry. Hence a large proportion

Table 11.8: ROC Closure Rates for Inter-regional and Foreign Manufacturing Plant Moves, 1966-71 and 1972-5

Sub-divisions	1966 - 71				1972 - 5				1966 - 75			
	Domestic Movers		Foreign Movers		Domestic Movers		Foreign Movers		Domestic Movers		Foreign Movers	
	Per Cent	Quotient	Per Cent	Quotient	Per Cent	Quotient	Per Cent	Quotient	Per Cent	Quotient	Per Cent	Quotient
Development Areas[a]	21.5	1.17	14.6	1.21	11.4	1.68	8.2	1.82	18.5	1.28	12.0	1.28
South-East	13.3	0.72	11.3	0.93	4.2	0.62	0.0	0.00	11.5	0.79	8.1	0.86
Rest of UK[b]	16.4	0.89	7.9	0.65	4.1	0.60	0.0	0.00	11.6	0.80	5.0	0.53
United Kingdom	18.4	1.00	12.1	1.00	6.8	1.00	4.5	1.00	14.5	1.00	9.4	1.00

Notes:

[a] North, Scotland, N. Ireland, Wales.

[b] All other regions.

of foreign-owned movers are in fact in the indigenous inter-regional category and could have contributed to the higher indigenous closure rate.

Development area closure rates for both indigenous and foreign movers have been consistently above those of the South-East and the rest of the United Kingdom throughout the period, and the closure quotients suggest a widening of this gap between 1972 and 1975 (Henderson, 1979). In fact all five non-surviving foreign movers between 1972 and 1975 involved moves to locations in the development areas, and 18 out of 29 non-surviving foreign-owned movers between 1966 and 1975 had development area locations. The relatively high concentration in the development areas of closures of the greenfield plants of foreign-owned firms is also shown by the closure quotients. Most of the remaining non-surviving foreign-owned plants had locations in the South-East and some may well represent transfers rather than true closures owing to the idiosyncrasies of the recording procedure used to compile the data.[16] Although a higher proportion of UK-owned movers failed to survive in the development areas as a whole, this was not the case in the Northern region, where 21 per cent of foreign openings and 15 per cent of indigenous openings closed between 1966 and 1975.

The *ROC* figures suggest, therefore, that foreign-owned greenfield investment has been much less stable in the development areas than in other parts of the United Kingdom, and that differential closure rates are likely to have made a contribution towards the convergence of the rate of growth of employment in foreign-owned manufacturing plants in these regions compared to the rest of the country after 1971. As the *ROC* covers new investment only, it is also likely to understate the involvement of overseas companies in closures, which on recent evidence is much more likely to be associated with acquisition investment (Fothergill and Gudgin, 1979; Smith, 1979; Healey, 1981). This being the case, the contribution of closures to changing patterns of foreign investment is likely to have been even more significant, particularly if, as Northern region evidence indicates, foreign take-over investment has recently become relatively more important in the development areas.

Conclusion and Summary

Any conclusions based upon existing official data sources relating to inward manufacturing investment must necessarily be tentative. This arises mainly from the restricted definitions of foreign investment that have been adopted which produce a high and increasing amount of understatement in official statistics. For example, total employment in foreign-owned manufacturing plants in the Northern region in 1973 was 50 per cent higher than the official figure suggests. To some extent, this understatement may reflect time-lags and delays in monitoring procedures but, in the case of both new and take-over investment, it is certainly definitional; investment through an existing UK subsidiary of an overseas company is not classified as foreign. Even where new investment originates directly from the parent, it is still not classified as being of foreign origin if the company already has an existing UK plant. The implications of this for this analysis are obvious; both greenfield and acquisition investment defined in this way are becoming progressively understated. As more foreign companies establish subsidiaries or branch plants in the United Kingdom, any further investment on their part will not be classified as foreign. A degree of understatement of this magnitude is clearly unacceptable, and as time goes on the *ROC* will become less and less satisfactory as a data source to measure inward investment. The same argument clearly applied to the acquisition data of Section M7 of the *Business Monitor*. The first conclusion of this chapter must be that a change in the definitional base of both data sources is essential for future analysis.

These data problems obviously hold implications for the present analysis. Clearly there are no grounds for expecting any spatial variation in the degree of understatement, although it is likely to have been more pronounced during the early 1970s than during the 1960s. It is thus not possible to say with any degree of certainty that foreign greenfield investment diminished during the early 1970s. In fact, alternative data sources such as SCOMER (Scottish Manufacturing Employment Record) provide evidence of an increased level of foreign-owned plant movement into Scotland between 1971 and 1975 (Scottish Economic Planning Department, 1980) even though the average employment size of these plants was below the 1960s level. If the *ROC* can be accepted as a satisfactory index of foreign greenfield investment, however, the conclusion that the development areas received a higher share of new foreign-owned plants during the early 1970s seems reasonably firm. It is therefore difficult to accept the theory that the reduced level of regional assistance and the increase in the geographical coverage of regions with intermediate area status after 1970 had a significant impact upon the redirection of *foreign* greenfield investment away from the development areas after 1971, unless a higher proportion of foreign moves to the intermediate and non-assisted areas were misclassified than moves to the development areas.

A further possibility is that differential employment growth rates between foreign-owned plants in development areas and foreign-owned plants based elsewhere in the UK made a substantial contribution to regional convergence during the 1970s. This is the component of change on which there is least evidence. Evidence for the North and Merseyside, however, suggests divergence rather than convergence, with high levels of plant mobility in the late 1960s having created a large population of immature branch plants in the development areas with the capacity for expansion during the early 1970s. Conversely, the *ROC* data indicate a relatively low level of foreign greenfield investment in the South-East and Yorkshire-Humberside between 1966 and 1971. Both of these regions experienced large absolute increases in foreign manufacturing employment after 1971 which are therefore unlikely to have resulted from 'in situ' expansion of previously established plants. This observation must again be qualified owing to the degree of under-statement of new foreign investment inherent in the *ROC* data.

If foreign-owned companies have been less responsive to regional policy changes then UK-owned firms in their locational decisions, as seems likely in view of the size of the firms involved (Holland, 1976) and their greater degree of locational flexibility (Vernon, 1972), we are left with relatively low foreign acquisition rates and high closure rates in the development areas as the most likely explanations of the post-1971 change. This chapter has shown that, in spite of the re-cession, the value of net inward foreign acquisition investment has continued to rise, and accounted for almost half the total value of net inward investment between 1972 and 1975. Undoubtedly much of this take-over investment was outside the manufacturing sector, but the proportion is impossible to determine. For example, the high level of foreign activity in the financial sector (Graham, 1979) does not pre-clude the possibility that many acquired non-manufacturing companies would have substantial interests in the manufacturing sector. It is also impossible to determine from existing data sources whether foreign take-over investment has been increasing at a faster rate than new investment, although there is some indication of a decline in the value of net capital expenditure by foreign-owned companies between 1971 and 1973.

On the spatial distribution of inward investment mergers, however, more definite conclusions can be reached. In the 1970s at least, take-overs by foreign manufacturers have primarily involved UK companies based in the more developed regions of the country, particularly the South-East and West Midlands. However, the closeness of the relationship between the level of foreign take-over activity and increases in foreign manufacturing employment is likely to depend upon the extent to which the acquired firms have the bulk of their manufacturing activity in the same region as their headquarters. For acquisitions of smaller firms this relationship will be fairly close but, since inward investment mergers generally involve larger national companies operating on a multiregional basis, the strength of the relationship depends upon the extent to which larger UK companies concentrate their activities in the country's more developed regions. A recent study by Watts (1979) has shown that in 1972 the thirteen largest private-sector manufacturing enterprises in the UK had half of their UK employment in the South-East and West Midlands regions alone, and only 14 per cent in the development areas. On this evidence a fairly close relationship is to be expected between acquisition investment by foreign-owned companies and regional employment change. Only in the development areas, which have relatively low levels of indigenous control (Firn, 1975; Smith, 1978), are employment increases in foreign-owned plants resulting from take-overs likely to be the result of the acquisition of branch plants whose control is external to the region. But even in the Northern region, the majority of foreign-acquired plants were owned by indigenous companies before take-over.

Except in the case of the Northern region, it is difficult to say whether foreign take-over activity became relatively more significant during the 1970s, owing largely to the deficiencies of foreign acquisition data for the 1960s. It is of course difficult to generalise from experience of one region, but employment increases in foreign-owned manufacturing plants through acquisition would seem likely to have been at least as high and probably higher outside the development areas during the 1970s. An obvious advantage of take-over investment in the more developed parts of the UK economy is the avoidance of IDC controls which only apply to new investment. An obvious advantage of acquisition through an existing UK subsidiary is that it avoids much of the controversy which can be associated with inward investment mergers. The considerable understatement of the level of foreign take-over activity in the UK in the *Business Monitor* (M7) figures is one indication that a great deal of acquisition investment by foreign companies is carried out in this manner.

Finally, this chapter has shown that new foreign investment in the development areas has been less stable than elsewhere in the United Kingdom, particularly since 1972. Some caution is necessary in attributing an important role to differential closure rates in the inter-regional convergence of foreign-controlled employment growth rates after 1971; first, because of the small absolute number of non-surviving foreign plants in the *ROC* data and, second, because evidence from other sources suggests that the main escalation of foreign-owned plant closures in the development areas occurred after 1975. Nevertheless, in view of the understatement of foreign-owned openings in the *ROC*, foreign-owned closures are also likely to be under-represented. The higher incidence of foreign-owned manufacturing plant closures in the development areas between 1972 and 1975 may be related to two factors: first, their increased peripherality with regard to the market of the EEC after 1973, and, second, the increased importance of acquisition as opposed to greenfield investment after 1971. Both sets of circumstances may have encouraged foreign companies to focus their rationalisation strategies on these peripheral regions during the recent recession.

Acknowledgements

I would like to thank Professor J.B. Goddard, Alfred Thwaites and Peter Nash for their helpful comments on an earlier draft of this chapter. I also owe a debt of gratitude to John Graham of the Office of Fair Trading who provided data on inward investment mergers.

Notes

1. Throughout this chapter the term 'development areas' refers strictly to the North, Scotland, Wales and Northern Ireland, except where indicated otherwise.

2. Net inward investment is the total value of the retained profits of foreign companies in the UK, the net inflow of funds from overseas and the net value of share and loan capital acquired.

3. Net inward acquisition investment represents the value of expenditure by foreign companies on acquiring the share and loan capital of UK businesses (including minority holdings) net of any divestment of foreign holdings to UK companies.

4. Net capital expenditure is the value of expenditure on new and existing fixed assets (including land) and includes the value of government grants received.

5. This table contains data abstracted from Section M7 of the *Business Monitor (Acquisitions and Mergers of Industrial and Commercial Companies)* which, as will be shown later, considerably understates the level of inward investment through take-overs.

6. The abolition of Investment Grants in 1970 and the intention to phase out the Regional Employment Premium by 1974.

7. In this case all areas with the appropriate level of assistance.

8. This source identifies all new greenfield investment in each region and the origin of this investment by UK sub-regions and overseas sources.

9. This list of proposed inward investment mergers was checked for implementation using *Who Owns Whom* (Dun and Bradstreet).

10. In the case of the Northern region, only one-third of the foreign-owned openings between 1966 and 1971 were classified as being of foreign origin. It is therefore probable that an even smaller proportion were classified as foreign between 1972 and 1975.

11. This figure assumes employment in foreign-owned openings to have been understated by a factor of four between 1972 and 1975.

12. Total net inward investment is the value of all investments by overseas companies in the UK, less the value of any disinvestment to UK companies.

13. Although column 5 of Table 11.6 is headed 'Net Take-overs', the 34 plants acquired by foreign companies between 1963 and 1973 represent an absolute gain to the foreign sector. Only one of the 1963 foreign-owned plants was sold off to a UK company and this did not survive until 1973.

14. Supplemented, after 1973, with employment figures derived from directory and newspaper sources.

15. It is not possible, however, to assess employment losses from closures from the *ROC* because only employment at the end year is given.

16. The DI record a closure in the region of origin when a complete transfer of activities to a new location takes place.

12 INTERNATIONAL TOURISM AND MULTINATIONAL CORPORATIONS IN THE PACIFIC: THE CASE OF FIJI

S.G. Britton

Introduction

The very rapid growth of international tourist travel has been one of the most notable phenomena of recent decades. Between 1950 and 1974 global international tourist arrivals increased eightfold from 25 million to 213 million, with an annual increase of over 9 per cent over the period from 1961 to 1971 (Schmoll, 1977; Robinson, 1976). This mushrooming demand for overseas travel has been a direct reflection of transformations that have occurred in advanced Western economies. Of total tourist movements in 1973, 91 per cent took place between and within Europe and North America (Robinson, 1976). The social and economic changes responsible for these developments have been the widespread improvement of employment conditions, the accompanying massive extension of demand for, and creation of, consumer goods and a similar growth of service industries as new avenues for capital accumulation. With respect to the specific causes for the rapid growth of tourism, three factors can be identified. These are: the increased opportunities for individual recreation (for example shorter working hours, higher incomes, paid holidays); the revolutions in air transport and communications technologies (for example wide-bodied jet aircraft, computerised reservations systems); and what Mandel (1975) calls the 'civilising function of capital', the extension of cultural and individual needs (for example individual enrichment from experiencing other cultures).

Paralleling this growth of mass tourism, however, has been a change in the way travel experiences have been organised. With the sheer growth in the volume of tourists after 1950, a distinct travel industry as such has evolved to create the infrastructure necessary to meet the demand for recreational travel. The consequence of the development of a tourist industry has been that the travel experience has taken on an increasingly standardised form. This is because, along with the general proliferation of consumer services, the travel experience has been subject to three pervasive economic forces within advanced capitalist societies. That is, the organisation of tourist travel has increasingly reflected the almost universal extension of commodity production into the service sector, the general tendency towards the centralisation and concentration of capital and the internationalisation of capital (Barrett-Brown, 1974; Radice, 1975; Mandel, 1975). In short, as international recreational travel has become an industry, the travel experience itself has evolved into a commodity form.

The International Tourist Industry: the Corporate Context

The transformation of individualised travel into a commodity form occurred with the introduction of inclusive or packaged tours in the mid-1960s (Burkhart and Medlik, 1974). This new concept brought together the conflicting psychological needs of tourists for novelty as well as security in strange environments (Cohen, 1972) and the latent tendency for commercial enterprise to reconstitute individual touring as a standardised, repeatable and marketable product. By incorporating such qualities, the package tour substantially reduced the cost of travel, broadened the potential tourist market and created a new source of surplus generation by giving maximum opportunity for tourism companies to control tourist expenditures. The standardisation and marketability of the tourist product through volume control also enhanced the efficient use of transport and accommodation capacities owned by tourism corporations. But for the various types of packaged travel, the viable operation of the current generation of wide-bodied jet aircraft, large hotel complexes, cruise ships and touring coach fleets would be more tenuous. Mass tourism thus represents the convergence of individuals' desire to engage in relatively frequent overseas travel and commercial imperatives to recoup massive capital outlays on technological innovations necessitated by corporate competition.

The tourist industry itself is a conglomerate of many diverse economic sectors such as accommodation, entertainment, retailing, banking and transport. These activities require selective modification and co-ordination to meet the requirements of tourists. With consistent increases in the volume of tourist travel and its profitability, the industry has become far more competitive. Through the processes of concentration (the reduction and amalgamation of competing firms) and centralisation (the reduction and amalgamation of competing capitals), the key integrative force within international tourism has thus become those large companies capable of organising, co-ordinating, creating and marketing the diverse inputs that constitute the various tourist products available. Three trends have contributed to the increasing importance of what amounts to corporate organisation within the tourist industry.

The first of these has been the growth in size of companies and their amalgamation into larger corporations, as firms sought to gain economies of scale through matching up the tourist seating capacities of aircraft, hotels and ground transport. Very large tour companies are obviously able to extract more favourable contract terms from airlines and hotel operators due to the large tourist numbers which the tour wholesalers can direct. (The same principle is also applicable to airline and hotel operators in their dealings with each of the other components of the industry). Large size also means that these companies have access to substantial funds with which to launch all-important promotional campaigns for their products, and enables them to take full advantage of expensive technologies such as computerised reservation and ticketing systems. This trend has facilitated the concentration of control of the industry within the hands of fewer and fewer companies. In the United Kingdom, for example, the three largest tour companies sold 50 per cent of all inclusive tours in 1972 (Young, 1973). Accompanying this increasing concentration has been the global spread of corporate tourist interests. This tendency is epitomised by the world-wide networks of Hilton, Regency-Hyatt, Holiday Inns, Intercontinental and other hotel chains. In the South Pacific an example is provided by the growth of South Pacific-Properties Ltd (SPP), a Hong Kong subsidiary of the Arab-owned Triad Investments Corporation. SPP extended its South-East Asian, Seychelles and Egyptian hotel interests in 1976 with the purchase of the English Trust Houses Forte hotel group. By 1978 SPP had bought out Travelodge Australia Ltd, giving it control of 61 hotels in Australia, New Zealand, Fiji, Tahiti and Papua New Guinea. In January 1980, construction of a further four South-East Asian hotels was started in East Malaysia, with further sites still to be selected in Singapore and the Philippines (*Australian*, 30 August 1978; *New Zealand Herald*, 2 February 1980).

The second organisational trend has been the vertical integration of various tourist services into larger corporate entities. In particular this integration has occurred between airlines, hotel chains and travel agencies. Airlines have found it both convenient and profitable to own sufficient hotel room capacity at their ports of call to accommodate the large numbers of passengers under their control. Thus Pan American

Airways owns the Intercontinental hotel chain. Similarly, in 1979 Ireland's Aer Lingus airline, which already owned the US-based Dunfey Hotel Group, purchased the Italian-based Ciga luxury hotel chain. Equally common is the amalgamation within one company of travel agency, wholesale package tour, ground tour and hotel operations. The Tourist Corporation of New Zealand, for example, oversees such functions in New Zealand itself and also in Fiji and the Cook Islands.

The other important trend that has become evident is the penetration of the industry by non-tourism capital. Whether the motivation is to control distribution or 'to secure the average rate of profit for the largest volume of capital' (Mandel, 1975, p. 389), this intervention increases the dominance of large companies. For example, partly as a consequence of centralisation, the traditional role of travel agents has been undermined over the last decade. Notably, this has been due to take-overs by banks, with their captive clientele, accessible locations and credit and computer facilities. For instance, Barclays Bank is now the principal shareholder of Thomas Cook and Sons, one of the world's largest tour companies. Recent years have also seen petroleum companies, department stores and supermarket chains enter the package tour retailing market and breweries have become very active in the purchase of hotel chains. In the United States, RCA has added Hertz Car Rentals to its electronics, records, finance and publishing interests, and the ITT conglomerate now includes the Avis Rent-a-Car and Sheraton Hotel groups.

These three trends within the industry, greater unit size, increasing horizontal and vertical integration and the penetration of non-tourism capital, have important repercussions for the internal organisation and structuring of the industry. Internal organisation directly shapes the nature of links between the various components of the industry. With regard to the spatial expression of international tourism, the most important link is that between the product marketing agencies in tourist source countries and the tourist facilities in destination countries. Given the tendencies towards the concentration and centralisation of commercial power within the tourism companies of the core metropolitan economies, the inclusion of Third World countries within international tourism typically involves external corporate controls and, more and more frequently, the presence of multinational companies.

Corporate Linkages between Metropolitan and Periphery Tourism Industries

The international tourism system, in similar fashion to other manifestations of metropolitan multinational enterprise, can be envisaged as a three-tiered hierarchy (Hymer, 1972). At the apex are metropolitan market countries in which are located the headquarters of those transport, finance, hotel and tourism supplying companies which dominate the lower levels of the industry hierarchy (Figure 12.1). At the intermediate level, in the tourist destinations of the underdeveloped periphery countries, are the branch offices and associate commercial interests of metropolitan firms operating in conjunction with their local tourism counterparts. At the base of the pyramid lie those small-scale tourism enterprises of the destination country which are marginal to, but dependent upon, the tourist companies of the intermediate level.

Since metropolitan enterprises are actually located within the principal tourist markets, they have direct contact with tourists. They therefore control the key link in the tourist flow chain. Given the nature of tourist travel, particularly in packaged form, tourists may not know the type of holiday they want, nor may they be definite about which destination(s) they wish to visit (Burkhart and Medlik, 1974). A tropical island holiday, for example, may be enjoyed in any one of a dozen Pacific Island destinations. This situation puts industry intermediaries between the tourist client and the destination countries in a pivotal position. It allows metropolitan tourism corporations to influence the volume of tourist flows to any one market (where subsidiary tourist companies may be owned). It also encourages foreign interests to become directly involved in the destination country tourist industries, especially since their capital resources, expertise, market connections and control over tourist flows give them overwhelming competitive advantages relative to local tourism operatives. Only countries having substantial government involvement, such as Singapore, appear to be able to overcome such competition. The apparent market competence of these metropolitan companies also renders them 'natural' recipients of destination government aid, co-operation and subsidisation (Hiller, 1977). From the perspective of a nascent Third World industry, integration with foreign tourism capital appears both beneficial and necessary.

Metropolitan companies are, therefore, in a strong position to dictate the manner in which a peripheral tourist destination will be deve-

Figure 12.1: The Articulation of Third World Destinations within the International Tourist Trade

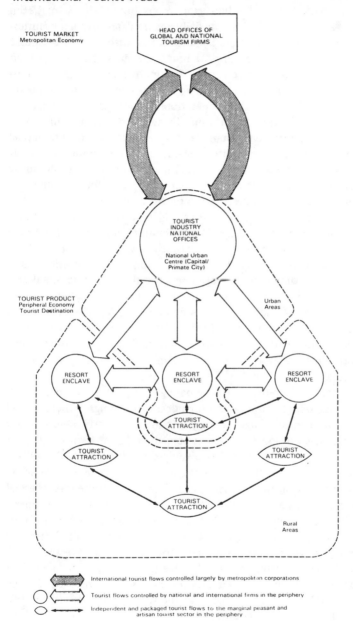

TOURIST MARKET
Metropolitan Economy

HEAD OFFICES OF
GLOBAL AND NATIONAL
TOURISM FIRMS

TOURIST
INDUSTRY
NATIONAL
OFFICES

National Urban
Centre (Capital/
Primate City)

TOURIST PRODUCT
Peripheral Economy
Tourist Destination

Urban
Areas

RESORT
ENCLAVE

RESORT
ENCLAVE

RESORT
ENCLAVE

TOURIST
ATTRACTION

TOURIST
ATTRACTION

TOURIST
ATTRACTION

TOURIST
ATTRACTION

Rural
Areas

International tourist flows controlled largely by metropolitan corporations

Tourist flows controlled by national and international firms in the periphery

Independent and packaged tourist flows to the marginal peasant and
artisan tourist sector in the periphery

loped and articulated within the international system. Metropolitan tour companies and airlines are the principal agencies in the creation of tourist marketing and advertising promotions. These marketing strategies, along with tourists' partially manipulated expectations and the transportation modes used by airline and wholesale tour operators, all help determine the type of tourist product that is created in underdeveloped countries. The more that metropolitan firms promote a destination, the more incentive there is for these firms to ensure the stability and viability of their operations through direct commercial participation within the destination. In addition, because of the inability of agricultural and manufacturing producers in the underdeveloped economies to guarantee the quality and continuity of supply of inputs appropriate for 'international luxury standard' tourist facilities, there is a strong reliance on imported supplies for both the construction and operation of destination tourist facilities.

A series of feedback loops is thus evident within the international tourism industry (Figure 12.2). The promotion and advertising strategies of metropolitan tourism corporations play a significant role in shaping tourist expectations. These expectations tend to conform to a type of tourist product and travel experience that best suits the priorities of these tourism firms. These priorities in turn are the key determinants of the type of tourist facilities developed in Third World tourist destinations. Not surprisingly, since such facilities are best planned, constructed and managed by those tourism firms with international experience, there is every incentive for metropolitan corporations to invest in Third World tourist facilities.

Underdeveloped countries participating in the international tourist trade are thus obliged to accept a high degree of foreign ownership and leakage of foreign exchange earnings. At the very least, there is likely to be a high level of expatriate management and control of key sectors of periphery tourist industries (for example Bryden, 1973). This situation is exacerbated by the fact that tourist travel is most commonly undertaken in package tour forms, since it means that the international and internal movement of tourists can be controlled by foreign operators. It has been found (ESCAP, 1978), for instance, that where tour packages consist of a foreign air carrier, but include local hotel and other group services, destination countries receive on average 40-45 per cent of the inclusive tour retail price paid by the tourists in their home country. If both the airline and hotels are owned by foreign companies, only 22 to 25 per cent of the retail tour price will be forwarded to the destination country.

Figure 12.2: Tourist Industry Linkages Responsible for the Generation of Tourist Flows

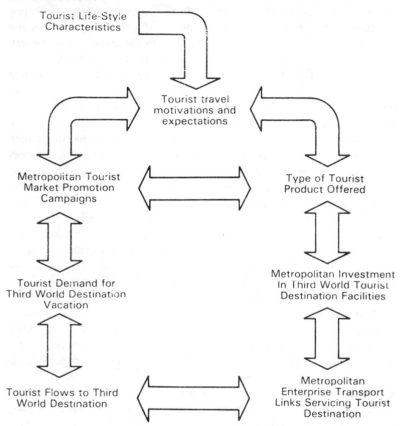

Such an industry structure ensures that Third World destinations have a largely passive and dependent role in the international system. Foreign multinational companies directly serve, and partially create, the demand and the means by which tourists consume Third World tourist products. Destination countries, on the other hand, are the recipients of tourists. They provide the novelty and superficial rationale for an overseas holiday. While this dichotomy refers to two poles in a continuum, there are varying degrees of foreign and local participation in any one country and any one tourism sector at that destination. But this does not negate the contention that the central problem for destinations in the periphery is the inequitable relationships inherent in this international system. Immobile tourism facilities in tourist destinations must rely on foreign corporations to supply both the tourist environment and the tourists to ensure viability. The flow of tourists to these destinations is achieved by either gaining the co-operation of foreign interests or by national bargaining power over factors affecting the profitability of these foreign interests. For, in the final analysis, metropolitan tourism corporations could direct tourists to alternative destinations. The influence and negotiating power of destination countries is further weakened by the fact that control of a very high proportion of tourist flows is in the hands of only a few corporations in each metropolitan market.

This problem was recently demonstrated during negotiations over airline practices on South-East Asian travel routes. The introduction of very low fares between Europe and Australasia by Qantas and British Airways led to the restructuring of flight networks between the metropoles and the Association of South East Asian Nations (ASEAN: Thailand, Malaysia, Singapore, Indonesia and the Philippines). The effect of these metropolitan airlines over-flying ASEAN destinations is potentially great, since the low-fare tickets impose financial penalties on stop-over tourists, and exclude or undercut ASEAN airlines from flying similar low-budget routes, thus seriously threatening the flow of tourists into South-East Asia.

This example of the conflict of interests between ASEAN countries and metropolitan airlines is indicative of the inconstancy of the spatial patterning of tourist flows. This is a direct manifestation of the inherently inequitable balance of commercial power between metropolitan and periphery tourist operators. That this inequity may be expressed so directly in the organisation and rearrangement of transportation networks is a reminder of the origins of the tourist industry in many Third World countries.

Historically the expansion of metropolitan capital into the Third World was closely associated with the development of transportation networks (Harvey, 1975). Foreign penetration of the periphery was, and still is, highly selective, and has led to a similarly selective distribution of transportation networks. Hence, with technological revolutions in transport as the basis of mass tourism, those peripheral economies with appropriate colonial infrastructure networks (for example Kenya) or those located on new transport networks established by metropolitan enterprises (for example Fiji, Bali) were most likely to be incorporated into the international tourism trade. The potential for ex-colonies to develop as tourist destinations, however, is relatively limited. Since from the airline, travel and tour companies' point of view other metropolitan countries have always been the most important markets (Bryden, 1973), those ex-colonial Third World countries which straddled inter-metropole flight sectors were most likely to be perceived as new and viable stop-over points. This has produced quite distinct Third World tourist flow patterns. The tourist industries in ASEAN countries, for example, initially developed as stop-over points on European-Australasian flights. The international air connections between Europe and Africa also closely reflect past ties between individual European powers and their former colonies, as a casual investigation of European overseas airline networks shows (for example Air France, British Airways). In the Pacific, Australasian and North American tourists fly (albeit in relatively small numbers) through a number of stop-over destinations: the ex-British colony of Fiji, the ex-New Zealand protectorates of Western Samoa and Cook Islands, the French colonies of Tahiti, New Caledonia and New Hebrides, the American State of Hawaii, the protectorate of American Samoa or the US strategic bases in Micronesia. As the ASEAN example shows, however, the establishment of transport connections by metropolitan interests is now matched by a capacity to promote alternative routes that are more appropriate to changing corporate requirements.

To summarise, the tourist industry in underdeveloped countries is likely to be controlled by foreign multinational companies, if not directly owned by these companies, since the protection of their commercial interests will be ensured by co-operative members of local elites. The overall direction of capital accumulation within the system is likely to be from the small-scale (peasant and artisan) sectors at the base of the tourism hierarchy (for example handicraft vendors, dance groups, shopping guides, street hawkers) up to the primary tourism sectors in the periphery (for example resort hotels, tour operations, travel agencies, wholesalers), and ultimately to the controlling metropolitan tourism corporations (for example headquarters of hotel, tour, travel agency companies, international airlines, tour wholesalers, manufacturers of tourist shopping goods). This is due to the lower orders of the tourism hierarchy being integrated in such a way as to render them functional to the commercial interests of those sectors above them (Britton, 1979). Hence the structure of the industry both internationally and nationally has a tendency towards monopolistic organisation, with control of key processes within tourism being further concentrated in the hands of metropolitan tourism capital. How this industry structure manifests itself within the periphery can be illustrated by a brief case study of the South Pacific island of Fiji.

Multinational Tourism Corporations in Fiji

After the Second World War, Fiji became a refuelling point for metropolitan airlines on trans-Pacific routes. With the subsequent recognition of its tourism potential, the colony was promoted and incorporated as a tropical island holiday package by North American West Coast, Australasian and British tourism interests, particularly the airlines. From 1963 to 1977 gross tourism receipts rose from $3.6 million to an estimated $79.8 million. Since 1968, the industry has been responsible, on average, for 31.5 per cent of Fiji's gross export earnings. Tourism has therefore helped the economy overcome one of the most serious adverse structural legacies of the colonial era — dependence on a very narrow range of export commodities. Up until the early 1960s, at least 60 per cent of total export receipts in any one year were from only one source — sugar. As late as 1964, 95.9 per cent of domestic exports and 77.5 per cent of total export receipts were derived from just three commodities: sugar, coconuts and gold. In 1977 these products still accounted for 90.9 per cent of domestic exports and 55 per cent of total exports (Bureau of Statistics, 1979).

The structure and internal dynamics of Fiji tourism, however, are such that they seriously reduce the net financial advantages the industry brings to the economy. As in many underdeveloped countries, the Fiji economy is dominated by foreign capital. Overseas firms account for approximately 80 per cent of all business turnover, with Australian firms contributing 60 per cent of that total (Annear, 1973). In 1977 foreign corporations accounted for 65.6 per cent of tourism retail turnover, and European and Indian Fiji citizen-owned enterprises accounted for a further 14.3 per cent and 15.3 per cent of turnover respectively. Indigenous Fijian-, Public-, Chinese- and Polynesian-controlled enterprises generated only 4.6 per cent of total turnover. A very high leakage of tourism earnings can be attributed to this substantial degree of foreign involvement. In 1975, 70 per cent of tourism-generated foreign exchange was lost in the form of payments for industry imports, foreign staff salaries and company profit repatriation, and the consumption of imports by locals from disposable income made available by tourism (Central Planning Office, 1975). The four key sectors of Fiji tourism between them illustrate some of the processes associated with multinational companies that have contributed to these patterns of income flow and industry control.

The Hotel Sector

Between 1960 and 1978 the number of tourists visiting Fiji rose thirteenfold from 14,272 to 184,000. After an initial expansion of tourist hotel rooms (excluding those with a predominantly local clientele) from 220 to 1,050 during the ten years from 1960, a serious shortage of accommodation occurred. With the apparently buoyant long-term prospects for Fiji tourism, hotel construction was substantially increased to take full advantage of very high short-term demand. Of the 3,274 tourist hotel rooms (44 hotels) available in 1977, 67 per cent were built during the 'boom' years of 1970-5. This large-scale, spontaneous, speculative and unplanned expansion was primarily undertaken by foreign capital. In 1977 foreign companies controlled 27 resort hotels and 62 per cent of Fiji's tourist hotel rooms: 65 per cent of this capacity was built between 1970 and 1975. The most important component of this sector was provided by five multinational companies: Cathay Hotels Ltd (Singapore), Fiji Resorts Ltd (USA), Regent International Hotels Ltd (USA), South Pacific Properties Ltd (Hong Kong) and the Tourist Corporation of Fiji Ltd (New Zealand). Between them, these companies controlled 18 hotels and 53.4 per cent of tourist rooms.

Table 12.1: Fiji Tourist Hotel Sector: Distribution of Rooms and Turnover by Ownership, 1976 (estimates A$)

Ownership[a] Category	Number of Rooms	Per Cent of Rooms	Gross Turnover	Per Cent of Turnover
Foreign company	2,170	58.0	19,745,617	64.5
Expatriate	59	1.6	348,697	1.1
European	598	15.8	4,854,951[b]	15.8
Indian	507	13.4	3,415,654	11.2
Fiji public co.[c]	347	9.3	1,679,364	5.5
Chinese	46	1.2	589,380[b]	1.9
Fijian	15	0.04	13,000	0.04
	3,742	100.0	30,646,663	100.0

Notes: a Foreign companies are those estimated to have a 50 per cent or more non-Fiji ownership of shares and/or foreign management contracts. Expatriates are non-Fiji citizens, but are recognised Fiji residents (usually of long standing). Europeans, Indians, Chinese and Fijians are all Fiji citizens. Fiji public companies are government-supported, Fiji-owned companies with public share subscriptions.

b These hotel groups derive a high proportion of their turnover from liquor and restaurant sales to local residents.

c This total includes 3,274 tourist hotel rooms and 468 hotel, motel, hostel and boarding house rooms serving a predominantly local clientele.

The distribution of hotel-sector income is directly related to control over accommodation plant (Table 12.1). In 1976 foreign companies were responsible for 65.6 per cent of total accommodation sector turnover with the five foreign hotel chains accounting for 41.3 per cent of that total (and 63 per cent of total foreign hotel company turnover).

Apart from the large-scale acquisition of freehold land (for example 3,900 ha by South Pacific Properties) and the dominance of expatriates in managerial posts (accounting for 57 per cent of foreign hotel management positions in 1976), the operation of foreign hotel companies has several other important implications for Fiji. Only large companies are able to construct highest-quality holiday accommodation and support the promotion campaigns that induce tourists to stay in such accommodation. In addition, except for a few local European concerns, only foreign hotels have direct ownership or commercial contract links to travel agencies, airlines and tour wholesalers in the tourist market countries. There is therefore a set of linkages built into the tourist industry that channels tourists to the advantage of foreign hotel companies. For example, a New Zealand hotel chain operating its own travel agencies in New Zealand can direct New Zealand tourists to its own Fiji hotels. Similarly, an American-owned hotel can make favourable contract arrangements, owing to its large size and reputation with one of the two or three key Australian tour wholesalers. The important implication of these arrangements is the inability of small-scale indigenously owned hotels to compete for a more substantial share of the tourist market.

Apart from their obvious commercial viability, based on market power and astute management, foreign hoteliers provide a clear example of the political influence of foreign tourism capital. This influence is particularly revealed in the provision of generous investment incentives. On the advice of tourist industry representatives, a Hotel Aids Ordinance was introduced by the Colonial government of Fiji in 1964. This ordinance contained provisions for cash grants of up to 7 per cent of hotel construction costs, tax-deductible depreciation allowances on capital costs of new construction against profits over 15 years, or as an alternative, a sum equal to 55 per cent of capital expenditure able to be written off against annual chargeable income tax until such time as the sum has been fully exhausted. These investment incentives have proved particularly advantageous for foreign hotels. Fiji tax laws already allowed unrestricted repatriation of company profits, along with the standard 33 per cent company tax being further reducible by various rebates. The additional benefits provided by the

Hotel Aids Ordinance have meant that virtually no taxes have since been paid by the large hotel companies. Indeed, the Ordinance obliged the Colonial and the subsequent Independent governments after 1970 to reimburse hotel companies to the sum of A$715,500 in cash grant payments, and a further A$13,750,000 was reimbursed under the 55 per cent investment allowance scheme between 1966 and 1975. Of the total of A$14,465,500, 79.7 per cent was claimed by foreign companies. Other sources of (comparatively cheap) local public finance have also been successfully tapped by foreign firms. Of the A$27.5 million loaned by the Fiji National Provident Fund for tourism purposes, 89.1 per cent went to foreign and local European-owned hotels. In this way, foreign tourism capital has been able to acquire substantial shares of the cheaper local capital market.

A final point to be made on the repercussions of foreign investment concerns Japanese hotel capital. Since 1972 there has been cautious and planned penetration into Fiji by several large Japanese industrial conglomerates including the Taisei Corporation, Tokyo Ocean Development and Engineering Co. Ltd, and Nichimen Co. Ltd. Through either the purchase or construction of tourist resorts, these conglomerates, representing over 30 Japanese industrial companies, have gained entry into Fiji's limited secondary manufacturing economy. Given the probable convergence between the country's future development needs and the capacity of such Japanese corporations, there is the possibility that these corporations will come to successfully dominate key sectors of the Fiji economy (Keith-Reid, 1977).

The Travel and Tour Sector

In Fiji this sector involves 43 enterprises. Nine companies provide retail travel agency and wholesale tour co-ordination and operation functions. Eleven are tour companies offering either scenic excursions or static (display) tourist attractions. Nine are ground transport companies and 14 others operate inter-island sea cruise tours and water taxi services. In 1977 these 43 firms had 87 retail outlets (excluding hotel tour desks).

It is possible to identify two key structural differences between these subsectors. First, companies can be divided between those essential for tourists since they provide travel between airports and tourist accommodation and between one hotel and another (as within a tour package) and those which provide services peripheral to these essential tourist movements, i.e. additional recreational travel activities. Retail travel agents, tour co-ordinators, ground transport companies and 'water taxi' services belong to the former category, while tour operators, tourist attraction operators and cruise tours belong to the latter group.

Second, enterprises can be categorised according to those responsible for the organisation and co-ordination of tourist movements (both to and within Fiji) and those which simply provide the means for tourists to travel or experience local attractions. The first group includes travel agencies/tour co-ordinators and larger ground transport companies directly linked via extensive communication and ownership networks to overseas operations, accommodation companies and/or airlines. Tour operators, cruise boat companies and smaller ground transport companies, on the other hand, are concerned solely with the movement of tourists already landed in Fiji.

While travel agents/tour co-ordinators are the most important component (by virtue of their control over tourist flows), so the 14 foreign firms are the most important ownership element. Moreover, foreign companies predominate in the key activities. In particular, they control 6 out of the 9 travel agency/tour co-ordinator companies and half the ground transport companies.

Foreign involvement in travel and tour activities is largely an extension of the commercial interests of Australian, New Zealand and United Kingdom wholesale travel agencies (for example Kings Tours (Aus), Trans Tours (NZ), Union Travel (NZ), Atlantic and Pacific Travel (UK), United Touring Co. (UK)). These companies incorporate Fiji into well established world-wide marketing networks. By locating branch agencies in Fiji they are able to co-ordinate and control client activities both from the tourist market and tourist destination ends of package tour schedules. A similar process had occurred within the ground transport group. Foreign companies in this sector (which are mostly metropolitan retail travel agencies/tour co-ordinators) have invested heavily in car and minibus fleets. Control by one such multinational company (the Australian subsidiary of the British-owned United Tour Company Ltd) of coach seating capacity has given it a monopoly over the country's tourist road routes and hence of inter-hotel transfer movements made by tourists. Foreign rental car firms are again extensions of international corporations. Operating as either independent enterprises in partnership with local companies (Tasman and Mutual from New Zealand) or with other foreign interests (Avis, Hertz and Kays from Australia), these companies dominate hire and rental car activities. Avis Rent-a-Car Ltd alone owns nearly 40 per cent of all rental cars operated in Fiji.

As a consequence of their control of key functions, foreign companies in 1977 accounted for 60 per cent of total sector receipts (Table 12.2), and local European companies for another 35 per cent. The remaining 4.3 per cent was shared between Indian, Fijian and other operators.

Table 12.2: Fiji Travel and Tour Sector: Distribution of Activity by Ownership Categories, 1977 (estimates A$)

Ownership Category	Number of Firms	Per Cent of Retail Outlets (n = 87)	Per Cent of All Vehicles (n = 580)	Total Turnover	Per Cent Turnover
Foreign	14	40.2	73.3	8,240,125	59.6
Expatriate	1	1.1	1.0	110,000	0.8
European	15	36.8	6.4[a]	4,850,780	35.2
Indian	5	12.6	18.8	381,500	2.8
Fijian	6	6.9	0.2	67,000	0.5
Other	2	2.3	0.3	140,000	1.0
	43	100.0	100.0	13,789,405	100.0

Note: [a] Consists primarily of inter-island cruise boats.

From this brief empirical discussion of the hotel and travel and tour sectors, two generalisations can be made. The first is the existence of an industry hierarchy. Whether based on the ownership of hotel rooms and transport units, or on the control of key components of the tourist travel experience, there is a clear dominance of those enterprises that are backed by foreign capital. Under them in descending order of importance are local European, Indian and, finally, Fijian enterprises.

The second generalisation is that this hierarchy is determined by both the differential importance of certain types of services within the sectors and the differential access by various ownership categories to essential inputs and linkages. The dominance of foreign hotel companies, for example, is based on their control of accommodation plant built to serve tourists rather than local clientele needs. Similarly, foreign and local European dominance of the travel and tour sector is determined by their ownership of activities which are pivotal in the organisation and direction of tourist movements. Complementing the strategic importance of these dominant groups is the fact that through the size of their operations, their commercial astuteness and their political and international market linkages, they are able to gain access to critical inputs. In particular, they have access to the best industry expertise, market contacts in metropolitan countries, extensive inter-industry communication networks that allow co-ordination and sale of attractive products, and extensive capital resources. This access has enabled them to gain control over the greater proportion of the total tourist receipts from these sectors. This ability of foreign companies to dominate strategic commercial links is further demonstrated within the tourist shopping and international transport sectors.

The Duty-free Shopping Sector

While the hotel, travel agency and tour sectors are the preserve of foreign and to a lesser extent local European companies, activities such as tourist retail shops are occupations held by indigenous small-scale entrepreneurs. Opportunities for the creation of these activities are one of the more important benefits that tourism brings to Fiji's labour surplus economy. In 1977, 192 tourist retail shopping outlets employed 926 people: 153 of these shops specialised in duty-free consumer goods. Indian proprietors ran 83.3 per cent of these outlets, foreign and European firms 15.1 per cent. The remaining three enterprises (1.5 per cent) were Chinese- and Fijian-owned. However, the implied correspondence between the degree of local (especially Indian) participation and the extent of financial gain accruing to indigenes is misleading. The reason for this lies in the pricing and marketing structure imposed by overseas suppliers and local wholesaling companies.

Fiji's geographic isolation and small market result in relatively high transport costs and the inability of importers (wholesalers) to obtain discounts from bulk purchases. However, irrespective of these costs, Fiji's duty-free trade would remain relatively uncompetitive due to the activities of multinational companies. Virtually all tourist goods are manufactured outside Fiji. Thus, in 1975, 73.7 per cent of the value of electrical and photographic items came from Japan. Australian, European and South-East Asian based companies accounted for 89.4 per cent of jewellery and perfumery goods. Australia, India, South-East Asia and United Kingdom companies supplied 73.1 per cent of souvenir items.

For a Fiji wholesaler, three indenting options are available: direct purchase from the manufacturer, direct purchase from a manufacturer's regional marketing subsidiary or direct purchase from 'independent' metropolitan companies controlling regional distribution rights of various products. The monopsonic rights these supply agencies have over specific brand names have important implications for the duty-free shopping sector.

These external agents determine which regional supplier a Fiji importer indents from. Examples can be found where products (such as photographic films) supplied from an Australian subsidiary of a European or American company are only available to Fiji importers from New Zealand marketing agents. By forcing importers to purchase through lower-order regional outlets, distributing agencies gain the multiple benefits of charging additional mark-ups, increasing the cost of goods to Fiji importers and reducing Fiji's attraction as a duty-free port.

Manufacturers, on the other hand, can directly control the marketing of their products in Fiji by establishing their own wholesale and retail outlets. Such direct marketing takes two forms. A corporation such as Philips Electrical International Ltd retails directly to the public through a Fiji branch of its New Zealand subsidiary. The prices charged in Fiji are such that the duty-free port does not offer prices likely to undermine prices in Australia — the company's main regional market. Alternatively, to reduce expenses incurred in direct retailing, manufacturers like Sanyo Electric Trading Co. Ltd supply direct to a select Fiji importer (often itself a foreign firm) and have a company agent *in situ* to act as a market liaison. Information on competitors' prices and tourist demand is relayed back to the parent company. Manufacturers can, therefore, export shipments of goods to Fiji with a built-in cost factor designed to maximise either the market share or the price a product will bear on the tourist market. In either case, the landed cost of goods in Fiji works to the benefit of the manufacturer, and not necessarily to the advantage of Fiji importers and retailers.

The result of these practices has all too often been the inability of Fiji retailers to offer Australian tourists duty-free goods at prices significantly below those prevailing in Australia. Products sold by Philips Electrical, for example, were priced identically in Fiji and Australia in 1977-8. In some cases, however, Fiji *wholesale* prices (including importers' mark-ups) were above Australian *retail* prices. For example, the wholesale prices of two Hanimex pocket cameras were $29.50 and $49.50 in Fiji. The retail prices of these same models in Australian discount stores were $29.50 and $49.50 respectively. A Polaroid Instamatic camera cost A$36.20 wholesale in Fiji and A$35.80 retail in Australia. Similarly a type of Agfa film wholesaled for A$3.75 in Fiji retailed for A$3.95 in Australia. Such a price structure has proved damaging to Fiji's duty-free sales and has undermined the viability of duty-free trading for the majority of the proprietors involved.

To many Indian retailers, however, it is the Fiji-based importers who are responsible for their uncompetitive position. Of approximately 140 brand-name product lines familiar to Australian, New Zealand and North American tourists, the distribution of 122 was controlled by 19 importing companies. Consisting of 7 foreign- and 12 Indian-owned firms in 1977,[1] these companies were responsible for an estimated 79 per cent of all imported duty-free items. The very strong position of these firms (many of which have their own retail outlets) has enabled them to impose average wholesale mark-ups ranging from 40 to 60 per cent. Retail shop proprietors are then left in a situation where they have to negotiate prices with tourists. With average retail gross profit mark-ups of between 8 and 15 per cent, the net incomes of many small retailers barely exceed subsistence levels.

Table 12.3: Fiji Tourist Shopping Sector[a]: Distribution of Gross Turnover, 1977 (estimates A$)

Intermediary	Number of Firms	Per Cent of Firms	Turnover	Per Cent of Turnover
1 Indian firms (net retail wholesale income)[b]	139	90.8	3,226,440	12.1
2 Foreign-European firms (net retail, wholesale income)[b]	6	3.9	1,688,117	6.3
3 European artisan firms (net income)[b]	5	3.3	88,293	0.3
4 Chinese and Fijian firms (net retail income)[b]	3	2.0	11,280	0.1
5 Foreign stock suppliers and transport firms[c]			15,200,000	57.1
6 Fiji-owned stock suppliers[d]			203,624	0.7
7 Government revenues (taxes, import duties)			5,232,353	19.6
8 Net wages and salaries of approx. 750 employees			989,793	3.7
	153	100.0	26,639,900	100.0

Notes:
a. Coverage includes duty-free enterprises as well as European and Indian retailers of handicrafts (i.e. tourist shops not selling duty-free goods).
b. Less turnover derived from 5-8.
c. Less turnover derived from 7.
d. Less turnover derived from 7-8.

For the duty-free sector as a whole, it is therefore evident that metropolitan companies have been the principal beneficiaries (Table 12.3). Out of the total retail turnover of A$26.6 million in 1977, foreign companies accounted for 63.4 per cent. Of this, 57 per cent went to metropolitan manufacturing, distributing and transport companies. A further 6.3 per cent constituted net income of foreign-owned, Fiji-based importing firms and retail outlets.

The International Air Transport Sector

Unless a tourist destination has adequate international transport services it will be unable to attract sufficient tourists to fill hotel rooms and tour transport fleet seats. In Fiji, international air carriers are the single most important capacity restraint within the tourist industry. Metropolitan airlines have become the force determining tourist flows into Fiji and, potentially, the most important influence on the type and extent of services offered by hotels and tour companies. Airlines have acquired this degree of control through their ability to determine the relative accessibility of Fiji as a destination and the volume of tourists able to be transported there.

To international airlines, small island destinations are relatively unimportant when it comes to the allocation of seating capacity. Conversely, by far the most important destinations are other metropolitan countries. Corporate (and, indirectly, government) airline strategies reflect the highest priority given to these markets. Any rationalisation of trans-Pacific air services by airlines is, therefore, likely to be at the expense of smaller stop-over destinations. It is exactly this situation that Fiji has faced since the early 1970s.

Between 1973 and 1976 a 45.2 per cent reduction in scheduled flights occurred into and out of Fiji, with a concomitant 11.2 per cent decline in actual seating capacity. Despite a steady growth in tourist numbers since 1976 after a stagnant period between 1973 and 1976 (due to the global decline in the world economy), the deterioration in air services has continued. Three factors were, and still are, responsible for this situation. First, the introduction of larger jet aircraft (B747s and DC-10s) has both reduced the number of flights needed to serve the same volume of tourist demand and, because of increased aircraft range, reduce the importance of Fiji as a stop-over point. Second, the onset of global fuel shortages and price rises led to the withdrawal of four foreign carriers from the Fiji sector (American Airlines, Air India, British Airways and Lan Chile). These withdrawals have not only left fewer tourist seats available for Fiji-bound passengers, but reduced competition between the remaining five carriers. As it was, the spatial arrangement of Pacific air services was such that each airline had relative dominance within discrete sectors, while still competing for the major metropolitan markets. In 1978, after the withdrawal of the other four carriers, 80 per cent of scheduled airline seats on the Fiji sector were controlled by Air New Zealand and Qantas, with a further 11 per cent held by Pan Am.

The third factor concerns the deregulation of international aviation services in the Pacific. The consequent increased competition between major carriers (now including Continental Airlines) on the key flight routes between Australasia and North America has induced greater over-flying of stop-over destinations, particularly by Qantas and Pan Am. Air New Zealand, in the meantime, has laid foundations for using the Cook Islands as an alternative stop-over point for its Auckland to Los Angeles flights. Given its management control of the regional carrier Polynesian Airways and its joint partnership in the Rarotongan Hotel, Air New Zealand has a virtual monopoly of ground and air seating capacity in the central South Pacific region. To exacerbate matters for Fiji, the introduction of drastically reduced air fares in the Pacific has heightened the attractions of the long-distance metropolitan destinations for tourists relative to those of the stop-over island countries.

The political and economic implications of such airline activities can become very serious for small, vulnerable island states. The Fiji government is obviously at a disadvantage in its capacity to enter into negotiations with metropolitan governments and airline corporations from a position of strength. Two quotations from the Managing Director of Pan American Airways in Sydney reveal the extent of this relative powerlessness:

> An example of the importance of tourism to the economy of an island state was provided recently by Fiji. During a dispute between Fiji and the United States, landing rights for a major carrier were cancelled in Fiji for a 3 month period. Business slackened, hotel occupancy dropped off, and the net result was a substantial increase in governmental and public appreciation and support of tourism [and air lines].

and

> I would suggest that it is difficult to separate air transportation from

tourism. Thus, if a decision is made against tourism [by a Pacific Island state], then the decision is also not to have air transportation (Clark, 1977, pp. 37 and 102: author's additions in brackets).

With their power to change the frequency of scheduled flights, the differential routing of flights and consequently the physical and monetary accessibility of a country, airlines render tourist flows into Fiji highly susceptible to their corporate priorities (or the priorities of their respective governments). At the same time, airlines can impede efforts by small states to maintain any real political independence.

Conclusion

The extensive benefits accruing to foreign capital from Fiji tourism have resulted from the way these interests have incorporated Fiji into the international tourist trade. Multinational tourism companies have been the prime movers in the establishment of international tourism transport links to Fiji, the development of tourism ground facilities and the creation of Fiji's tourist image. The concentration of commercial power by foreign tourism capital has been achieved through control over key industry inputs. These controls include finance, tourism technology, expertise, access to tourist markets and influence over tourist preferences and expectations. Such companies also control the distribution of international tourist flows, accommodation room capacity, internal transport fleets and tourist shopping sector stock supplies. Moreover, such commercial power is concentrated in the hands of relatively few companies. In 1977, three foreign corporations controlled 92 per cent of international airline seating capacity, five foreign companies controlled Fiji-bound international cruise-ship operations, five foreign hotel chains were responsible for 46 per cent of total accommodation stock and 42 per cent of turnover, and six foreign travel and tour companies accounted for nearly 70 per cent of tour fleet vehicles and 58 per cent of that sector's turnover.

The pre-eminence of metropolitan companies in the international tourist industry gives them the competitive advantages and commercial motivation to dominate similarly second-order tourism functions in the periphery. However, the reason for the ease with which this penetration of a Third World tourist industry has been achieved also lies in the historical evolution of the international economy. The development of tourism in many underdeveloped countries originated from the extension of already-present foreign industrial and mercantile (colonial) capital, or inflows of new foreign tourism capital that have sought to penetrate a profitable strategic growth sector in these neo-colonial economies (Amin, 1976; Obergón, 1974). In Fiji, the introduction of tourism originated from the extension of foreign interests already present in Fiji's colonial economy. Currently operating foreign airline companies, duty-free stock importers, financial institutions, accommodation sector suppliers, owners of freehold land and companies controlling sectors of Fiji's internal transport networks were all active in Fiji before independence. With prior economic growth based on sugar, copra and gold exports, the development of Fiji as a tropical island tourist destination can be seen as simply an extension of a process whereby Fiji has been articulated with the international economy in forms instigated and defined by multinational companies. At various times in the past, it was firms such as the Colonial Sugar Refining Co., the Emperor Gold Mining Co., Lever Bros. and Burns Philp (South Seas) Ltd that ensured the subordination of Fiji's economic development to the interests of Anglo-Australasian industrial capital. In the latest phase of the country's development, multinational tourism companies are one of the key forces effective in reshaping Fiji's underdeveloped status.

Note

1. One firm, controlled by Jardine Matheson Ltd of Hong Kong, has subsequently been re-purchased by local European interests.

13 INTERNATIONAL CAPITAL, INTERNATIONAL CULTURE

J.R. Peet

'Our music goes around the world and I hope it brings us all a little closer' — closing cliché, US 'Emmy Awards', 1979.

'And now stay tuned as beautiful Barbi Benton plays an aspiring sex goddess, next on Fantasy Island' — American Broadcasting Corporation, 18 October 1980.

Introduction

This chapter examines the power of the multinational corporation from a perspective different from the one that is normally found in the conventional literature. The integration of national economies into the capitalist world system, a process in which the multinational corporation is the main institutional actor, is a research theme of great importance, yet it is also one with great diversionary potential, for it is a theme which may disguise as much as it reveals. Issues of the class compositions and ownership systems of the integrated economies may be bypassed via an exclusive focusing on the question of national capital versus international capital, enabling 'policy conclusions' to be reached that merely support semi-state-controlled national capitalism in place of a scarcely controllable international capitalism. Entire dimensions of understanding are seldom integrated into the limited economic analyses of this question. For example, while the (nation) state nearly always forms a component of the analysis of world economic integration, the nature of the state under capitalism is not usually discussed, hence it is merely *assumed* to be antagonistic to 'global corporations [which] must be regulated to restore sovereignty to government' (Barnett and Muller, 1974, p. 375). An economics which remains within capitalist assumptions, or an approach which remains exclusively economic, cannot provide the understanding necessary to comprehend the present changes in the world system. Nor can it guide the concerted mass action which might combat the concentrated force already present in the multinational corporation.

There is a tendency, present to some degree in virtually all thinking

275

about corporations, multinational or not, to see them operating under an autonomous dynamic, yet also exercising a concerted power. Such a universal tendency must contain some truth; but it is an easy truth, and therefore cannot go to the heart of a matter which, even superficially, can be seen to be complex. First, the evident power of the multinational corporation should not be confused with an ability to transcend the structuration of action by the existing total dynamic of the world capitalist system, nor with an independent ability drastically to change that dynamic. Corporate activity must be seen as a sequence of reactions to a structural context only partially understood and controlled by even the mightiest institution. This places the emphasis of analysis on the corporation as specificity of a totality, an emphasis which entails three main interconnected levels of analysis — the internal structure and dynamic of the specific institution, the composition and movement of the total structure of which it is a specific version, and the changing relation between specificity and totality. Totality, here, is obviously the world system of social formations, and the analysis closest to being adequate to its understanding can only be found in the recent work of Amin (1974; 1976; 1980), Frank (1979), Wallerstein (1974) and others (for example Fröbel, Heinrichs and Kreye, 1980). Hence the need for a synthesis between the institutional analysis of the multinational corporation and world systems analysis, with the latter being interpreted in its mode of production formulation rather than in its ideological form, for example, as merely a system of 'interdependent development' (Brookfield, 1975). Some elements of this general context will be made evident by the first part of the main body of this chapter which discusses international capital.

Second, we should discuss the idea of a concert of corporate action and power. Evidence of meetings of the heads of corporations, interlocking directorships between corporations and between them and financial institutions, etc., is simultaneously revealing and mystifying. This kind of work is revealing in its compilation of the minutiae of corporate machination — who gets together with whom to do what to whom by which means. It is mystifying in that it again assumes a corporate power to do almost anything to anyone as though by fiat; further, uncovering the detail of corporate decision-making is so delicious that the researcher develops a taste only for it, and not for the more general cultural context in which both 'corporate manipulation' and 'common action' take place. For an understanding of this context we must look at the development of a world-synthetic consciousness and culture which increasingly structures the minds and actions of world managers, workers and consumers alike. Understanding this development involves integrating analyses of particular corporate manipulative practices, as in for example the development of corporate advertising on a world scale (for example Janus and Roncaglio, 1979), with the more general analyses of ideology and false consciousness (Althusser, 1971; Jakubowski, 1976; Barrett, Corrigan, Kuhn and Wolff, 1979). The beginning of such an integration, as the theoretical basis of the internationalisation of capitalist culture, will be made in the second part of this chapter.

The analytical theme uniting the two main components of the chapter is the situating of the relative autonomy of movement of a part of society (here the multinational corporation) within, as a component of, and determined by a totality which is not some separate 'Being for itself' but is, precisely, the historical accumulation and present systems of interactions of such components. It is to Althusser's (1969, pp. 89-128) merit that he re-opened the debate on the combination of structural determination with the relative autonomy of the instances of a structure; it is to his detriment that his formulation of that combination could believably be described as 'an orrery of errors' (Thompson, 1978, especially pp. 272-95).

International Capital

The study of the multinational cannot begin with corporation triumphant, but must place its growth and spatial extension of action within the development of the mode of production of which it now forms the most significant component. Failure to situate it in this way leads to the fetish of autonomous multinational corporative movement mentioned in the introduction to this chapter. There is scarcely room here to describe the development of international capitalism, from the transition from feudalism to the present late-monopoly stage. Such a history could, however, be pieced together from the Marxist and neo-Marxist literature. My objective is to indicate some of the main constituents of this analysis and their relations within a perspective which emphasises the *geography* of capital accumulation and underdevelopment (Harvey, 1975).

Centre and Periphery

The development of a world centre of the accumulation of capital is predicated on two, interlocking bases. First, at the centre, the mass separation of labour from ownership of the objective conditions of existence and the purchase of labour as a commodity by the owners of capital previously accumulated in feudal exchange activities created the requisite class relations for the retention of surplus value in the hands of what became the owners of the means of *production* (Marx, 1967, vol. 1, ch. VII, part VIII; Marx, 1973, pp. 447-512). At first, surplus value was increased absolutely by forcefully extending the length of the working day. But, as Brenner (1977, pp. 30, 68) in particular has emphasised, the *distinguishing* feature of capitalism was that it required the owners of the means of production to increase surplus value through the expansion of relative, as opposed to absolute, surplus labour. The increased surplus made possible through improving labour productivity (and thus shortening the labour time necessary for the reproduction of the labour force) was forced by competition into further improvements in labour productivity through mechanisation. As Marx continues:

> There appears here the universalizing tendency of capital, which distinguishes it from all previous stages of production. Although limited by its very nature, it strives towards the universal development of the forces of production, and thus becomes the presupposition of a new mode of production, which is founded not on the development of the forces of production for the purpose of reproducing or at most expanding a given condition, but where the free, unobstructed, progressive and universal development of the forces of production is itself the presupposition of society and hence of its reproduction; where advance beyond the point of departure is the only presupposition. This tendency – which capital possesses, but which at the same time, since capital is a limited form of production, contradicts it and hence drives it toward dissolution – distinguishes capital from all earlier modes of production (Marx, 1973, p. 540).

It is within the context of this necessary dynamic of the capitalist mode, as distinguished from all previous modes of production, that we can fit the second basis for the development of centre in Western Europe.

This second basis is the appropriation and accumulation by the centre of surplus value, created by labour in the world periphery (Frank, 1969; Wallerstein, 1974), and transferred through processes ranging from direct, forceful expropriation (Marx, 1967, p. 751) to the hidden mechanisms of unequal exchange (Emmanuel, 1972). The Brenner position on surplus flows is not to deny that there was a long-term transfer from periphery to centre, but to emphasise the development of a class system in the centre which ensured that surplus value was re-invested in production rather than spent on cathedrals (Brenner, 1977, p. 67). By accepting this emphasis on class we can put the two bases of the centre's economic development into synthetic relation: surplus value from the periphery played an essential role in the original 'primi-tive accumulation' and subsequently provided a continuing input via unequal exchange; but emphasis is also laid on the changing class system as it evolved in Western Europe.

Once the question of the origins of centre and periphery has been clarified, we can examine subsequent developments in terms of the laws of motion of capital of the centre, the penetration, partial breakdown and reorientation of the pre-capitalist modes of the peripheral regions, and the 'spatial dialectic' between these two movements occurring in different (though changing) geographical macro-regions (Peet, 1978). All three aspects of this development have been examined by Amin. While Amin's formulation is so elaborate as to preclude a short sum-mary, we can outline some of the main features of his conception of development and underdevelopment, and the more specific model he presents of the global accumulation of capital (Amin, 1974a; 1974b; 1976, especially pp. 72-8, 191-7; 1977).

Amin *essentially* extends the Baran-Sweezy-Frank line of analysis beyond the level reached by these writers. The development of world capitalism, and the corresponding systems of relations between centre and periphery, are divided into mercantile, industrial revolution and imperialist monopoly stages. Relations between centre and periphery played vital roles in the genesis of capitalism. International trade be-tween periphery and developing centre was the main element in world exchange, with internal exchange in the centre mainly distributing the luxury goods and crafts derived from the periphery, and trade playing a crucial part in the disintegration of feudalism and development of capitalism in the centre. With the industrial revolution, trade settled into the familiar exchange of industrial for agricultural products within what became a relatively fixed pattern of international specialisation. As centre countries other than Britain were industrialised, trade in manufactured and mineral products developed between these countries, and the pattern of trade split into two groups of exchanges with differ-ing functions: exchange between centre and periphery and internal exchange within the centre. Up to this time there had been little export of capital. The formation of monopolies made this possible from about 1870-90 onwards. Again, capital exports must be distinguished between those going to young countries of the central type and those to the periphery. In the periphery these investments made possible changes in specialisation towards goods produced by modern capitalist enterprise with a high productivity and it is these modern sectors, the expressions of *capitalist* development, which provide three-quarters of the periphery's exports to the centre. The capitalist mode of production, which dominates the social formations of the periphery, was thus originally stimulated from without and continues to be anchored in the centre — hence the presence of what Amin calls 'peripheral capitalism' as compared with 'capitalism of the centre'. But whereas in the centre the capitalist mode of production is not merely dominant, but becomes exclusive (i.e. mode of production and social formation coincide), peripheral capitalism is based on the external market and pre-capitalist modes are not destroyed but transformed and subjected to the dominant mode. Peripheral social formations remain articulations of several modes, with the nature of articulation, and the typical level of underdevelopment, varying regionally depending on the originally dominant mode, and the time of incorporation into the world capitalist system.

For Amin there is a fundamental difference between the model of self-reliant accumulation at the centre and extraversion in the periphery, hence he rejects a linear theory of 'stages of development'. The determining relationship of the self-centred system links the production of mass consumption with that of capital goods (intended for the production of consumption goods) with external relations playing a marginal role (Figure 13.1).

Figure 13.1: Amin's Model of Centre and Periphery

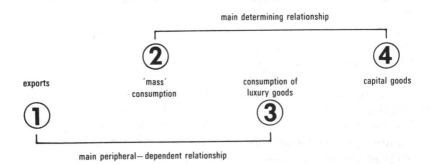

main determining relationship

② ④

exports — 'mass' consumption — consumption of luxury goods — capital goods

① ③

main peripheral—dependent relationship

In the periphery the main relationship is between an externally generated export sector, which because of unequal exchange provides low returns to labour, and the consumption of luxury goods by the ruling classes of incorporated modes and the national bourgeoisie and the state bureaucracy allied with the dominant monopolies. The export sector requires capital-intensive investments which only the transnational oligopolies are in a position to provide and which constitutes the material basis for technological dependence. This scheme characterises the first phase of use of the periphery under imperialism, that is the colonial and semi-colonial form of domination.

The engine of change in the second phase was the anti-imperialist national liberation movement which ended in 'victory' under bourgeois leadership. The triumphant national bourgeoisie then embarked upon a strategy of import-substitution industrialisation designed to provide luxury goods, a strategy which continues to distort the allocation of resources to the detriment of the production of mass consumption goods. The marginalisation of the masses ensures a minimum wage rate in the export and luxury goods sectors. The economy remains 'externally propelled' despite its diversification, industrialisation, etc.

The crisis of this second phase of imperialism was opened by the demand for a 'new international economic order' — that is a rise in the real prices of raw materials exported by the periphery which could finance a new stage of industrialisation involving large-scale exports of manufactured products to the centre. Amin regards this demand as presently led by the national bourgeoisies of the Third World and leading not to the development of mature capitalist formations, but to a new form of unequal exchange:

> The reason, a quite fundamental one, is that the new division of labor would be based on the export by the periphery of cheap manufactured goods, i.e., goods for which the advantage of low wages (bearing in mind comparative productivities) makes it possible to raise the rate of profit in the world system as a whole. The world-wide equalization of profit would then modify relative prices and hence would conceal this extra transfer of value from the periphery to the center. In other words, the new division of labor would perpetuate and worsen unequal exchange. Furthermore, this unequal division of labor would perpetuate the distorted pattern of demand in the peripheries to the detriment of mass consumption, just as in the previous phases. Therefore, the development of the world system would remain fundamentally unequal, and external demand would

still be the main motive force propelling this still dependent type of development (Amin, 1977, pp. 13-14).

Internally it would perpetuate agricultural backwardness, continuing to base industrial accumulation on extortions from the rural world in real terms (rural-urban migration) and financial terms (heavy taxation, unfavourable internal terms of trade, etc.). The contemporary industrialisation of parts of the Third World is thus, in Amin's analysis, merely a new phase of the long-existing process of underdevelopment.

Centralisation and Internationalisation of Capital

Using Amin's account of the development of the phases of centre-periphery relations as historical background, we can now focus on certain particularly crucial aspects of this development, beginning with the relation between the capitalist mode of production and the concentration, centralisation and internationalisation of capital.

Built into Marx's 'general law of capitalist accumulation' are the tendencies towards the concentration and centralisation of capital. Concentration refers to the relatively slow process by which surplus value is re-invested to produce a greater concentration of means of production and labour under the control of individual capitalists. Centralisation refers to a much faster change in the distribution of already concentrated capital brought about by competition via scale of production, aided by the credit system, and enabling industrial capitalists to further extend the scale of their operations (Marx, 1967, vol. 1, pp. 624-8). The theme of centralisation of capital is developed further by Lenin, who sees the end of the nineteenth century as a period of cartelisation taking place within a fusion between industrial and finance capital. The profits, which monopolisation makes possible, accumulate to create a superfluity of capital which cannot find 'profitable' investment and is exported to the periphery - - hence at the end of the nineteenth century the export of commodities, typical of the competitive stage, is replaced by the export of capital as the typical feature of monopoly capitalism. The world is divided into spheres of influence of the monopolist countries which search especially for sources of raw materials. Intensification of the struggle by central national states for the partition of the world is seen as the geopolitical origin of the First World War (Lenin, n.d.).

Lenin's focus on the end of the nineteenth century as the crucial phase of transition from competitive to monopoly capitalism was taken up by Baran and Sweezy (1968), whose analysis emphasises monopoly as issuing from the tendency for the rate of profit to fall under capitalism. For them, the main advantage of the large firm is its ability to be a price maker rather than a price taker — hence the tendency for the surplus to rise and the shifting of the focal problem to one of absorption of the rising economic surplus under monopoly capitalism. Sohn-Rethel (1971) sees the tendency for the rate of profit to fall (specifically in the 'great depression' of 1873-96) as promoting two kinds of reaction: an expansion of markets and opening of new territories and fields for capital investment — that is imperialism, a path followed especially by Britain and France; and an increase in the rate of exploitation at home via modernisation and 'rationalisation' (Taylorism) in the United States and, later, Germany. Hence, in the Marxist theory, centralisation and concentration of capital and imperialism are related, inherent developments of the capitalist mode of production.

The latter, external aspect of the capitalist mode has been theorised by Palloix (1975; 1977) in terms of the 'internationalisation of capital' proceeding through the internationalisation of the separate circuits of capital. The circuit of commodity capital, in which money takes the form of commodities only, was the first to be internationalised — indeed, as we have seen, the mercantile form of simple commodity circulation was international in scope prior to the development of capitalist *production*. The internationalisation of the circuit of money capital, that is international investment or the export of capital, begins with the stage of monopoly. And the third, ultimate stage is the internationalisation of productive capital, that is international production by transnational firms and the spread of capital as a social relation. Hence the capital of the 500 largest US firms employs an international labour force of almost the same size as their national labour force. In addition, 'hegemonic' US capital ensures its reproduction by intersecting with the self-expansion of national capitals, that is 'dominated' capital, both that acting as 'relay' capital (for example Western European) and local (for example Third World) capital. But Palloix's aim is not merely to perform a functional analysis of this phenomenon, an analysis which he says leads in the direction of the chains of dependence which became apparent during internationalisation. Rather the aim is a structural analysis, one that 'reveals the real *capitalist* content of internationalisation: *the law of uneven development*' (Palloix, 1977, p. 22). The idea is to relate the operation of the international and national economies not as two alternate realities, but as 'two phenomena which constantly mirror each other, exemplifying each other in their own historic development because they are both shaped and moulded by capital' (Palloix, 1977, p. 23). In Palloix's structural analysis, internationalisation has its roots in the law of uneven development — it ensures the reproduction of world-wide inequalities as a condition for increasing the rate of surplus value. Internationalisation of capital is not merely the international purchase of labour power, but also the international differentiation of the working class.

> Thus in its international aspect, capital prevents any unity of the international working class by dividing up different working classes, taking advantage of areas of uneven development and amplifying existing schisms. The internationalization of capital is antagonistic to the international class struggle of the proletariat which attempts to re-establish the unity of the working class (Palloix, 1977, p. 23).

We can take from this discussion the idea of the periodisation of central capital's use of the international periphery, and thus the basis of the particular nature of the transnational institution's activities in the Third World. Drawing together Amin's, Lenin's and Palloix's contributions, the three main periods are: (1) a first period when the centre drew commodities produced in use-value-dominated modes in the periphery and transnational companies operated in a mercantile capacity; (2) a second period of the export of capital, made possible by monopolisation of centre economies, in which multinational companies became involved in the production of agricultural and mineral commodities in the periphery; (3) the contemporary period of the internationalisation of the main social relation of capitalism, the integration of at least parts of the world's labour force directly into the process of the self-expansion of capital, and multinational corporations increasingly producing manufactured goods using the abundant cheap labour of the Third World. These periods are not mutually exclusive, in that the earlier ones continue to the present, nor are they evenly present in all regions: as we shall see, the last phase, particularly represented by the growth of industrial production for the world market, has been only selectively 'diffused' into certain regions. Nevertheless, this last phase will be emphasised as being particularly significant.

Uneven Development and the Geography of Class Struggle

Social formations dominated by the capitalist mode of production develop unevenly under the impetus of thousands of atomistic decisions by owners and controllers of the means of production in the context of millions of reactions to those decisions by the working class, as direct producers and consumers, and by the state. Even initially, capitalism rose to dominance in only certain social formations (Brenner, 1976). Within the mode, different sectors pass through its historical stages (manufacturing, modern competitive industry, monopoly industry) at different speeds; likewise, the regional economies dominated by these sectors develop in an uneven way. This uneven development is utilised by the leading economic sectors to reproduce their dominant position.

Uneven development, however, should be seen as the outcome not merely of different capitalist decisions, but of those decisions in the context of the geography of the struggle between capital and labour. While the emphasis of Marxian theory has been on class struggle on the macro-level and cast in terms of essential ownership of the means of production, other recent work (Braverman, 1974; Brecher, 1972; Nichols, 1980, Part V; Friedman, 1977) has begun to examine worker resistance *within* the labour process. In Friedman's (1977, Chapters 4, 6, 9, 17) analysis, when the worker sells his or her labour power for a fixed period, what is actually exchanged is *capacity for labour*. The amount of labour which is then extracted from the worker is limited by laws and customs established by class struggle in the society as a whole and within particular firms and industries. In the monopoly sector of advanced capitalist economies, workers have been able, through struggle, to 'raise the value of their labour power'. On the side of labour, this was made possible by the drying up of the latent reserve army of the rural areas and the growth of worker resistance from the late nineteenth century onwards. On the side of capital, competition was limited by monopoly power, and a larger surplus thus made available to buy off labour resistance. Following Emmanuel (1972), Friedman also argues that workers in advanced countries were able to raise the value of their labour power because surplus was transferred from the underdeveloped countries via unequal exchange. (It should be noted here that Friedman (1977, p. 268) unconventionally redefines 'value of labour power' to mean 'the labour time necessary to keep workers' labour power (as a class) available to capitalists'.)

In Friedman's analysis (1977, p. 131) the major aim of worker resistance has been self-protection from reserve army pressures. To explain adequately the historical origins of differential reserve army pressure we can see these labour reserves, in the layers specified by Marx (1967, vol. 1, pp. 640-8), as emanating from several pre-capitalist modes of production variously articulated with the capitalist mode in the social formations dominated by that mode. Lipietz (1980, pp. 63-5), for example, briefly examines what he calls a '"domestic quasi-mode of production", functioning as an auxiliary to the capitalist mode' and representing a principal labour reserve. But a richer source of cheap labour can be found flowing from the articulation between agricultural petty commodity production and the capitalist mode of production. The two aspects of this articulation of importance are: (1) an unequal exchange between the two which favours industry and promotes the stagnation of small agricultural production; (2) the transfer of cheap labour from stagnated agriculture to industry. Damette (1980) and Carney (1980) widen this latter aspect of labour supply to include areas previously dominated by earlier stages in the development of the capitalist mode (mining, old industrial areas) and now discarded. The theme of these contributions is to link cheap labour supply and pressure of the reserve army on the active industrial army to the differential articulation of modes of production and the phases of geographical development of the capitalist mode.

Continuing this work, we can now approach more closely a Marxist explanation of recent changes in the geography of capitalist production, and especially the internationalisation of capital. From the analytical viewpoint of uneven development, and basing his analysis on the tendency for the rate of profit to fall, Damette sees three ways for firms to make surplus profits: technical advance; a more favourable geographical location; and greater exploitation of the labour force. The third of these has assumed greater importance and, under the additional impact of state policy, has resulted in the 'hypermobility of capital' as the source of 'the most important laws of the organization of space under State Monopoly Capitalism' (Damette, 1980, p. 85). Similarly, from his analysis of class struggle, Friedman (1977, p. 140) concludes that the spatial form of the hypermobility of capital is that

> Large companies, particularly in the last few decades, have been shifting their new investments to where they can take advantage of immigrant workers: to less developed regions of developed countries, or to less developed countries. There wages are lower, workers are poorly organised and often the local state offers to bolster Direct Control strategies with coercive labour laws.

My own formulation (Peet, 1977, 1978, 1979) of the pressures behind the mobility of capital is cast in terms not only of the geography of class struggle, but of a series of contradictions inherent in the capitalist mode, which mature, intersect and form complexes as that mode matures. Contradictions are revealed in a succession of 'social and environmental problems' in areas long occupied by capitalism. An increasing share of the society's surplus value, and indeed of the entire material and intellectual effort of the society, has to be devoted to containing these problems, while a sophisticated diversionary ideology is also necessitated particularly by the fact that such problems *can* only be (barely) contained and not solved. The seriousness of the crisis of advanced capitalism can only be understood if it is realised that its contradictions are located in the conditions of existence of the entire mode of life: that is, they occur in the social relations and the relation with physical environment which enable the material reproduction of life. Specifically, in the case of production institutions, these contradictions impinge in the form of a raising of the costs of production (higher wages, more union resistance, higher taxes, etc.) in the old regions of capitalism. As it is not even possible for particular institutions to engage the originating societal causes of the 'problems' which they experience, some capitalist firms take the course of re-investment in a succession of peripheries (regional, national, international), and others are then forced to follow by a competitive pressure which remains even under quasi-monopoly (Cypher, 1979). The most recent manifestation of a geographic movement at least as old as the late-nineteenth-century relocation of the US cotton textile industry is the internationalisation of productive capital in manufacturing industry. Let us conclude this section by briefly looking at the resulting geography of industrial production.

Figure 13.2 shows a pattern of decline in manufacturing employment that is almost exactly confined to the old industrial heartland of Western Europe and the north-eastern United States (United Nations, 1970; United Nations, 1979). Hence, the countries with an average annual decline in persons engaged in manufacturing of greater than 0.5 per cent per year between 1965 and 1975 were Belgium (−1.2 per cent), Denmark (−0.9 per cent), West Germany (−0.8 per cent), Italy (−4.1 per cent), Netherlands (−2.0 per cent), Switzerland (−4.2 per cent) and the United Kingdom (−2.4 per cent), and in the United States, New England (−1.1 per cent), the Middle Atlantic (−1.7 per cent) and East North Central (−0.6 per cent) regions. Although France (−0.05 per cent) is missing from this list, it can be seen that industrial decline is almost exactly coterminal with the original industrial heartland. Second, the map shows that rapid industrial growth (10 per cent or more per annum 1965-75) is limited to a few countries (Hong Kong, Malaysia,

Figure 13.2: Growth of World-wide Manufacturing Employment, 1965-75

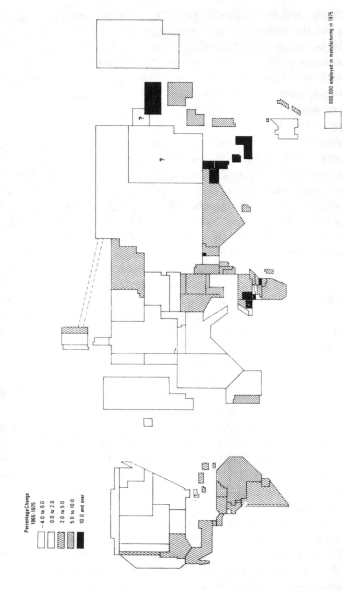

Percentage Change
1965-1975
-4.0 to 0.0
0.0 to 2.0
2.0 to 5.0
5.0 to 10.0
10.0 and over

800,000 employed in manufacturing in 1975

Source: *UN Statistical Yearbook*, 1970-9.

Singapore, Indonesia, South Korea and Taiwan) in South-East Asia (data for the other rapid-growth countries shown on the map are unreliable). The overall pattern of world manufacturing employment remains one dominated by the industrial heartland of Europe, North America and Japan; with Mexico, Brazil and Argentina now also as major employers, and South-East Asia as the area of dramatic change. We are *not*, therefore, witnessing the widespread industrialisation of the periphery, only of certain parts of it, in countries with quite small populations. The economic consequences of export-led industrialisation in these countries have been shown to be limited in terms either of indigenous capitalist development or meeting the needs of Third World workers and peasants (Landsberg, 1979). Even so, as integral components of the world capitalist economy, these countries have to be tightly integrated into capitalist culture; as indeed have all areas of the periphery used by capitalist production. It is to this cultural aspect of world capitalism that we now turn.

International Culture

In Marxist theory, human cultures are founded in the historically specific ways in which the material reproduction of life is achieved – in Hall's (1977, p. 318) terms, 'culture refers to the arrangement – the *forms* – assumed by social existence under determinate historical conditions.' The emphasis here will be on the consciousness component of culture or, as Marx (1969a) put it, the 'entire superstructure of distinct and peculiarly formed sentiments, illusions, modes of thought and views of life' which arises on the basis of 'different forms of property, upon the social conditions of existence'. The illusory aspect of consciousness, referred to by Marx, stems from the limiting conditions which definite levels of the development of the productive forces, and forms of social interactions between producers, place on the formation of human conceptions, ideas, etc.: 'The phantoms formed in the human brain are . . ., necessarily, sublimates of the material life-process' (Marx, 1969b, p. 25). In the early stages of the development of the forces of production, nature 'appears to men as a completely alien, all-powerful and unassailable force' yielding natural religion and a limited form of social consciousness – 'herd-consciousness' (Marx, 1969b, pp. 32-3). With increased productivity and the division of labour, a more emancipated consciousness becomes possible. But as the development of exchange begins to equate the human labours which create commodities, as it becomes possible for labour to be understood as the basis of value, the process of production is simultaneously mystified by the relation between the producers assuming the fantastic form of a relation between their products – what Marx (1967, pp. 71-6) calls the fetishism of commodities. False consciousness thus arises from a necessary but fundamental misunderstanding of the natural and social conditions of human existence.

In addition, in class societies the means of the production of ideas are controlled by the class which is the ruling material force – that is, in so far as 'they rule as a class and determine the extent and compass of an epoch . . . they do this in its whole range, hence among other things they rule also as thinkers, as producers of ideas, and regulate the production and distribution of the ideas of their age' (Marx, 1969b, p. 47). The resulting dominant, or in Gramsci's phrase hegemonic, ideologies are particular (ruling) class versions of the fundamentally false consciousness of an era. They become 'hegemonic' when accepted as descriptors of the order and causes of things, when people are induced by them into acquiescence that the existing life is natural, good and just (Kellner, 1978, pp. 48-50). At their core, hegemonic ideologies are supportive theories of the existing order. But they are also prescriptive of attitudes and behaviour, and thus come to be the ideational bases of whole ways of being a person. Mass culture thus comes to be underlain by ideology produced on behalf of the existing order and in the interests of the extant ruling class.

Captains of Consciousness

There is a tendency, at this point, for discussions of hegemonic ideology to slip into versions of manipulation theory – the idea that there is a class of mind managers which wilfully manipulates the masses into an acceptance of the *status quo* (Ben-Horin, 1977, pp. 10-22). For example, Horkheimer and Adorno's (1972, pp. 120-67) discussion of the 'culture industry' provides a sophisticated version of manipulation theory. They argue that the culture industry, controlled economically and technologically by monopoly capital, uses psychotechnology in mass-producing 'ready-made clichés' to overpower the consumer, stunting her or his powers of imagination, turning participants into listeners and observers amenable to central control. The direct producers of culture are pressured into conformity – hence the artist must fit into business life as aesthetic expert – so that cultural production comes to consist of a constant reproduction of the same thing. The consumers of culture thus have the freedom to choose what is always the same. As a result, their every action bears witness to

> man's attempt to make himself a proficient apparatus, similar (even in emotions) to the model served up by the culture industry. The most intimate reactions of human beings have been so thoroughly reified that the idea of anything specific to themselves now persists only as an utterly abstract notion: personality scarcely signifies anything more than shining white teeth and freedom from body odor and emotions (Horkheimer and Adorno, 1972, p. 167).

The problem with this account is that it over-simplifies the production of culture at one end of the process and its automatic effect at the other, even while disclosing an essential truth about the profound influence of the culture industry in late capitalism. The first of these deficiencies can be further exemplified by Ewan's work on the development of 'modern advertising' in the United States. Ewan sees advertising as a response to two crises of capitalism: first, the rise of labour militancy in the late nineteenth century evoked 'a cultural apparatus aimed at defusing and neutralizing potential unrest' in the forms of 'human engineering' within the workplace and the development of 'an ideology of consumption' beyond it (Ewan, 1976, p. 12); second, the development of mass productive capacity necessitated a mass market, one which cut across differences of region, taste, need and class to produce men and women 'habituated to respond to the demands of the productive machinery' (Ewan, 1976, p. 25). The solution to both was the production, via advertising, of a *commodity self*, that is people habituated to buying as a solution to their problems as encountered in industrial capitalism. However, this 'solution' was functional beyond production and consumption. Embedded within it was the propagation of support for corporate capitalism as a mode of social organisation, of consumption as an alternative to other modes of change, as alternative to class thinking, and as the focus of a conception of a good life. 'Only in the instance of an individual ad was consumption a question of *what to buy*. In the broader context of a burgeoning commercial culture, the foremost political imperative was *what to dream*' (Ewan, 1976, p. 109). This 'imperialization of the psyche' initiated in the 1920s came into full force in the economic boom of the post-war era, especially in the 1950s when television provided the ideal vehicle for the diffusion of a consumerist mentality, that is 'a vision of freedom which continually relegated people to consumption, passivity and spectatorship' (Ewan, 1976, p. 213). The resulting conformism was disrupted during the 1960s, but advertising has responded by incorporating the appearances of resistance into mass culture, generating new commodity markets out of 'resistance' to commodityisation, even incorporating anti-corporate sentiment into advertisements for corporate products!

This account again displays deep insight into the effects of advertising. Its deficiencies lie in its analysis of how the necessities of capitalism, as general system, come to be met by advertising, as specific ideological institution. The analytical need here is to achieve an explanation which relates specific institutional action to the dynamic of the totality, yet does not rely on the naïve notion that advertising deliberately sets out to 'save capitalism'. Advertising has the particular intention of selling products. Myriad attempts to sell more products then amount to a more general ideology which has a mass effect. But the links between systemic necessity, particular institutional intention and general ideological effect must be effectively made: as yet, Ewan has not made these links.

In a broader, related analysis, Enzensberger (1974, pp. 11-12) argues that the main function of the 'consciousness industry' (radio, cinema, television, recording, advertising, public relations, newspapers, fashion and industrial design, propagation of religious and other cults, tourism, etc.) is *not* to sell particular products but to 'sell' the existing order:

> Material exploitation must camouflage itself in order to survive; immaterial exploitation has become its necessary corollary. The few cannot go on accumulating wealth unless they accumulate the power to manipulate the minds of many . . . What is being abolished in today's affluent societies, from Moscow to Los Angeles, is not exploitation, but our awareness of it.

Focusing on the role of the communications media in promoting consumerism, Enzensberger argues that the attractive power of mass consumption is based not on the dictates of false needs, but on the falsification of real and legitimate ones, while the media owe their power not to any sleight of hand but to 'the elemental power of deep social needs which came through even in the present depraved form of those media' (Enzensberger, 1974, p. 111). In this latter point Enzensberger is quite right — the powerful effect of the media is derived from the falsification of deep social needs which continue to exist, continue to demand fundamental rather than ideological satisfaction. Again, however, Enzensberger's analysis of the consciousness industry relies on deliberate manipulation in the interest of preserving the general order.

Let us examine 'consciousness manipulation' in a little more detail. On the one hand we have the consciousness industry manufacturing ideological products. Because this industry holds the central position in late capitalism, it can use the attractions of high monetary return and mass adulation to employ the most 'creative' minds, the most beautiful bodies, the most skilled technicians to produce technicolored, stereophonic pieces of edited false consciousness which are continually projected into the minds of people living at the centre of world capitalism with the use of the most sophisticated 'communications' technology ever known. The techniques used involve particularly the provision of manufactured 'experience' in audio and visual formats which replicate, and especially exaggerate, real events, intervening between everyday sensory experience and the process of consciousness formation by providing ready-formed but inaccurate generalisations (the clichés referred to by Horkheimer and Adorno). After a certain period, the mind comes to prefer such exaggerated, edited, 'perfectized' forms of 'experience' over the more mundane real experience. The result has been to produce not only new forms, but perhaps also new levels of false consciousness, levels so deep as to produce a fantasy prism between direct experience and the mind; rose-coloured spectacles which almost totally prevent a critical consciousness from developing in reaction to societal contradiction. Rather than particular ideologies having particular effects, violent television programmes promoting individual violent acts, etc., the emphasis here is on the long-term effects of the replacement of real experience by manufactured, exaggerated 'experience'. This has produced a people whose lives are dominated by the pursuit of the latest cultural (ideological) fetish and the acquisition of the commodities, commodity activities and commodity personalities which are inevitably attached to that fetish.

On the other hand, no matter how sophisticated the techniques of ideological production, the consciousness industry must also retain a connection with the real structure of life: that is, it must relate to real events and people's fears and aspirations, as its essential source of power and the guiding direction (however indirect) of its dynamic. We can only understand the basis of false consciousness in terms of a mode of the production of life whose conditions of existence are in a state of ultimate contradiction. The relation with nature and the social relation between people, which combine to make the production of life possible, are inherently contradictory in the capitalist mode. As that mode develops, contradictions intensify and interact, to form an unsolvable complex manifested in social and environmental problems which invade all aspects of life at the epicentre of the world capitalist system. The unsolvable nature of these problems means that they must not be thought in real terms, for this would lead in the direction of revolutionary consciousness (that is one aimed at overthrowing 'the basis of the entire existing system' – Marx and Engels, 1969b, p. 42); yet they must be thought, and they must appear in mass consciousness and culture. Hence they can only be 'thought' in fantasy form. Both the producers of cultural products and the consumers of these products thus share a fascination with fantastic versions of the effects of unsolvable societal contradictions: this fascination comes out, for example, in the production of a popular culture which endlessly revolves around such themes as violence and death, commodity destruction, cults of mysterious forces, escape and escapade in space, super technology and super-powerful human beings. Because these are only fantastic versions of fragments of contradiction, they cannot deal satisfactorily with the fears aroused by their source. But this leads only to further exaggeration, a more extreme fetish, more powerful technologies used to reproduce endless variations on the same theme. The end result of this escalating process might be called 'super-culture' had the word 'super' not already been superseded. We should, instead, call the resulting culture by its own favourite description: hence we are now in the phase of 'ultra-culture'.

Ultra-culture is differentiated from its predecessors mainly by the degree of its deliberate, highly technological manufacture, not of course as a whole, but as carefully prepared individual clichéd components launched on to the 'market of minds' under the impetus not of a centrally planned decision but thousands of 'spontaneous' decisions informed by the profit motive. These particular cultural clichés interact to form a system, which changes as new versions of clichés appear, become dominant, and (rapidly) disappear. Both the manufactured individual clichés and the cultural totality formed by their interaction are conditioned by the economic structure of the mode of production: the dynamic of the whole mode, structure and superstructure can only be understood in terms of societal contradiction, partial response to contradiction and the continued but altered maturation of contradiction. However, while the dynamic of the economic structure conditions the development of culture, there is a tendency also for culture, and especially its consciousness aspect, to achieve a greater autonomy than, for example, the political instance of the superstructure. For, while there is no other original source of consciousness than social being,

consciousness   nd
developing in t   ıst.
Specifically, th   the
components of   ives
of previous, a   ure.
Hence while t   ) the
dictates of the   ffect
their consume   material contradi   ʒ and
comprehendii   alisa-
tion. And ye   ested
with all the   rough
the media, s   ', or a
tune careless   ext. So
it is that c   Orwell's
sense of pla   g culture
producing 'ı

The Interna

The geography of culture is rooted in the different ways ше people of the earth reproduce their material existence under different levels of development of the productive forces, under different social relations of production, and with different social relations to varying physical environments. But in addition, the culture formed in a given social and material context is often found beyond the confines of that environment. The fundamental basis of mass culture diffusion is the economic use made of one social formation by another. As part of an overall process of economic domination, the hegemonic culture of the dominating power prevails over dominated cultures, producing synthetic versions from the interaction of itself and the local cultures, over wide stretches of conquered space. Further, the relative autonomy of the cultural instance often is translated, in spatial terms, into the extension of cultural hegemony beyond the arena of economic use, or political control, so that a dominant formation's area of cultural hegemony may be larger than its economic or political domains. This can be seen in the wide diffusion into the periphery of the 'ultra-culture' developed in the crucible of intense contradiction at the centre of world capitalism.

From its very beginning, capitalism has been a world system, in terms of flows of materials, labour and capital. From its beginning also centre-capitalist ideologies have both accompanied, and spread beyond, the use of resources and people in a series of widening peripheries. The religious ideology developed in the capitalist centre has always tended to extend beyond the domain of significant economic use. By comparison, the imposition of a 'colonial mentality', under which colonial people were taught to imitate the dominator's cultural models, vividly described by Fanon (1968), Memmi (1965), Friere (1972) and Constantino (1978) involved a more intense contact and thus at least political control by the dominant power. The recent intensification in the centre's use of peripheral resources, markets and labour has been accompanied by an intensification of cultural domination. But even beyond the arena of significant economic use, elements or imitations of the ultra-culture can be found: for example in Peruvian villages, peasants too poor to buy transistor radios carry stones painted black as 'status items' (Barnett and Muller, 1974, p. 177). My own field work in the remote Lau Group of Fiji (Peet, 1980) also indicates a considerable penetration of 'Western' artefacts and forms of behaviour even in remote village communities only tenuously integrated into the world economy — here also the ubiquitous transistor radio is a powerful vehicle of diffusion.

This process of the penetration of hegemonic culture can be analysed at various levels and under a number of approaches. The most obviously 'geographic' approach is via 'flows' of influence down the urban hierarchy or between regions. Thus Gould and Johnson (1980a; 1980b) have begun to examine flows of television programmes described as 'the most powerful verbal and visual form of international communication ever created'. Their research is cast not only in terms of origins and destinations, but more importantly in terms of the structure of television programming, structure being defined as the intersection between 'backcloth' (subject-matter) and 'traffic' (way in which the subject-matter is treated). This latter aspect inevitably raises the question of the 'value structures' which inform classifications of television programmes — a question which they hardly answer satisfactorily by designing an analytical device which allows individual countries to 'describe programmes on the basis of their own value structures' (1980b, p. 189). In addition, programme flows must be set in the context of the institutional matrix which informs and performs the transfer of cultural materials: that is, which corporations are involved in the physical transfer process, for what reasons, etc. Without at the very least this institutional component the purely geographic concept of 'flow' tends to abstract from the real transfer mechanisms involved.

Various aspects of the 'diffusion' of hegemonic culture have been examined elsewhere. Methodologically, most are variations of an institutional analysis within a more general dependency framework. They emphasise the multinational activities of centre advertising, 'communications' and other consciousness industries. Thus Janus and Roncàglio (1979) link the multinationalisation of industry with global dissemination of international advertising agencies, most of which originated in the United States, and more generally with changes in the functions of the mass media, the development of consumerism and effects on the 'whole fabric of society and especially on choices of development strategies'. Golding (1978) has analysed the international publishing industry, now dominated by international corporations with local subsidiaries, in terms of 'cultural dependency as the complement . . . to economic dominance'. Varis (1976) and Guback (1974) have looked at the activities of international media corporations in the flow of films: ' "Hollywood" keeps half the cinemas in the non-socialist world supplied with films' – and also television programmes (see also Varis, 1974; de Cardona, 1975), radio programmes, records and cassettes and printed material. Masmondi (1979) and Harris (1974; 1976) have examined the international news networks providing 80 per cent of the world news flowing overwhelmingly from centre to periphery, so that peripheral people find out what is happening in the periphery via news from the centre. And a number of studies have examined the organisation and the effects of international tourism on indigenous culture – hence Perez (1975, p. 140), speaking of the West Indies, concludes:

The very culture passes into dependency on tourist patronage. Art, music, dance, and literature become the patrimony of an expanding tourist economy. In the process, artistic expression in the West Indies loses its integrity and, indeed, its relevance to the West Indian experience.

Hence the evidence of 'cultural imperialism', instituted especially by the multinational media corporations, has thus been abundantly established. This is so evidently the case that the main need is not for further institutional studies, but for models which can synthesise the materials available within a political economic framework (Mattelart, 1979).

As Horkheimer and Adorno (1972, pp. 122-6) argued, the monopolies of the culture industry operate under the domination of the leading sectors of industry which employ them. As pointed out in the first part of this chapter, the leading sectors now operate at a world scale, using world resources and labour, and needing the world market to exhaust their resulting output. The need, increasingly, is for a world population which responds to the dictates of the international corporations – a homogenised mass of people who respond in predictable ways to the inducements of the world capitalist economy. But how is such a 'systemic need' realised under conditions of atomistic, self-serving decision-making? It is realised by mental adherence to capitalist culture, the 'ultra-culture' described earlier. That is, the diffusion of the artefacts and behaviours of a powerful, fetishised way of life, one which comes to be preferred over indigenous culture, transforms the world's people into latent cogs in the capitalist production and consumption machine. This preference for capitalist culture is then concretely realised by purchase of its most important artefacts – clothing, radios, televisions, music, films, automobiles, etc. Hence while mental adherence is widespread, concrete realisation of adherence varies with money income. Rather than describing the variation in adherence/realisation in terms, for example, of a distance decay function, we should instead look at the more fundamental determinants of differential adherence to, and realisation of, the hegemonic culture of the centre.

For the sake of simplicity, we could divide the periphery into two types of dependent social formations. First, there are formations in which the original mode(s) of production are subjected to the capitalist mode, yet remain as the basis for commodity production. Second, there are formations in which capitalist relations of production are now being instituted. In the first, the indigenous culture retains a functional relation to its original (but changed) material basis, hence adherence to capitalist culture is countered by a viable cultural alternative. In addition, money incomes tend to be small, so that the realisation of adherence is blocked at least for the mass of the population. In the second type of formation the capitalist mode is more completely dominant and is the main determinant of cultural adherence, while the higher money incomes which result from direct employment by capitalist enterprise make the concrete realisation of this adherence more fully possible. Such realisation of a culture can, in turn, be expected to reinforce its adherence in consciousness. Hence we can predict two levels of domination by hegemonic culture, specified in terms of adherence and realisation, and dependent ultimately on the degree and type of economic use of a peripheral formation by central capitalism. The peripheries which are intensively used by central capitalism, especially those in which capitalist social relations of production are being instituted, as in the export platforms of the new manufacturing zone in South-East Asia, should also be areas of the domination of capitalist culture in terms of adherence in consciousness and the realisation of this adherence in terms of purchases of commodities, styles of life, forms of behaviour, etc. Peripheries which are not intensively used, or in which the original mode of production is maintained as source of exported commodities, should be areas of lower mental adherence to central capitalist culture, and a lower degree of realisation of this culture in terms of purchases of its artefacts, change in life-style and behaviour.

This discussion has focused on the cultural forms developed at the centre of world capitalism, their movement over space and their effects on cultures associated with pre-capitalist modes of production. It has not taken into account the specific contents of indigenous cultures and the differential resistance implied by these contents, for that would be impossible at this level of generalisation. But while this crucial ingredient of the analysis is missing, what has been presented does enable an understanding of the economic sources of the process of cultural domination and integration, especially the tendency towards the transformation of the culture of the centre into world culture under the economic impetus of the internationalisation of capital.

International Capital, International Culture

Focusing on the multinational corporation as the main institutional actor represents an advance towards a more exact, realistic analysis of the economic geography of the world. But it is important also that the insights derived from this analytical advance should not prevent a further movement towards placing this institution into the more general structure of which it forms a component part. Failure to do so yields an over-emphasis on the autonomy of action and overwhelming manipulative power of the corporation triumphant, an emphasis which has enough truth to maintain it, but which misses other more fundamental insights. The multinational activities of centre-corporations must instead be seen in the context of the development of the world capitalist system. This is a system which first is capitalist, and must be understood as such — this means tying institutional analysis into the more profound theory of the structure of the capitalist mode of existence. Specifically, large corporations must be seen as the modern institutional form of the capitalist mode of production; they are the most recent manifestation of a process which has a long history. And second, the world capitalist system is a geographic phenomenon, one which operates in space and re-forms spatial content through its action. Capitalism is a system which develops unevenly in space, continually making centres and peripheries, with relations of dependence and exploitation between the peoples in these different types of region. International monopoly capitalism can thus be comprehended by tying the institution 'multi-national corporation' into a systemic process operating in space, a process understood simultaneously in terms of economic structure and space.

This chapter has examined two aspects of the process of the internationalisation of capitalism: the internationalisation of capital; and the internationalisation of capitalist consciousness and culture. Capital must be understood not as neutral money, but as the product of a certain class relation — an exploitative relation between owners of the means of production and labour deprived exactly of these means. It must, therefore, be understood in terms both of apparent forms and origin, hence its analysis must also be historical. But as the school of thought represented by Frank, Amin and Emmanuel has shown, capital of the centre must *also* be understood as an accumulation based in part on exploitative relations between centre and periphery, so its analysis must instantaneously be geographic. Hence through a historical geography of the capitalist mode of production we can place the present tendency towards internationalisation of monopoly capital in the context of inherent movements of capitalism towards concentration and centralisation of capital and the history of relations between capitalist centre and pre-capitalist periphery. Further, as the relation between capital and labour is primarily one of exploitation and struggle over surplus, we can examine the movement of capital from the additional perspective of the geography of class struggle. And finally, as capitalism is a mode of the production of life which is contradictory, destroying its conditions of existence at the same time as it exists by them, we can examine movements in the world system in terms of the formation in space of complexes of contradictions, attempts to escape the crisis phenomena emanating from these contradictions, and their re-formation elsewhere. Hence the objective, only partially fulfilled, is to place the institution 'multinational corporation' into the general structure of the capitalist system.

But this general structure of capitalism must be more than a purely economic structure, for the mode of the production of life is, surely, exactly that — the production of all aspects of life, its politics, its culture and its forms of consciousness. Different economic structures are the bases of different ways of being human, of different types of human relations, of different contents of the mind and ways of reasoning about these contents. Specifically, the movement of centre capitalism into a period of increasing contradiction, the invasion of crisis into everyday life, has produced a powerful response in the realm of consciousness and culture. This response has not primarily been one of dealing with the origins of crisis in societal contradiction, via revolutionary politics, but rather has been one of handling crises through creating the requisite forms of false consciousness. Contradiction informs contemporary consciousness, provides it with material and fuel, gives it its overwhelming power; but simultaneously consciousness diverts into fantasy forms of the comprehension of contradiction. A fascination with the effects of contradiction — death, violence, destruction — and with fantastic ways of escaping from contradiction — space, super-human beings, supra-human forces — becomes the main content of contemporary ultra-culture, while at the same time the origins of these effects, and real ways of dealing with originating forces, are continually evaded. And this must be the case if social and environmental problems emanate from contradiction in the conditions of existence.

The existing literature on the production of ultra-culture at the centre, and its dissemination into the peripheries, is in the tradition of institutional analysis. This over-emphasises the freedom of action, and the manipulative potential, of what are, admittedly, powerful particular institutions. The crunch comes when these models attempt to deal with intention, when atomistic institutions pursuing individual goals supposedly fuse into a structure responding to systemic needs. Hence the attempt in the latter part of this chapter to place the actions of the institution into the context of the movement of the totality.

Internationalisation of the economic operation of the capitalist system must be accompanied by political and cultural domination. The connection between the economic structural, and the political and cultural superstructural, instances of internationalisation are complex indeed. Centre economic use of the resources and people of the periphery may be seen as the primary determinant of the degree of adherence to, and realisation of, centre culture. But this determination is not one in which a specific type and intensity of economic use exactly determines a specific type and intensity of cultural imperialism. In particular centre culture has a power, and fluidity in space, which enable it to capture significantly the hearts and minds of people only tenuously connected with the world capitalist economic system. The implications of this power and spatial fluidity are profound. The direction is one of

homogenisation of world culture, the making of the world's people into brown, black and yellow jealous imitators of American super-people. And if this process of cultural integration is successful, the consequence is that everyone, not just the people of the centre, becomes involved in the fantastic escape from what are becoming world-wide contradictions in the conditions of human existence.

REFERENCES

Aaronovitch, S., and Sawyer, M.C. (1975) *Big Business: Theoretical and Empirical Aspects of Concentration and Mergers in the United Kingdom*, Macmillan, London

Aboyade, O. (1968) 'Industrial Location and Development Policy: the Nigerian Case', *Nigerian Journal of Economic and Social Studies*, 10(3), 275-302

Abumere, S. (1978) 'Multinationals, Location Theory and Regional Development: Case Study of Bendel State of Nigeria', *Regional Studies*, 12, 651-64

Aglietta, M. (1979) *A Theory of Capitalist Regulation: the US Experience*, New Left Books, London

Aharoni, Y. (1966) *The Foreign Investment Decision Process*, MIT Press, Cambridge, Mass.

Alford, J. (1979) 'Australian Labour, Multinationals and the Asian-Pacific Region', *Journal of Australian Political Economy*, 6, 4-23

Aliber, R.Z. (1970) 'A Theory of Direct Investment' in C.P. Kindleberger (ed.), *The International Corporation*, MIT Press, Cambridge, Mass., pp. 17-34

— (1971) 'The Multinational Enterprise in a Changing World' in J.H. Dunning (ed.), *The Multinational Enterprise*, George Allen and Unwin, London, pp. 49-56

Althusser, L. (1969) *For Marx*, Penguin, Harmondsworth

— (1971) 'Ideology and Ideological State Apparatuses' in L. Althusser, *Lenin and Philosophy*, Monthly Review Press, New York, pp. 127-86

Amin, S. (1974a) *Accumulation on a World Scale: a Critique of the Theory of Underdevelopment*, 2 vols., Monthly Review Press, New York

— (1974b) 'Accumulation and Development: a Theoretical Model', *Review of African Political Economy*, 1, 9-26

— (1976) *Unequal Development*, Monthly Review Press, New York

— (1977) 'Self Reliance and the New International Economic Order', *Monthly Review*, 29(3), 1-21

— (1978) *The Law of Value and Historical Materialism*, Monthly Review Press, New York

— (1980) *Class and Nation, Historically and in the Current Crisis*, Monthly Review Press, New York

Annear, P. (1973) 'Foreign Private Investment in Fiji' in A. Rokotuivuna, *Fiji — a Developing Australian Colony*, International Development, North Fitzroy, Melbourne, pp. 39-49

Ansoff, H.I. (1965) *Corporate Strategy*, McGraw-Hill, New York

Ardagh, J. (1977) *The New France*, Penguin, Harmondsworth

Arpan, J., and Ricks, D. (1975) *Directory of Foreign Manufacturers in the United States*, School of Business Administration, Georgia State University, Atlanta

Arrighi, G., and Saul, J.S. (1973) 'Nationalism and Revolution in Sub-Saharan Africa' in G. Arrighi and J.S. Saul (eds.), *Essays on the Political Economy of Africa*, Monthly Review Press, New York, pp. 44-102

Ashcroft, B., and Ingham, K.P.D. (1979) 'Company Adaptation and the Response to Regional Policy: a Comparative Analysis of the MNC Subsidiaries and Indigenous Companies', *Regional Studies*, 13, 25-37

Ashford, N. (1979) 'South Africa and the Threat of Economic Sanctions', *Optima*, 28, 139-51

Australia and New Zealand Banking Group (1979) *Annual Report*, Melbourne

The Australian (1981) 22 October

Australian Bureau of Statistics (1979) *Foreign Investment 1977-78* (Catalogue No. 5305.0), Australian Government Publishing Service, Canberra

— (1980) *Overseas Trade, Australia: Comparative and Summary Tables*, Australian Bureau of Statistics, Canberra

Averitt, R.T. (1968) *The Dual Economy*, Norton, New York

Ayeni, B. (1979) 'Spatial Dimensions of Manufacturing Activities in Nigeria', unpublished paper, Department of Geography, University of Ibadan, Nigeria

Baer, W. (1965) *Industrialization and Economic Development in Brazil*, Homewood, Chicago

Baffoe, F. (1978) 'Some Aspects of the Political Economy of Economic Cooperation and Integration in Southern Africa', *Journal of Southern African Affairs*, 3, 327-42

Bailey, M. (1977) 'Few Firms Step Out of Line to Invest in Transkei', *New African Development*, 11, 237

Bambrick, S. (1979) *Australian Minerals and Energy Policy*, Australian National University Press, Canberra

Banaji, J. (1977) 'Modes of Production in a Materialist Conception of History', *Capital and Class*, 3, 1-44

Banas, G. (ed.) (1961) *O Capital Estrangeiro no Brasil*, Editora Banas, Rio de Janeiro

— (ed.) (1962) *A Industria de Material Eletrico e Eletronico 1962*, Banas, São Paulo

Bank of New South Wales (1979) *Annual Report*, Sydney

The Banker (1978) 'Pacific Basin Survey', December 1978, 43-82

— (1979a) 'Survey of 30 World Banking Centres', 129, April 1979, 49-127

— (1979b) 'The Top 300', 129, June 1979, 87-149

Baran, P., and Sweezy, P. (1968) *Monopoly Capital*, Monthly Review Press, New York

Barna, T. (1962) *Investment and Growth Policies in British Industrial Firms*, Cambridge University Press, London

Barnett, R.J., and Muller, R.E. (1974) *Global Reach*, Simon and Schuster, New York

Barrett, M., Corrigan, P., Kuhn, A., and Wolff, J. (eds.) (1979) *Ideology and Cultural Production*, Croom Helm, London

Barret-Brown, M. (1974) *The Economics of Imperialism*, Penguin, Harmondsworth

Bater, J.H., and Walker, D.F. (1974) 'Aspects of Industrial Linkage: the Example of the Hamilton Metalworking Complex, Ontario', *Revue de Géographie de Montreal*, 28, 233-43

Beddgood, D. (1978) 'New Zealand's Semi-Colonial Development: a Marxist View', *The Australian and New Zealand Journal of Sociology*, 14, 285-9

Ben-Horin, D. (1977) 'Television without Tears: an Outline of a Socialist Approach to Popular Television', *Socialist Revolution*, 35, 7-35

Benson, J.K. (1978) 'The Interorganisational Network as a Political Economy' in

L. Karpik (ed.), *Organisation and Environment*, Sage, London, pp. 69-102

Bergsman, J. (1970) *Brazil: Industrialization and Trade Policies*, Oxford University Press, London

Blackbourn, A. (1968) 'The Location of American Manufacturing Plants in Canada' in S.P. Chatterjee and S.P. Das Gupta (eds.), *Selected Papers, 21st International Geographical Congress*, National Committee for Geography, Calcutta, pp. 53-6

—— (1972) 'The Location of Foreign-owned Manufacturing Plants in the Republic of Ireland', *Tijdschrift voor Economische en Sociale Geografie*, 63, 438-43

—— (1974) 'The Spatial Behaviour of American Firms in Western Europe' in F.E.I. Hamilton (ed.), *Spatial Perspectives on Industrial Organization and Decision-making*, John Wiley, London, pp. 245-64

—— (1978) 'Multinational Enterprises and Regional Development: a Comment', *Regional Studies*, 12, 125-7

Blackburn, R., and Mann, M. (1979) *The Working Class and the Labour Market*, Macmillan, London

Blausten, R. (1976) 'Foreign Investment in the Black Homelands of South Africa', *African Affairs*, 75, 208-23

Bluestone, B., and Harrison, B. (1980) 'Why Corporations Close Profitable Plants', *Papers for a New Society*, 7, 15-23

Bolton Committee (1971) Committee of Inquiry on Small Firms, *Report*, Cmnd 4811, HMSO, London

Bozzoli, B. (1978) 'Capital and the State in South Africa', *Review of African Political Economy*, 11, 40-50

Braverman, H. (1974) *Labour and Monopoly Capital*, Monthly Review Press, New York

Brecher, J. (1972) *Strike!* Fawcett Publications, Greenwich, Connecticut

Brenner, R. (1976) 'Agrarian Class Structure and Economic Development in Preindustrial Europe', *Past and Present*, 70, 30-75

—— (1977) 'The Origins of Capitalist Development: a Critique of Neo-Smithian Marxism', *New Left Review*, 104, 25-92

Brewer, A. (1980) *Marxist Theories of Imperialism. A Critical Survey*, Routledge and Kegan Paul, London

Brighton Labour Process Group (BLPG) (1977) 'The Capitalist Labour Process', *Capital and Class*, 7, 3-26

Britton, J.N.H. (1976) 'The Influence of Corporate Organization and Ownership on the Linkages of Industrial Plants: a Canadian Enquiry', *Economic Geography*, 52, 111-14

—— (1977) 'Canada's Industrial Performance and Prospects under Free Trade', *Canadian Geographer*, 21, 351-71

—— and Gilmour, J.M. (1978) *The Weakest Link*, Science Council of Canada, Ottawa

Britton, S.G. (1979) 'Tourism in a Peripheral Capitalist Economy: the Case of Fiji', unpublished PhD thesis, Australian National University, Canberra

—— (1980) 'The Evolution of a Colonial Space-economy: the Case of Fiji', *Journal of Historical Geography*, 6, 251-74

Bronte, S. (1981) 'The end of the Foreign Banks' Tokyo Idyll', *Euromoney*, January 1981, 53-69

Brookfield, H. (1975) *Interdependent Development*, Methuen, London

Brown, J.L., and Schneck, R. (1979) 'A Structural Comparison between Canadian and American Industrial Organizations', *Administrative Science*

Quarterly, 24, 24-47

Bryden, J.M. (1973) *Tourism and Development: a Case Study of the Common-wealth Caribbean*, Cambridge University Press, London

Buckley, P.J., and Casson, M. (1976) *The Future of Multinational Enterprise*, Macmillan, London

Burawoy, M. (1979) *Manufacturing Consent*, University of Chicago Press, Chicago

Burkhart, A.J., and Medlik, S. (1974) *Tourism: Past, Present and Future*, Heinemann, London

Burr, R. (1978) 'The Changing World of Foreign Banks', *The Banker*, April 1978, 45-54

Caloren, F. (1978) 'The Logic of Layoffs and Factory Closures' in F. Caloren, M. Chossudousky and P. Gingrich, *Is the Canadian Economy Closing Down?* Black Rose, Montreal

Carmichael, C.L. (1977) 'Employer Labour-force Adjustment to Changing Market Conditions, with Special Respect to Declining Demand', *Working Paper 2*, Department of Geography, London School of Economics

—— (1978) 'Local Labour Market Analysis: its Importance and a Possible Approach', *Geoforum*, 9, 127-48

Carney, J. (1980) 'Regions in Crisis: Accumulation, Regional Problems and Crisis Formation' in J. Carney, R. Hudson and J. Lewis (eds.), *Regions in Crisis: New Perspectives in European Regional Theory*, Croom Helm, London, pp. 28-59

Casetti, E. (1972) 'Generating Models by the Expansion Method: Applications to Geographical Research', *Geographical Analysis*, 4 (1), 81-91

Caves, R.E. (1971) 'International Corporations: the Industrial Economics of Foreign Investment', *Economica*, 38, 1-27

Chandler, A.D. (1962) *Strategy and Structure: the History of the American Industrial Enterprise*, MIT Press, Cambridge, Mass.

—— (1977) *The Visible Hand*, Harvard University Press, Cambridge, Mass.

—— (1980) 'The Growth of the Transnational Industrial Firm in the United States and the United Kingdom: a Comparative Analysis', *Economic History Review*, 33, 396-410

—— and Daems, H. (1974) 'Introduction – the Rise of Managerial Capitalism and its Impact on Investment Strategy in the Western World and Japan' in H. Daems and H. Van der Wee (eds.), *The Rise of Managerial Capitalism*, Nijhoff, The Hague, pp. 1-34

Channon, D.F. (1973) *The Strategy and Structure of British Enterprise*, Allen and Unwin, London

Chapman, K. (1974) 'Corporate Systems in the United Kingdom Petrochemical Industry', *Annals, Association of American Geographers*, 64, 126-37

Chossoudovsky, M. (1978) 'Is the Canadian Economy Closing Down?' in F. Caloren, M. Chossudovsky and P. Gingrich (eds.), *Is the Canadian Economy Closing Down?* Black Rose, Montreal

Clark, G.L. (1981) 'The Employment Relation and Spatial Division of Labour: a Hypothesis', *Annals, Association of American Geographers*, 71, 412-24

—— (1982) 'Fluctuation and Rigidities in Local Labour Markets', *Environment and Planning A*, 14, forthcoming

Clegg, S. (1980) 'Restructuring the Semiperipheral Labour Process' in P. Boreham and G. Dow (eds.), *Work and Inequality. Volume One. Workers,*

Economic Crisis and the State, Macmillan, Melbourne, pp. 28-53
—— and Dunkerley, D. (1980) *Organisation, Class and Control*, Routledge and Kegan Paul, London
Cohen, E. (1972) 'Towards a Sociology of International Tourism', *Social Research*, 39(1), 164-82
Colclough, C., and McCarthy, S. (1980) *The Political Economy of Botswana*, Oxford University Press, Oxford
Cole, R.V. (1979) 'The Anatomy of Credit for Pacific Island Nations', unpublished paper presented for 1979 ANU Development Studies Centre Seminar Series 'The Island States of the Pacific and Indian Oceans: Anatomy and Development', 19 July 1979
Coles, J., and Cohen, R. (1975) *South African Subimperialism*, United Nations African Institute for Economic Development and Planning, CS/25289, Dakar
Commercial Banking Company of Sydney Ltd (1979, 1980) *Annual Report*, Sydney
Commercial Bank of Australia (1980) *Annual Report and Notice of Meeting*
Committee of Inquiry into the Australian Financial System (Mr J.K. Campbell, Chairman) (1980) *Interim Report*, Australian Government Publishing Service, Canberra
Commonwealth Bank (1980) *Annual Report*, Sydney
Commonwealth Secretariat (1978) *The Mineral Industry of Namibia: Perspectives for Independence* (Consultant R. Murray), The Commonwealth Secretariat, London
Conference of Socialist Economists (CSE) (1976) 'The Labour Process and Class Strategies', *CSE Pamphlet No. 1*, Conference of Socialist Economists, London
Connor, J.M., and Mueller, W.F. (1977) *Market Power and Profitability of Multinational Corporations in Brazil and Mexico*, Report to the Senate Subcommittee on Multinational Corporations, Government Office, Washington
Constantino, R. (1978) *Neo-colonial Identity and Counter Consciousnes*, Merlin Press, London
Cooper, D. (1976-7) 'The Selebi-Phikwe Strike, Botswana, 1975: the State, Mine Workers and the Multinationals' in *The Societies of Southern Africa in the 19th and 20th Centuries, Vol. 8*, Collected seminar papers No. 22, University of London Institute of Commonwealth Studies, London, pp. 143-60
Cooper, M.J., and Sorenson, A.D. (1980) 'The Decision to Go Off-shore: an Analysis of Motives and Methods in a Sample of Australian Transnationals', unpublished paper presented at IAG Industrial Geography Study Group, Newcastle, NSW, February 1980
Cordell, A.J. (1971) *The Multinational Firm, Foreign Direct Investment and Canadian Science Policy*, Science Council of Canada, Background Study No. 22, Information Canada, Ottawa
Corina, M. (1970) 'A German Precedent', *The Times*, 2 January 1970, p. 19
Coriot, B. (1980) 'The Restructuring of the Assembly Line: a New Economy of Time and Control', *Capital and Class*, 11, 34-43
Cronin, T.E. (1979) *Industrial Conflict in Modern Britain*, Croom Helm, London
Cronje, G., and Cronje, S. (1979) *The Workers of Namibia*, International Defence and Aid Fund for Southern Africa, London
Crough, G. (1979) *Transnational Banking and the World Economy*, Transnational Corporations Research Project, University of Sydney

Crozier, M. (1964) *The Bureaucratic Phenomenon*, Tavistock, London

Crum, R.E., and Gudgin, G. (1977) *Non-production Activities in UK Manufacturing Industry*, EEC Commission, Brussels

Crush, J.S. (1977) 'Swaziland: Development, Dependence and Interdependence', paper presented to the Special Session on Southern Africa, Association of American Geographers Annual Meetings, Salt Lake City

—— (1979) 'The Parameters of Dependence in Southern Africa: a Case Study of Swaziland', *Journal of Southern African Affairs*, 4, 55-66

Cunningham, S. (1981) 'Multinational Enterprises in Brazil: Locational Patterns and Implications for Regional Development', *Professional Geographer*, 33, 48-62

Cushman, R.E. (1976) 'Sources and Uses of Capital in the Asian Region', *Euromoney*, May, supplement, p. 13

Cyert, R.M., and March, J.G. (1963) *A Behavioural Theory of the Firm*, Prentice-Hall, Englewood Cliffs, New Jersey

Cypher, J. (1979) 'The Internationalization of Capital and the Transformation of Social Formations: a Critique of the Monthly Review School', *Review of Radical Political Economics*, 11(4), 33-49

Dahl, R.A. (1957) 'The Concept of Power', *Behavioural Science*, 2, 201-15

Daily Telegraph (1980a) 29 August

—— (1980b) 29 August

—— (1981) 9 November

Damette, F. (1980) 'The Regional Framework of Monopoly Exploitation: New Problems and Trends' in J. Carney, R. Hudson and J. Lewis (eds.), *Regions in Crisis: New Perspectives in European Regional Theory*, Croom Helm, London, pp. 76-92

Davies, G., and Thomas, I. (1977) *Overseas Investment in Wales*, Christopher Davies, Swansea

Davies, R. (1979) 'Capital Restructuring and the Modification of the Racial Division of Labour in South Africa', *Journal of Southern African Studies*, 5, 181-98

—— Kaplan, D., Morris, M., and O'Meara, D. (1976) 'Class Struggle and the Periodisation of the State in South Africa', *Review of African Political Economy*, 7, 4-30

Davis, E.W., and Yeomans, K.A. (1974) *Company Finance and the Capital Market:a Study of the Effects of Firm Size*, Cambridge University Press, Cambridge

Davis, M.D. (1973) *Game Theory: a Non-technical Introduction*, Basic Books, New York

Davis, S.I. (1981) 'International Bank Expansion: Time for a Reassessment', *The Banker*, 131(663), 63-70

Dean, W. (1969) *The Industrialization of São Paulo 1880-1945*, University of Texas Press, Austin

de Cardona, E. (1975) 'Multinational Television', *Journal of Communication*, 25(2), 122-7

Delegation à l'Amenagement du Territoire et à l'Action Régionale (DATAR) (1974) *Investissements Etrangers et Amenagement du Territoire*, Documentation Française, Paris

De Smidt, M. (1966) 'Foreign Industrial Establishments Located in the Nether-

lands', *Tijdschrift voor Economische en Sociale Geografie*, 57, 1-19
– – (1968) 'Foreign Industrial Establishments in the Netherlands', *Tijdschrift voor Economische en Sociale Geografie*, 63, 438-43
Department of Decentralisation and Development (1976) *Overseas Performance of Australian Multi-national Companies* (Parts A, B and C), Department of Decentralisation and Development, Sydney, NSW
Devine, P.J., Jones, R.M., Lee, N., and Tyson, W.J. (1979) *An Introduction to Industrial Economics*, George Allen and Unwin, London
Dicken, P. (1977) 'A Note on Location Theory and the Large Business Enterprise', *Area*, 9, 138-43
—— and Lloyd, P.E. (1976) 'Geographical Perspectives on United States Investment in the United Kingdom', *Environment and Planning A*, 8, 685-705
—— (1979) 'The Contribution of Foreign-owned Firms to Regional Employment Change: a Components Approach with Particular Reference to North-West England', *Working Paper 8*, North West Industry Research Unit, University of Manchester
——, —— (1980) 'Patterns and Processes of Change in the Spatial Distribution of Foreign-controlled Manufacturing Employment in the United Kingdom, 1963-1975', *Environment and Planning A*, 12, 1405-26
Dieques, M. Jnr (1964) *Imigracao, Urbanizacao, Industrializacao*, Cento Brasileiro de Persquises Educacionais, Rio de Janeiro
Dike, K.O. (1956) *Trade and Politics in the Niger Delta, 1830-85*, Oxford University Press, Oxford
Downie, J. (1958) *The Competitive Process*, Duckworth, London
Dun and Bradstreet (1978/9a) *Who Owns Whom: United Kingdom and Republic of Ireland*, vols. 1 and 2, Dun and Bradstreet, London
—— (1978/9b) *Who Owns Whom: North America*, Dun and Bradstreet, London
Dunning, J.H. (1958) *American Investment in British Manufacturing Industry*, Allen and Unwin, London
Dunning, J.H. and Pearce, R.D. (1981) *The World's Largest Industrial Enterprises*, Gower, Farnborough, Hants
Eatwell, J. (1971) 'Growth, Profitability and Size: the Empirical Evidence' in R. Marris and A. Wood (eds.), *The Corporate Economy, Growth, Competition and Innovative Power*, Macmillan, London, pp. 400-7
Economic and Social Commission for Asia and the Pacific (ESCAP) (1978) 'The Formulation of Basic Concepts and Guidelines for Preparation of Tourism Sub-Regional Master Plans in the ESCAP Region', *Transport and Communications Bulletin*, 52, 33-40
The Economist (1969a) 6 December 1969, 106
—— (1969b) 13 December 1969, 86
—— (1969c) 20 December 1969, 76
—— (1980a) 'ICI – Helped and Hurt by North Sea Oil', 15 March, 75.
—— (1980b) 'The Axeman Cometh', 18 October, 95-6
—— (1980c) 'Same Old Story Only Worse', 24 May, 96-8
—— (1980d) 'Dow Shalt Not Pass?', 19 April, 70-1
—— (1980e) 'ICI – The Empire Strikes Back', 16 August, 76-7
—— (1980f) 'Between the Devil and the Deep North Sea', 26 January, 100-1
—— (1981a) 'British Industry', 4 July, 73-6
—— (1981b) 'The Chemical Industry Reacts', 26 September, 82-3
—— (1981c) 'Taking up the Slack', 6 June, 73-4
—— (1981d) 'Oil Industries Never Die, They Only Fade Away', 3 January, 48-9
—— (1981e) 'ICI: Not Out of the Wood Just Yet', 1 August, 55

—— (1981f) 'Fraser Threatens Firms with Freedom', 4 April, 83
—— (1981g) 'Cycling off the Edge of a Cliff', 15 August, 57-8
—— (1981h) 'Cheap Coal for ICI's Bathtub', 4 July, 23
—— (1981i) 'ICI's Search for a New Imperial Wizard', 31 October, 69-70
Edwards, R. (1979) *Contested Terrain: the Transformation of the Workplace in the Twentieth Century*, Basic Books, New York
Ehrensaft, P. (1976) 'Polarized Accumulation and the Theory of Dependence: the Implications of South African Semi-Industrial Capitalism' in P.C.W. Gutkind and I. Wallerstein (eds.), *The Political Economy of Contemporary Africa*, Sage, Beverly Hills, pp. 58-89
Emmanuel, A. (1972) *Unequal Exchange*. Monthly Review Press, New York
Enzensberger, H.M. (1975), 'The Industrialisation of the Mind', *Urban Review*, 8, 68-75
Epstein, B. (1971) *Politics of Trade in Power Plant*, Atlantic Trade Study, Trade Policy Research Center, London
—— and Mirow, K.R.U. (1977) 'Impact of Restrictive Practices by Multinational Companies on the Industrialization Programs of Developing Countries. Electrical Equipment in Brazil: a Case Study', prepared for UNCTAD, United Nations, Geneva
Erlandsson, U. (1975) *Foretagsutveckling och utrymmesbehov*, CWK Gleerup, Lund
Ettinger, S. (1973) 'The Economics of the Customs Union between Botswana, Lesotho, Swaziland and South Africa', unpublished PhD thesis, University of Michigan
Evans, A.W. (1973) 'The Location of the Headquarters of Industrial Companies', *Urban Studies*, 10(3), 387-95
Ewan, S. (1976) *Captains of Consciousness: Advertising and the Social Roots of the Consumer Culture*, McGraw-Hill, New York
Fagan, R. (1980) 'The Internationalisation of Capital: a Perspective on Stephen Hymer's Work on Transnational Corporations' in R. Peet (ed.), *An Introduction to Marxist Theories of Underdevelopment*, Department of Human Geography, Publication HG14, Australian National University Press, Canberra, pp. 175-80
Fair, D. (1979) 'The Independence of Central Banks', *The Banker*, 129 (October), 31-41
Fair, T.J.D., Murdoch, G., and Jones, H.M. (1969) *Development in Swaziland*, Witwatersrand University Press, Johannesburg
Faith, N. (1972) *The Infiltrators: the European Business Invasion of America*, Dutton, New York
Fanon, F. (1968) *The Wretched of the Earth*, Penguin, Harmondsworth
Far Eastern Economic Review (1980a) 'Banking '80', 4 April 1980, 40-104
—— (1980b) 'Merchant Banking '80', 19 September 1980, 56-100
Feddersen, K. (1974) *German Subsidiary Companies in the United Kingdom*, German Chamber of Commerce, London
—— (1976) *German Subsidiary Companies in the United Kingdom*, German Chamber of Commerce, London
—— (1978) *German Subsidiary Companies in the United Kingdom*, German Chamber of Commerce, London
Federal Trade Commission (1923) *Report on the Radio Corporation of America*, Government Printing Office, Washington, DC

—— (1928) *Report on the Supply of Electrical Equipment and Competitive Conditions*, Government Printing Office, Washington, DC

Fieldhouse, D.K. (1978) *Unilever Overseas: the Anatomy of a Multinational*, Croom Helm, London

Fiji, Government of (1975) *Fiji's Seventh Development Plan, 1976-1980*, Central Planning Office, Fiji

—— (1979) *Current Economic Statistics*, July 1979, Bureau of Statistics, Suva

Financial Times (London) (1977a) 25 November

—— (1977b) 16 December

—— (1978) 6 March

—— (1981) 29 June

Firn, J.R. (1975) 'External Control and Regional Development: the Case of Scotland', *Environment and Planning A*, 7, 393-414

First, R., Steele, J., and Gurney, C. (1972) *The South African Connection: Western Investment in Apartheid*, Temple Smith, London

Fisk, C., and Riminger, F. (1979) 'Non-parametric Estimates of LDC Repayment Prospects', *Journal of Finance*, 34(2), 429-38

Fitzgerald, T.M. (1974) *The Contribution of the Mineral Industry to Australian Welfare*, Australian Government Publishing Service, Canberra

Forbes, D.K. (1982) 'Energy Imperialism and a New International Division of Resources: the Case of Indonesia', *Tijdschrift voor Economische en Sociale Geografie*, 73, forthcoming

Forer, P. (1978) 'A Place for Plastic Space?', *Progress in Human Geography*, 2(2), 230-67

Fothergill, S., and Gudgin, G. (1979) 'The Components of Rural Growth and Urban Decline in the East Midlands: 1968-75', *Working Note 573*, Centre for Environmental Studies, London

Frank, A.G. (1969) *Capitalism and Underdevelopment in Latin America*, Penguin, Harmondsworth

—— (1979a) *Dependent Accumulation and Underdevelopment*, Monthly Review Press, New York

—— (1979b) 'Unequal Accumulation: Intermediate Semi-peripheral and Sub-imperialist Economies', *Review*, 2, 281-350

Frank, C.R., and Cline, W.R. (1971) 'Measurement of Debt Servicing Capacity: an Application of Discriminant Analysis?', *Journal of International Economics*, 1, 327-44

Franko, L.G. (1976) *The European Multinationals*, Harper and Row, London

Fransman, M. (1977) 'The State and Development in Swaziland 1960-1977', unpublished PhD dissertation, University of Sussex

Friedman, A. (1977a) *Industry and Labour: Class Struggle at Work and Monopoly Capitalism*, Macmillan, London

—— (1977b) 'Responsible Autonomy versus Direct Control of the Labour Process', *Capital and Class*, 1, 43-57

Friedman, H., and Meredeen, S. (1980) *The Dynamics of Industrial Conflict: Lessons from Ford*, Croom Helm, London

Friere, P. (1972) *Pedagogy of the Oppressed*, Penguin, Harmondsworth

Fröbel, F., Heinrichs, J., and Kreye, O. (1977) 'The Tendency Towards a New International Division of Labour', *Review*, 1, 73-88

——, ——, —— (1980) *The New International Division of Labour*, Cambridge University Press, Cambridge

Gallie, D. (1978) 'In Search of the New Working Class: Automation and Social

312 *References*

Integration within the Capitalism Enterprise', *Studies in Sociology*, 9, Cambridge University Press, Cambridge
The Globe and Mail (Toronto) (1979) 10 December
Goddard, J.B. (1975) *Office Location in Urban and Regional Development*, Oxford University Press, London
—— and Smith, I.J. (1978) 'Changes in Corporate Control in the British Urban System, 1972-77', *Environment and Planning A*, 10, 1073-84
Golding, P. (1978) 'The International Media and the Political Economy of Publishing', *Library Trends*, 26, 453-66
Good, D., and Williams, M. (1976) *South Africa: the Crisis in Britain and the Apartheid Economy*, Anti-Apartheid Movement, London
Goodwin, W. (1965) 'The Management Center in the United States', *The Geographical Review*, 55(1), 1-16
Gort, M. (1969) 'An Economic Disturbance Theory of Mergers', *Quarterly Journal of Economics*, 83, 624-42
Gorz, A. (ed.) (1976) *The Division of Labor: the Labor Process and Class Struggle in Modern Capitalism*, New Jersey Humanities Press, Atlantic Highlands
Gould, C. (1964) *The Last Titan. Perceival Farquar. American Entrepreneur in Latin America*, Institute of Hispano-American and Lugo-Brazilian Studies, Stanford
Gould, P., and Johnson, J. (1980a) 'The Content and Structure of International Television Flows', *Communication*, 5(1) 43-63
—— and Johnson, J. (1980b) 'National Television Policy: Monitoring Structural Complexity', *Futures* (June), 178-90
Government of Canada (1972) *Foreign Direct Investment in Canada*, Information Canada, Ottawa
Graham, J. (1979) 'Trends in UK Merger Control', *Trade and Industry*, 14 September
Gramsci, A. (1968) *Prison Notebooks*, Lawrence and Wishart, London
Great Britain, Board of Trade (1968) *The Movement of Manufacturing Industry in the United Kingdom, 1945-65*, HMSO, London
Great Britain, Department of Industry (1979a) *Business Monitor, PA 1002, 1975*, HMSO, London
—— (1979b) *Business Monitor: M7 Acquisitions and Mergers of Industrial and Commercial Companies*, HMSO, London
Green, R.H. (1979) *Namibia: a Political Economic Survey*, Discussion Paper No. 144, University of Sussex, Institute of Development Studies, Brighton
—— (1980) 'The Unforgiving Land – Basis for a Post Liberation Programme in Namibia', *Bulletin, Institute of Development Studies*, 11(4), 72-6
Gregory, G. (1979) 'Foreign Banking in Japan: in Search of a Broader Role', *The Banker*, 129 (June), 37-40
Gripaios, P. (1977a) 'Industrial Decline in London: an Examination of its Causes', *Urban Studies*, 14, 181-9
—— (1977b) 'The Closure of Firms in the Inner City', *Regional Studies*, 11, 1-6
Grundy, K.W. (1976) 'Intermediary Power and Global Dependency: the Case of South Africa', *International Studies Quarterly*, 20, 553-80
Guback, T.H. (1974) 'Film as International Business', *Journal of Communication*, 24(1), 90-101
Gurr, R. (1977) 'Invest in Lesotho – Where the Growing is Good' in R. Gurr (ed.),

Transnational Corporations and Developing Countries, Lesotho National Development Corporation, Maseru, pp. 254-64

Hakam, A.N. (1966) 'The Motivation to Invest and the Location Pattern of Foreign Private Industrial Investments in Nigeria', *Nigerian Journal of Economics and Social Studies*, 1, 49-65

Håkanson, L. (1979) 'Towards a Theory of Location and Corporate Growth' in F.E.I. Hamilton and G.J.R. Linge (eds.), *Spatial Analysis, Industry and the Industrial Environment. Volume I. Industrial Systems*, John Wiley, Chichester, pp. 115-38

Hall, S. (1977) 'Culture, the Media and the "Ideological Effect" ' in J. Curran, M. Gurevitch and J. Woollscott (eds.), *Mass Communication and Society*, Edward Arnold, London, pp. 315-48

Hamilton, F.E.I. (1976) 'Multi-national Enterprise and the European Economic Community', *Tijdschrift voor Economische en Sociale Geografie*, 67, 258-78

—— (1981) 'International Systems: a Dynamic Force Behind International Trade', *Professional Geographer*, 33, 26-35

—— and Linge, G.J.R. (eds.) (1979) *Spatial Analysis Industry and the Industrial Environment. Volume 1. Industrial Systems*, John Wiley, Chichester

——, —— (eds.) (1981) *Spatial Analysis, Industry and the Industrial Environment: Volume 2. International Industrial Systems*, John Wiley, Chichester

Hancock, G., and Lloyd, S. (1980) 'Processing for Export; Africa's Industrial Free Zones' in *Africa Guide*, World of Information, Saffron Walden, pp. 47-9

Hannah, L. (1976) *The Rise of the Corporate Economy*, Methuen, London

—— and Kay, J.A. (1977) *Concentration in Modern Industry, Theory, Management and the UK Experience*, Macmillan, London

Hansen, N. (1981) 'Mexico's Border Industry and the International Division of Labour', *Annals of Regional Science*, 15(2), 1-12

Harris, P. (1974) 'Hierarchy and Concentration in International News Flow', *Politics*, 9(2), 159-65

—— (1976) 'International News Media Authority and Dependence', *Instant Research on Peace and Violence*, 6(4), 148-59

Harrison, R.T., Bull, P.J., and Hart, M. (1980) 'Space and Time in Industrial Linkage Studies', *Area*, 12, 333-8

Harvey, C. (1974) 'British Investment in Southern Africa', *Journal of Southern African Studies*, 1, 52-73

Harvey, D. (1973) *Social Justice and the City*, Edward Arnold, London

—— (1975) 'The Geography of Capitalist Accumulation: a Reconstruction of the Marxian Theory', *Antipode*, 7(2), 9-21

Healey, M.J. (1981) 'Location Adjustment and the Characteristics of Manufacturing plants', *Transactions, Institute of British Geographers*, 6 (4), 394-412

Helleiner, G.K. (1981) *Intra-firm Trade and the Developing Countries*, Macmillan, London

—— and Lavergne, R. (1979) 'Intra-firm Trade and Industrial Exports to the United States', *Oxford Bulletin of Economics and Statistics*, 41, 297-310

Henderson, R.A. (1979) *An Analysis of Closures amongst Scottish Manufacturing Plants*, Discussion Paper 3, Economics and Statistics Unit, Scottish Economic Planning Department, Edinburgh

Hexner, E. (1946) *International Cartels*, University of North Carolina Press, Chapel Hill

Hickson, D.J., Hinings, C.R., McMillan, C.J., and Schwetter, J.P. (1974) 'The Culture-free Content of Organization Structure: a Trinational Comparison', *Sociology*, 8, 59-80

Hiller, H.L. (1977) 'Industrialism, Tourism, Island Nations and Changing Values' in B.H. Farrell (ed.), *Social and Economic Consequences of Tourism in the South Pacific*, University of California, Santa Cruz, pp. 115-21

Hoare, A.G. (1975) 'Foreign Firms and Air Transport: the Geographical Effect of Heathrow Airport', *Regional Studies*, 9, 349-68

Hobsbawm, E. (1968) *Industry and Empire*, Penguin Books, Baltimore, Maryland

Holland, S. (1971) *Sovereignty and Multinational Companies*, Fabian Tract 409, Fabian Society, London

—— (1976) *Capital Versus the Regions*, Macmillan, London

Hood, N., and Young, S. (1980) *European Development Strategies of U.S.-Owned Manufacturing Companies Located in Scotland*, HMSO, Edinburgh

Horkheimer, M. and Adorno, T.W. (1972) *Dialectic of Enlightenment*, Herder and Herder, New York

Horst, T. (1974) 'The Theory of the Firm' in J. Dunning, *Economic Analysis and the Multinational Enterprise*, Praeger, New York, pp. 31-46

Hudson, R. (1981) 'The Development of Chemicals Production in Western Europe in the Post-war Period', paper presented to XXI Annual Congress of the European Regional Science Association, Barcelona, 25-28 August

Hughes, J. (1980) *The Internationalisation of Japanese Finance: a Preliminary Assessment*, Australian National University Australia-Japan Research Centre Research Paper 69

Hunter, A. (1961) 'Restrictive Practices and Monopolies in Australia', *Economic Record*, 37, 25-52

Hymer, S. (1960) 'The International Operations of International Firms: a Study of Direct Investment', unpublished PhD dissertation, Massachusetts Institute of Technology

—— (1972) 'The Multinational Corporation and the Law of Uneven Development' in H. Radice (ed.), *International Firms and Modern Imperialism*, Penguin, Harmondsworth, pp. 39-62

—— and Pashigian, P. (1962) 'Firm Size and Rate of Growth', *Journal of Political Economy*, 70, 557-63

Imperial Chemical Industries Limited (ICI) (1970-80) *Annual Reports*, London

—— (1981) *ICI Worldwide*, ICI Public Relations Department, London

Innes, D. (1978) 'Imperialism and the National Struggle in Namibia', *Review of African Political Economy*, 9, 45-59

—— (1980) 'Monopoly Capital and Imperialism in Southern Africa: the Role of the Anglo-American Group', unpublished PhD thesis, Department of Comparative Politics, University of Sussex

International Metalworkers Federation, World Automotive Council (n.d.) press release on auto-parts sourcing in Europe

International Organization (1979) Special Issue on 'Dependence and Dependency in the Global System', 32(1), 1-300

Ishigaki, K., and Fujita, M. (1981) *The Development of International Business by Japanese Banks*, Australian National University Australia-Japan Research Centre Research Paper 86

Jakubowski, F. (1976) *Ideology and Superstructure in Historical Materialism*, Allison and Busby, London

Janus, N., and Roncaglio, R. (1979) 'Advertising, Mass Media and Dependency',

Development Dialogue, 1, 81-97

Jao, Y.C. (1979) 'The Rise of Hong Kong as a Financial Centre', *Asian Survey*, 19(7), 674-94

Jazairy, I, Kuin, P., and Somaria, J. (1977) 'Transnational Enterprises' in J. Tinbergen (co-ordinator), *Reshaping the International Order: a Report to the Club of Rome*, New American Library, New York, pp. 355-69

Johns, S. (1973) 'Botswana's Strategy for Development: an Assessment of Dependence in the Southern African Context', *Journal of Commonwealth Political Studies*, 11, 214-30

Jonathan, L. (1977) 'The Transnational Corporation – Help or Hindrance to National Development?' in R. Gurr (ed.), *Transnational Corporations and Development Countries*, Lesotho National Development Corporation, Maseru, pp. 1-6

Jones, R., and Marriott, D. (1970) *Anatomy of a Merger*, Bedford Square, London

Journal of Industry and Commerce (1977) 'Australian Multinationals – How They Fare Overseas', March

Kaplan, D. (1977) 'Capitalist Development in South Africa: Class Conflict and the State' in T. Adler (ed.), *Perspectives on South Africa*, African Studies Institute, University of Witwatersrand, Johannesburg, pp. 96-131

—— (1979) 'Toward a Marxist Analysis of South Africa', *Socialist Review*, 48, 117-37

Karpik, L. (1977) 'Technological Capitalism' in S. Clegg and D. Dunkerley (eds.), *Critical Issues in Organization*, Routledge and Kegan Paul, London, pp. 41-71

—— (1978) 'Organizations, Institutions and History' in L. Karpik (ed.), *Organization and Environment: Theory, Issues and Reality*, Sage, London, pp. 15-68

Kast, F.E., and Rosenzweig, J.E. (1974) *Organization and Management: a Systems Approach*, McGraw-Hill Kogakusha, Tokyo

Keeble, D. (1976) *Industrial Location and Planning in the United Kingdom*, Methuen, London

Keegan, W.J. (1974) 'Multinational Scanning: a Study of the Information Sources Utilized by Headquarters Executives in Multinational Companies', *Administrative Science Quarterly*, 19, 411-21

Keith-Reid, R. (1977) 'The Talking over Japan is on the Move in Fiji', *Pacific Islands Monthly*, 48(11), 65-6

Kellner, D. (1978) 'Ideology, Marxism and Advanced Capitalism', *Socialist Review*, 42, 37-65

Kemper, N.J., and de Smidt, M. (1980) 'Foreign Manufacturing Establishments in the Netherlands', *Tijdschrift voor Economische en Sociale Geografie*, 71, 21-40

Kilby, P. (1969) *Industrialization in an Open Economy: Nigeria 1945-1966*, Cambridge University Press, Cambridge

Kiljunen, K. (1980) 'Namibia: the Ideology of National Liberation', *Bulletin, Institute of Development Studies*, 11(4), 65-71

Killick, A. (1981) 'Euromarket Recycling of OPEC Surpluses: Fact or Myth?', *The Banker*, 131(659), 15-23

Kindleberger, C. (1965) *Economic Development*, McGraw-Hill, New York

—— (1969) *American Business Abroad*, Yale University Press, New Haven, Connecticut

Knickerbocker, F.T. (1973) *Oligopolistic Reaction and Multinational Enterprise*, MIT Press, Cambridge, Mass.

Knight, K. (1976) 'Matrix Organization – a Review', *Journal of Management Studies*, 13, 111-30

Krümme, G. (1981) 'Making it Abroad: the Evolution of Volkswagen's North American Production Plans' in F.E.I. Hamilton and G.J.R. Linge (eds.), *Spatial Analysis, Industry and the Industrial Environment. Volume 2. International Industrial Systems*, John Wiley, Chichester, pp. 329-56

Labasse, J. (1975) 'The Geographical Space of Big Companies' *Geoforum*, 6, 113-24

Lall, S. (1974) 'Less Developed Countries and Private Foreign Direct Investment: a Review Article', *World Development*, 2(4/5), 43-8

—— (1978) 'The Pattern of Intra-firm Exports by US Multinationals', *Oxford Bulletin of Economics and Statistics*, 40, 9-21

Landsberg, M. (1979) 'Export-led Industrialization in the Third World: Manufacturing Imperialism', *Review of Radical Political Economics*, 11(4), 50-63

Lanning, G. (1979) *Role of Transnational Mining Corporations in the Plunder of South Africa's Mineral Resources*, United Nations Centre Against Apartheid Notes and Documents, Sem 3/79

—— and Mueller, M. (1979) *Africa Undermined: Mining Companies and the Underdevelopment of Africa*, Penguin, Harmondsworth

Leff, N. (1968) *The Brazilian Capital Goods Industry 1929-64*, Harvard University Press, Cambridge, Mass.

Legassick, M. (1974) 'South Africa: Capital Accumulation and Violence', *Economy and Society*, 3, 253-91

—— (1977) 'Gold, Agriculture and Secondary Industry in South Africa, 1885-1970: from Periphery to Sub-metropole as a Forced Labour System' in R. Palmer and N. Parsons (eds.), *The Roots of Rural Poverty in Central and Southern Africa*, University of California Press, Berkeley, pp. 175-200

—— and Hemson, D. (1976) *Foreign Investment and the Reproduction of Racial Capitalism in South Africa*, Anti-Apartheid Movement, London

—— and Innes, D. (1977) 'Capital Restructuring and Apartheid: a Critique of Constructive Engagement', *African Affairs*, 76, 437-82

—— and Wolpe, H. (1976) 'The Bantustans and Capital Accumulation in South Africa', *Review of African Political Economy*, 7, 87-107

Lenin, V.I. (n.d.) 'Imperialism, the Highest Stage of Capitalism', *Selected Works*, Volume 5, Martin Lawrence, London

Lesotho, Kingdom of (1975) *Second Five Year Development Plan 1975/76-1979/80*, 2 vols., Government Printer, Maseru

Lewis, D. (1975) 'Direct Foreign Investment and Linkages in a Less Developed Country', *Botswana Notes and Records*, 7, 81-8

Leyland (1964) in P.J. Devine *et al.* (1979)

Leys, R. (1979) 'Lesotho: Non-development or Underdevelopment: Towards an Analysis of the Political Economy of the Labour Reserve' in T.M. Shaw and K.A. Heard (eds.), *The Politics of Africa: Dependence and Development*, Longmans and Dalhousie University Press, London, pp. 95-129

Linge, G.J.R., and Hamilton, F.E.I. (1981) 'International Industrial Systems' in F.E.I. Hamilton and G.J.R. Linge (eds.), *Spatial Analysis, Industry and the Industrial Environment. Volume 2. International Industrial Systems*, John Wiley, Chichester, pp. 1-117

Lipietz, A. (1980) 'The Structuration of Space, the Problem of Land and Spatial

Policy' in J. Carney, R. Hudson and J. Lewis (eds.), *Regions in Crisis: New Perspectives in European Regional Theory*, Croom Helm, London, pp. 60-75

Lipton, M. (1976) 'British Engagement in South Africa: is Constructive Engagement Possible?', *South African Labour Bulletin*, 3(3), 10-48

Litvak, I.A., Maute, C.J., and Robinson, R.D. (1971) *Dual Loyalty*, McGraw-Hill of Canada, Toronto

Litvak, L., De Grasse, R., and McTigue, K. (1978) *South Africa: Foreign Investment and Apartheid*, Institute for Policy Studies, Washington, DC

Logan, M.I. (1972) 'The Spatial System and Planning Strategies in Developing Countries' in J. Blunden, *Regional Analysis and Development*, Harper and Row, London, pp. 283-91

Lumsden, A., and Corina, M. (1969) 'An Unexpected Splash of Colour', *The Times*, 3 December 1969, 27

Luz, N.V. (1975) *A Luta Pela Industrializanao do Brasil*, Omega, Sao Paulo

Mabogunje, A.L. (1968) *Urbanization in Nigeria*, University of London Press, London

—— (1978) *On Developing and Development 1977*, University of Ibadan Lectures, Ibadan, Nigeria, pp. 65-99

Macintosh, A.S. (1963) *The Development of Firms*, Cambridge University Press, London

McAleese, D., and Counahan, M. (1979) ' "Stickers" or "Snatchers"? Employment in the Multinational Corporation During the Recession', *Oxford Bulletin of Economics and Statistics*, Special Issue, 41, 345-58

McConnell, J.E. (1980) 'Foreign Direct Investment in the United States', *Annals, Association of American Geographers*, 70, 259-70

McDermott, P.J. (1976) 'Ownership, Organization and Regional Dependence in the Scottish Electronics Industry', *Regional Studies*, 10, 319-36

—— (1977) 'Overseas Investment and the Industrial Geography of the United Kingdom', *Area*, 9, 200-7

McKern, R.B. (1976) *Multinational Enterprise and National Resources*, McGraw-Hill, New York

McLoughlin, P. (1978) *Regional Policy and the Inner Areas*, Reading Geographical Papers, 64

McNee, R.B. (1974) 'A Systems Approach to Understanding the Geographic Behaviour of Organisations, Especially Large Corporations' in F.E.I. Hamilton (ed.), *Spatial Perspectives on Industrial Organisation and Decision Making*, John Wiley, London, pp. 47-76

McPhee, A. (1926) *The Economic Revolution in British West Africa*, Frank Cass, London

Magubane, B. (1979) *The Political Economy of Race and Class in South Africa*, Monthly Review Press, New York

Malecki, E.J. (1975) 'Examining Change in Rank-Size Systems of Cities', *The Professional Geographer*, 27(1), 43-7

Mandel, E. (1975) *Late Capitalism*, New Left Books, London

Markowitz, H.M. (1970) *Portfolio Analysis*, Yale University Press, New Haven, Connecticut

Marris, R. (1964) *The Economic Theory of 'Managerial' Capitalism*, Macmillan, London

—— (1972 Supplement) 'Why Economics Needs a Theory of the Firm', *Econo-*

mic Journal, 82, 321-41

Martin, J.E. (1973) 'Industrial Employment and Investment in a Frontier Region: the Franco-German Example', *Geography*, 58, 55-8

Marx, K. (1967) *Capital*, 3 vols., International Publishers, New York

—— (1969a) 'The Eighteenth Brumaire of Louis Bonaparte' in K. Marx and F. Engels, *Selected Works*, Volume 1, Progress Publishers, Moscow, pp. 394-487

—— (1969b) 'The German Ideology' in K. Marx and F. Engels, *Selected Works*, Volume 1, Progress Publishers, Moscow, pp. 16-30

—— (1973) *Grundrisse*, Penguin, Harmondsworth

Masmondi, M. (1979) 'The New World Information Order', *Journal of Communication*, 29(2), 172-85

Massey, D., and Meegan, R.A. (1979) 'The Geography of Industrial Reorganisation', *Progress in Planning*, 10, 155-237

Matsebula, M.S. (1979) 'Tax Incentives in Botswana, Lesotho and Swaziland: a Case for Policy Harmonization and Regearing', *Journal of Southern African Affairs*, 4, 45-54

Mattelart, A. (1979) *Multinational Corporations and the Control of Culture*, Harvester, Sussex

Mattle, A.J. (1981) 'Eurobonds – an Appeal for Leadership', *The Banker*, 131 (662), 107-9

Meeks, G. (1977) *Disappointing Marriage: a Study of the Gains from Merger*, Cambridge University Press, Cambridge

—— and Whittington, G. (1975) 'Giant Companies in the United Kingdom', 1948-69', *Economic Journal*, 85, 824-43

——, —— (1977) in P.J. Devine *et al.* (1979)

Memmi, A. (1965) *Colonizer and the Colonized*, Orion Press, New York

Merkle, J.A. (1980) *Management and Ideology: the Legacy of the International Scientific Management Movement*, University of California Press, Berkeley

Miastre, G. (1976) *Géographie des Mass-Media*, Les Presses de l'Université du Québec, Montreal

Milkman, R. (1979) 'Contradictions of Semi-peripheral Development: the South African Case' in W.L. Goldfrank (ed.), *The World System of Capitalism: Past and Present*, Sage, Beverly Hills, pp. 261-84

Mingret, P. (1970) 'Les Investissements Americain en Belgique', *Revue de Géographie de Lyon*, 243-78

Monopolies [and Restrictive Practices] Commission (1957) *Report on the Supply and Exports of Electrical and Allied Machinery and Plant*, HMSO, London

Moran, T. (1978) 'Multinational Corporations and Dependency: a Dialogue for Dependistas and Nondependistas', *International Organization*, 32, 79-100

Morgan, A.D. (1979) 'Foreign Manufacturing by UK Firms' in F. Blackaby (ed.), *De-industrialisation*, Heinemann, London, pp. 78-94

—— and Blanpain, R. (1977) *The Industrial Relations and Employment Impacts of Multinational Enterprises: an Enquiry into the Issues*, OECD, Paris

Mosley, P. (1978) 'The Southern African Customs Union: a Reappraisal', *World Development*, 6, 31-43

Nakase, T. (1981) 'Some Characteristics of Japanese-type Multinationals Today', *Capital and Class*, 13, 61-98

National Bank of Australasia Ltd (1979) *Annual Report and Notice of Annual General Meeting*, Melbourne

Newfarmer, R.S. (1978) The International Market Power of Transnational Corporations: a Case Study of the Electrical Industry, report prepared for UNCTAD

—— and Mueller, W.F. (n.d.) *Multinational Corporations in Brazil and Mexico: Structural Sources of Economic and Noneconomic Power*, Report to the Subcommittee on Multinational Corporations, Government Printing Office, Washington, DC

Ngwenya, M.A.R. (1977) 'Do Transnational Corporations Influence Development Policy Objectives and If So, What are the Consequences on Well-being' in R. Gurr (ed.), *Transnational Corporations and Developing Countries*, Lesotho National Development Corporation, Maseru, pp. 57-76

Nichols, T. (ed.) (1980) *Capital and Labour: Studies in the Capitalist Labour Process*, Fontana, London

—— and Beynon, H. (1977) *Living with Capitalism: Class Relations and the Modern Factory*, Routledge and Kegan Paul, London

North West Economic Planning Council (1978) *Economic and Social Trends*, North West Economic Planning Council, Manchester

Nunn, S. (1980) *New Openings of Manufacturing Industry 1966-75*, Economics and Statistics Division, Department of Industry, London

Nukse, R. (1953) *Problems of Capital Formation in Underdeveloped Countries*, Blackwell, Oxford

Nyathi, V.M. (1975) 'South African Imperialism in Southern Africa', *African Review*, 5, 451-71

Obergón, A.Q. (1974) 'The Marginal Pole of the Economy and the Marginalised Labour Force', *Economy and Society*, 3(4), 394-428

O'Brien, P. (1980) 'The New Multinationals. Developing Country Firms in International Markets', *Futures*, August 303-15

O'Farrell, P.N. (1975) *Regional Industrial Development Trends in Ireland, 1960-1973*, Industrial Development Authority of Ireland, Dublin

Onimode, B. (1978) 'Imperialism and Multinational Corporations – a Case Study of Nigeria', unpublished seminar paper, Department of Economics, University of Ibadan, Nigeria

Overseas Investment Commission (1980) *Investing in New Zealand*, Wellington

Palloix, C. (1975) *L'Economie Modiale Capitaliste et les Firmes Multinationales*, Tome 2, Maspero, Paris

—— (1976) 'The Labour Process: from Fordism to Neo-Fordism' in Conference of Socialist Economists, *The Labour Process and Class Strategies*, CSE Pamphlet No. 1, Conference of Socialist Economists, London, pp. 46-67

—— (1977) 'The Self Expansion of Capital on a World Scale', *Review of Radical Political Economy*, 9(2), 1-28

Palmer, R., and Parsons, N. (eds.) (1977) *The Roots of Rural Poverty in Central and Southern Africa*, University of California Press, Berkeley

Pan American Union (1903) *Bulletin*, March

Passer, H.C. (1953) *The Electrical Manufacturers: 1875-1900*, Harvard University Press, Cambridge, Mass.

Peet, R. (1977) 'Editorial: Interaction of the Environmental and Spatial Contradictions during Late Capitalism', *Antipode*, 9(2), front and back covers

—— (1978) 'Materialism, Social Formation and Socio-spatial Relations: an Essay in Marxist Geography', *Cahiers de Géographie du Québec*, 22 (September), 147-57

—— (1979) 'Societal Contradiction and Marxist Geography', *Annals, Association of American Geographers*, 69(1), 164-9

—— (1980) 'The Consciousness Dimension of Fiji's Integration into World Capitalism', *Pacific Viewpoint*, 21, 91-115

Penrose, E. (1959) *The Theory of the Growth of the Firm*, Blackwell, Oxford

Perez, L.A. Jnr (1975) 'Tourism in the West Indies', *Journal of Communication*, 25(2), 136-43

Perman, R. (1979) 'The Dangers Facing Industry in Scotland', *Financial Times*, 9 November 1979

Perrons, D.C. (1981) 'The Role of Ireland in the New International Division of Labour: a Proposed Framework for Regional Analysis', *Regional Studies*, 15, 81-100

Pettman, R. (1979) *State and Class. A Sociology of International Affairs*, Croom Helm, London

Phillips, E. (1974) 'State Regulation and Economic Initiative: the South African Case', *International Journal of African Historical Studies*, 7, 227-54

Plasschaert, S.R.F. (1979) *Transfer Pricing and Multinational Corporations: an Overview of Concepts, Mechanisms and Regulations*, Saxon House, Farnborough

Pred, A.R. (1974) 'Major Job-providing Organizations and Systems of Cities', *Resource Paper No. 27*, Commission on College Geography, Association of American Geographers, Washington, DC

Rabey, G.F. (1977) *Contraction Poles: an Exploratory Study of Traditional Industry Decline within a Regional Industrial Complex*, Discussion Paper 3, Centre for Urban and Regional Development Studies, University of Newcastle-upon-Tyne

Radice, H. (ed.) (1975) *International Firms and Modern Imperialism*, Penguin, Harmondsworth

Ramsay, H. (1981) 'An International Participation Cycle: Variations on a Recurring Theme', paper presented to Conference on Organisation, Economy, Society: Prospects for the 1980s, Brisbane, 16-19 July

Ray, M. (1965) *Market Potential and Economic Shadow: a Quantitative Analysis of Industrial Location in Southern Ontario*, Research Paper 101, Department of Geography, University of Chicago

—— (1971) 'The Location of US Manufacturing Subsidiaries in Canada', *Economic Geography*, 47, 389-400

Reader, W.J. (1970) *Imperial Chemical Industries: a History. Volume 1. The Forerunners, 1870-1926*, Oxford University Press, London

Recenseamento de 1920 (1920) V, part 3, Brasil

Rees, J. (1972) 'The Industrial Corporation and Location Decision Analysis', *Area*, 4, 199-205

—— (1978) 'On the Spatial Spread and Oligopolistic Behavior of Large Rubber Companies', *Geoforum*, 9, 319-30

Reid, S.R. (1976) *The New Industrial Order: Concentration, Regulation and Public Policy*, McGraw-Hill, New York

Reuber (1973) *Private Foreign Investment in Development*, Oxford University Press, London

Richardson, G.B. (1964) 'The Limits to Firms' Rates of Growth', *Oxford Economic Papers*, 16, 9-25

Richardson, K. (1981) 'Poised for Attack', *ICI Magazine*, 59, 84-7

Robinson, H. (1976) *A Geography of Tourism*, Macdonald and Evans, London

Robinson, J. (1979) 'MNC's and the EC', *Europe*, 216, 7-10

Robinson, J.N. (1981) 'Is it Possible to Assess Country Risk?', *The Banker*, 131 (659), 71-9

Rogerson, C.M. (1974) 'The Foreign Branch Plant in South Africa', *South African Geographer*, 4, 335-9

—— (1978) 'Corporate Strategy, State Power and Compromise: Television Manufacture in Southern Africa', *South African Geographical Journal*, 60, 89-102

—— (1980) 'The Structural and Spatial Fabric of Industrialization in the Republic of South Africa', paper prepared for IGU Commission on Industrial Systems, Tokyo meeting

—— (1981a) 'Industrialization in the Shadows of Apartheid: a World-systems Analysis' in F.E.I. Hamilton and G.J.R. Linge (eds.), *Spatial Analysis, Industry and the Industrial Environment: Volume 1. International Industrial Systems*, John Wiley, Chichester, pp. 395-421

—— (1981b) 'Spatial Perspectives on United Kingdom Investment in South Africa', *South African Geographical Journal*, 63

—— (1981c) 'Patterns of Indigenous and Foreign Control of South African Manufacturing', *Social Dynamics*, 7

—— and Pirie, G.H. (1979) 'Apartheid, Urbanization and Regional Planning in South Africa' in R.A. Obudho and S. El-Shakhs (eds.), *Development of Urban Systems in Africa*, Praeger, New York, pp. 323-44

Rose, M. (1975) *Industrial Behaviour: Theoretical Developments since Taylor*, Allen Lane, London

Rowley, A. (1978) 'Hong Kong Moves up Market', *The Banker*, December 1978, 55-8

—— (1981) 'Anatomy of Japan: the Financiers', *Far Eastern Economic Review*, 8-14 May, 61-8

Rugman, A. (1981) *Inside the Multinationals. The Economics of Internal Markets*, Croom Helm, London

Ruz, R. (1974) *O Telefone*, CTB, Rio de Janeiro

SADE (1968) *Le Dynamique Industriel en Alsace, dans le Pays de Bade et dans la Région Baloise*, SADE, Strasbourg

Salt, J. (1967) 'The Impact of the Ford and Vauxhall Plants on the Employment Situation of Merseyside 1962-65', *Tijdschrift voor Economische en Sociale Geografie*, 58, 255-64

Sampson, A. (1973) *The Sovereign State: the Secret History of ITT*, Hodder and Stoughton, London

Samuels, J.M., and Chester, A.D. (1972) 'Growth Survival and the Size of Companies 1960-9' in Carling, K. (ed.), *Market Structure and Corporate Behaviour*, Gray Mills, London

Schelling, T.C. (1980) *The Strategy of Conflict*, Harvard University Press, London

Schmoll, G.A. (1977) *Tourism Promotion*, Tourism International Press, London

Schollhammer, H. (1974) *Locational Strategies of Multinational Firms*, Pepperdine University, Los Angeles

School of Economic and Financial Studies, Macquarie University (1976) 'Australian Enterprises Overseas', unpublished manuscript

Scottish Economic Planning Council (1980) 'Overseas Investment in Scottish Manufacturing Industry', *Scottish Economics Bulletin*, 20, 10-15

Seidman, A. (1970) 'Old Motives, New Methods: Foreign Enterprise in Africa Today' in R.W. Johnson and C.H. Allen (eds.), *African Perspectives*, Cambridge University Press, Cambridge, pp. 251-72

—— (1977) 'Post World II Imperialism in Africa: a Marxist Perspective', *Journal of Southern African Affairs*, 2, 403-25

—— (1979) 'Why US Corporations Should Get Out of South Africa', *Issue*, 9(1/2), 37-41

—— and Makgetla, N. (1978) *Activities of Transnational Corporations in South Africa*, United Nations Centre Against Apartheid, Notes and Documents, 24/79

—— and O'Keefe, P. (1980) 'The United States and South Africa in the Changing International Division of Labour', *Antipode*, 12(2), 1-16

—— and Seidman, N. (1977) *US Multinationals in Southern Africa*, Tanzania Publishing House, Dar-es-Salaam

Selwyn, P. (1975) *Industries in the Southern African Periphery*, Westview, Boulder

Semple, R.K. (1973) 'Recent Trends in the Spatial Concentration of Corporate Headquarters', *Economic Geography*, 49(4), 309-18

Shafer, D.M. (1979) *The Wiehahn Report and the Industrial Conciliation Amendment Act: a New Attack on the Trade Union Movement in South Africa*, United Nations Centre Against Apartheid, Notes and Documents, 25/79

Simon, H.A. and Bonini, C.P. (1958) 'The Size Distribution of Business Firms,' *American Economic Review*, 48, 607-15

Singh, A. (1973) in P.J. Devine *et al*. (1979)

—— (1975) 'Take-overs, Economic Natural Selection and the Theory of the Firm', *Economic Journal*, 85, 497-515

Skully, M. (1978) 'Profits Up Down-under', *The Banker*, 128, December, 75-7

—— (1979) 'Getting Your Bank to Work for You Overseas', *Rydges*, April, 26-8

—— (1980) 'Foreign Banking in New York City: the Australian Bank Agencies', *The Bankers' Magazine of Australasia*, 94, 205-12

—— (1981a) 'The Australian Banks in London: a Brief History', *The Bankers' Magazine of Australasia*, 95, 44-7

—— (1981b) 'The Australian Banks in London: a Move to Corporate Banking', *The Bankers' Magazine of Australasia*, 95, 94-7

Sloan, A.E. (1964) *My Years with General Motors*, Doubleday, Garden City, New York

Smith, B. (1978) 'Australian Mineral Development, Future Prospects for the Mining Industry and Effects on the Australian Economy' in W. Kasper and T.G. Parry (eds.), *Growth, Trade and Structural Change in an Open Australian Economy*, Centre for Applied Economic Research, University of New South Wales, Sydney, pp. 130-55

Smith, I.J. (1978) *Ownership Status and Employment Change in Northern Region Manufacturing Industry, 1963-73*, Discussion Paper 7, Centre for Urban and Regional Development Studies, University of Newcastle-upon-Tyne

—— (1979) 'The Effect of External Takeovers on Manufacturing Employment Change in the Northern Region between 1963 and 1973', *Regional Studies*, 13, 421-37

Sohn-Rethel, A. (1971) 'Mental and Manual Labour in Marxism' in S. Hall and P. Walton (eds.), *Situating Marx*, Human Context Books, London

—— (1976) 'The Dual Economics of Transition' in Conference of Socialist Economists, *The Labour Process and Class Strategies*, CSE Pamphlet No. 1, Conference of Socialist Economists, London, pp. 26-45

South (1981a) 'The Sea Up for Grabs', 7 May, 20-4

—— (1981b) 'Big Money for Big Business', 11, October, 70-1

——'(1981c). 'TNCs: Tipping the Trade Balance', 11, October, 73

South Africa, Republic of (1970) *Third Report of the Commission of Enquiry into Fiscal and Monetary Policy in South Africa*, Government Printer, Pretoria, RP87/1970

—— (1978) *Census of Manufacturing 1976: Statistics According to Major Groups and Subgroups*, Government Printer, Pretoria, Report No. 10-21-32

South Africa, Union of (1958) *Commission of Enquiry into Policy Relating to the Protection of Industries*, Government Printer, Pretoria, UG 36-1958

Souza, L.I.H. (1962) 'A Historia de Industria Eletrica no Brasil' in G. Banas (ed.), *A Industria de Material Eletrico e Eletronico 1962*, Banas, São Paulo, 64-76

Stanworth, M.J.K., and Curran, J. (1976) 'Growth and the Small Firm – an Alternative View', *Journal of Management Studies*, May, 95-110

Stein, S. (1957) *The Brazilian Cotton Manufacture: Textile Enterprise in an Underdeveloped Area*, Harvard University Press, Cambridge, Mass.

Stetson, C.P. Jnr (1980) 'The Reshaping of Corporate Financial Services', *Harvard Business Review*, 58, September-October 134-42

Stewart, J.C. (1977) 'Australian Company Mergers, 1960-1970', *The Economic Record*, 53, 1-29

Stewart, J.S. (1976) 'Linkages and Foreign Direct Investment', *Regional Studies*, 10, 245-58

Stilwell, F.J.B. (1980) *Economic Crisis, Cities and Regions*, Pergamon, Sydney

Stocking, G.W., and Watkins, M.W. (1946) *Cartels in Action*, Twentieth Century Fund, New York

Stopford, J.M., and Wells, L.T. (1972) *Managing the Multinational Enterprise*, Basic Books, New York

—— Dunning, J.H., and Haberich, K.O. (1980) *The World Directory of Multinational Enterprises*, Sijthoff and Noordhoff, Netherlands

Sullivan, L. (1980) *The Role of Multinational Corporations in South Africa*, South African Institute of Race Relations, Johannesburg

Sunday Times (1980a) 2 March

—— (1980b) 26 October

Tan, A. (1978) 'The Philippines: New Windows on the World', *The Banker*, vol. 128, December, 61-5

Taylor, M.J. (1975) 'Organisational Growth, Spatial Interaction and Location Decision-making', *Regional Studies*, 9, 313-23

—— and Thrift, N.J. (1979) 'Guest Editorial', *Environment and Planning A*, 11, 973-5

——, —— (1980) 'Finance and Organizations: Towards a Dualistic Interpretation of the Geography of Enterprise', unpublished seminar paper, Department of Human Geography, Australian National University

——, —— and Thrift, N.J. (1981a) 'The Historical Geography of Financial and Industrial Organization: a Submodal Approach', unpublished seminar paper, Department of Human Geography, Australian National University

——, —— (1981b) 'Some Geographical Implications of Foreign Investment in the Semi-periphery: the Case of Australia', *Tijdschrift voor Economische en Sociale Geografie*, 72, 194-213

——, —— (1981c) 'British Capital Overseas: Direct Investment and Firm Development in Australia', *Regional Studies*, 15, 183-212

——, —— (1982) 'The Geography of Industrial Transformation: an Approach', *Progress in Planning*, forthcoming

Teriba, P., Edozien, E.C., and Kayode, M.O. (1972) 'Some Aspects of Ownership and Control Structure of Business Enterprise in a Developing Economy', *Nigerian Journal of Economic and Social Studies*, 14 (1), 1-20

Teulings, A.W.M. (1975) *Philips, Gestiedenis en Praktijk van een Wereld-Concero (Philips, History and Practice of a World-wide Corporation)*, Van Gennep, Amsterdam

—— (1981) 'The Internationalization Squeeze: Double Capital Movement and Job Transfer within Philips – Worldwide', paper presented to the Organization, Economy, Society Conference, Brisbane, July 1981

Tharakan, M. (1980) *The New International Division of Labour and Multinational Companies*, Saxon House, Farnborough

Thomas, M.D. (1980) 'Explanatory Frameworks for Growth and Change in Uninational and Multinational Firms', *Economic Geography*, 56, 1-17

Thomas, W.A. (1978) *The Finance of British Industry 1918-1976*, Methuen, London

Thomas, W. (1978) *Economic Development in Namibia: Towards Acceptable Development Strategies for Independent Namibia*, Kaiser Verlag, Munich

Thompson, E.P. (1978) *The Poverty of Theory and Other Essays*, Merlin Press, London

Thrift, N.J. (1979) 'Unemployment in the Inner City: Urban Problem or Structural Imperative? A Review of the British Experience' in D. Herbert and R.J. Johnston (eds.), *Geography and the Urban Environment. Volume Two*, John Wiley, Chichester, pp. 125-226

—— (1980) 'Fröbel and the New International Division of Labour' in R. Peet (ed.), *An Introduction to Marxist Theories of Underdevelopment*, Department of Human Geography, Publication HG14, Australian National University Press, Canberra, pp. 181-9

The Times (1980) 15 October

—— (1981a) 27 February

—— (1981b) 14 April

The Times 1000 (1979) Times Newspapers, London

Topik, S. (1968) 'Economic Nationalism and the State in an Underdeveloped Country, Brazil 1889-1930', unpublished PhD dissertation, University of Texas at Austin

Townsend, A.R. (1981) 'Geographical Perspectives on Major Job Losses in the UK 1977-80', *Area*, 13, 31-8

Tucker, K. (1981) *Traded Services in the World Economy*, Bureau of Industry Economics' Working Paper 16

Ullman, E.L. (1958) 'Regional Development and the Geography of Concentration', *Papers and Proceedings of the Regional Science Association*, 4, 179-98

UNESCO (1978) *Transnational Corporations in World Development: a Reexamination*, United Nations, New York

United Kingdom Board of Trade (1947) *Survey of International and Internal Cartels 1944-1946*, vol. 2, Part III, 1947, 'Electrical Machinery and Apparatus', Board of Fair Trading, London (released in 1975)

United Nations (1970) *UN Statistical Yearbook 1969*, United Nations, New York

—— (1979) *UN Statistical Yearbook 1978*, United Nations, New York

US Bureau of the Census (1952) *United States Census of Population: 1950. Vol. II. Characteristics of the Population*, US Government Printing Office, Washington, DC

—— (1962) *United States Census of Population: 1960. Vol. I. Characteristics of the Population*, US Government Printing Office, Washington, DC

—— (1973) *United States Census of Population: 1970. Vol. I: Characteristics of the Population*, US Government Printing Office, Washington, DC

—— (1976) 'Estimates of the Population of Metropolitan Areas, 1973 and 1974, and Components of Change since 1970', *Current Population Reports; Population Estimates and Projections*, Series P-25, No. 618

US Government (1946) *Industrial Reference Service*, US Department of Commerce, December

Utrecht, E. (1978) 'The Political Economy of ASEAN', *Journal of Australian Political Economy*, 2, 46-66

Vaitsos, C. (1973) 'Foreign Investment Policies on Economic Development in Latin America', *Journal of World Trade Law*, Nov./Dec.

—— (1974a) *Intercountry Income Distribution and Transnational Enterprises*, Clarendon Press, Oxford

—— (1974b) 'Income Distribution and Welfare Considerations' in J. Dunning (ed.), *Economic Analysis and the Multinational Enterprise*, George Allen and Unwin, London, pp. 300-41

Van den Bulcke, D., Boddewyn, J.J., Martens, B., and Klemmer, P. (1979) *Investment and Divestment Policies of Multinational Corporations in Europe*, Saxon House, Farnborough

Van der Wees, G. (1981) 'Multinational Corporations, Transfer of Technology and the Socialist Strategy of a Developing Nation: Perspectives from Tanzania' in F.E.I. Hamilton and G.J.R. Linge (eds.), *Spatial Analysis, Industry and the Industrial Environment: International Industrial Systems*, John Wiley, Chichester, pp. 529-47

Varis, T. (1974) 'Global Traffic in Television', *Journal of Communication*, 24(1), 102-9

—— (1976) 'Aspects of the Impact of Transnational Corporations on Communication', *International Social Science Journal*, 28, 808-30

Vernon, R. (1966) 'International Investment and International Trade in the Product Cycle', *Quarterly Journal of Economics*, 80, 190-207

—— (1970) 'Foreign Enterprises and Developing Nations in the Raw Materials Industries', *American Economic Review*, 60, 122-6

—— (1971) *Sovereignty at Bay: the Multinational Spread of US Enterprises*, Penguin, Harmondsworth

—— (1972) *Restrictive Business Practices: the Operation of Multinational United States Enterprises in Developing Countries, their Role in Trade and Development*, United Nations, New York

—— (1978) *Storm Over the Multinationals*, Harvard University Press, New York

—— (1979) 'The Product Cycle Hypothesis in a New International Environment', *Oxford Bulletin of Economics and Statistics*, 41, 255-68

Villela, A.V., and Wilson, S. (1975) *Politica do Governo e Crescimento da Economia Brasileira 1889-1945*, IPEA, Rio de Janeiro

Walker, D.F., and Bater, J.H. (eds.) (1974) *Industrial Development in Southern Ontario: Selected Essays*, Department of Geography, Faculty of Environmental Studies, University of Waterloo, Waterloo, Ontario

Walker, R., and Storper, M. (1980) *Technological Innovation, the Labour Process, and the Location of Industries: a Research Progress Report*, Department of Geography and Institute of Urban and Regional Development, University of California, Berkeley

——, —— (1981) 'Capital and Industrial Location', *Progress in Human Geography*, 5, 473-509

Wallerstein, I. (1974) *The Modern World System: Capitalist Agriculture and the Origins of the European World Economy in the Sixteenth Century*, Academic Press, New York

—— (1979) *The Capitalist World Economy*, Cambridge University Press, Cambridge

Ward, R.G., and Proctor, A. (eds.) (1980) *South Pacific Agriculture Choices and Constraints: South Pacific Agricultural Survey 1979*, Manila, Asian Development Bank in association with ANU Press, Canberra

Warneryd, O. (1968) *Interdependence in Urban Systems*, Regionkonsult Aktiebolag, Goteborg, Sweden

Warren, B. (1980) *Imperialism: Pioneer of Capitalism*, New Left Books, London

Watts, H.D. (1979) 'Large Firms, Multinationals and Regional Development: Some New Evidence from the United Kingdom', *Environment and Planning A*, 11, 71-81

—— (1980a), *The Large Industrial Enterprise: Some Spatial Perspectives*, Croom Helm, London

—— (1980b) 'The Location of European Investment in the United Kingdom', *Tijdschrift voor Economische en Sociale Geografie*, 71, 3-14

—— (1980c) 'Conflict and Collusion in the British Sugar Industry, 1924-8', *Journal of Historical Geography*, 6(3), 291-314

Weiss, L.W. (1974) 'Concentration – Profits Relationship and Antitrust' in J. Goldshmid, H.N. Mann and J.F. Weston (eds.), *Industrial Concentration: the New Learning*, Little, Brown and Co., Boston, pp. 184-232

Weiss, R. (1975) 'The Role of Parastatals in South Africa's Politicoeconomic System' in J. Suckling, R. Weiss and D. Innes (eds.), *The Economic Factor: Foreign Investment in South Africa*, Study Project on External Investment in South Africa and Namibia, London, pp. 55-91

Welsh Office (1978) *Welsh Economic Trends No. 5*, Welsh Office, Cardiff

Wertheimer, H.N. (1971) 'The International Firm and International Aspects of Policies on Mergers' in J.B. Heath (ed.), *International Conference on Monopolies, Mergers and Restrictive Practices*, HMSO, London, pp. 171-206

Weston, R. (1980) *Domestic and Multinational Banking*, Croom Helm, London

Wheelwright, E.L. (1980) 'The New International Division of Labour in the Age of the Transnational Corporation' in J. Friedmann, E.L. Wheelwright and J. Connell (eds.), *Development Strategies in the Eighties*, Monograph No. 1, Development Studies Colloquium, University of Sydney, Sydney, pp. 43-58

Whisson, M.G. (1980) 'The Sullivan Principles: Striking a Lost Chord', *Social Dynamics*, 6, 17-24

Widstrand, C. (ed.) (1975) *Multi-national Firms in Africa*, Scandinavian Institute of African Studies, Uppsala

Wileman, J.P. (1909) *Brazilian Yearbook*, G.R. Fairbanks, New York

Wilkins, M. (1970) *The Emergence of Multinational Enterprise: American Business Abroad from the Colonial Era to 1914*, Harvard University Press,

Cambridge, Mass.
—— (1974a) 'Multinational Enterprise' in H. Daems and H. Van der Wee (eds.), *The Rise of Managerial Capitalism*, Nijhoff, The Hague
—— (1974b) *The Maturing of Multinational Business from 1914 to 1970*, Harvard University Press, Cambridge, Mass.
—— and Hill, F.E. (1964) *American Business Abroad*, Wayne State University, Detroit
Williams, R. (1976) *Television*, Fontana, London
—— (1981) *Culture*, Fontana, London
Winai-Ström, G. (1975) 'The Influence of Multinational Corporations on Lesotho's Politics and Economics', *African Review*, 5, 473-97
—— (1978) *Development and Dependence in Lesotho, the Enclave of South Africa*, Scandinavian Institute of African Studies, Uppsala
Winter, I. (1978) 'The Post-Colonial State and the Forces and Relations of Production: Swaziland', *Review of African Political Economy*, 9, 27-43
Wolpe, H. (1972) 'Capitalism and Cheap Labour-Power in South Africa: from Segregation to Apartheid', *Economy and Society*, 1, 425-56
Wood, P.A. (1980) 'Industrial Geography', *Progress in Human Geography*, 44(3), 406-16
Yannopoulos, G.M., and Dunning, J.H. (1976) 'Multinational Enterprises and Regional Development: an Exploratory Paper', *Regional Studies*, 10, 389-99
Young, G. (1973) *Tourism: Blessing or Blight?* Penguin, Harmondsworth, Middlesex
Young, S., and Hood, N. (1977) *Chrysler UK: a Company in Transition*, Praeger, New York
Zeleny, J. (1980) *The Logic of Marx*, Basil Blackwell, Oxford
Zimbalist, A. (ed.) (1979) *Case Studies on the Labour Process*, Monthly Review Press, New York

NOTES ON CONTRIBUTORS

S. Abumere, Department of Geography, University of Ibadan, Ibadan, Nigeria

A. Blackbourn, Department of Geography, University of Windsor, Windsor, Ontario, Canada

S.G. Britton, Department of Geography, University of Auckland, Auckland, New Zealand

I.M. Clarke, Department of Human Geography, Research School of Pacific Studies, The Australian National University, Canberra, Australia

J. Hirst, Department of Human Geography, Research School of Pacific Studies, The Australian National University, Canberra, Australia

R.S. Newfarmer, Department of Economics, University of Notre Dame, Notre Dame, Indiana, USA

J.R. Peet, Graduate School of Geography, Clark University, Worcester, Massachusetts, USA

C. Rogerson, Department of Geography and Environmental Studies, University of the Witwatersrand, Johannesburg, South Africa

I.J. Smith, Centre for Urban and Regional Development Studies, University of Newcastle-upon-Tyne, Newcastle-upon-Tyne, UK

M.J. Taylor, Department of Human Geography, Research School of Pacific Studies, The Australian National University, Canberra, Australia

N.J. Thrift, Department of Human Geography, Research School of Pacific Studies, The Australian National University, Canberra, Australia

S. Topik, Department of History, Federal University of Rio de Janeiro, Niteroi, Brazil

H.D. Watts, Department of Geography, University of Sheffield, Sheffield, UK

SUBJECT INDEX

COMPANY INDEX

This is an ind^x of the *major* industrials and banks cited in the text. It includes information on (1) nationality and (2) ranking by size (assets) as found in the 1978 world top 800+ list compiled by Dunning and Pearce (1981).

AUTHOR INDEX